Özden Zeynep Oktav • Emel Parlar Dal •
Ali Murat Kurşun
Editors

Violent Non-state Actors and the Syrian Civil War

The ISIS and YPG Cases

Springer

Editors
Özden Zeynep Oktav
Faculty of Political Sciences
International Relations Department
Istanbul Medeniyet University
Istanbul, Turkey

Emel Parlar Dal
Faculty of Political Sciences
International Relations Department
Marmara University
Istanbul, Turkey

Ali Murat Kurşun
Faculty of Political Sciences
International Relations Department
Marmara University
Istanbul, Turkey

ISBN 978-3-319-67527-5 ISBN 978-3-319-67528-2 (eBook)
DOI 10.1007/978-3-319-67528-2

Library of Congress Control Number: 2017955952

Printed on acid-free paper

This Springer imprint is published by Springer Nature
The registered company is Springer International Publishing AG
The registered company address is: Gewerbestrasse 11, 6330 Cham, Switzerland

Testimonials

This timely volume by regional scholars and experts examines various aspects of the emergence and expansion of violent non-state actors in the Syrian/Iraqi conflict. The wealth of detail and approaches enhances our understanding of the transformation and dynamics of contemporary conflicts within and beyond the region.

Keith Krause

The Graduate Institute, Geneva

This volume contains a wealth of useful information on violent non-state actors in the Syrian conflict and their transnational dimensions and consequences and helps situate the Syrian experiences in a broader comparative and theoretical perspective.

Kristian Skrede Gleditsch

University of Essex & Peace Research Institute Oslo (PRIO)

This book is an excellent resource for those looking for an interdisciplinary account of VNSAs during the Syrian civil war. It makes a nice contribution to the study of violent non-state actors and poses a set of new and pressing questions.

Max Abrahms

Northeastern University

This book makes a valuable contribution both to the literature on terrorism and insurgency and to the measures and efforts needed to most effectively counter them.

Omar Ashour

University of Exeter

This volume marks a major contribution by analyzing the differences in the aims and nature of violent non-state actors like ISIS and the Kurdish YPG, in how they operate, and especially in the ways major and rising powers relate to them.

Charles T. Call

School of International Service at American University, Washington, DC

This book opens fascinating glimpses into contrasting forms of "state-like" governance established by non-state actors, ISIS and the Kurdish PYD. [...] It is an important source for students of the Syrian conflict, civil wars, failed states and hybrid governance.

Raymond Hinnebusch
Director Centre for Syrian Studies, University of St. Andrews

Contents

Reframing and Reassessing the VNSAs in Syrian Conflict: An Introduction

Özden Zeynep Oktav, Emel Parlar Dal, and Ali Murat Kurşun

In September 2014, the small northern Syrian city of Kobane became a battleground between the Islamic State in Iraq and Syria (ISIS) and the People's Protection Units (Yekîneyên Parastina Gel-YPG). The city was surrounded by ISIS fighters, resulting in a massive civilian movement toward the nearby Turkish border. However, back in September 2014, it would have been considered only a distant possibility that the events taking place in Kobane would change the fate of the Syrian war for not only these two major violent non-state actors (VNSAs) that have emerged from the ongoing Syrian conflict but also for regional and international actors engaged both diplomatically and militarily in the conflict. The events in Kobane also led to the crystallization of divergences between regional and major powers in their methods and use of local actors in their fight against ISIS. It has since become more apparent that the existing antagonisms and differing territorial objectives between ISIS and the YPG have the potential to be exploited by major actors, particularly the United States in further stages of the crisis.

Four months of intense combat between the YPG and ISIS in Kobane also laid bare what will be an important legacy of the civil war for the future of Middle Eastern politics in general and Syria in particular: the consolidation of violent non-state actors as active players on the ground. Although it is irrefutable that the course of the Syrian civil war has been marked by the proliferation of various armed actors, the 2014 Kobane battleground revealed the need to reconsider VNSAs from an analytical and comprehensive point of view. First, September 2014 showed that

Ö.Z. Oktav
Faculty of Political Sciences, International Relations Department, Istanbul Medeniyet University, Istanbul, Turkey
e-mail: ozoktav@yahoo.com

E. Parlar Dal (✉) • A.M. Kurşun
Faculty of Political Sciences, International Relations Department, Marmara University, Istanbul, Turkey
e-mail: emelparlar@yahoo.com; alimuratkursun@gmail.com

Ö.Z. Oktav et al. (eds.), *Violent Non-state Actors and the Syrian Civil War*,
DOI 10.1007/978-3-319-67528-2_1

the conflict in Syria is not only about the conflict between the regime and opposition groups but also between VNSAs, each of which is ready to fight for their causes and diverging political agendas. Second, it was only after the Kobane events that the struggles of the VNSAs in Syria began to be understood in their local and regional-global interaction contexts. The Syrian civil war has also proven that the differing strategies and priorities of actors involved in the Syrian picture may end up either generating additional tensions among themselves or establishing ad hoc coalitions on the shifting grounds of the conflict. Third, the Kobane events also demonstrated that ISIS and the YPG represent a new wave of Middle Eastern VNSAs. This new wave is marked by their hybrid characteristics, differing scopes, strategies, and tactics in terms of geopolitics, sovereignty, and interactions with the local government and regional and major powers when compared to the previous waves of Middle Eastern VNSAs such as the jihadist Al-Qaeda and the Marxist-ethnic nationalist PKK. Although initially portrayed as loose networks, VNSAs can act as solid geopolitical actors impacting the various calculus of both major and regional powers with regard the ongoing Syrian war. These three interconnected rationales drive the inquiry raised in this book project.

VNSAs in the Middle Eastern context are still an understudied and weakly explored field of research despite the existence of a growing literature on the topic, particularly on ISIS, in recent years. In the face of the 6-year Syrian civil war, VNSAs have emerged as an important topic in both the conflict/security and IR fields due to their changing nature, hybrid military strategies, and shifting geopolitics vis-à-vis state authority and neighboring states. The Syrian civil war gave birth to a wide range of new generation VNSAs, among which ISIS and the YPG are the most visible in terms of their spatiality, developed socialization networks, new forms of sovereignty challenging the legitimacy of the traditional nation-state, and new security threats and violence.

Given this background, ISIS as a global revolutionary nonethnic VNSA and the YPG as an ethnic and nationalist VNSA need to be further analyzed in terms of their goals, connections with the nation-state, other VNSAs acting on the ground and strategies of warfare, as well as the changing conditions catalyzing their contagion to other regions and states. Based on this, this book intends to present a comprehensive approach to the conceptual and empirical study of contemporary VNSAs. In doing so, it will first attempt to produce a more integrated conceptual classification of VNSAs, borrowing from previous classifications made by different conflict scholars, and will then try to offer a comprehensive portrait of ISIS and the YPG as the new generation of VNSAs. Second, the focus will shift to the specificities of ISIS and the YPG which make them different from previous VNSAs in the Middle East. Here, a three-layered framework of *actorness*, *powerfulness*, and *effectiveness* will be employed in order to position these two actors in the Middle Eastern and Syrian contexts and to assess their distinctive characteristics and behaviors distinguishing them from the old generation VNSAs. Third, the book will explore how the actorness, powerfulness, and effectiveness of ISIS and the YPG have been constructed and reconstructed within the deepening Syrian civil war. Finally, the book's focus will shift to how global and regional actors have envisaged the rise of these two new VNSAs and thus attempts to grasp their converging and diverging approaches and strategies toward the groups in the context of the Syrian civil war.

1 Reclassifying VNSAs: From Old Typologies to New Typologies

The reconceptualization and reclassification of VNSAs is not an easy task due to the existence of various categories based on their most significant characteristics and key dimensions. This study first aims to briefly present the existing literature on various VNSA typologies classifying them in terms of their objectives—actors, outreach, and transcendental scope. Second, the focus will be on placing ISIS and the YPG into the existing classifications of VNSAs.

1.1 An Overview of the Existing Literature on VNSA Typologies

Although restricted, the existing literature on VNSAs has so far produced various definitions, categories, and typologies. Although it is useful to have multiple conceptual avenues for assessing VNSAs, the literature needs an agreed typology, especially in light of their increasing relevance in contemporary world politics. The aim here is not to propose a new typology of VNSAs but rather to explore contemporary VNSAs' actorness, powerfulness, and effectiveness using an integrated approach and the cases of ISIS and the YPG. The current literature uses similar typologies with a changing number of categories. For instance, Keith Krause and Jennifer Miliken (2009, p. 204) classify non-state armed groups under the following five categories: insurgent groups, militant groups, urban gangs and warlords, private militias, police forces, and security companies and transnational groups. Phil Williams (2008, pp. 9–17) however uses seven categories: warlords, militias, paramilitary forces, insurgencies, terrorist organizations, criminal organizations, and youth gangs. Ersel Aydınlı (2016) uses a framework based on six categories: insurgents, domestic militant groups, warlords/urban gangs, private militias/military companies, terrorists, and criminal organizations. Natasha Ezrow (2017) tabulates 11 types of VNSAs: de facto states, political organizations with militant wings, insurgencies, terror organizations, terror networks, marauding rebels, warlords, organized crime, gangs, private security companies, and paramilitaries. Another categorization by Troy Thomas, Stephen Kiser, and William Casebeer (2005, p. 18) classifies VNSAs under six categories: warlords with private armies, transnational criminal organizations, militant religious organizations, ethno-nationalist groups, emergent set of eco-warriors and anti-globalizationists, and anarchists.

Diverging classifications in the literature point to the lack of consensus among scholars due to the inclusion or exclusion of certain types of VNSAs such as private military companies, which are considered to be regulated by states, and maritime pirates, which rarely challenge state authority. However, most scholars are in broad agreement on the following classifications: warlords, militias, paramilitary forces/military companies, insurgencies, terrorist organizations, and criminal organizations/gangs.

VNSAs may also be examined in terms of the agendas they pursue. In this regard, the literature divides VNSAs into two categories based on their motivating and driving factors with an eye toward understanding their ideological/practical framework: transcendental and transactional VNSAs. While transactional VNSAs mainly focus on economic profit maximization, transcendental VNSAs follow political, religious, or moral pathways (Thomas et al. 2005, p. 122). It is possible to further examine transcendental VNSAs based on the value sets they are attached to. For instance, Ezrow (2017) classifies their values under four categories: liberation, separatist, reform/revolutionary, and religious/traditional. Similarly, based on political aims, VNSAs may adopt either "a political–mostly social-revolutionary or ethno-nationalistic agenda and view themselves as 'future armies' of a liberated population" (Schneckener 2006, p. 25). Likewise, A. Guelke (1995) also identifies groups on the basis of their ideologies since they may be informed by left or right wing, social revolutionary, or nationalistic or religious ideologies.

A more simplified categorization of transcendental VNSAs may give a better understanding considering their interwoven aims, scope, and ideologies and can be divided as global revolutionary VNSAs and ethno-nationalist VNSAs. Global revolutionary VNSAs appear to be more motivated by universalist and religious ideologies than the nationalist ideologies of ethno-nationalist VNSAs. Among existing global revolutionary VNSAs, Salafi jihadi movements such as Al-Qaeda and ISIS are prominent as they seek to reinforce their religious ideology, vision, and doctrine in the eyes of all Muslims through military operations in both Western and Muslim territories (Forest 2009, p. xvi). With ISIS as the most contemporary and influential example of such groups, current global revolutionary VNSAs are also seen as "state-building revolutionaries" seeking to challenge established norms through radical extremism (Walt 2015, p. 42). In addition to Salafi jihadist revolutionary VNSAs, transcendental VNSAs also include revolutionary Marxist groups such as the National Liberation Army (ELN) in Colombia. The scope of ethnonationalist VNSAs is narrower, however, as they do not aim to foster the global overthrow of established norms and institutions but rather to pursue nationalist-driven goals of separatism or greater autonomy. Ethnic nationalists such as the Basque Fatherland and Liberty (ETA) in Spain, PKK in Turkey, PYD-YPG in Syria, and others in Chechnya, Kashmir, Mindanao, and Sri Lanka are good examples of transcendental VNSAs with ethno-nationalist ideologies and existential codes that use terrorist means to achieve their goals (Thomas 2010). Ethnonationalism, the most widespread type of nationalism, underlines the importance of a common ethnic background for the formation of an organic nation. In this regard, the main objective of ethno-nationalist VNSAs is the creation of a separate state or a quasi-state (Stepanova 2008, pp. 39–40). One of the most distinguishing characteristics of ethno-nationalist VNSAs is their commitment to a certain piece of territory regarded as their homeland. In fact, the source of political violence generated by ethno-nationalist VNSAs is directly related to this territorial understanding (Brown 1993, p. 5).

1.2 *Whither a New Generation of VNSAs? Typologizing ISIS and the YPG*

Given the conceptual framework given above, this section aims to investigate the categories of VNSAs which best allow for the conceptualizing of ISIS and the YPG and to position them in the wider classification of VNSAs. The transformation and evolution of VNSAs over time also give some clues to their multiple roles and overlapping identities. For instance, ISIS evolved from an insurgent group to a terrorist organization with clandestine and criminal links. As seen in Table 1, ISIS today gives the appearance more of a terrorist organization than an insurgency. This means that among its three overlapping categories of terrorist organization, insurgency, and criminal organization, the category of terrorist organization outweighs the two others in terms of output or impact. In the YPG case, the group better fits into the category of insurgencies in terms of impact, although it also carries the characteristics of a paramilitary force and a terrorist organization. The YPG's organic links with the PKK, which is considered a terrorist organization by Turkey, the United States, and the EU, and its inclusion of a significant number of PKK fighters of Turkish origin also gives it a hybrid identity, at least in the eyes of Turkey. On the other hand, with the recent US decision to arm the SDF, which is mainly composed of YPG fighters, and the US Administration's plan to use YPG forces in the Raqqa operation against ISIS in the summer of 2017, the YPG has gained status as a paramilitary force. The use of the YPG by the United States as a viable local actor against ISIS is also a good indicator of the gradual evolution of status of VNSAs in the eyes of outside actors. Regardless of whether the US engagement with the Syrian Kurds in the Raqqa operation is merely an ad hoc coalition or will be part of a long-term strategy, this move clearly proves that perceptions of VNSAs vary from actor to actor depending on national interests. The recognition of VNSAs by outside actors as a local partner also helps them gain a certain degree of legitimacy in the eyes of international society.

Second, the present study also classifies ISIS and the YPG in terms of their geographical outreach. As indicated in Table 1, while ISIS is a global revolutionary and jihadist VNSA, the YPG may be considered a local ethno-nationalist actor with

Table 1 VNSA typology of ISIS and YPG

		ISIS	YPG
Objective/actors	Insurgency	+	+++
	Terrorist organization	+++	+
	Criminal organization	++	
	Paramilitary forces		+
Outreach	Global revolutionary	+++	
	Ethno/nationalist		+++
Transcendental scope	Religious/jihadist	+++	
	Anarchist/Marxist		+++

+++, best fit; ++, fit; +, least fit

limited regional ambitions. In fact, ISIS's actions have so far proved it to not only be a local or a regional phenomenon but to aim to propagate its so-called revolution against the infidels. Indeed, the presence of affiliates across the globe and the scope of its actions further illustrate that it has been able to generate global repercussions. ISIS, in addition to its activities in Syria and Iraq, has so far claimed responsibility for terrorist attacks in six European countries (Belgium, Denmark, France, Germany, Sweden, and the United Kingdom) and caused the death of approximately 300 people in Turkey as a global revolutionary actor effectively using violent extremism as a propaganda tool against non-Muslims and Muslims (as seen in the case of attacks in Turkey). In contrast, the YPG shows characteristics of a more limited VNSA in terms of its geographical outreach and, as a narrow and ethnic-based VNSA with limited territorial and expansionist aims, when compared with ISIS, does not enact terrorist attacks outside its region.

Third, as the Table 1 also suggests, this study further looks at the transcendental scope of ISIS and YPG by classifying the ideological frameworks in which they operate. In this regard, as shown in Table 1, ISIS pursues jihadist ideology, while the YPG's ideology is rather anarchist/Marxist. Grounded on Salafist ideology, ISIS's jihadism includes various elements of extremism and radical terror. This also separates ISIS from Al-Qaeda which has not used violent extremism as a communication tool as frequently and efficiently as does ISIS, thanks to various social media networks. It is apparent that the YPG's Marxist ideology is far from creating a broader impact on either the regional or international levels and lacks effective propaganda channels. However, the YPG's direct links with the PKK, a Marxist separatist Kurdish terrorist organization fighting against Turkey since the 1980s, utilize the PKK's existing propaganda tools and existing links with both Europe and other regional actors. The phenomenon of women fighters, for instance, constitutes a source of sympathy for the YPG and PKK in the eyes of Western political and media circles.

2 Locating the New Generation of VNSAs in the Middle East: A Three-Layered Analysis of ISIS and the YPG

Drawing on the embedded typology of ISIS and the YPG in Table 1, it is possible to offer a three-layered framework to assess their distinguishing characteristics and behaviors: actorness (territoriality and geopolitical codes and community building), powerfulness (financial resources and funding and recruitment and propaganda tools), and effectiveness (regional engagements and international engagements and legitimacy) (see Table 2). This three-staged approach will be beneficial for conceptualizing ISIS and the YPG as new generation VNSAs with different specificities from their predecessors. In addition, this proposed three-layered framework accounts for a better analysis of these two VNSAs by locating them as distinct groups among the various types of VNSAs in the Middle East since their actorness,

Table 2 Key characteristics of the new generation of VNSAs

New generation of VNSAs		
Actorness	Powerfulness	Effectiveness
Territoriality and geopolitical codes	Financial resources and funding	Regional engagements
Community building	Recruitment and propaganda tools	International engagements and legitimacy

powerfulness, and effectiveness have indeed taken precedence over the existing VNSAs in the region.

It is apparent that ISIS and YPG's distinguishing characteristics come from their ability to fulfill their actorness, powerfulness, and effectiveness to a greater degree than other VNSAs currently do in the region. A closer look at the subcategories of actorness, powerfulness, and effectiveness given in Table 3 provides an overview of how these two actors construct their agency differently from their predecessors and contemporaries in the region.

2.1 Actorness

2.1.1 ISIS

Territoriality and Geopolitical Codes

Both ISIS and the YPG have managed to construct and pursue their geopolitical aims far more than the any other VNSAs in the Middle East. In this regard, the ISIS case presents an overarching model based on a set of *geopolitical codes* that is limitless and open to expansion regardless of ethnic, sectarian, or religious distinctions. With the aim of establishing the Islamic caliphate, ISIS pursues a systematically established geopolitical pattern with an objective toward establishing its governance architecture in seized territories (Zelin 2016, p. 1). The existence of such a geopolitical pattern aiming at enforcing a state-like governance provides ISIS with a distinct sense of territoriality rendering its geopolitical imagination a more embedded one rejecting the idea of territorial control only as a means of survival. That is, to say that, although most other VNSAs tend to perceive territory as an area of shelter distant from the forces they fight against, the ISIS case in particular is distinctive as its perception of territoriality is much more focused on constructing actorness by controlling territory and imposing a set of governing rules on the population. ISIS's evolving strategy from an insurgent group to an actor bearing quasi-state geopolitical codes also paves the way for the building of communities pledging allegiance, albeit forced. Therefore, by viewing territory not only as a shelter but also an opportunity to engage in administrative activities, ISIS has proved that its geopolitical codes go beyond the idea of survival and extend

Table 3 ISIS and YPG's distinguishing characteristics

		ISIS	YPG
Actorness	Territoriality and geopolitical codes	– Open to expansion regardless of ethnic, sectarian, and religious divisions – Territorial control for administrative practices – Aggressive geopolitical behavior	– Not expansionist, limited with clear ethnic divisions – Construction of an anti-extremist stance – Defensive geopolitical behavior
	Community building	– Universal network-based community – Regardless of territorial togetherness – Enforcing the idea of citizenship	– Ethnic (Kurdish) community – Territory-based community building
Powerfulness	Financial resources and funding	– Territorial control and use of natural resources and criminal revenues – Sales of illicit oil – Taxes and confiscations	– Fundraising, regular and voluntary contributions – Oil sales – Revenue from the existing channels of the PKK
	Recruitment and propaganda tools	– Appeal to different groups and nationalities – Members of Saddam Hussein's defeated army, defectors from Syrian rebel groups, new recruits from Iraq and Syria, global Internet recruits – Foreign fighters from 85 countries – Members and affiliates outside of Iraq and Syria – Media institutes such as Al-Furqan and Al-Hayat – Digital magazines such as Dabiq, Rumiyah – Almost 90,000 Twitter users	– Mandatory military duty – Alleged forcible recruitments – Limited number of foreign and female fighters – Limited propaganda – Recruitment websites – Leftist political networks
Effectiveness	Regional engagements	– Regional territorial control in Syria, Iraq, Egypt, Libya, Afghanistan, and Nigeria – Spillover effects into the neighboring countries, most notably Turkey – Instrumentalization of ISIS for legitimization of proactive involvement (Iran, Turkey)	– Not perceived as a security threat by the all countries in the region – Turkey's perception of YPG as a national security threat – Ambiguous but neutral stances of regional countries – Neither overt support nor objection from regional actors like KRG and Iran

(continued)

Table 3 (continued)

		ISIS	YPG
	International engagements and legitimacy	– The refugee crisis (Turkey-EU refugee deal) – Deterioration of the relations between regional and major powers (Turkey, Russia, United States) – Delegitimization of the UN (fail of Geneva talks, counterterrorism strategies) – Diminishment of the EU's global actorness – Not a legitimate actor	– Increasing autonomy and legitimacy after the Kobane events – Open US support and arms supply – Coordination with Russia in the fight against ISIS – Not seen as a terrorist group albeit the organic relations with PKK – Open US military support – Russian willingness to include it in the Geneva talks

all the way to proto-statehood, although one not likely to be internationally recognized (Katagiri 2015, p. 547).

Community Building

What is noteworthy here is that ISIS's state-like geopolitical representation is a direct product of its jihadist ideology which also offers a ground for *community-building* practices. In this regard, rather than pursuing control within limited boundaries, ISIS's jihadist geopolitical codes encourage it to imagine an open-ended structure that does not recognize ethnic, sectarian, and religious divisions but rather aims for expansion as far as possible to establish a full-functioning Islamic caliphate. Thus, through this jihadist geopolitical code, ISIS seeks a universal community understanding based on worldwide acceptance from Muslims and even calls for a mass immigration to the territories under its control (Bunzel 2015, pp. 32–33). Therefore, it is possible to argue that ISIS perceives all Muslims, even those not living under its controlled territories, as its natural community that should obey orders issued from its ranks. Furthermore, the community-building practices of ISIS make use of the previous grievances of Sunnis living in Syria and Iraq by providing them a sense of favorable citizenship under its control (Pollard et al. 2015, p. 14). A universal community-building understanding is important as, although territorial control and administration is a distinct characteristic of these new generations of VNSAs, it first enforces the idea of a network community based on "ideological projects" (Lia 2015, p. 34) regardless of territorial attachment and second provides ISIS with universal attraction for its sympathizers which in turn helps it supply financial and personnel resources from all over the world.

2.1.2 YPG

Territoriality and Geopolitical Codes

In line with the distinctive characteristic of establishing a solid actorness of the new generation of VNSAs, the YPG has also grounded its moves on a nuanced set of *geopolitical codes* enabling it to benefit from the course of the civil war. Its pragmatic decision to not take a clear position between the regime and the rebel forces in the beginning of the civil war provided the YPG with a sense of geopolitical flexibility facilitating its ascent as a rational actor in the eyes of external powers. As ISIS has likewise developed a territorial understanding going beyond the previous VNSA perceptions on territoriality, YPG has assigned a meaning to its relations with the territory. Again, as a characteristic of these new generations of VNSAs, the YPG also perceives territory as an opportunity to rehearse state-like activities. However, as opposed to the open-ended geopolitical pattern of ISIS, the YPG has so far executed a more limited understanding of geopolitical actorness confined within certain boundaries in the north of Syria. Although the existence of a narrow-scoped geopolitical actorness can be explained by the relative material weakness of the YPG, the historical background of Kurdish political demands contributes to the YPG's limited geopolitical actorness to a larger degree in the sense that certain ethnic and geographic bounds have always limited the Kurdish geopolitical imagination. In this regard, the YPG has sought to construct its geopolitical actorness grounded on defensive behavior as the last and only group to defy radicalism and extremism on the ground. In doing so and by gaining legitimacy from both the local population and external powers, the YPG has also managed to engage in administrative activities in the territories it controls, Rojava in particular, through its political branch, the PYD. In this context, with administrative activities such as providing security and public services (Khalaf 2016, p. 10), the YPG and, to a limited degree, the PYD have also undertaken a quasi-state-like geopolitical actorness in the north of Syria. Furthermore, the PYD-YPG presents a decentralized understanding of territorial administration based on cantons (Cemgil 2016) which also reflects the idea of the strong relation between the community and territory.

Community Building

Therefore, it is possible to argue that there is a strong sense of a community understanding and a *community-building* practice observed in the YPG case. However, again, this is a much more limited understanding of community that is directly attached to the population living in the territories under its control. In this regard, the YPG has presented a restricted regional network as opposed to ISIS's universal network-based community understanding. The YPG's sense of community is generally presented as if it is grounded on a secular understanding embedded in Kurdish ethnic nationalism which is also open to other religious and ethnic communities in Syria. For instance, the Yazidis under the SDF also give the appearance of acting with the Syrian Kurds, particularly in the fight against ISIS. Whether the Yezidi-YPG cooperation may be temporal or not, it seems clear that this coalition is a good sign of the way in which the Syrian Kurds construct their community in Syria on a broader geopolitical basis than has generally been predicted. Indeed, added to the victories gained against ISIS and historical Kurdish political demands in the region, such a flexible inclusivity in terms of community-building practices gives the PYD-YPG a greater legitimacy in the eyes of the local population. Therefore, although constructed on a narrower framework, the PYD-YPG seems to draw its territorial understanding with its community-building practices in a much more practical and flexible manner.

2.2 *Powerfulness*

2.2.1 ISIS

Financial Resources and Funding

Different from its predecessors, ISIS has created a self-sufficient economic model based on its territorial control which makes it an independent actor. In addition to exploiting natural resources, minerals, raw materials from oil to agricultural products, and industrial and commercial activities, the group obtains revenues from criminal activities such as extortion, kidnapping and ransom, and antiquities trafficking, as well as donations. Another important part of the group's funding comes from the extortion of the population living in the territories it invades in the form of taxes, fees, and confiscations for use in financing the administration of the territories under its control, military actions, and political and military diffusion to other territories. As a self-sustaining actor, ISIS is not dependent on major donors like its predecessors (for instance, Al-Qaeda and its franchises). As its funding comes predominately from internal sources, counterterrorism finance measures of Western governments are hampered. The financing of terrorism such as private Gulf Donations and other private contributions to ISIS and other groups in Syria, such as the Al-Qaeda affiliate Jabhat Al-Nusra, is under strict surveillance by the US Administration. However, there also exist some allegations indicating that some Arab countries (for instance, Saudi Arabia and Qatar) are involved in the financing of ISIS.

Today, most of ISIS's revenue comes from the sale of illicit oil, a small number of donors, and criminal enterprises. Before the start of the international coalition air campaign against ISIS in August 2014, the group operated 60% of Syria's oil fields and sold 50,000 barrels in Syria, at approximately $40 per barrel on the black market. It is also striking to note that ISIS only produces a fifth of the fields' total capacity in Iraq and Syria, although Syrian oil production only produced 10% of its capacity before the war began. The group also makes use of preexisting black market routes and the smuggling networks inherited from the Saddam era. In 2015, international coalition air strikes hobbled ISIS's financing sources, particularly their access to and sale of natural resources and ability to realize transactions, and thus increased its extortion revenue. With the intensification of international coalition and Russian air strikes since October 2016 and ISIS's military setbacks, a significant decrease in its revenue may also be expected in 2017. The correlation between ISIS's territoriality and its access to natural sources is high, and the group aims to expand its territory to reach new financing resources. This point also clearly shows how ISIS's economic model is different from that of Al-Qaeda, which is based on donations from individuals rather than its own self-sufficient resources. Unlike other VNSAs in the Middle East which are rather dependent on state sponsors, donors, or abuses of charity, ISIS is also engaged in a significant number of criminal enterprises in both Iraq and Syria.

Recruitment and Propaganda Tools

ISIS's successful methods of recruiting individuals ready to kill and die for their cause are one of the most important factors behind its quick territorial advancement in Iraq and Syria. Its ability to appeal to a range of different groups and nationalities is remarkable, and released videos and leaked information point to the fact that ISIS has been able to gather a diversified group of people including those from the West and Central Asia. John Graham identifies four categories of recruits that ISIS focuses on: members of Saddam Hussein's defeated army, defectors from Syrian rebel groups, new recruits from Iraq and Syria, and global Internet recruits (Graham 2015). The main bulk of ISIS forces fighting on the ground come from the first three categories due to their ready presence on the ground in the region and have helped ISIS emerge as an important phenomenon. Many accounts report that the members of Saddam Hussein's army dismantled after the US invasion constitute the core body of ISIS. Drawing on this core body of fighters, ISIS has been able to effectively engage in recruiting foreign members flowing into Syria. Most recent reports suggest that ISIS has recruited almost 30,000 fighters from 85 countries including EU countries, the United States, Canada, Australia, and Russia, with the highest numbers of recruits coming from Tunisia, Saudi Arabia, Russia, Turkey, and Jordan (Benmelech and Klor 2016). Such numbers far exceed those recruited by any other previous generation VNSAs. Several studies have sought to understand the motivations behind foreign fighters joining ISIS and report that their main motivation appears to be based on a search for identity and purpose (Barrett et al. 2015, p. 6). Furthermore, what rendered the group globally effective is that global recruits are not necessarily coming to fight in the Syrian territories but are also ready to engage in terrorist activities around the world. These recruits join external ISIS networks without any direct links to Iraq and Syria. However, they provided ISIS with the ability to commit terrorist attacks in cities such as Brussels, Istanbul, Paris, and Manchester. Here, social media and online communication and propaganda tools seem to be the most efficient mediums for recruiting members abroad. As Charlie Winter argues, ISIS creates a kind of "echo chamber" in order to trigger a radicalization process for the potential targets on social media networks (Winter 2016, p. 6). Indeed, ISIS has an established strategy for disseminating information and propaganda through print and digital media tools. To this end, ISIS has even founded an institute named Al-Furqan to produce media including CDs and magazines, and the center Al-Hayat produces multilingual products

(Cunningham et al. 2015, pp. 3–4). Another influential medial tool published by ISIS circles is the digital magazine *Dabiq*, which also indoctrinates an alternative vision (Ingram 2016, pp. 459–460). Added to this, the extensive use of Twitter helps ISIS to send its message to the world. Research on the utilization of Twitter by ISIS indicates up to 90,000 ISIS supporters on Twitter (Berger and Morgan 2015, p. 9). Recent analyses further illustrate that the narrative used in social media by ISIS circles has shifted from being focused on local issues to a more global narrative (Cunningham et al. 2015, p. 8).

2.2.2 YPG

Financial Resources and Funding

Contrary to ISIS, PYD-YPG's financial sources remain unclear, and it is not possible to identify reliable information outlining the details of its financial governance. However, based on the existing info, PYD-YPG's financial sources are a combination of fundraising, petrol sales, and existing channels with the PKK. The group's fundraising mechanism seems to be efficient in the sense that it manages to create a working and systematic mechanism for collecting basic expenses. The charter of the PYD gives important clues about how it makes use of regular contributions, voluntary donations, and various fundraising mechanisms. The sixth article of the charter suggests that the necessary financing is provided through two interconnected mechanisms: annual and monthly subscription fees of the members and supporters, which are determined voluntarily, and donation campaigns, voluntary business, and investments (Acun and Keskin 2016, p. 43). Although these official mechanisms seem to be the only reliable information to explain the YPG's financial sources, it is possible to speculate that the territorial control in Syria also provides further economic means. In this regard, oil revenues are also collected, although to a lesser extent than by ISIS, since PYD-YPG's territorial consolidation enabled it to take control of petrol sales and smuggling activities. Similarly, it is also reported that the PYD-YPG has the ability to produce electricity by the use of dams and power plants it controls such as the Tishrin Dam and Rumeilan power plant (Orhan 2016, p. 12; Khaddour 2017).

Given the existing links with the PKK, it can also be claimed that the YPG also benefits from the PKK's financial sources and funding. It is an acknowledged fact that the PKK has long been involved in narcotics/illegal drug trafficking and has control over a wide drug trafficking network based in Europe and has managed to generate a significant amount of financial revenues. Since the YPG appears to act as a franchise of the PKK (Soner et al. 2017), having adopted its doctrine, administrative practices, recruitment, and military strategies, it is possible to argue that there is also a flow of financial resources. Furthermore, it has already been brought to light that donations are made to the PKK through various foundations and associations based in Europe from sympathizers and it would not be a stretch to assume that YPG is also a beneficiary. On the other hand, since the Kobane events, the YPG has gradually become a viable local partner of the United States and has captured land from ISIS, thanks to US air strikes, military assistance, and training. Washington's recent decision to provide heavy military equipment to the SDF, the umbrella organization that is more than three-quarters YPG forces, has placed the YPG as the leading actor on front lines in a possible Raqqa operation. The fact that YPG became the biggest beneficiary of American military assistance seems to have boosted its confidence to move beyond Syria in pursuit of their aim for autonomy (Sly 2017).

Recruitment and Propaganda Tools

After the attack on Kobane by ISIS in 2014, the YPG adopted a law on mandatory military duty in July of that year, requiring at least one member of each family to join the army for a fixed period of 6 months. The law was to be managed and enforced by a special committee of the PYD (Acun and Keskin 2016, p. 24). This mandatory military duty was presented as a moral and societal responsibility. The requirement was enforced for Syrian Kurdish male citizens between the age of 18 and 30, and exceptions were made for families with only one male child. Kurdish women are permitted to enter the army on a voluntary basis. That this law was passed strongly indicates that the YPG seeks to have a regular army under its control similar to those of nation-states with the aim of reinforcing its own defense.

Although the law does not exempt Arabs and Christians living in the areas under the PYD's control, recruitment has been contained to only the Kurdish Muslim population (KurdWatch 2015). As cited in the KurdWatch Report, it has been claimed that the PYD remains reluctant in conscripting Arabs and Christians so as not to create tensions with the representatives of Arab tribes. In addition, the PYD's possible recruitment of Arabs also increases the risk of conflict with the Syrian regime's military forces who expect Arabs living in Kurdish areas to join the Syrian Army. However, the KurdWatch Report also indicates that Christian militias living in PYD-controlled areas are randomly recruited due to the PYD's limited cooperation with the YPG.

As the report suggests, the PYD has apparently engaged in developing a strict recruitment regime for the cantons under its administration by issuing new family registers with the aim of collecting more precise information about the family compositions and by detaining young Kurds who have not yet been registered (KurdWatch 2015, pp. 9–10). On the other hand, there are also some claims that the YPG utilizes forcible conscription and child soldiers. Human Rights Watch reported some human rights violations in 2014 in the area of child soldiers, where recruitment of those under 18 has been observed in Kurdish-controlled territories. However, the report also underlines that, starting from 2013, the YPG General Command issued an order prohibiting child recruitment under the age of 18 (Human Rights Watch 2014, p. 27).

Compared to ISIS, YPG fighters are mostly local, rather than foreign. However, it has been reported that in 2014 the YPG also called for foreign fighters to join the struggle against ISIS. Those foreign volunteers that joined the YPG were mainly those sympathetic to the PKK, militia coming from Matthew VanDyke's Sons of Liberty International (a not-for-profit business that trains Christian militias in northern Iraq) and a few other Western and Asian veterans (Harp 2017). Here it must be stressed that the driving force behind the attractiveness of the YPG in the eyes of foreign volunteers is the fact that YPG's cadres seem to pursue Marxist and hard-core leftist political ideologies (The Carter Center 2017). It must also be added that the YPG has a web recruitment in English to inform foreign fighters of route to Rojava.

Linked to this, it must also be underlined that the YPG also uses effective propaganda channels via various social media apparatus including recruitment sites, Facebook and Twitter accounts. However, compared to ISIS, their communication channels do not appear to be formal or institutionalized. Another distinguishing point between ISIS and the YPG in terms of use of social media is that YPG's lack of a global indoctrination and comprehensive propaganda strategy prevents it from becoming effective in the area of social communication. In fact, compared to ISIS, the narrow-scoped local VNSA YPG does seem to feel the necessity of launching an aggressive propaganda campaign to attract more supporters. The relatively positive perception of the YPG in the Western media, thanks to the widespread coverage of female fighters, also enforces its legitimacy in the Western world.

2.3 *Effectiveness*

2.3.1 ISIS

Regional Engagements

Against this backdrop of the practical utilization of the means of actorness and powerfulness, ISIS has pursued an effectiveness strategy to generate regional and international reactions. Among these, *regional interactions* were the most apparent as ISIS was able from the beginning to control a large swath of territory ranging from Syria and Iraq to Egypt, Libya, Nigeria, and even Afghanistan. Although current estimates suggest a significant decrease in territories controlled by ISIS (Dobbins and Jones 2017, p. 55), the regional chaos it has generated is distinct in the sense that no other VNSA has been able to produce such regional effectiveness. A comprehensive look at the presence of affiliates and terrorist activities claimed by ISIS suggests that the group's effectiveness has been felt in almost every country in the region, including Lebanon, Jordan, Saudi Arabia, Turkey, Libya, Egypt, Nigeria, Algeria, and Yemen (Lister 2014, pp. 32–34). It is possible to argue that ISIS has made a huge impact on the domestic and foreign policies and national security considerations of regional states and has destabilized the Middle Eastern regional order of fragile balances among regional and major powers. The direct spillover effects of the conflict generated by ISIS into neighboring countries, most notably Turkey, have shaken their domestic policies by creating security vulnerabilities (Parlar Dal 2017). In the Turkish case, a significant domestic politics transformation regarding its own Kurdish peace process has occurred as a result of these spillover effects, and the country has experienced increasing political polarization due to the increasing opposition directed toward its Syrian policy in general and its open border policy in particular. In addition to the impact on domestic politics, ISIS has become a source of tension among regional countries due to their controversial policies and disagreements on how to respond to the threats posed by ISIS. The presence of such a radical extremist terrorist organization at their borders has led regional countries, for instance, Iran, to instrumentalize ISIS in an attempt to legitimize their proactive policies toward Syria in the eyes of the Western and other regional countries. Thus, using ISIS to legitimatize their presence in the Syrian scene, most actors in the region have looked for greater autonomy in Syria for their attempts to counter ISIS: Iran has mobilized Hezbollah militias, the United States has begun to use YPG forces as a proxy, Russia has initiated military operations, and Turkey launched its own Euphrates Shield operation in September 2016. Related to this, the idea that any concrete advancement toward a peaceful solution in such regional crises is not possible without the effective engagement of regional powers through regional initiatives has been a lasting legacy from the fight against ISIS.

International Engagements and Legitimacy

The effectiveness of ISIS is also felt at the *international level* directly and through various indirect results affecting world politics from the Syrian civil war. Indeed, the intensified regional quagmire generated by ISIS has triggered both direct visible international effects and paved the way for generation of transformations in the policies and stances of international actors and organizations. Among these direct visible effects, the most prominent has been the refugee crisis resulting from the mass migration triggered by the advance of ISIS in Syria toward the neighboring countries of Turkey, Jordan, and Lebanon as well as Europe. Indeed, neighboring countries have been used mainly as passage routes by refugees aiming to reach European countries. This mass migration generated significant debate in European capitals due to the unwillingness or inability of most to welcome such a large number of Syrians. Although the refugee crisis led to an initial rapprochement between Turkey and the EU leading to a refugee deal, both the deal and the relationship between the two eventually became dysfunctional. This failure can be considered an initial signal of the further deterioration of relations between regional and major powers over the fight against ISIS. For instance, with US policy in flux in Syria, Turkey instead approached Russia, a fact that further deepened the divide between Russian and US interests in their efforts at countering ISIS. However, both the United States and Russia were able to eventually reach a mutual acceptance of the others' strategy against ISIS. For Turkey though, this understanding led to the further isolation of Turkey on the ground. The quick expansion of ISIS appeared to reveal the fact that international organizations do not possess the adequate flexibility or means to counter such an extremist threat. The UN's inactive attitude in face of the events in Syria and the atrocities of ISIS and the ineffectiveness of the Geneva talks and UN counterterrorism efforts have further weakened the UN's legitimate actorness in the eyes of regional actors. Similarly, the EU also faces legitimacy issues as its Syrian policies and long-standing counterterrorism strategies were not effective against the ISIS threat or in solving the crisis.

2.3.2 YPG

Regional Engagements

The YPG was able to generate impacts at the *regional level* as a new generation VNSA capable of affecting regional affairs. It is first important to note that the YPG does appear to be perceived as a significant and comprehensive security threat across the region as does ISIS. However, among countries in the region, only Turkey perceives the YPG as a substantial threat to its national security. The reason behind such a view is directly related to the perception Turkey has of its own Kurdish population, stemming from its long-standing struggle with the PKK, which has explicit organic ties with the YPG. For this reason, Turkey not only perceives the YPG as a national security threat but also argues that it is a terrorist organization that should be regionally and internationally fought against. Furthermore, having identified the YPG as a terrorist organization, Turkey's Syrian policy has been heavily influenced by the YPG's victories against ISIS on the ground as these victories provided the group with further international legitimacy and support. However, it is possible to argue that the YPG's ascendance as a legitimate and supported actor on the ground did not trigger a significant perceptual transformation in the foreign policy behavior of the other regional powers. What is striking about the other regional countries' perception of the YPG is their wait-and-see attitude based on neutrality. However, while turning a blind eye, it is not possible to argue that they follow Turkey in pursuing a negative strategy toward the YPG. Thus, although there are clear ethnic ties, the Kurdistan Regional Government in Northern Syria has not explicitly declared overt support to the YPG. Iran has not shown a clear strategic pattern regarding the ascendance of the YPG as a solid actor on the ground. However, Iran had previously demonstrated with its stance about the PKK in the past that it could easily make use of such organizations in its political calculations of regional rivalries. Similarly, Iran's uncertain attitude of the YPG can easily be explained by such a strategy based on a regional rivalry with Turkey within the Syrian scene.

International Engagements and Legitimacy

At the level of *international effectiveness*, there has been an upsurge in the perception of PYD/YPG as a legitimate actor in the Syrian scene. Initially, the ISIS phenomenon also helped the Syrian Kurds increase their autonomy and legitimacy, and the Kobane events led to the changing of local balances in Syria, allowing the PYD/YPG to become an increasingly viable local partner for the United States and the international coalition in the fight against ISIS. Seen as a legitimate actor, the United States has provided the YPG with a significant number of arms, over strong objection from Ankara. Such open support is important in the sense that it demonstrates how a VNSA, different from the previous generations, can be considered internationally to be a reliable partner and receive arms despite objection from a NATO ally. Again, notwithstanding the concerns raised by Turkey, YPG forces are considered to be the main reliable actor on the ground in almost every strategic calculation planned by the United States against ISIS. Russia also regards the YPG as a legitimate actor in the fight against ISIS and has shown willingness to cooperate with the group by establishing a military observation zone in Afrin. Indeed, Russia has shown its willingness to include the PYD-YPG in the Geneva talks as well. In this regard, the PYD-YPG has become a focus of attention in the Syrian civil war and the fight against ISIS for both the United States and Russia. Both parties show their willingness to rely on the YPG on the ground and to provide them with either explicit or covert support. Therefore, among the many groups searching for actorness in the Syrian quagmire, the YPG has emerged as the only actor able to earn such support and international legitimacy.

3 From Global to Regional: ISIS and the YPG in the Syrian Civil War

Acknowledging the necessity of a framework for the understanding and positioning of VNSAs in the Syrian context, this book aims to inject some fresh ideas into the academic analysis of contemporary VNSAs in the post-Arab Spring Middle East. Drawing on the abovementioned framework grounded on actorness, powerfulness, and effectiveness, the book first intends to decode ISIS's and the YPG's actorness. First, the four subthemes of actorness, *territoriality*, *geopolitical codes*, *interaction*, *and warfare strategies*, are discussed. Second, the powerfulness of our two VNSAs is examined in two chapters on recruitment of foreign fighters and on financing and natural resources. Third, the book goes beyond this scope and delves into the assessment of major and regional powers' evolving policies and strategies toward ISIS and the YPG over the course of the Syrian civil war. In the first stage of this assessment, the authors explore the American, Russian, and European engagement with the VNSAs using multiple conceptual and empirical perspectives. In the second stage, the focus shifts to the policies, strategic adjustments, and challenges of the two regional actors, Iran and Turkey, with regard the ISIS and the YPG. A key dynamic that runs through the entire book is the nuanced three-staged insight to the new generation of VNSAs that came to emerge from the Syrian civil war and its analytical path connecting the three-layered framework of *actorness*, *powerfulness*, and *effectiveness*.

3.1 Decoding "Actorness" of ISIS and the YPG

Territoriality

In his contribution to this book entitled "Contested Geographies: How ISIS and YG Rule 'No-Go' Areas in Northern Syria," Akın Ünver examines in detail the linkage between weak states and the changing understanding of territoriality of the new generation of VNSAs by delving into the ISIS and YPG cases. Ünver deals with

VNSA territorial administration practices in the Syrian civil war, from the perspective of the Islamic State (ISIS) and People's Protection Units (YPG). Departing from the argument that these two VNSAs, one religious and the other ethnonationalist, offer a good comparison in how they administer and run no-go zones, as well as how they establish control and sustain it at the expense of the Syrian central government, Ünver reveals that ISIS and the YPG offer two different—and competing—understandings of administration. The first is rooted in an extreme interpretation of religion, and the second is a social-economy model which attempts to create a "safe zone" free from those extreme interpretations.

Ünver in detail explains these differences in which they address common challenges of administering no-go zones. In doing so, Ünver argues that ISIS begins by infiltrating a contested territory (where authority of the central government is weak) and setting up sleeper cells that gather information and collect intelligence. By contrast, the YPG's self-identified zone of control is more limited and includes areas only with high percentage of Kurds. Furthermore, Ünver points to the differences between the populations living in the territories ISIS and the YPG control. According to Ünver, while ISIS rules over a large territory with a mostly suppressed/intimidated populace, the YPG rules over a smaller swath of territory with higher consolidation in support. This means that YPG has less incentive to develop pre-territorialization (sleeper cells, intelligence) methods such as those developed by ISIS and instead focus on post-territorial ones. Furthermore, Ünver speculates that ISIS's defenses will withdraw back to its core areas where it enjoys a higher level of support from the local populace, increasing its ferocity in fighting. For the YPG case, Ünver argues that the group will likely settle for a long-term administration within a limited area.

Geopolitical Codes

In the chapter that follows entitled "Making Sense of the Territorial Aspirations of ISIS: Autonomy, Representation, Influence," Hakan Mehmetcik and Ali Murat Kurşun analyze ISIS's geopolitical codes applying the three-layered framework of autonomy, representation, and influence borrowed from Ersel Aydinli in order to assess the degree to which ISIS has so far presented and pursued a territorial understanding as a non-negligible agency on the ground. Applying these three conceptual tools, Mehmetcik and Kurşun look at ISIS's, representation, regeneration, and organizational management strategies, capacity to act independently from states' support or persecution and impacts on politics in pursuit of problematizing ISIS's state formation and evaluating the group's potential actorness with a focus on its nuanced territorial understanding.

By demonstrating the group's organizational, fundraising, and regeneration capacities, the authors argue that, as the international fight against ISIS has intensified, the group's autonomy has weakened. Mehmetcik and Kurşun further point to the fact that by providing alternative visions (ummah) and concrete services such as security, etc., ISIS has been able to ground its autonomy on a flexible foundation helping it to act as an entity somewhere between a non-state- and state-like actor.

As a second layer of analysis, the authors take up the representation of ISIS by delving into the different sets of territories designed to:

1. Defend and expand missions in the first-tier area, namely, in Iraq and Syria
2. Establish alliances and create disorder and conflict to build a pre-territorial control in the second-tier area, namely, in Libya, Afghanistan, Egypt, Yemen, and Mali
3. Generate alliances and inflict lone-wolf attacks in the third-tier area, basically every possible place beyond the first- and second-tier areas

In the final analysis, Mehmetcik and Kurşun argue that ISIS has been able to create many transformative developments, pulling great power focus from the overreaching war and straining relations among allies, regional countries, and different political/religious sects. In this final layer of influence, the chapter scrutinizes the ability of ISIS to create major disruption and political instability from Europe to Far East Asia by creating refugee flows and generating ultra-national, Islamophobic waves of policies and a new and deadly wave of terror attacks. Drawing on the empirical results obtained from the application of the abovementioned three-layered framework, Mehmetcik and Kurşun conclude that, in addition to the military fight against the group, the struggle to defeat ISIS should also focus on local dynamics for success in the long run with the understanding that one way or another ISIS has been able to generate autonomy, representation, and influence on the ground.

Interdependence
Although much effort has been devoted to understanding the actorness of VNSAs on their own settings, a more practical approach is needed to understand how their mutual interactions and interdependence contribute to the construction of their actorness. Based on this, Fred H. Lawson's chapter "The Islamic State versus the Popular Protection Units: Reciprocal Mobilization of Violent Non-State Actors in the Syrian Civil War" provides such a comprehensive approach by looking at the question of how radical Islamist formations took the lead in the struggle against the Ba'th Party-led government in the popular uprising in Syria in March 2011 which transformed into civil war and how these Islamist militants pose a severe threat to the country's ethno-sectarian minorities, both directly by attacking their most vulnerable members and indirectly by inflicting substantial collateral damage during the course of repeated clashes between the radical Islamists and rival anti-government forces. In doing so, Lawson argues that these ethno-sectarian minorities, in response to the growing danger, organized militias to defend their respective communities, particularly in the northern and northeastern provinces.

To Lawson, the YPG, as the largest of these communal militias, steadily expanded its area of operations in the face of violent confrontations with radical Islamists, creating a situation in which the YPG's efforts to protect predominantly Kurdish areas provoked redoubled attempts by the Kurdish community's adversaries to overcome those measures. In this regard, Lawson argues that this belligerent interaction left the Kurds no more secure than they had been before, thereby constituting a classic conflict spiral. Turning to the ISIS case, Lawson contends that a parallel dynamic took shape in the spring of 2013, when ISIS became involved in the Syrian conflict. Hence, YPG cadres engaged in running battles against ISIS fighters not only in the northeast but also in the northern marches of Aleppo and al-Raqqah provinces as well. Based on this argumentation, Lawson concludes that reciprocal mobilization among the radical Islamists, Kurdish activists, and ISIS resulted in the consolidation of sizable territorial domains under the control of these three actors, which marked the ascendance of violent non-state actors as the primary protagonists in the Syrian civil war.

Warfare

In addition to the question of on which geopolitical codes and interaction types these new VNSAs construct their actorness, it is important to understand which methods and tactics they use in their prolonged conflicts with each other under civil war conditions in order to point out the consequent combined nature of the warfare happening on the ground. To that end, Özlem Kayhan Pusane's chapter "How to Profile PYD/YPG as an Actor in the Syrian Civil War: Policy Implications for the Region and Beyond" begins with an analysis of the concepts of "hybrid war," "hybrid threat," and "hybrid adversary." Drawing on the understanding of hybrid non-state actors both as organizations that can integrate regular and irregular forces, tactics, and strategies in armed confrontations and as entities that carry state-like features and challenge those states that they are placed in, Kayhan Pusane delves into the PYD-YPG for which the demarcation between the state and non-state actorness is blurred.

Debating these issues, Kayhan Pusane looks at how the PYD/YPG is a non-state actor with sophisticated state-like political features on one hand and how it is an effective local military force on the ground which combines conventional and irregular capabilities on the other hand. Departing from the argument that the PYD/YPG presents a key example to explain different dimensions and characteristics, Kayhan Pusane questions the factors behind the YPG's increasing influence on regional and international politics with an eye toward the concepts of hybrid war, threat, and adversary. After scrutinizing the perceptions of the PYD/YPG by the Syrian regime, other Kurdish actors in Syria and Iraq, regional actors such as Turkey, Iran, and Israel, and international actors such as the United States and Russia, Kayhan Pusane concludes that the actorness of the PYD/YPG has some limitations in the sense that almost all of the other actors engaged in dubious relationships with the group, mainly due to its hybrid characteristics.

3.2 Decoding "Powerfulness" of ISIS and the YPG

Financing Natural Resources

The use of natural resources as a financing methodology appears to be among the most debated issues in the VNSA literature and has drawn significant attention in the Syrian context as well. İbrahim Mazlum's chapter "ISIS as an Actor Controlling Water Resources in Syria and Iraq" makes an analysis of ISIS's strategic use of water as objectives and weapons of war in Syria and Iraq. Drawing on the argument that controlling natural resources such as water for political and economic purposes motivated ISIS's moves during the Syrian crisis, Mazlum goes further by arguing that ISIS tended to occupy the water resources and systems, especially large dams and water facilities, in order to engage in activities such as electricity generation and irrigation and to provide public services to the population.

Mazlum further looks at the use of water resources as weapon of war for offensive and defensive military purposes. Moreover, Mazlum illustrates that ISIS also attempted to threaten the other regions beyond its reach with weaponization of water such as downstream by flooding. Mazlum concludes by arguing that the Syrian civil war and the crisis in Iraq show the capability of new generation of VNSAs in the example of ISIS to effectively weaponize natural resources as strategic tools.

3.3 Decoding "Effectiveness" of ISIS and the YPG

3.3.1 Global Interactions

United States and Russia

As outlined in the previous section, since the ability to enact global effectiveness is one of the most important distinguishing characteristics of the new generation of VNSAs, a comparative look at the US engagement with ISIS and the YPG is helpful in order to gauge the degree to which they have been able to generate repercussions at the global level. Helin Sarı Ertem's "'Surrogate Warfare' in Syria and the Pitfalls of Diverging US Attitudes Towards ISIS and PYD" probes the reasons why the United States has lacked a credible counter strategy against the new generation of VNSAs by taking the internal and external dynamics into account. For Sarı Ertem, one of the most important reasons for the missing counter strategy stems from Washington's own pragmatic tendency of applying ambiguous policies changing from one VNSA to another. In doing so, as Sarı Ertem claims, the United States sows the seeds of confusion and distrust among regional allies and, as the chapter further argues, that the generation of such a confusion and distrust might lead to the creation of new threats posed to regional allies giving rise to further rivalries, which in turn might be costlier for the future interests of the United States in the region. Drawing on the concept of "surrogate war" as a means to minimize the burden of warfare with a limited engagement, Sari Ertem's chapter gives a bird's-eye view of the discussions of the reasons and consequences of the Obama administration's noninterventionist stance during the Syrian crisis with a view toward explaining the emergence and/or strengthening of VNSAs, including ISIS, the YPG, Lebanese Hezbollah, Jabhat Al-Nusra and Jabhat Fatah Al-Sham, etc., while rendering them into more significant political actors that are hard to ignore.

In order to examine the pitfalls of the US surrogate warfare, Ertem looks at the US decision to support the YPG as a solid actor on the ground in the fight against ISIS by arguing that it not only generates the abovementioned ambiguity but also contributes to the worsening of its relations with Turkey. In return, as the chapter explains, such an approach triggers further Turkish military involvement in the Syrian quagmire, which would worsen the situation in the region. Sari Ertem concludes her chapter by analyzing the effectiveness of this surrogate warfare pursued in the Obama era and further speculates the possibilities of a radical change in the US policy toward ISIS and the YPG under the Trump administration.

In his chapter entitled "External Actors and VNSAs: An Analysis of the United States, Russia, ISIS and PYD/YPG," Doruk Ergun argues that states have long interacted with VNSAs at varying capacities and with numerous motivations. The author argues that as a result of the Syrian war, Moscow and Washington seem to have found a common enemy with the VNSA ISIS while also finding a partner in the VNSA YPG. While both strive for "statehood" in the general sense, ISIS constitutes an antithesis to nation-states as seen clearly in its territorial expansion in Iraq and Syria and its attempts to roll back international humanitarian standards in the areas under its control and to inspire followers and other VNSAs across the globe. On the other hand, as underlined by the author, the PYD aims to achieve international legitimacy and recognition and presents a very rare case of a VNSA that has managed to cooperate with both Russia and the United States at the same time.

The author goes further by arguing that both VNSAs have transcended their pure military function and gained normative characteristics. He contends that ISIS has become a cause against which the international community can rally against, whereas the PYD has gained an unprecedented popularity with its overwhelmingly positive representations of female Kurdish fighters in both Western and Russian media outlets for their role in the fight against ISIS. Indeed, while recruits of American and Russian origin migrating to Syria to fight under ISIS ranks have been viewed as a major homeland security challenge and as a "radicalization" threat, fighters that joined the ranks of PYD have not been seen in this light. Another point the author underlines is the existence of variations in the dealings of the United States and Russia with ISIS and YPG separately. To the author, the United States sees the fight against ISIS as a natural extension of their fighting against transnational jihadist terror organizations, particularly Al-Qaeda. Regarding the PYD, the author notes that the Obama administration eventually turned to the PYD, similar to its decision to collaborate with the Iraqi Kurds in the 2003 Iraq War. In the view of the author, while different agencies in Washington, most notably the State Department and Pentagon, have differing priorities, over time, the Washington's anti-ISIS strategy on the ground has now become dependent on the PYD.

Regarding Russia's policies toward ISIS and the YPG, the author argues that although Russia remains among the top three "exporters" of foreign fighters to ISIS ranks, this has not been Moscow's primary motivation for intervening in Syria. In the final analysis, the author underlines that Russia's military intervention has had a set of goals, including, but not limited to, ensuring the permanence of the Assad regime or any other pro-Russian entities in Syria, increasing its military and political presence in the Middle East as an alternative to the United States, impeding NATO's freedom of movement in Syrian airspace, and breaking the Western imposed isolation after its annexation of Ukrainian territories. With regard to

Russia's policy on the PYD, the author stresses that Russia's maintenance of close ties with the YPG has served three main purposes. First, Russia prevented the YPG from falling under the complete sway of the United States. Second, the YPG's ability to cooperate and coexist with the Assad regime increased its attractiveness in the eyes of Russia, and thanks to this, Afrin was used to gradually cut the access of rebel groups to Aleppo with their lifeline in the Turkish border. Third, the ties with the PYD have also served as a counterweight against Turkey. As a consequence, the author underlines the functionality and the utility for Russia of using YPG as a local partner in the Syrian battlefield.

European Union

Although unable to pursue a substantial practical strategy in the course of the Syrian civil war, the European Union (EU) should also be analyzed in terms of its broader strategies in the Syrian civil war and its ability to pursue a solid framework for engaging with the new generation of VNSAs fighting in Syria. To this end, Yonca Özer and Fatmanur Kaçar's chapter entitled "The EU's Stance Towards VNSAs in Dealing with the Syrian Crisis and its Effects" unpacks the EU's technical approach laid down in its regional strategy for Syria and Iraq and highlights that the EU grounds its policies for dealing with the Syrian crisis on three main pillars: humanitarian assistance, prevention of regional spillovers, and fighting terrorism. By locating the EU as one of the most disputed actors as a result of the global effects of the new generation of VNSAs on the refugee flow and security challenges, Özer and Kaçar draw on the external and internal reasons driving the EU's strategies to cope with these VNSAs by looking at the consequent transformations observed in the EU's counterterrorism policies particularly after the terrorist attacks experienced in EU capitals. Drawing on the changing nature of threats posed to the EU, Özer and Kaçar look at how the "crisis-driven" approach of the EU counterterrorism policies has been transformed to respond to the ISIS threat within the framework of the EU's foreign policy priorities by discussing its actorness and identity.

By zeroing in on the ISIS case as a direct security threat to the EU's actorness on the global stage, the authors present an overview of the main challenges posed to the EU from its members, neighbors, and external powers as a result of its ineffectiveness in handling the crisis without giving a base to the global questioning of its actorness. In doing so, Özer and Kaçar argue that the rise of the VNSA threat, and of ISIS in particular, has once again laid bare that the EU's actorness is highly contentious when it comes to coping with nontraditional security challenges. Furthermore, the chapter takes up the questions of how the VNSAs have affected the EU's security/threat perceptions and its search for cooperation with other players in the region and how the EU takes the security and sovereignty concerns of regional countries such as Turkey into consideration in order to demonstrate why the EU had to cooperate with Turkey in applying its counterterrorism policy. Here, the authors also draw particular attention to the PYD/YPG case in order to assess how its partners' differing perceptions and calculations about these new VNSAs affect the EU's ability to pursue a global actorness through its counterterrorism policies.

3.3.2 Regional Interactions

Iran

As one of the most important regional actors engaging with VNSAs on the ground, Iran draws on its historical experience of engaging with the groups and has thus been able to pursue a nuanced policy with regard to the VNSAs in the Syrian civil war. Özden Zeynep Oktav's chapter "Understanding Iran's Approach to Violent Non-State Actors: ISIS and YPG Cases" sets the framework for assessing the network of VNSAs that Iran has attempted to manipulate as a result of its isolation in international society and diminishing maneuvering capacity vis-à-vis global actors. In doing so, Oktav's chapter presents a retrospective analysis of Iranian engagement with ISIS and the YPG during the course of the Syrian civil war with an eye toward linking the role of effective engagement with these VNSAs in Iran's evolving posture in the international system and its relations with the United States. Drawing on the argument that Iran has a long tradition of making use of VNSAs, Oktav probes the reasons behind Iran's inclination toward the organizations by introducing the "counter stigmatization" concept to the debate.

In her contribution, Oktav further argues that there has emerged a different dimension in the Iranian involvement with VNSAs after the rapid expansion of ISIS in Iraq and Syria. To Oktav, Iran's different response to ISIS is important in the sense that it has also generated a transition in the perception of Iran in Washington. In this regard, the chapter proceeds with the analysis of these consequences and Iran's shifting policies with a special emphasis on its transition from being a part of the "axis of evil" to another status, being "the last best hope" of Washington. In the final analysis, Oktav delves into the YPG case by portraying it as the elephant in the room in the Middle East by arguing that it will be the YPG that will come to the forefront again once the conflicts in Syria and Iraq end. The author further argues that the YPG rather than ISIS will become the main proxy in determination of the fate of Syria and Iraq in the future.

Turkey

Among the various spillover cases of the Syrian civil war, Turkey appears to be the most affected. Emel Parlar Dal's chapter entitled "The Contagion of the Syrian Civil War into Turkey Under the Impact of ISIS and YPG Cases: Conditioning Factors and Diffusion Mechanisms" looks at the Syrian civil war's contagion into Turkey by putting ISIS and the YPG at the core of the narrative. Parlar Dal's chapter addresses the question of how ISIS and the YPG brought the Syrian conflict into Turkey by also looking at the driving factors that triggered the overall contagiousness of the Syrian civil war. In her contribution, departing from the argument that contagion process of civil wars need to be examined both in terms of conditions and mechanisms, the author first attempts to empirically analyze the structural, political, economic-social, and cultural/perceptional factors laying the groundwork for the contagion of the Syrian civil war and second analyzes in detail the direct and indirect diffusion mechanisms through which ISIS and the YPG spread the consequences of the Syrian civil war into Turkey. In doing so, Parlar Dal looks at the effect of *bad neighborhood(s)*, *interaction opportunities and ties*, and *conflict characteristics* as direct mechanisms and *new tactics or strategies, new ideas and delegitimization of previous approaches, revised expectations about the likely behavior of key outside actors*, and *revised expectations about the chances of success as indirect mechanisms* of the diffusion.

After a close investigation of these, Parlar Dal illustrates that during the contagion process into Turkey, political and structural factors were more influential than economic-social and cultural-perceptional ones. The author goes further by arguing that among the direct mechanisms of the diffusion, bad neighborhood and interaction opportunities and ties played greater roles in the diffusion via ISIS and the YPG, while new tactics or strategies and new ideas and delegitimization of previous approaches catalyzed the process. In the final analysis, Parlar Dal draws particular attention to the transformations experienced in Turkish domestic and foreign policy behaviors due to the impact posed by the ISIS and the YPG on Turkey. To the author, Turkey had to undergo a striking process of behavioral transformation including further internal polarization, stalling of its Kurdish peace process, tighter domestic security measures, rapprochement with Russia, and the construction of an autonomous and preemptive security role in the Syrian scene. Finally, Parlar Dal concludes that the rise of the VNSA phenomenon with regard to the Syrian civil war accelerated the diffusion process of the civil war into Turkey and posed obliged Turkey to face with significant challenges both in terms of domestic and foreign policy issues.

In Guise of Conclusion

Since the onset of the first popular revolts in the late 2010, the Middle East has entered a new phase of political, economic, social, and demographic transformation of which the consequences for both the region and the entire world appear to be irreversible and deep-rooted. The optimism for the Arab Spring has been gradually replaced by a rising pessimism, particularly with the start of the Syrian conflict, one of the bloodiest and most tragic civil wars in the world history with estimated 400,000 deaths, 6.3 million displaced people, and 5 million of Syrian refugees in Europe and neighboring countries (CNN Library 2017). The Syrian conflict has also been marked by the inability, incapacity, and unwillingness of the West and Western institutions to effectively respond to this deepening crisis through the use of national and multilateral mechanisms. Another irreversible consequence of the Syrian civil war is the arrival of a new type of VNSAs on the scene with new forms of geopolitical actorness and means making them different from the other acting VNSAs in both the Middle East and the world. The existence of such a parallelism between the transformation of the Middle East and the emergence of new generation VNSAs also pushes us to rethink concepts such as sovereignty, territoriality, weak states, legitimacy, international justice, cosmopolitanism, and humanitarianism in relation with changing international politics.

The present book, by putting ISIS and the YPG at the core of its narrative, seeks to draw attention to the transformation observed in the IR literature in general and in Middle Eastern IR in particular. Acknowledging the fact that the VNSA phenomenon as one of the pioneers of this transformation is nothing new, these new generations of VNSAs differ from the previous ones in the sense that their novelties manifest themselves through the triple framework of actorness, powerfulness, and effectiveness, which is the detailed focus of this book. Since such a transformation is now irrevocable, the responses and policies taken by the states and international society against these VNSAs seem to be more determinant than ever. Given the lack of common understanding and coordinated response, it is almost certain that this new generation of VNSAs is able to undermine the existing perceptions of state sovereignty, which in turn could have a solid impact on the future of the states and the international system as a whole. What is more, as experienced in many cases, the inability to form a sustained regional order in the Middle East will most likely continue to adversely affect the entire international system. In view of the fact that the contemporary world order is composed of distinct or connected regional orders having converging and diverging normative settings, it is of vital importance to understand and assess how these new generations of VNSAs will affect or further prevent the reformation of the Middle Eastern regional order.

Although not attempting to provide a complete picture of the new generation of VNSAs, the contributions in this volume offer both analytical and empirical insights into the study of VNSAs and the Syrian civil war in general and of ISIS and the YPG in particular. Addressing the cases of ISIS and YPG, this book seeks to provide a set of new conceptual and analytical tools to improve our understanding of the new generation of VNSAs in the Syrian civil war context. By advancing a new framework based upon the triad of actorness, powerfulness, and effectiveness, the contributions that make up this book take a deeper look at the study of VNSAs by inquiring into the rationales of how these new generations of VNSAs construct their identities on visionary imaginations, how they transform their imagined visions into effective means to be utilized in the trajectory of their power consolidation, and how they make use of their consolidated power to enact regional and global impacts.

Outputs of the Book

In a nutshell, the main findings of this book can be summarized in four points of reconsideration. *First*, above all, the general framework of this book points almost exclusively to the need to address the new generation of VNSAs within civil war contexts. Since most of the existing works do not attempt to attach the ascendance of the new generation of VNSAs to the civil war conditions, such an approach is novel and seems to be one of the most persuasive approaches for understanding not only the proliferation of the VNSAs but also to make sense of how they can render the fate of civil wars into prolonged international conflicts. To put it another way, as some of these VNSAs gain strength in civil war conditions, the international community perceives some of them as reliable actors on the ground to be supported with the aim of giving an end to the civil wars in which they operate. Similarly, by giving rise to the emergence of legitimate proxy VNSAs, such an attitude not only prolongs the civil war but also paves the way for further compartmentalization of the international community itself.

Second, the chapters of this book provide compelling arguments in support of the view that these new generations of VNSAs have the ability to appeal to a greater number of people around the world with the help of effective use of their identities and means. In doing so, these new generation VNSAs have built their own audiences around the world in contrast to the rather limited representation of the previous generations. For instance, the empirical evidence provided in this book suggests that ISIS has been able to build such an audience through its emphasis on jihadism/caliphate with the help of the most violent extremist and radical means used by VNSAs so far. The YPG on the other hand has pursued its outreach strategy through its Marxist ideology. Put broadly, the typology of VNSAs the world is witnessing is one that is able to succeed in building audiences and gaining supporters around the world in different ways. Linked to this, the degree to which they have been able to transnationalize their actorness—most notably in the ISIS case—is also of great importance for understanding the diffusion processes of civil wars into neighboring countries. Indeed, contagion processes of the civil wars through the increasing violence of these VNSAs closely affect both domestic and foreign policies of neighboring countries and major powers. Again, in parallel to the increasing actorness of these VNSAs, the international community shifts its attention from the broader issues of addressing the atrocities and problems in these weak state structures to combatting these VNSAs themselves. In return, such a shift in the attention of the international community allows these VNSAs to act as a counter effective phenomenon by further prolonging the survival of such failed regimes themselves.

The *third* output that can be deduced from this book is related to the relation between the ineffectiveness of global counterterrorism strategies and further regeneration of VNSAs. Since there has been a lack of a total global counterterrorism strategy capable of dealing these new VNSAs a death blow, the loose efforts executed so far have served no purpose beyond their further mobilization through greater anger generation. Put another way, each fruitless effort to counter these VNSAs triggers a more eager perusal of their territorial, recruitment, and funding mechanisms. Therefore, the key thing to remember here is that the individual counterterrorism efforts pursued by countries such as the United States, Russia, Turkey, and Iran should be channeled into a more coordinated and global strategy for the sake of preventing distraction of efforts and regeneration of VNSAs. Likewise, what is further needed is the reconsideration of the legal and practical aspects of global counterterrorism efforts to be pursued by organizations such as the UN and NATO in order to lay the groundwork for a coordinated and legitimate struggle with them.

Last but not least, based on the overall framework of this book, it seems pertinent to suggest that the new generation of VNSAs should be approached from more multidisciplinary perspectives. Particularly, the study of new generation VNSAs from the perspectives of only conflict or counterterrorism studies fails to accomplish the creation of an overall analysis of the broader picture of their actorness, powerfulness, and effectiveness. In this regard, by also going beyond the sole IR perspective, these new generations of VNSAs should be examined on the basis of the various concepts outlined in this book project. For instance, an economic perspective based on international political economy literature is highly needed to assess their engagements while recruiting personnel, running economic networks including the management of natural resources and raising funds. Moreover, anthropological and sociological perspectives can also further serve to understand questions such as the human mobility and ideological transformation generated by these new VNSAs and the cultural alterations in the areas they control. Provided that, further research is needed to draw together the different lenses used by different perspectives in order to yield purposeful results about the current situation and the future of the new generation of VNSAs and their broader roles in regional and global affairs.

Further Research

The main inspiration behind this book was to understand how a comprehensive analysis of the ascent of ISIS and the YPG in the Syrian civil war context can serve to further the study of VNSAs in general by offering a framework proposing new components for understanding the new generation of VNSAs by looking at the degree to which they are able to self-accomplish themselves in terms of ideational, structural, and functional settings. Indeed, each of the individual chapters of this book is designed to propose and understand these new components in either a detailed or a combined manner using the examples of ISIS and the YPG. To this end, the overall framework of this book further attempts to develop a viable understanding of the new generation of VNSAs within the IR literature by offering empirical insights to their own interactions and to their engagements with regional and global actors.

Contemporary coverage of VNSAs is composed of various reports, op-eds, and analyses looking at the topic from a narrow state-centric perspective, constituting an obstacle to the birth of new avenues of research on the relevant topic which are more integrating in terms of their methodology and scope. Such a less state-centric approach seems to be vital in locating these VNSAs in the existing IR and conflict literature. On the other hand, it must be emphasized that the current scholarship on VNSAs lacks studies combining conflict studies and IR literature. This book seeks to fulfill this lacuna by its IR-sponsored conflict approach. In fact, this twin approach seems to facilitate the study of various VNSAs on both a comparative and interrelational basis.

After all, what emerges from this collection is that more research should be devoted to the nexus between VNSAs and civil war. Although this book covers a wide range of topics related to VNSAs, ranging from their geopolitical codes/territoriality, financial means, recruitment and propaganda tools, and regional and global engagements, there still exists additional room for further research into the new generation of VNSAs, especially in the Middle Eastern context. Recent studies on VNSAs in the Middle East lack a multidimensional integrated approach to the topic and rarely provide new theoretical and conceptual insights to the assessment of this new generation of actors. Rather, they mostly consist of facts or actor-based analysis preventing scholars from deepening their analysis with a wide range of perspectives. Last but not least, with all its limitations in mind, this book intends to go beyond the existing studies with its nuanced analytical approach and engage in opening a new debate on the study of the new generation of VNSAs in the global context in general and in the Middle East context in particular. In this regard, a special focus on ISIS and the YPG using the three-pronged framework of actorness, powerfulness, and effectiveness may also be applied to the study of other VNSAs in both the Middle East and other geographies and thus may construct an appropriate analytical tool for further research on VNSAs in the context of civil war.

References

Acun, C., & Keskin, B. (2016). *PKK'nın Kuzey Suriye Örgütlenmesi: PYD, YPG*. SETA.

Aydinli, E. (2016). *Violent non-state actors: From Anarchists to Jihadists* (1st ed.). Abingdon: Routledge.

Barrett, R., Berger, J., Ghosh, L., Schoenfeld, D., el-Shawesh, M., Skinner, P. M., et al. (2015). *Foreign fighters: An updated assessment of the flow of foreign fighters into Syria and Iraq*. The Soufan Group. Accessed June 11, 2017, from http://soufangroup.com/wp-content/uploads/2015/12/TSG_ForeignFightersUpdate3.pdf

Benmelech, E., & Klor, E. F. (2016). *What explains the flow of foreign fighters to ISIS?* National Bureau of Economic Research. Accessed June 11, 2017, from http://www.nber.org/papers/w22190

Berger, J. M., & Morgan, J. (2015). *The ISIS Twitter census: Defining and describing the population of ISIS supporters on Twitter* (No. 20). Center for Middle East Policy at Brookings. Accessed June 11, 2017, from https://www.brookings.edu/wp-content/uploads/2016/06/isis_twitter_census_berger_morgan.pdf

Brown, M. E. (1993). *Ethnic conflict and international security*. Princeton, NJ: Princeton University Press.

Bunzel, C. (2015). *From paper state to Caliphate: The ideology of the Islamic State* (No. 19). Washington, DC: Center for Middle East Policy at Brookings.

Cemgil, C. (2016). The republican ideal of freedom as non-domination and the Rojava experiment: "States as they are" or a new socio-political imagination? *Philosophy and Social Criticism, 42* (4–5), 419–428. https://doi.org/10.1177/0191453715624959

CNN Library. (2017, May 26). *Syrian civil war fast facts*. http://cnn.it/2r7FbFm

Cunningham, D., Everton, S. F., & Schroeder, R. (2015). *Social media and the ISIS narrative*. Accessed June 11, 2017, from http://calhoun.nps.edu/handle/10945/53059

Dobbins, J., & Jones, S. G. (2017). The end of a Caliphate. *Survival, 59*(3), 55–72. https://doi.org/10.1080/00396338.2017.1325596

Ezrow, N. (2017). *Global politics and violent non-state actors*. Thousand Oaks, CA: SAGE.

Forest, J. J. F. (2009). *Influence warfare: How terrorists and governments fight to shape perceptions in a war of ideas*. Westport, CN: Praeger Security International.

Graham, J. (2015, December 29). Who joins ISIS and why? *Huffington Post*. http://www.huffingtonpost.com/john-graham/who-joins-isis-and-why_b_8881810.html

Guelke, A. (1995). *The age of terrorism and the international political system*. London: I.B. Tauris.

Harp, S. (2017, February 14). The Anarchists vs. the Islamic State: On the front lines of Syria with the young American radicals fighting ISIS. *Rolling Stone*. http://rol.st/2rXzrRY

Human Rights Watch. (2014). *"Maybe we live and maybe we die" recruitment and use of children by armed groups in Syria*. Human Rights Watch.

Ingram, H. J. (2016). An analysis of Islamic State's Dabiq magazine. *Australian Journal of Political Science, 51*(3), 458–477. https://doi.org/10.1080/10361146.2016.1174188
Katagiri, N. (2015). ISIL, insurgent strategies for statehood, and the challenge for security studies. *Small Wars and Insurgencies, 26*(3), 542–556. https://doi.org/10.1080/09592318.2014.989672
Khaddour, K. (2017, April 23). *How regional security concerns uniquely constrain governance in Northeastern Syria*. http://ceip.org/2qzqOgO
Khalaf, R. (2016). *Governing Rojava: Layers of legitimacy in Syria*. London: Chatham House.
Krause, K., & Milliken, J. (2009). Introduction: The challenge of non-state armed groups. *Contemporary Security Policy, 30*(2), 202–220. https://doi.org/10.1080/13523260903077296
KurdWatch. (2015). *Forcible recruitments and the deployment of child soldiers by the Democratic Union Party in Syria* (No. 10). KurdWatch.
Lia, B. (2015). Understanding Jihadi proto-states. *Perspectives on Terrorism, 9*(4), 30–41.
Lister, C. (2014). *Profiling the Islamic State* (No. 13). Brookings Doha Center. http://brook.gs/2sqHkzG
Orhan, O. (2016). *Syrian Kurds: Current political/military situation and foreign affaris* (No. 48). ORSAM.
Parlar Dal, E. (2017). Impact of the transnationalization of the Syrian civil war on Turkey: Conflict spillover cases of ISIS and PYD-YPG/PKK. *Cambridge Review of International Affairs*, 1–25. https://doi.org/10.1080/09557571.2016.1256948
Pollard, S. E., Poplack, D. A., & Casey, K. C. (2015). Understanding the Islamic State's competitive advantages: Remaking state and nationhood in the Middle East and North Africa. *Terrorism and Political Violence*, 1–21. https://doi.org/10.1080/09546553.2015.1108310
Schneckener, U. (2006). Fragile statehood, armed non-state actors and security governance. In A. Bryden & M. Caparini (Eds.), *Private actors and security governance* (pp. 23–40). Münster: LIT Verlag.
Sly, L. (2017, July 1). U.S. military aid is fueling big ambitions for Syria's leftist Kurdish militia. *The Washington Post*.
Soner, B. A., Aslan, Ö., & Kıyıcı, H. (2017). *PKK's regional franchise of terror*. International Center for Terrorism and Security Studies.
Stepanova, E. (2008). *Terrorism in asymmetric conflict: Ideological and structural aspects*. Oxford: Oxford University Press.
The Carter Center. (2017). *Foreign volunteers for the Syrian Kurdish forces*. http://bit.ly/2sqH0ks
Thomas, T. S. (2010). *Beyond pain: Coercing violent non-state actors*. U.S. Air Force Academy, Institute for National Security Studies. Accessed June 11, 2017, from http://www.usafa.edu/app/uploads/Thomas-Coercing-VNSA.pdf
Thomas, T. S., Kiser, S. D., & Casebeer, W. D. (2005). *Warlords rising: Confronting violent non-state actors*. Lanham, MD: Lexington Books.
Walt, S. M. (2015, November/December). ISIS as revolutionary state. *Foreign Affairs*, 94, 42–51.
Williams, P. (2008). *Violent non-state actors and national and international security*. International Relations and Security Network. Accessed June 11, 2017, from https://www.files.ethz.ch/isn/93880/VNSAs.pdf
Winter, C. (2016). *An integrated approach to Islamic State recruitment*. The Australian Strategic Policy Institute. Accessed June 11, 2017, from https://aspi.org.au/publications/an-integrated-approach-to-islamic-state-recruitment/SR88_IS-recruitment.pdf
Zelin, A. Y. (2016). *The Islamic State's territorial methodology* (No. 29). The Washington Institute for Near East Policy.

Part I
Actorness

Contested Geographies: How ISIS and YPG Rule "No-Go" Areas in Northern Syria

H. Akın Ünver

1 Introduction

Why do civil wars create "no-go zones" and how do they enforce these territorialities? By exploring how these "no-go zones" are formed, we can understand how legitimacy can be localized and prevent standing armies from challenging these territorialities during civil wars and localized low-intensity conflicts. Syrian Civil War in a good case study in theorizing these no-go zones as state weakness has created a number of strong violent non-state actors (VNSAs) operating within their own territorial bounds.

In fact, no-go zones have been around for centuries, under empires, kingdoms, and states that were suffering from different levels of weakening of the central authority. Brigands, bandits, and rebels have populated these no-go zones, conducting their own taxation, extortion, and recruitment operations. In modern study of war, VNSA no-go zones became important once again following the end of the Cold War, as the threat perception shifted from global to local (Buzan 2008; Dobbie 1994; Rousseau and Garcia-Retamero 2007; Russett 1994). Dormant pressures of identity and legitimacy became unearthed by the removal of a global nuclear threat, and countries that contained various levels of suppressed disenfranchisement began suffering from separatist movements. This new internal threat forced the states to devise military-only solutions that have paradoxically enabled the strengthening and deepening of VNSAs—especially where grievances are shared by a large portion of the minority. These VNSAs, in turn, have successfully established and enforced no-go zones in areas where their ethnic or religious kin predominantly lived. Not only in rural areas but also within cities, districts, and

H.A. Ünver (✉)
Kadir Has University, Istanbul, Turkey
e-mail: akin.unver@khas.edu.tr

Ö.Z. Oktav et al. (eds.), *Violent Non-state Actors and the Syrian Civil War*,
DOI 10.1007/978-3-319-67528-2_2

even individual streets, these no-go zones have turned into de facto micro administrations with their own taxation, recruitment, and, in some cases, legal systems.

The scholarship on weak and failed states has grown considerably cautious since the inception of the Syrian Civil War, a far cry since Gerald Helman and Steven Ratner wrote a blueprint article in 1992 on how the United States could "put back" together failed states (Helman and Ratner 1992). With the academic and policy wisdom shifting away from favoring intervention, the combined systemic shift and state weakening in Iraq and Syria may well generate a bloody, yet long-term opportunity for the transnational rise of Kurdish nationalism. Even though the effects of Kurdish nationalism will not be transformative in strong states like Iran and Turkey, it will nonetheless have long-term implications where there are strong Kurdish actors in weak states such as Iraq and Syria. Mikaelian and Salloukh use the Hezbollah in Lebanon as such a case study, whereby strong non-state actors within weak states lead to quasi-statelets and parallel decision-making bodies (Salloukh and Barakat 2015).

Syrian Civil War became a microcosm of observing how VNSAs form, operate, and establish their own territorialities. One perspective on VNSA formation was introduced by Robert I. Rotberg, who approached state weakening as a contagious phenomenon, whereby the ripple effect of state weakening in one country spills over into adjacent countries (Rotberg 2004). Rotberg furthers his argument by underlining the fact that the cause of state weakening—unearthing of identity-related dormant grievances—travel well across closer distances, triggering similar reactions in its neighborhood. These reactions can both be vertical and exist within an administrative entity, and also horizontally—across adjacent countries. This was diagnosed best by Anthony Vinci, who demonstrated how VNSAs expand as a response to state weakness, spilling over into the borders of neighboring countries. In Vinci's view, the extent to which a VNSA spreads is determined by the level of grievances and disenfranchisement experienced by the same identity group in its immediate territorial environment. This has indeed been the case with the Islamic State in Iraq and Syria (or ISIS or Daesh) and Democratic Union Party, PYD (*Partiya Yekîtiya Demokrat*, along with its military wing, YPG—*Yekîneyên Parastina Gel*, or People's Protection Units) who emerged from the dual state weakening in Syria and Iraq. It also gives us a good idea on why they compete horizontally (with other non-state armed groups) and vertically (with the standing armies of states they inhabit) not only through armed confrontation but also practices or administration, taxation, and territorial control.

1.1 Theorizing ISIS and YPG's Territorialization

Both state and non-state territorialization build upon the foundational literature of Sack (1986), Vandergeest and Peluso (1995), Sivaramakrishnan (1997), Buch-Hansen (2003), Wadley (2003), and Roth (2008) to argue for an understanding of state territorialization as a dynamic, negotiated, and historically contingent phenomenon that goes beyond negotiations and interactions among state and non-state actors. In establishing the classical literature on territorial methodology, Sack (1986) engages in a critical inquiry against biological determinists, who viewed territorialization as an adaptive behavior, whereby individuals and cultures form long-term power relations through administration, territorial practice, and identity cohesion. Vandergeest and Peluso (1995) later mounted a second critique against political scientists who claimed that territorialization is merely "international" or "external" engagement, which is negotiated with adjacent population units only. To debunk this thinking, Vandergeest and Peluso introduce "internal territorialization," which conceptualizes how groups develop territorial methodology not only against external units but also through in-group dynamics, such as administration and lawmaking. Following this literature, Ribot and Peluso (2003), Li (2007), and Sikor and Lund (2009) further the argument by emphasizing on legal territorialization, land rights, and administrative practice as different components of territorial methodology.

There is an observable norm diffusion and transmission between VNSAs and states they fight with. Indeed, most VNSAs copy recruitment, training, strategy, administration, and taxation practices of the states. The mechanics of state-VNSA norm transmission was conceptualized by Klaus Schlichte, who observed how prolonged secessionist conflicts create two mirror images with similar core skills and complementary strategies that create a persistent stalemate (Schlichte 2009). In Schlichte's view, a well-organized state security and military apparatus—by itself—is not enough to end secessionist conflicts, as VNSAs mirror similar organization as a survival strategy. As long as the foundational grievance of the VNSA persists and if it can create its own no-go zone with a standing administration, it simply evolves in the face of a capable military force, mimicking and adapting to the very armed force it is fighting. The very military/security measures states take to subdue such groups, without making progress in political representation, also paradoxically strengthen them, as new military knowledge, equipment, and training types travel well within a single border, in addition to such equipment being lost or stolen in conflict. However, over time, non-state armed groups also start to mimic the states they are fighting with, along with their ceremonial, symbolic, and mobilization procedures. This is why many armed non-state groups use symbols associated with the states they are fighting against, flags, anthems, and, in some cases, their own currency, to foster group cohesion and acceptance. The methodical use of these symbols become more commonplace, as armed groups begin administering territory and population, thus becoming the main security providers of that area (Podder 2013). In turn, such non-state groups become proto-statelets and engage in a horizontal competition of territorial control with states. However, these symbols are not merely for internal consumption. In the past, in what is termed as "passport wars" between Israel, Palestine, and other Arab countries, the usage of term "Palestine" along with its flag and the passport itself were heavily contested, leading to the wider internationalization of the Palestinian issue (Fiddian-Qasmiyeh 2016).

One of the reasons why no-go zones materialize is because of the local support in favor of VNSA that is controlling it. In that, successful provision of services such as security and basic goods and services renders VNSAs' competitors to state control in their respective territories and prevents state security personnel to enter, seize, and hold them. Robert Bunker specifies a three-step process on how this works in northern Syria, where:

- Decline in the supply of state protection, gradually assuming a more permanent lack of capacity. This also follows prolonged lack of state capacity in providing services, administration, and legal oversight in the said region.
- Gradual increase in demand for security from the locals, which, coupled with long-standing lack of service provision, assumes a quasi-rebellious character.
- Emergence of local VNSAs who offer this protection in exchange for local loyalties, fulfilling some basic functions of administration along the way (Bunker 2014).

If three conditions are met, then local VNSAs take over the functions of the state and behave like the central authority it dislodged. This has profound implications on the Weberian notion of legitimacy (states as the legitimate sources of the use of force) as well as Westphalian understanding of sovereignty and nonintervention (social contract between the state and the state as the sole provider of security). The latter further brings questions regarding foreign intervention and spills into the literature on responsibility to protect (R2P).

Syria and Iraq—among other states that suffer from instability—therefore brings us to the question: are central governments still the main source of stability in international relations? What happens if a central government destabilizes itself and starts exporting instability into its adjacent territories by exacerbating existing divisions, ethnic, or religious? Usually indiscriminate and excessive force, following extended political disagreements over identity problems that cover a large demography, paradoxically leads to a weakening of state control in a particular territory. The use of force then follows the law of diminishing returns, as the state descends into a vicious circle of launching gradually higher-cost operations with increasingly lower percentage of objectives met, often intensifying the level of discontent in the region. When grievances against the state intensify and the vicious circle of extreme force and continued violence continue, the local populace gets divided, often between those that still feel loyal to the state and those that seek alternative sources of localized statehood, in the form of newly emerging VNSAs (Milliken and Krause 2002). Thus, a new symbiotic relationship emerges between VNSAs and parts of the population, with implications on ideology, politics, and daily life of the territory. Shifting loyalties from state to non-state actors not only generates further violence but also opens up the territory from external military intervention, citing a lack of legitimate central authority and the spillover effect of the chaos there.

David Kilcullen conceptualizes no-go zones as the perfect expression of this suspense in state weakening. These areas don't have to be on the margins of a country (i.e., close to its borders)—some no-go zones can be located within major cities as well, evidenced by French suburbs, slums of Rio de Janeiro, and Molenbeek in Brussels—among other examples (Kilcullen 2015). Kilcullen's "theory of competitive control" is important, not only in terms of how no-go zones are established but also on how they are sustained. The theory of competitive control stipulates that in a conflict setting, the armed actor which the population believes to be the better side in establishing a predictable, consistent, and wide-spectrum normative system, namely, a "set of behavioral rules correlated with a set of predictable consequences" of control, is most likely to dominate that population in its residential area and develop legitimacy. In the absence of a central authority, VNSAs that best simulate the functions of a state—security, taxation, goods, and services—in a predictable and regular fashion, will steer the loyalties of that population. Kilcullen has a paradoxical view of VNSAs. He believes that VNSAs both corrupt the social fabric of a society by undermining order, but, in a different chapter, argues that VNSAs emerge as a direct result of state weakening—that's why it is hard to locate where Kilcullen situates the responsibility of the chaos that emerges with VNSAs. "Conflict entrepreneurs," in Kilcullen's view, expedite the process of state weakening through both armed violence and also through exploiting the grievances of deprived and forgotten populace, turning their grievances into violent resistance against the state.

No-go zones are becoming an increasingly problematic aspect of international security and counterinsurgency as wars between states become rarer and states increasingly fight with insurgencies within or across the immediate border. Regardless of whether they are supportive of, or against, Western military intervention, all non-state armed groups have demonstrated similar patterns of behavior with regard to establishing alternative regimes and localized control zones. RAND defines "ungoverned spaces" as "... failed or failing states, poorly con-trolled land or maritime borders, or areas within otherwise viable states where the central government's authority does not extend" (Rabasa et al. 2007). The US Department of Defense on the other hand offers this definition:

> A place where the state or the central government is unable or unwilling to extend control, effectively govern, or influence the local population, and where a provincial, local, tribal, or autonomous government does not fully or effectively govern, due to inadequate governance capacity, insufficient political will, gaps in legitimacy, the presence of conflict, or restrictive norms of behavior... the term 'ungoverned areas' encompasses under-governed, misgoverned, contested, and exploitable areas as well as ungoverned areas. (Lamb 2008)

The study of no-go zones in war zones (or in urban settings) gives us great insight on how issue and policy compartmentalization occur between central authorities and VNSAs. For example, a non-state group can provide local security, food, and garbage disposal, whereas a state can still be providing electricity, water, and banking services. This equilibrium between state and non-state administration can range from ghettoization, where non-state groups maintain security in small districts and streets, to full state collapse, where non-state actors provide all components of administration, including infrastructure, municipality, and financial services. One of the best examples to this was the case of Mosul, where civil servants continued to receive salaries from Baghdad, long after the capture of the city by ISIS. It was only in October 2015 that Baghdad decided to cut off salaries of Iraqi officials serving in parts of Iraq controlled by the Islamic State. The decision to cut funding was intended to remove one source of funding to ISIS, as well as preventing the organization to get credit from the administrative daily operations funded by Baghdad. ISIS, in turn, began using this decision for its own propaganda purposes, making the case against populations under its control that Baghdad had "abandoned" them (Colest 2015). Indeed, the relationship between states and VNSAs over no-go zones is usually blurry. State and non-state actors can actually cooperate in administering and running a territory, while remaining adversaries over the security control of the same area.

1.2 Religion and Ethnicity: Expansion and Zone Selection Mechanics of ISIS and YPG

ISIS and YPG offer two different—and competing—understandings of administration; the first rooted in an extreme interpretation of religion and the second a social economy model, which attempts to create a "safe zone" free from those extreme interpretations. YPG's zone of control—Rojava, in northern Syria—gradually expanded through the organization's ground operations, assisted by US airstrikes, often at the expense of ISIS. Eventually, YPG's aim is to create an autonomous and self-administered federal territory, through an uninterrupted territorial belt stretching across the Turkish-Syrian border. Turkey's Operation Euphrates Shield, which penetrated into ISIS-held stronghold in al-Bab, largely ended YPG's bid to unify its cantons, but nonetheless, YPG still controls a great part of northeastern border of Syria. ISIS, on the other hand, emerged first in the Sunni-held Anbar province in Iraq and simultaneously expanded into Syria in the second half of 2014. ISIS defines its territoriality as deeply rooted in Sharia and establishes order in the predominantly Sunni areas of Syria and Iraq through the strict enforcement of religious rules. Aaron Zelin has conducted one of the earliest inquiries into how ISIS administers, by dividing it into two phases (pre-territorial and post-territorial). In pre-territorial, ISIS employs methods such as intelligence gathering and sleeper cell implantation, while in post-territorial, it focuses on administrative practices such as moral policing and services provision. So far, ISIS methodology isn't substantially different from YPG, which also focuses on municipality work and infrastructure construction (Zelin 2016).

What makes ISIS and YPG different is the detail in which they address common challenges of administering no-go zones. ISIS begins infiltrating into a contested territory (where authority of the central government is weak) and setting up sleeper cells that gather information and collect intelligence. In the first phase, they also start bribing local clans for their loyalty and start recruiting and training potential insurgents. Once the first phase—coined by ISIS as *dawa*, or "cause"—yields desired results, and the local populace turns receptive to ISIS influence, then the dominant tribes and power brokers in the region pledge allegiance (*baya*) to ISIS leader Abu Bakr al-Baghdadi and set up dedicated training camps for the use of ISIS. Once a territory is seized by ISIS and becomes a no-go zone, the second phase begins when ISIS initiates outreach programs toward the wider segment of the local populace through "soft" methods like games, competitions, and coffee gatherings, gradually intensifying the tone and scope of the outreach into direct propaganda and image building (Charters 2014). This is done by a dedicated PR office, which logs the details of the population and households into a central roster, especially paying close attention to powerful tribes and houses (Dabiq 2017: 32). Once ISIS succeeds in presenting a positive image of itself in the no-go zone, it proceeds into employing two key aspects of administration: security provision and legal oversight. The group's provision of security and its ability to resolve long-standing tribal disputes in the no-go zone—if successful—reinforces the group's challenge against the central authority and can present itself not just as an occupying force but also as a better administrator that the local populace should support (Zelin 2016). One ISIS defector, using the pseudonym "Abu Ahmed," outlined how different parts of the local society were co-opted into ISIS through uncommon ways: "Many of the lowest parts of society jumped to join ad-Dawlah in the first days. For instance, a women who was running [a brothel] joined ad-Dawlah [... later becoming ...] the emir of the *hisbah* [morality police]" (ICSVE 2015).

YPG has a different approach to pre-territorial control. While ISIS aims to unite all Sunni areas of Syria and Iraq under a single banner, YPG's self-identified zone of control is more limited and includes areas only with high percentage of Kurds (Pusane 2017). However, while ISIS rules over a large territory with mostly suppressed/intimidated populace, YPG rules over a smaller swath of territory with higher consolidation in support. This means that YPG has less incentive to develop a pre-territorialization (sleeper cells, intelligence) like the one developed by ISIS and instead focus on post-territorial methods. One exception to this rule emerged as YPG started to expand into territories beyond the immediate Kurdish hinterland in northern Syria and began spilling over into territories with considerable Arab population (Perry 2015). While YPG control spread rapidly across predominantly Kurdish towns, where the group employed its social economy model, as it started expanding beyond Tal Abyad, this expansion slowed down, forcing YPG to think of multiethnic administrative compositions and setting up new military offshoots such as the SDF (made of Arabic volunteers).

In traditional Kurdish geopolitics, a hypothetical Kurdistan would be completely landlocked and would be at the mercy and goodwill of its neighbors for trade and survival. The Syrian Civil War changed this thinking. Once ISIS was defeated at Kobani, the Kurdish cantons of Afrin, Kobani, and Jazira would unite along the border, creating a singular territorial reality, resting at the edge of Turkey's Hatay province—which would be the only gap that would prevent a unified Rojava from accessing the Mediterranean Sea (Unver 2016). Not only would the Kurdish belt's access to the Mediterranean would be an immense geopolitical goal that would render unification and state building, it would also open up KRG oil fields to naval export without having to deal with neighboring Turkey, Syria, Iraq, or Iran. A key detail about the Syrian Democratic Forces, SDF—a renamed version of YPG—is that its official flag is a map of Syria, which contains Turkey's Hatay province; however, several Syria experts this author interviewed noted that the same map of Syria is used by the majority of factions fighting in Syria, including those supported by Turkey.

Overall, ISIS and YPG's expansion dynamics reveal and inherit from their geopolitical ambitions. While ISIS seeks to unite an Arab-Sunni hinterland into one single caliphate, YPG seeks to unite ethnic-Kurdish lands of northern Syria into one, uninterrupted belt, with autonomous and representative canton-type administrations. Therefore, ISIS expansion strategy follows the logic of religious conquest and picks its battles in areas where receptivity toward Sharia will be greater—or at least, resistance to it smaller. YPG on the other hand follows a predominantly ethnic trajectory in no-go zone selection, which is aimed toward ruling over predominantly Kurdish areas along the border. Although YPG has partnered with Arab and other ethnic groups in Syria to form the Syrian Defense Forces (SDF) to further this territorial link, areas under SDF control are substantially smaller than those controlled by YPG alone. This difference in target selection and expansion mechanics also tells us a lot about how both groups rule and administer their no-go zones.

1.3 Hisbah and Kolkhoz: Two Schools of Thought in Running No-Go Zones

Hisbah is a rule in Islamic administration whereby the ruler has to promote good deeds and prevent wrongdoing in order to maintain order and run the society at optimum efficiency. In terms of ISIS territorial practice, hisbah is the third phase after the successful completion of the first (intelligence, sleeper cell, and information networks) and second (public relations, network deepening, and introduction of earlier phases of "soft" control) phases. In hisbah, ISIS assumes a direct confrontational posture, converting the territory into a "war economy," where penalties and stricter interpretation of Sharia start to emerge as administrative practice (Ingram 2015). Hisbah is largely understood in culturalist terms as a street vendor selling rotten food is treated in a similar fashion to a woman who doesn't wear the niqab properly. Other features of this control phase are militants carrying heavier weapons (as intimidation) and putting ISIS black flags in visible parts of the town, including propaganda posters in public places (Speckhard and Yayla 2015). Municipality projects are also not forgotten in this phase, as ISIS derives its administrative legitimacy through maintaining electricity and water grid, along with constructing new mosques, shops, and parks. As a form of communicating to the local populace that ISIS' arrival effectively ends the conflict and provides safety (one of the most welcome changes to a population under prolonged duress), the group also restarts industries (quarries, poultry farms, glass, brick, and wood workshops) that halted due to conflict. Mass production of food—especially bread, rice, and potato—is also one of the final phases of ISIS administrative practice (al-Tamimi 2015). In one anecdote, ISIS Caliph Baghdadi got into a car accident. The driver in the other car didn't recognize Baghdadi and threatened him to take him to court. Baghdadi agrees and appears in the court together with the man, being handed over a financial penalty by the judge under Baghdadi's rule (Weiss and Hassan 2015: 337).

Kolkhoz on the other hand is an early twentieth-century Soviet concept, which shares similarities with its Israeli counterpart kibbutz in establishing self-administering communities with little or no connection to a nation's capital (Abashin 2017). Having transformed into Western daily life in the form of "cooperatives," both kolkhoz and kibbutz follow the principle of "social economy"—a combination of cooperatives across economic sectors in order to meet basic supplies of food and fuel (Utting 2015). The idea of self-governing farming collectives has thus been central to Rojava's political economy and act as a pivot toward possible statehood. The logic of social economy is that it is a self-sustaining unit of production and living, which is built to endure regardless of whether the Kurds succeed in gaining statehood or not. In the case of success, these territories will be the centers of their respective provincial administration, supporting other towns and villages around it. If Syrian Civil War ends in favor of Damascus, however, these self-administering zones will still be largely autonomous as they will be "off the grid," seeking little—if any—supply and infrastructure aid from the central government. In that, Rojava revolution has also been—among other things—a land reappropriation project from former government-controlled fiefdoms into self-governing farming collectives that feed their immediate neighborhoods. The self-sufficient nature of these collectives also brings in the debate on the abolishment of currency altogether, befitting its socialist credentials (Cemgil 2016). In late 2014, for example, Derik town (within Jazira canton) started distributing salaries on a need basis (such as the number of dependents) rather than merit, later spilling over into food and aid distribution practices (Solomon 2014).

As the level of analysis problem in modern conflicts are reduced to the size of cities and even districts, understanding competition for territorial control through administrative practice is key. In that, a military-only thinking of both organizations prevents a proper contextualization of why they have sustained popular support and social base. Both groups construct authority based on coercive, persuasive, and administrative approaches in which intertwined and dynamic processes of conflicts coexist. In comparing and contrasting both groups' territorial methods, two layers of analysis are required: population-economy (resources) and centralization-autonomy (type of rule). This is important because both variables determine how far these groups expand and how long they can hold their no-go zones.

Population and territory-wise, ISIS is dominant. It controls a population close to 7 million—Iraq and Syria combined—and has a large territory, even though it shrunk in the last year from 90,800 km^2 (35,000 mi^2) to 68,300 km^2 (26,370 mi^2) (Gartenstein-Ross 2015; Yeung 2016). In Syria, the most concentrated ISIS population centers are Raqqa (around 1 million) and Deir ez-Zor Province (also around 1 million) in Syria, whereas in Iraq these are Ninawa Province (1,480,000) and parts of Kirkuk, including al-Dibs, Daquq, and Hawija (525,000). For PYD-controlled areas, on the other hand, one of the earliest measurements of population was 4.6 million as of late 2014, based on New World Academy report, although a more recent census has been unforthcoming. Even with the 2014 figure, an important majority of those are thought of as internally displaced people. In Rojava, the most populated cantons are Jazira (1.5 million), Kobani (1 million), and Afrin (1.3 million) as of May 2014 (Canton Based Democratic Autonomy of Rojava 2014; Maur and Staal 2015). Both groups control similar sizes of population and, in that regard, identifying a clear long-term demographic winner is difficult at this point. At a time when a proper census is unforthcoming, a statistical survey on the birthrates—a reliable measurement of long-term demography—is also hard to conduct. Therefore, based on available data, ISIS and Rojava seem to be tied down in a draw over competition for demographic superiority. Nonetheless, the territorial gains of PYD at the expense of ISIS in Syria and the rollback of ISIS in Iraq is likely to change this picture.

Finances of a no-go zone are often harder to measure, and evidence on this is usually produced by traders and merchants who can report from within these zones. Collecting this information, Financial Times ran one of the deepest accounts of ISIS finances in its own no-go zones, identifying two levels of economic management. These two levels refer to two symbiotic economies, one for the use of ISIS members and the other, for the use of outsiders (Jones and Solomon 2015). The "insider economy," geared toward ISIS members, is priced at half of most goods priced toward the outsiders (Dabiq 2016). Yet, it is important to underline that when talking about an "ISIS economy," it is still a war economy, based on conquest and wartime production, as with most no-go zone economies are (Caris and Reynolds 2014). In that, ISIS pays little attention in improving the level of economy itself; it consumes existing economy through confiscation, reappropriation, and extortion, or selling rent commodities such as oil or antiquities (Solomon and Jones 2015). A governor (*wali*) is in charge of all economic activities, counseled by a Zakat Council, which oversees economic policy, collection of tax, and designating taxation amount based on loyalty and financial capacity of taxpayers (Pagliery 2015). Tax is extracted in the form of cash, grain, or cotton, depending on the type of estate and production capacity of the taxpayer. A 2.5% base tax is deducted from all businesses, and an additional 5–10% is added based on the quality and quantity of production of a business. As with all no-go zone economies, ISIS also runs an economy on the edge, proofed against attack, siege, and sanctions. This is done by structuring local economy in a way that any external pressure or sanction will first hurt the most vulnerable parts of the society—rather than ISIS members—in order to deter such pressures on humanitarian concerns (Colas 2017). This mimics ISIS defenses and base networks, which are established within or close to dense civilian areas to deter aerial bombardment. Eventually, this creates a hybrid political-economic war administration where defections are minimized and external pressures hurt the group least.

Our evidence on YPG-controlled areas is clearer, given YPG and PYD's policy of explaining "Rojava revolution" to outsiders. Therefore, the literature has both curated and uncurated (insider accounts) versions of how Rojava economy runs. However, due to the federal and decentralized nature of Rojava, a single, unitary economic policy is hard to track, given how individual cantons run different levels and strands of economic policy. Common themes are expressed in the Rojava constitution, which asserts democratic autonomy, instead of a unitary and centralized nation-state (Canton Based Democratic Autonomy of Rojava 2014). The constitution tries to find a common ground between "not being opposed to the state" and "not seeking to form a state," mainly because of its priority of not provoking neighboring Turkey, Iraq, and the Syrian government into an all-out military operation. One of the main differences between ISIS and YPG approaches to ownership is that YPG seeks to pursue a hybrid of private property and collective communalization, depending on the necessities of different cantons it administers (Yousef 2016). One common difference is that instead of collecting taxation in the form of zakat, YPG-run economies focus on collective production—collective consumption dynamic, geared toward the ultimate goal of eliminating currency from the economy. These administrative experiments, however, are applied in no-go zones that are distant to the immediate battlefield, whereas a stricter and more centralized administration is followed in territories that are close to active combat.

1.4 Evaluating the Success of No-Go Zones: Which Model Is Sustainable?

Population, resources, and the administrative capacity of the ruling VNSA determines the level of success of any no-go zone. Population and territory size must be proportional as models which favor the former over the latter will succumb into the problems of overpopulation, starvation, and internal riots. In contrast, if a no-go zone territory is too large for its population, then it will be hard to defend and hold against outside attacks. To that end, it is difficult to tell whether ISIS or YPG will rule over long-term no-go zones, even though ISIS has a larger population and a larger territory. From a purely population and territory point of view, ISIS has roughly 95 people per 1 km^2 area of land under its control, whereas YPG has around 300 people per the same measure of area it controls.[1] This implies that YPG will be able to hold its territory for longer periods of time compared to ISIS, within current population and territory under its control. In their approach to economy as well, ISIS policy of conquest economy (confiscations, extortion, and rentierism) will eventually dwindle its resources if their wars continue for a long time. YPG, on the other hand, has largely succeeded in establishing a collective farming and local autonomy regime—at least in a number of pilot areas—which gives them a slight

[1]These figures were collected from Maur and Staal (2015), Pagliery (2015), and Solomon and Jones (2015).

advantage over ISIS in the long run as well. While ISIS controls a larger population, its rigid conquest economy creates too many disenfranchisements away from these territories, inevitably leading to economic shrinkage. Indeed, ISIS has already begun banning travels outside its control zones (Dar al-Harb) following large numbers of defections of people whose properties were confiscated from cities under its control.

ISIS seems to have already fallen into a trap which is often shared by other conquest economies—which is, if conquest stops, so will the economy. ISIS war economy largely focuses on exploiting existing resources and level of economic production, rather than expanding and developing them. YPG, on the other hand, seems to be more understanding of the necessity of attracting capital, rather than overtax or restrict the movement of goods and services. However, its co-op economy may run into bigger problems as territory and population expands into a size, which may require more efficient financial planning. In addition, YPG itself is not immune from accusations of extortion and other abuses of power, ("Under Kurdish Rule: Abuses in PYD-run Enclaves of Syria" 2014) which may complicate its bid to emerge as a more progressive and accommodating alternative to ISIS. Nonetheless, both ISIS and PYD have effectively filled in the need for the administration of basic goods and services in a conflict setting, providing security, food, and basic activities of livelihood to an otherwise ungoverned territory.

In terms of political administration, ISIS favors direct centralization, whereas PYD is the complete opposite, advocating canton-style autonomy. Aymenn Jawad al-Tamimi made a detailed account of the evolution in ISIS' administration, tracking it back to 2006, when the group was a fringe organization in Iraq (al-Tamimi 2015). ISIS adopts a mixture of technocratic and ideological approach to appointments, where "important" ministries such as oil and health were headed by engineers and doctors with due specialization. By 2014, ISIS had already developed an administrative model with 14 "ministries," including education, resources, currency, PR, and agriculture. Strong cultural adherence is required in the application of such administration, such as a common policy on zakat or other practices such as the closure of businesses during prayer times. In the application of administration, harsh justice and rigid religious-legal apparatus have helped to bring order in ISIS-controlled places that have suffered from extended fighting. ISIS's centralization becomes easier to enforce as warring sides have been fully polarized across clear-cut trenches, unlike the fragmented picture that emerged soon after the Iraq War in 2003. Also, the populace is more war-weary now compared to 2003 and is more receptive to the idea of harsh justice in exchange for security and basic stability. In that, the structure of ISIS administration has a clear-cut hierarchy, where Caliph is the ultimate source of authority, which rules over a cabinet of advisors. In turn, the Caliph has two deputies, one for Syria and one for Iraq, each of which rule over 12 governors in Syria and 12 in Iraq. A separate Shura Council, which administers religious and military affairs, counsels both the Caliph and his deputies (Thompson and Shubert 2015).

Rojava, on the other hand, has a different structure, which follows an interlinked setup of institutions that address administration at different levels (Canton Based

Democratic Autonomy of Rojava 2014). While different cantons have individual models, the best-defined example is the Jazira administration, where Executive Council acts as a government with 22 ministries, with a Kurdish President and two deputies—one Arab and one Syriac. A Judicial Council oversees legal processes, whereas a Supreme Constitutional Court and High Commission of Election act within a checks and balances system (Khalaf 2016). For the Legislative Council, made up of 101 members, and the Judicial Council, Supreme Constitutional Court (which is responsible for determining the constitutionality of laws enacted by the Legislative Assembly), and High Commission of Elections, there is a gender quota of at least 40% in women. In addition, there is also a Local Administration Council, which handles local affairs in ten cities of the Jazira Canton. Yet, the planned structure is currently lagging behind due to the persistence of the conflict and the proximity of population centers to active combat (Charter of the Social Contract in Rojava (Syria) 2014). In addition, despite an autonomous and loosely linked decision-making, the "Rojava project" is still viewed by critics as a "PYD project" (Glioti 2016; Baher 2016; Grojean 2000; Rudaw 2013), which prevents further consolidation and unification (Wilgenburg 2016). Other criticisms exist in terms of Rojava project being "too ethno-nationalist," as well as denouncement for being too rigid from its ideological standpoint and its harsh stance against other local Kurdish political parties.

2 Conclusion

No-go zones will become even more important in scholarly research in the coming years as conflicts and tensions will be transmitted from the global level to local (Oktav et al. 2017). Syria will be subject to further analyses on non-state actors, their fighting capabilities, recruitment, as well as how they run no-go zones and establish their own anti-access points. These no-go zones will remain important regardless of the outcome of the Syrian Civil War, as if the war is won by the Syrian Armed Forces; these self-administering units will still remain in tension with the central authority. Over time, these self-administering units may actually be the hubs of renewed revolts against Damascus. Indeed, in Kilcullen's words: "whichever actor takes on the wider range of capabilities, covering more of the spectrum from persuasion to coercion" (Kilcullen 2015: 48) will dominate a particular territory, uproot central state authority, and redirect the loyalties of the local populace.

Neither ISIS nor YPG have developed these administrative models overnight. ISIS inherits militant administrative models that go back to the Iraq War of 2003, where numerous no-go zones emerged throughout the country. From the lessons of these largely failed no-go zones, ISIS has fine-tuned its approach, detailing its expansion, intelligence gathering, propaganda, and administration practices. "Rojava experiment" on the other hand goes back to the 1990s, when the PKK established a large network of no-go zones within southeastern Turkey and northern Iraq. ISIS territorial practice is perhaps better fine-tuned, given the sheer size of territory and population it has to administer and local notables it has to keep in line. There is a direct hierarchy in ISIS model and a clear-cut standard operating procedure, with good population diagnostics. YPG's territory is more minimalist, although it rules over a high population density compared to ISIS. This brings in the need for local and autonomous solutions to unforeseen problems, which is why Rojava constitution emphasizes decentralization and collective economy.

However, the debate on the survivability of both models comes under increased scrutiny when adjacent states are brought into the equation. Neither Turkey nor Iraq or Syrian government—or foreign intervention on the part of Russia and the United States—seems to grant ISIS a minimalist scope of territory for the group to rule permanently. Eventually, as ISIS dwindles into a smaller territory, its defense will withdraw back to its core areas where it enjoys higher level of support from the local populace, increasing its ferocity in fighting. It is so far unclear as to how a solution, which seeks the elimination of ISIS through a war of attrition or "let it rot" approach, will materialize, or whether ISIS will be able to transform its economy into a more sustainable nature by then. Similar questions can be addressed toward YPG, but given a similar chance of ruling over a minimal area versus going into an all-out defense against outside intervention, YPG will likely settle for a long-term administration within a limited area. If that happens, the way it has structured its economic model will be more advantageous than ISIS, which is based on a constant momentum of conquest.

Bibliography

Abashin, S. (2017). Stalin's rais: Governance practices in a central Asian Kolkhoz. *Central Asian Survey, 36*, 131–147.

Baher, Z. (2016). Our attitude towards Rojava must be critical solidarity. *LibCom*. Retrieved March 2, 2017, from https://libcom.org/library/our-attitude-towards-rojava-must-be-critical-solidarity

Brenner, N. (1999). Beyond state-centrism? Space, territoriality, and geographical scale in globalization studies. *Theory and Society, 28*(1), 39–78.

Buch-Hansen, M. (2003). The territorialization of rural Thailand: Between localism, nationalism and globalism. *Tijdschrift voor Economische en Sociale Geografie, 94*(3), 322–334.

Bunker, R. (2014). *The emergence of feral and criminal cities: U.S. Military Implications in a Time of Austerity*. Land Warfare Papers No: 99W. Arlington, VA: The Institute of Land Warfare.

Buzan, B. (2008). *People, states & fear: An agenda for international security studies in the post-cold war era*. Colchester: ECPR Press.

Caris, C. C., & Reynolds, S. (2014). *ISIS Governance in Syria*. Institute for the Study of War. Retrieved March 4, 2017, from http://www.understandingwar.org/sites/default/files/ISIS_Governance.pdf

Cemgil, C. (2016). The republican ideal of freedom as non-domination and the Rojava experiment: "States as they are" or a new socio-political imagination? *Philosophy & Social Criticism, 42*, 419–428.

Charters, J. (2014). Enforcing sharia in Raqqa: The Islamic State'. *Independent Journal Review*. Retrieved March 4 2017, from http://ijr.com/2014/08/167051-life-isis-religious-police-brutal-merciless/

Colas, B. (2017). What does Dabiq do? ISIS hermeneutics and organizational fractures within Dabiq magazine. *Studies in Conflict and Terrorism, 40*(3), 173–190.

Colest I. (2015). Despair, hardship as Iraq cuts off wages in Islamic State cities. *Reuters*. Retrieved March 2, 2017, from http://www.reuters.com/article/us-mideast-crisis-iraq-salaries-idUSKCN0RW0V620151002

Dobbie, C. (1994). A concept for post-cold war peacekeeping. *Survival, 36*, 121–148.

Fiddian-Qasmiyeh, E. (2016). On the threshold of statelessness: Palestinian narratives of loss and erasure. *Ethnic and Radical Studies, 39*(2), 301–321.

Fukuyama, F. (2004). *State-building: Governance and world order in the 21st century*. Ithaca, NY: Cornell University Press.

Gartenstein-Ross, D. (2015). How many fighters does the Islamic State really have? *War on the Rocks*. Retrieved March 4, 2017, from https://warontherocks.com/2015/02/how-many-fighters-does-the-islamic-state-really-have/

Glioti, A. (2016). Rojava: A libertarian myth under scrutiny. *Al Jazeera*. Retrieved March 2, 2017, from http://www.aljazeera.com/indepth/opinion/2016/08/rojava-libertarian-myth-scrutiny-160804083743648.html

Grojean, O. (2000). The production of the new man within the PKK. *European Journal of Turkish Studies, 8*. Retrieved March 4, 2017, from https://ejts.revues.org/4925

Helman, G. B., & Ratner, S. R. (1992). Saving failed states. *Foreign Policy*. Retrieved March 4, 2017, from http://foreignpolicy.com/2010/06/15/saving-failed-states/

Ingram, H. J. (2015). The strategic logic of Islamic State information operations. *Australian Journal of International Affairs, 69*(6), 729–752.

Jones, S., & Solomon, E. (2015). Isis Inc: Jihadis fund war machine but squeeze "citizens". *Financial Times*. Retrieved March 4, 2017, from https://www.ft.com/content/2ef519a6-a23d-11e5-bc70-7ff6d4fd203a

Khalaf, R. (2016). *Governing Rojava; Layers of legitimacy in Syria*. London: Chatham House Research Papers.

Kilcullen, D. (2015). *Out of the mountains: The coming age of the Urban Guerrilla*. New York: Oxford University Press.

Krasner, S. D., & Pascual, C. (2005). Addressing state failure. *Foreign Affairs, 84*(4), 153–163.

Lamb, R.D. (2008). Ungoverned areas and threats from safe havens. *Ungoverned areas project*. Washington DC: Office of the Under Secretary of Defense for Policy

Li, T. M. (2007). *The will to improve: Governmentality, development and the practice of politics*. Durham, NC: Duke University Press.

Lund, A. (2015). *What if no one is winning the war in Syria?* Carnegie Middle East Centre. Retrieved March 4, 2017, from http://carnegie-mec.org/diwan/60078

Maur, R., & Staal, J. (Eds.) (2015). *Rojava: Stateless democracy*. Utrecht: New World Academy.

Mazarr, M. J. (2013). The rise and fall of the failed-state paradigm. *Foreign Affairs*. Retrieved March 4, 2017, from https://www.foreignaffairs.com/articles/2013-12-06/rise-and-fall-failed-state-paradigm

Milliken, J., & Krause, K. (2002). State failure, state collapse, and state reconstruction: Concepts, lessons and strategies. *Development and Change, 33*(5), 753–774.

Oktav, Ö. Z., Parlar Dal, E., & Kursun, A. M. (2017). Reframing and reassessing the VNSAs in Syrian conflict: An introduction. In O. Z. Oktav, E. Parlar Dal, & A. M. Kursun (Eds.), *Violent non state actors and the Syrian civil war: The ISIS and YPG cases*, Springer.

Osiander, A. (2001). Sovereignty, international relations, and the Westphalian Myth. *International Organization, 55*(2), 251–287.

Pagliery, J. (2015). Inside the $2 billion ISIS war machine. *CNN Money*. Retrieved March 4, 2017, from http://money.cnn.com/2015/12/06/news/isis-funding/

Peluso, N. L. (2005). Seeing property in land use: Local territorializations in West Kalimantan, Indonesia. *Geografisk Tidsskrift, Danish Journal of Geography, 105*(1), 1–15.
Peluso, N. L., & Vandergeest, P. (2001). Genealogies of the political forest and customary rights in Indonesia, Malaysia and Thailand. *The Journal of Asian Studies, 60*(3), 761–812.
Perry, T. (2015). Syrian Kurds' spending plans reflect rising ambition. *Reuters*. Retrieved March 4, 2017, from http://www.reuters.com/article/us-mideast-crisis-syria-kurds-idUSKCN0Q21BK20150728
Podder, S. (2013). Non-state armed groups and stability: Reconsidering legitimacy and inclusion. *Contemporary Security Policy, 34*(1), 16–39.
Pusane, O. K. (2017). How to profile PYD/YPG as an actor in the Syrian civil war: Policy implications for the region and beyond. In O. Z. Oktav, E. Parlar Dal, & A. M. Kursun (Eds.), *Violent non state actors and the Syrian civil war: The ISIS and YPG cases*, Springer.
Rabasa, A., Boraz, S., Chalk, P., Cragin, K., Karasik, T. W., Moroney, J. D. P., O'Brien, K. A., & Peters, J. E. (2007). *Ungoverned Territories*. Santa Monica, CA: RAND Corporation.
Ribot, J. C., & Peluso, N. L. (2003). A theory of access. *Rural Sociology, 68*(2), 153–181.
Rotberg, R. I. (Ed.). (2004). *When states fail: Causes and consequences*. Princeton, NJ: Princeton University Press.
Roth, R. (2008). Fixing the forest: the spatiality of conservation conflict in Thailand. *Annals of the Association of American Geographers, 98*(2), 373–391.
Rousseau, D. L., & Garcia-Retamero, R. (2007). Identity, power, and threat perception: A cross-national experimental study. *Journal of Conflict Resolution, 51*(5), 744–771.
Russett, B. (1994). *Grasping the democratic peace: Principles for a post-cold war world*. Princeton, NJ: Princeton University Press.
Sack, R. D. (1986). *Human territoriality: its theory and history*. Cambridge: Cambridge University Press.
Salloukh, B., & Barakat, R. (2015). *The politics of sectarianism in postwar Lebanon*. Chicago, IL: University of Chicago Press.
Sassen, S. (2005). When national territory is home to the global: Old borders to novel borderings. *New Political Economy, 10*(4), 523–541.
Schlichte, K. (2009). *In the shadow of violence: The politics of armed groups*. New York, NY: Campus Verlag.
Sikor, T., & Lund, C. (2009). Access and property: A question of power and authority. *Development and Change, 40*(1), 1–22.
Sivaramakrishnan, K. (1997). A limited forest conservancy in southwest Bengal 1894–1912. *Journal of Asian Studies, 56*(1), 75–112.
Solomon, E. (2014). Amid Syria's violence, Kurds carve out autonomy. *Reuters*. Retrieved March 4, 2017, from http://www.reuters.com/article/us-syria-kurdistan-specialreport-idUSBREA0L17320140122
Solomon, E., & Jones, S. (2015). Isis Inc: Loot and taxes keep jihadi economy churning. *Financial Times*. Retrieved March 4, 2017, from http://www.reuters.com/article/us-syria-kurdistan-spIsisInc:Lootandtaxeskeepjihadieconomychurningecialreport-idUSBREA0L17320140122
Speckhard, A., & Yayla, A.S. (2015). Eyewitness accounts from recent defectors from Islamic State: Why they joined, what they saw, why they quit. *Perspectives on Terrorism, 9*(6). Retrieved March 4, 2017, from http://www.terrorismanalysts.com/pt/index.php/pot/article/view/475/html
Tamimi, A. (2015). The evolution in Islamic State administration: The documentary evidence. *Perspectives on Terrorism*, *9*(4). Retrieved March 4, 2017, from http://www.terrorismanalysts.com/pt/index.php/pot/article/view/447/html
Thompson, N., & Shubert, A. (2015). The anatomy of ISIS: How the "Islamic State" is run. *CNN*. Retrieved March 4, 2017, from http://edition.cnn.com/2014/09/18/world/meast/isis-syria-iraq-hierarchy/
Unver, H. A. (2016). Schrödinger's kurds: Transnational kurdish geopolitics in the age of shifting borders. *Journal of International Affairs, 69*(2), 65–98.

Utting, P. (Ed.). (2015). *Social and solidarity economy: Beyond the fringe*. London: Zed Books.
van Wilgenburg, W. (2016). Kurdish national council in Syria condemns federalism declaration by Kurdish rival. *ARA News*. Retrieved March 4, 2017, from http://aranews.net/2016/03/kurdish-national-council-syria-condemns-federalism-declaration-kurdish-rival/
Vandergeest, P., & Peluso, N. (1995). Territorialization and state power in Thailand. *Theory and Society, 24*(3), 385–426.
Wadley, R. L. (2003). Lines in the forest: Internal territorialization and local accommodation in west Kalimantan, Indonesia (1865–1979). *South East Asia Research, 11*(1), 91–112.
Weber, M. (1922). *Wirtschaft und Gesellschaft: Grundriß der Verstehenden Soziologie*. Tübingen: JCB Mohr.
Weiss, M., & Hassan, H. (2015). *ISIS: Inside the army of terror*. New York, NY: Simon and Schuster.
Yeung, P. (2016). *Isis has lost an area of territory the size of Ireland*. Retrieved March 4, 2017, from http://www.independent.co.uk/news/world/middle-east/isis-territory-syria-iraq-latest-news-islamic-state-daesh-a7129421.html
Yousef, A. (2016). The social economy of Rojava. *FairCoop*. Retrieved March 4, 2017, from https://cooperativeeconomy.info/the-social-economy-in-rojava/
Zelin, A. Y. (2016). *The Islamic State's territorial methodology*. Washington, DC: Washington Institute for Near East Policy.

Online Sources

Break the Cross. (2017). *Dabiq Magazine*. Issue 17. Retrieved March 4, 2017, from https://azelin.files.wordpress.com/2016/07/the-islamic-state-e2809cdacc84biq-magazine-1522.pdf
Canton Based Democratic Autonomy of Rojava. (2014). Belgium: Kurdistan National Congress. Retrieved March 4, 2017, from https://peaceinkurdistancampaign.files.wordpress.com/2011/11/rojava-info-may-2014.pdf
Charter of the Social Contract: Self Rule in Rojava. (2014). Belgium: Kurdistan National Congress. Retrieved March 4, 2017, from https://peaceinkurdistancampaign.files.wordpress.com/2014/03/english-version_sc_revised-060314.pdf
ISIS defectors speak. (2015). *International center for the study of violent extremism (ICSVE)*. Retrieved March 4, 2017, from http://www.icsve.org/isis-defectors-speak-internet-memes/she-became-the-emir-of-the-hisbah/
Osman Ocalan. (2013). PYD will not allow power sharing in Syria. *Rudaw*. Retrieved March 4, 2017, from http://www.rudaw.net/english/middleeast/syria/20082013
The Danger of Abandoning Darul-Islam. (2016). *Dabiq Magazine*. Retrieved March 4, 2017, from https://azelin.files.wordpress.com/2015/09/the-islamic-state-e2809cdc481biq-magazine-11e280b3.pdf
Under Kurdish Rule. (2014). Abuses in PYD-run enclaves of Syria. *Human Rights Watch*. Retrieved March 4, 2017, from https://www.hrw.org/report/2014/06/19/under-kurdish-rule/abuses-pyd-run-enclaves-syria

Making Sense of the Territorial Aspirations of ISIS: Autonomy, Representation, and Influence

Hakan Mehmetcik and Ali Murat Kurşun

1 Introduction

The Middle East has not witnessed such extensive disarray since the end of World War I as it does today. As decades-old wars and conflicts resulting in destruction and violence show no signs of abating in the region, violent non-state armed actors (VNSAs) have become an important determinant of the ongoing crisis and affect regional and international trends. Amassing new-found revenue, support, institutions, and legitimacy in the civil wars, VNSAs increasingly follow the state-formation process by creating competing forms of authority, legitimacy, and capacities to existing states. The Islamic State of Iraq and al-Sham (ISIS) is a prime example in the region. Although ISIS is generally regarded as a global terrorist network that uses and abuses Islam, the very fact that the group has managed to gain substantial territorial control and declared a caliphate complicates the issue. Existing works generally deal with the question of whether ISIS is a terrorist group or a state-like phenomenon. When it comes to territory and territorial control, only insurgencies with military might and de facto states among the variety of VNSAs possess effective territoriality in theory. An insurgency group is generally defined as an armed struggle against existing state authority, while de facto states are those states without international recognition (Oktav et al. 2017). Yet, when it comes to ISIS, the group is more than an insurgency organization yet less than a de facto state in terms of territoriality and territorial control. The group has

H. Mehmetcik (✉)
Department of International Relations, Marmara University, İstanbul, Turkey
e-mail: hakan.mehmetcik@marmara.edu.tr

A.M. Kurşun
Faculty of Political Sciences, International Relations Department, Marmara University, Istanbul, Turkey
e-mail: alimuratkursun@gmail.com

Ö.Z. Oktav et al. (eds.), *Violent Non-state Actors and the Syrian Civil War*,
DOI 10.1007/978-3-319-67528-2_3

become essentially state-like by launching systemic military action and exercising effective control over territory but is not yet a semiautonomous actor. As a *trans*national terror network, ISIS has also managed to build networks consisting of different terror cells, alliances, and sympathizers by operating in partnership with both domestic and international actors. Thus, it exhibits a hybrid form of transnational terror network and insurgent traits. By establishing a government and declaring a caliphate, ISIS has challenged the conventional wisdom. Moreover, even though many have rejected ISIS as a sham, the group cannot be easily dismissed as it is in possession of sufficient money, fighters, weapons, and land to make a plausible case (McCants 2015, p. 201). Many studies have attempted to deal with the case of ISIS in a similar sense. For instance, Cronin suggests that with its sizeable number of well-equipped and trained fighters, control, and extensive funding compared to other similar VNSAs, "ISIS is a pseudo-state led by a conventional army" (Cronin 2015). According to Walt, with its hostility to the existing state system and prevailing international norms, use of ruthless violence to eliminate or intimidate rivals, indoctrination to enforce obedience, and their approach to inevitable victory, ISIS should be considered a "revolutionary state" (Walt 2015). Yayla and Spechard argue that ISIS mainly operates as "a police state" with a deep engagement with the Baathist intelligence apparatus (Speckhard and Yayla 2017). For Batchelor (2015), ISIS is more than a police state with its organization, ideological appeal, and military capacities. In Lia's account, ISIS is just another "proto-jihadist state" among dozens of similar cases throughout history, although far more successful (Lia 2015). Brands and Feaver underline that over the years the ISIS had become "the strongest, best-resourced and most ideologically potent "terrorist quasi-state" of the post-9/11 era" (Brands and Feaver 2017). A Rand Corporation report suggests that "ISIS is a hybrid insurgent-terrorist group" (Connable et al. 2017). Celso (2015) argues that ISIS, along with Boko Haram, represents a new wave of jihadi terrorism with territorial control. According to Cali (2014), ISIS is "the first modern transnational movement with a home base that it is fanatically determined to retain." There are many such accounts that refer to ISIS as a state-like organization in one way or another. Indeed, over the years, ISIS has managed to create a functioning state formation in Iraq and Syria despite being regarded as an anomaly. Even after a years-long collective fight against the group, it still occupies large amounts of territory in Iraq and Syria as of January 2017. The rush to begin state-building processes may not be the only feature that makes it distinct from other jihadi non-state armed groups, yet the ISIS case is important as the group represents many newly emerging trends or patterns for other ideological and irredentist VNSAs, whether they are jihadist or not.

Historically, territoriality and territorial control largely depend on the monopolization of the means of coercion, institutions, revenues, and legitimacy within a given territory. In this sense, the path from insurgency to state-like organization goes through building an operational army, establishing a centralized administration and local population support (Ünver 2017). By creating alternative imagined communities and providing new forms of security and welfare in a civil-war context, VNSAs operate as the functional equivalents of states with new forms of non-state sovereignty (Davis 2009). A closer examination of ISIS suggests that a parallel dynamic is at play in Iraq and Syria (Katagiri 2015). Even so, similar dynamics are far more common than generally recognized in other parts of the world such as Libya, Yemen, and Egypt. Indeed, state weakness in areas such as rule of law, security, health, justice, and local conflict management is punctuated by the presence of dispersed, fragmented, and overlapping structures that substitute for lacking state institutions. Thus, non-state actors cohabit, co-distribute, and co-deliver public goods and services in what has been described as hybrid or non-Weberian/non-Westphalian political formations (Podder 2014). These types of emerging non-state sovereignties are more observable in civil-war contexts (Aliyev 2017). Over the years, Syria, Iraq, Afghanistan, Libya, Mali, Yemen, and many other territories have become open laboratories in which these hybrid actors form their own local governance designs. These groups are the direct beneficiaries of conflicts and wars and gain greater territorial capacities, legitimation, and recognition. Therefore, their very existence as "non-state complex" is inseparable from the dynamics of wars in the region. In this sense, there is a wide range of similarities with other VNSAs and ISIS, such as political motivation for state-institutions setup; provision of defense, security, and sociopolitical services; multiple roles and functions via local, regional, and international alliances; organizational designs, recruitment patterns, and warfighting tactics; logistics; territorial control and attempts for recognition and legitimacy and rent-seeking activities within local, regional, and transnational levels; essentialist identities and exclusory ideologies; and a network of fund extractions over certain resources. Furthermore, the success or failure of the attempt significantly depends on external factors such as states' support or opposition and finance and fundraising opportunities. ISIS thus has become much more internationalist in its activities, receiving an overwhelming media and political attention. Lastly, with its relatively advanced weapons and command and control systems, the group is able to follow a territorially expansive agenda.

Indeed, ISIS will neither obtain statehood in a legal sense (Boyle 2015) nor be able to protect its territorial grip (Dobbins and Jones 2017). However, it will not evaporate even after it completely loses its home base in Iraq and Syria (Hassan 2016). That is, even if the group is defeated militarily, another group claiming legitimacy and statehood could emerge by controlling ISIS' base territory if the circumstances from which the group emerged continue. In this sense, no matter how inconvenient or ideologically fraught, the case of ISIS in terms of its territorial ambitions and broader effect needs a more comprehensive analysis to understand the group's effects on international relations. However, research on the group is still far less comprehensive when it comes to its level of agency as a VNSA. This chapter aims at providing a more empirically rich and theoretically parsimonious analysis of the general patterns and variables within the transition from insurgency to a state-like organization using the case of ISIS. To do this, we use the framework produced by Ersel Aydınlı in his book *Violent Non-state Actors: From Anarchist to Jihadists* (Aydinli 2016). Aydınlı's framework employs a three-layered analysis of autonomy, representation, and influence (ARI), on which the factors that drive the transformation from insurgency to a state-like organization can be traced. Briefly, autonomy refers to a VNSA's capacity to act independently from states' support, regeneration, and management strategies and influence politics. Thus, a higher level of autonomy leads to better representation and, in turn, higher influence. Yet, higher levels of influence result in either greater recognition or harsher opposition, which in turn alters the VNSAs' overall autonomy (Aydinli 2016, p. 151). Using this framework, this paper problematizes ISIS's revolutionary state formation and attempts to evaluate the group's potential actorness and identify its nuanced territorial understanding and wider impact. This analysis would help provide a better understanding of the dynamics of the interaction of the ARI factors and thus make more informed predictions for regional and global politics.

2 Autonomy: Distance from the State and International State System

The first layer in the ARI framework is autonomy, upon which VNSAs construct their "non-state complex" as a base for territorial control. Autonomy has two dimensions: local autonomy and autonomy from the international state system. Local autonomy refers to the ability to be removed from state support, intervention, or persecution. Thus, the main questions are: How far are they able to establish autonomy outside of the state(s)? Is their autonomy self-reliant in terms of being free from states' opposition or financial support? The second dimension of autonomy refers to the ability to remain removed from the international state system. Here the main question is if their autonomy is sovereignty-free in terms of being free from existing states' rules, regulations, and institutions. That is, how far are they capable of creating their own non-state sovereignty? If a VNSA is overdependent on states' financial, infrastructure, or military supports, withdrawal of that support could bring the end of their formation. Being able to maneuver among states on some issues while building self-reliance on other issues would indicate greater autonomy. In addition to being able to survive without state support, being able to survive states' active opposition and even fighting back are important determinants of non-state autonomy. In a similar sense, if a VNSA is able to distance itself from state-centric regime by creating new and alternative regime instruments and agencies such as means for money transfers or alternative mediums for oil trade, then its autonomy is much more capable of functioning independently.

Thus, at the autonomy layer, the first dimension to tackle is the question of how far ISIS is able to establish an autonomy outside of the Iraq and Syrian states' apparatus. Is its autonomy at this level self-reliant in terms of being free from these states' opposition and financial support? The former requires us to look at the ideological roots, administrative capacities, and territorial reach of ISIS in Iraq and Syria, while the latter is more associated with ISIS's finances and the multi-front and multi-actor nature of the fight against the group (Table 1).

In order to make sense of the ideological roots of ISIS's autonomy at this level, we have to first trace its social origins in the Iraqi and Syrian contexts. Even though it is generally acknowledged to be an offspring of global jihadi movements, ISIS

Table 1 Autonomy

Distance from state	Free from state involvement	Ideologically depends on an amalgam of Salafi/jihadi and Baathist elements as well as other tribal/sectarian factions. In this sense, its autonomy depends on (1) Sunni disenfranchisement, (2) local tribes' support, (3) preventing fundraising capacity and (4) attracting new members (foreign fighters) Therefore, the group has higher autonomy where it can step in and instrumentalize these factors. In such areas, ISIS operates as the functional equivalents of states with new forms of non-state sovereignty by creating alternative imagined communities and providing new forms of security and welfare in a civil-war context. In other areas where these factors are not potent enough, ISIS operates as a terror cell
	Able to survive state opposition	Since 2014, when the group peaked in its expansion, it has faced multi-actoral and multi-frontal war. Yet, ISIS probably is able to go underground and regroup again in areas where its autonomy is high. In this sense, once the international fight against the group lose its momentum, the group can reemerge, under other names since the current Iraqi and Syrian states both boost ISIS autonomy at the local domain International state opposition also diminishes ISIS's funding capacity since oil and taxation/extortion are their most important and stable sources of revenue. Both income sources however decline as territory shrinks
Distance from international system	Being sovereignty-free	Appealing to the Islamic "umma" understanding, ISIS claims superior political legitimacy and rejects the (1) existing international system and (2) existing borders and nation states In this sense, it has a sovereignty-free ideology, which was appealing for some of its members yet it has also escalated the fight against the group Over the years, ISIS cares less about territorial continuity and more about ideological and procedural continuity in its territoriality Even if the group loses its base territory in Iraq and Syria, it may be able to go underground and regroup again once the international fight against the group cease momentum

was born out of the tacit cooperation between Iraqi al-Qaeda and the Baathist regime of Saddam Hussein (Gerges 2016, pp. 339–343). Tribal groups in Iraq and later in Syria that cooperate, coexist, and coordinate with the group for a number of economic, political, and religious reasons must also be added to the equation. Therefore, ISIS represents an amalgam of jihadi/Baathist and transnational/regional actors that came together at the right time in the right place. As the American invasion produced local, regional, and international ruptures, the dismantling of the Baath Party and the army plunged Iraq into new sectarian and religious conflicts. Marginalized, disempowered, and largely discriminated Sunnis in the new Iraq, especially under the government of Nuri Al-Maliki (Al-Ali 2014), and increasing sectarian tensions in the course of the Syrian civil war created an opening for ISIS to step in and instrumentalize these conflicts. Thus, ISIS has flourished in the heartland of the Iraqi Sunni population, in places like al-Anbar, Tikrit, and Mosul. In the later phase, it easily spread toward other Sunni populated areas in Iraq and Syria. In this sense, even if the majority of the population under ISIS rule do not support its extreme radical views of Islam, they find it appealing as they face other repression, discrimination, and mob violence. ISIS's ideology and tactic are designed to take advantage of Sunni grievances as a source of funding, manpower, and legitimacy. When we look at the sudden transformation of ISIS from obscurity to a so-called caliphate, sectarian dissention plays a much greater role than any state support or state failure. For instance, ISIS territorial expansion slowed in November 2014 due to a number of factors such as increasing international support and coordination in the fight against the group. However, one of the fundamental reasons for this slowdown is that ISIS has begun to encounter non-Sunni towns, whose population staunchly resist it (Hashim 2014). In this sense, ISIS's ability to recruit, fund, and organize its quasi-state formation relies on ideological support given to the group by disenfranchised Sunnis at the local level. Therefore, ISIS is the direct beneficiary of the sectarian nature of the wars in Iraq and Syria (Bolton 2015). Thus, at the ideological level, the current Iraqi and Syrian states boost ISIS autonomy at the local level by prioritizing sectarian policies.

Furthermore, as tribes in this part of the world are central to political and social life and often act with their own interests, objectives, and strategies (Cigar 2012), ISIS was able to exploit the tribal system to enhance its status as an insurgency and forge quasi-alliances with these groups. In addition to logistical support, the tribal system helped ISIS establish a "semi-sovereign context" where it operates outside of the existing local states' authority by providing its own administration, police, judiciary, tax collection, and educational facilities (Zelin 2016). Unlike other jihadi proto-state examples, in addition to applying strict Islamic daily routines, rules, and customs as a part of the administrative body, ISIS also provides its own government practices, institutions, and servants (Wallace et al. 2015). Overall, ISIS defies the sovereign territorial authority of both Syria and Iraq by applying its own institutional and administrative control. Even though the group's autonomy varies in degrees and not in kind within different territorial contexts, from pre-territorial control to full territorial control, it consistently follows a pattern of systematizing, bureaucratizing, and formalizing of its governance structures (Zelin 2016). With these parallel structures, along with its ideological zeal, ISIS has managed to establish a strong autonomy within its core territory both in Iraq and Syria.

At the logistical level, apart from local tribal support, foreign fighters are one of the important elements of ISIS recruitment. Recruitment patterns are to be analyzed in the following representation part in detail, but here it is important to underline that the group has shown a terrifying ability to attract young/disenfranchised adventurers from other part of the world with its videotaped beheadings, mass executions, sex slaves, and promises of cash. This ability also has increased ISIS's autonomy at the local level. However, as territorial control diminishes and ISIS is almost entirely encircled with fighting forces, the group's recruitment momentum has stopped. Although the group still has the ability to oppose other rival actors as well as states with coordinated military operations, endurance of its political formations will eventually become extinct.

The funding of these operations is inspirable from the logistics of the group. ISIS' fundraising capacity has made it different from other transnational terror networks. According to some estimates, it has able to generate more than $2.4 billion annually (Martin and Solomon 2017). Oil and oil trade is one of the fundamental source of revenue. ISIS has consolidated its grip on oil supplies in Iraq and Syria with deliberate extension of its territorial control and established a smuggling network with revenues of $1–$5 million a day (Daragahi and Solomon 2014). Lacking stable external support, ISIS engages in narcotics, illicit trade, robbery, kidnapping, and extortion to finance its operation. In addition, it mostly relies on abusive taxation and extortion (Almukhtar 2015). ISIS's financial portfolio also includes a large amount of money looted from banks when it suddenly seized Mosul, as well as from the illicit trade of antiquities, jewelry, cars, machinery, and livestock from conquered residents. Through control of the main borders and transit roads, the group has been able to collect a large amount of tax on a daily basis. It even earns revenue from cotton and wheat grown in Raqqa (Cronin 2015). This large-scale funding ability is another factor that increases ISIS' autonomy at the local level. However, the main problem for the group is the fact that both oil and taxation/extortion, its two most important and stable sources of revenue, are declining as its territory shrinks. ISIS also must spend money fast in order to finance its military operation over dispersed territory. ISIL members have to be paid a salary, and ammunition, weapons, vehicles, fuel, and spare parts must be purchased. The group also pays for intelligence and security personnel (Crane 2015). Moreover, it still has to provide basic social services, health care, water, and electricity and maintain roads and sewage systems, as well as pay the wages of civil servants under its control (Lister 2016). Therefore, over the years, ISIS' financial autonomy has steadfastly diminished as the international fight against the group gains ground. Yet, as long as ISIS does not rely on states' sponsorship to fund its operational capacities militarily and administratively and can show the ability to cooperate, coexist, and coordinate with local tribes, its autonomy is relatively greater than other VNSAs.

At the autonomy layer, the second dimension is at the international level, where it must be asked if ISIS can act outside of the international state system, or in other words if it is sovereignty-free. Achieving territorial control over existing borders, ISIS greatly challenges the state system at the international level, regional nation states, and the balance of power (Panayiotides 2015). Indeed, since the end of Ottoman rule, ISIS has become "the most concerted challenge of all directed toward state-centrism of existing sovereign states" in the Middle East (Falk 2015). However, claiming that ISIS is somehow akin to current territorial states is misleading.

ISIS opposes the current state system and the historical roots of regional borders as they are inclined to see all Sunni Muslims as a single nation. In its earlier forms until 2006 under the name Jama'at al-Tawhid wa'al-Jihad or later as al-Qaeda in Iraq, the group initially focused on driving foreign forces from Iraq and preventing a Shia takeover. As the group grew with the withdrawal of American forces from Iraq, it started emphasizing the establishment of an Islamic State as one of its priorities. The Islamic State, declared in 2006 as *al-Dawla al-Islamiyya*, was initially presented as a state for Iraq's Sunni population, a Sunni zone between Kurdish and Shia semiautonomous zones. Yet, territorial nationalism does not sit well with jihadi ideology. As a matter of fact, ISIS has a practical nuance in its territorial understanding. This was evident in the early pronouncements of the group (Bunzel 2014). For instance, in the work entitled "Informing the People About the Birth of the Islamic State of Iraq," released via Furqan Media, ISIS's official media outlet, it was argued that "unlike modern Western states, Islamic State is not defined by absolute geographic boundaries, a monopoly on the use of violence, or bureaucratically-administered services. . .[rather] Islamic states is structured around pseudo-feudal allegiances from subject to Emir, shared ideological goals, and the execution of judicial proceedings" (Fishman 2007).

In this sense, ISIS initially started with the idea of establishing a state in fixed territory, yet soon moved beyond this by articulating a new type of *networked-territorial control* rather than *fixed border control*, which indicates a non-Westphalian territorial idea. Therefore, over the years it cared less about borders or territorial continuity and more about ideological and procedural continuity in its territoriality. This sort of understanding is in line with the Islamic tradition of "umma," which is the expression of Islamic cosmopolitanism and loyalty from Muslims independent of their location. In a similar sense, ISIS's territorial understanding, based on ideological and procedural continuity, relies on units that fight against enemies, administer the domain, and indoctrinate civil populations independently of clearly defined borders and battle lines. These units could be guerrillas, terrorists, computer hackers, individuals, clans, or warlords, and they operate independently and are organized as a network rather than a hierarchically bound group. What Brian Fishman (2007) calls fourth-generation governance can be found in ISIS's notion of the caliphate. With other Salafi-jihadist groups in other parts of the world declaring allegiance to ISIS as demanded by the group in its declaration of the caliphate, ISIS was able to expand its borders by seizing Ramadi, Iraq, the capital of Anbar province, in May 2015 (Hashim 2014). Since 2015, the group has also expanded its self-existence into Libya, capitalizing on domestic instability in that country since the fall of the Gaddafi regime. The same is true for the Egypt Sinai Peninsula and some parts of Mali and Afghanistan. In addition to these dispersed territorial autonomies in different parts of the world, ISIS has inspired more than 140 terrorist attacks in 29 countries other than Iraq and Syria (Lister et al. 2017). In this sense, ISIS autonomy as a sovereign organization is even higher than generally anticipated. Even though a tacit adhesion and recognition of ISIS' statehood may emerge in the Middle East, (Anderson 2016) ISIS has no interest in being accepted or recognized as a state (Falk 2015). On the contrary, the group claims a superior political legitimacy by discrediting those states that were imposed on the region after WWI. As the curse of Sykes-Picot, which has become a symbol of the fragmentation imposed upon the Middle East, continues to haunt the region (Wright 2016), ISIS' message of a unified Islamic State over the territory divided by the West is a stronger message than many existing Middle Eastern states' ideology. Therefore, ISIS has a resilient base to act outside of the existing state system at the ideological level that has increased its autonomy.

However, state opposition, especially international, against ISIS has provided the greatest setback to the group's agenda. In Syria, ISIS's territory lies relatively remote from the regime's key front lines such as Homs, Aleppo, Dara, and Damascus. This makes it less of a priority target for the Syrian regime. Thus, while the regime bombs and besieges other rebel-held territories, it permits a sense of normalcy and continuity in ISIS-held territories (Itani 2014). Along the course of the wars in Syria, ISIS has been used and supported by the regime of Bashar Al-Assad for different reasons (Baker 2015). The fact that ISIS does not face the same regime attacks is an important reason for its ability to establish its order and advance its political goals in Syria. However, the number of new battle front intensifies the fight against the group. In Iraq, the Iraqi army, consisting of Kurdish Peshmerga forces and Shia militias, along with coalition air support, has made significant progress retaking most of the city of Mosul, Iraq's second largest city which was captured by ISIS in 2014. Turkey, along with Syrian rebels, has sealed off its border completely with an operation into Syria capturing al-Bab. The offensive toward Raqqa, the so-called capital of the Caliphate, has intensified despite causing deep division and concerns among coalition partners. Efforts involving a number of regional and international countries and different coalitions have engendered mixed results over the last few years. Yet, ISIS has lost most of its territorial grip in Iraq and Syria and is largely contained, and many of its financing and recruiting capabilities have been degraded. On the other hand, ISIS's ability to go underground and regroup with different formations once it loses its territorial base in Iraq and Syria remains likely (Bill 2016; Lister 2017). A post-territorial ISIS would probably be a shadow of its former self, resembling another al-Qaeda-type terror network or a merger of the two groups (Miller 2017). However, the most important point here is that, as Hassan underlines, without the campaigns of a combined 60 nations, ISIS would be able to regroup as the Iraqi and Syrian forces have been unable to defeat the group on the ground on their own. In this sense, "taking territory away from them is such a temporary activity" (Hassan 2017). Hassan also highlights that a post-territorial ISIS would still be able to wage a full-fledged urban insurgency while maintaining its core operational structure. Moreover, as in the case of the Raqqa and Mosul offensives, both of which are conducted by mostly rival local forces, the post-ISIS era would result in new types of disenchantment that created the group in the first place.

3 Representation: Ability of Regeneration, Loyalty, and Management of Overstretch

The second layer in the ARI framework is representation, via which VNSAs create a united body of shared interests, values, and goals among its members. The layer is made up of two dimensions. In the first dimension, in addition to "shared community" and "identity," the critical questions are if they are able to maintain existing members by creating loyalty and attract new members. In the second domain, it is whether or not they are able to manage organizational/ideological overstretches. Being able to offer a common identity or unifying ideology among its member is an essential factor that makes VNSAs sustainable in the long run. In addition to keeping its members loyal to the cause, VNSAs should continuously supply constituents to keep itself active and meaningful. There are at least two logical limits of this regeneration. First, how far is the group able to generate loyalty among its members? That is, if the organization reaches organizational or ideological overstretch, generating loyalty becomes difficult. If loyalty to the group is gained through money incentives, when the group reaches the end of its ability to pay, loyalty would reach a point where it could not be sustained. For this reason, VNSAs' ability to meet its members' needs, whether monetary, ideological, or religious, is important for its sustainability. Second, regeneration potential is generally derived from the group's ideological or ethnic base. If a VNSA is restricted to a particular ethnic identity, its membership boundaries will be equally restricted by the number and geography of that ethnic group. If the group's ideology speaks for a larger population, then membership boundaries would be larger (Aydinli 2016, pp. 10–11).

Thus, representation for ISIS has at least three interlinked missions: recruitment, generating loyalty, and managing overstretch. Success in these three missions leads to a successful representation capacity. ISIS representation is also interlinked with the group's aims within different parts of the world. Iraq and Syria, and to certain degree Libya, are ISIS's first-tier target areas, where the group seeks to defend and expand its territorial control. Afghanistan, Egypt, Yemen, and Saudi Arabia are the group's second-tier target area, where the group attempts to establish affiliates and increase disorder to create a pre-territorial control by building alliances and infiltrating local communities. Algeria, the North Caucasus, and some part of the central and eastern Asia are the group's third-tier target areas, where it seeks to attack and polarize the existing local and regional dynamics. Beyond these three core tiers, ISIS tries to inflict lone-wolf attacks by indoctrinating sympathizers. All of these different missions require different regeneration patterns (Department of Defense 2015) (Table 2).

Accordingly, for its first mission in the interior ring, ISIS was a merger of jihadi/Baathist officials and tribe members (in the Libyan case, former Gaddafi officers) and transnational/regional actors. Here, total ISIS combat power estimates vary from a minimum of 9000 fighters to a maximum of 200,000 (Gartenstein 2015). However, the existing Baathist and jihadi organizations are ISIS' main source of

Table 2 Representation

Regeneration	Attracting new members	ISIS representation is also interlinked with the group's aims within different parts of the world. Iraq, Syria, and Libya are the ISIS's first-tier target areas, where the group seeks to defend and expand its territorial control. Here this depends on (1) old-regime soldiers and officials, (2) Sunni tribes, and (3) foreign fighters Due to the sociopolitical roots of the group, ISIS is recognized as one of the most successful organizations with its use of an extreme ideology and new media. However, the most important recruitment source for the group is the existing Sunni population that faces state repression, persecution, and violence in the first-tier area In the second- and third-tier areas, the group tries to establish affiliates and increase disorder to create a pre-territorial control by building alliances and infiltrating local communities and polarizing the existing local and regional dynamics In the outer rim, ISIS tries to inflict lone-wolf attacks by indoctrinating sympathizers. The group use extremist ideology encompassing a global network of scholars, websites, media outlets, and social media activities to reach and indoctrinate large numbers of people in the world
	Building recognition and establishing legitimacy	It has been able to build strong recognition and ideological legitimacy among some other jihadi organizations. For Sunni Muslims, even if they do not share ISIS' use of extreme violence, they sometimes see it as a better alternative than current regimes. Thus, foreign fighters that join ISIS are generally motivated by its propaganda on building Islamic States, while local forces join because it is generally the least worst option in the area, in particular in contrast to Bashar al-Assad's regime in Syria
	Maintaining membership and generating loyalty	There are different motivations for people joining the group in the first palace. For local members, internal factors such as repression, discrimination, and torture, etc. are more important than ideological appeals. Moreover, many of the local members join the group out of necessity and fear. For foreign fighters, the grand narrative at the ideological level is more appealing. Some of them also join the group with other motivations such as monetary incentives, etc. As such, ISIS has been able to gain support and generate loyalty among locals, while it has difficulties among foreign fighters, to whom the ability has been hardened as the group's territorial grip shrinks

(continued)

Table 2 (continued)

Managing overstretch	Organizational	Organizational overstretch is obvious especially among foreign and local fighters. In terms of managing overstretch at the operational level, there are also reports that these foreign fighters have become a liability rather than an asset. The differences between local and foreign fighters in terms of aims, priorities, expectations, and methods have assumingly created tensions The group tries to reduce tensions among fractions by removing foreign fighters from administrative and political positions and relegating these fighters to IT-related intelligence work, IED factories, and technical tasks
	Ideological	It has able to manage ideological overstretch due to extreme central control Yet, foreign fighters also create long-term strife among group members at the ideological level as they incline use of violence and heavy-handedness in the application of Sharia, which erodes its base support among locals

manpower, and it is generally accepted that the group has at least 35,000 well-trained and equipped fighters. After the USA's ill-fated decision to dismantle Saddam's Sunni majority army and other state bodies, these experienced soldiers and officers joined ISIS' ranks. The role of bitter and unemployed Iraqi soldiers and officers has been a powerful factor in the rise of the Islamic State ("Saddam Hussein's officer drew up ISIS master plan" 2015). They have provided administrative and logistic blueprints, spy networks, crucial links to the tribal system, commands and control mechanisms, and military strategy and tactics, all of which are important inputs in ISIS's bid to rule the caliphate (Coles and Parker 2015).

The most important manpower source for ISIS after Saddam-era officers is the Sunni population in the broader Middle East. ISIS has skillfully used Sunni disenfranchisement in Iraq, Syria, and beyond to recruit large numbers of Sunnis who experienced shame and frustration at the hand of Iraqi and Syrian governments. Indeed, ISIS' successes at regenerating among Sunni Arabs actually depend on many factors such as illegitimate and failing government structures, ongoing wars and crisis, increasing unemployment, etc. However, none of these are as important as the large number of disenfranchised young Arabs. Equipped with modern tools such as advance social media knowledge and propaganda techniques, ISIS was able to spread its core message of raw power and revenge for Sunni Muslims. When looking at the regions where ISIS has been able to declare provinces by inciting regional conflicts, infiltrating local communities, and merging alliances by building relationships with jihadist groups, almost all are young, male Sunni Muslims (Watkins et al. 2015). Insurgencies recruiting foreign fighters are a growing concern (Malet 2010), yet ISIS's case differs both in kind and in degree. Even though the disenfranchised young Muslims are the main target of the group, a web of motivations such as ideology, money, adventure, sex slaves, etc. can play a part. Over the course of ISIS' transformation from an insurgency to a proto-state, the number joining ISIS's rank from abroad is estimated in the thousands, a majority of which come from Sunni countries such as Tunisia, Saudi Arabia, Chechenia, Egypt, and Jordan (Bremmer 2017). ISIS is the single most important group that has succeeded in attracting such large numbers of foreign fighters. However, according to some experts, estimations of the number of foreign fighters are high. Numbers vary, yet the general consensus is that up to 30,000 foreigners have joined ISIS from more than 100 countries. Finally, the third source of manpower is foreign fighters coming from different parts of the world which are mainly operational in the third ring. In order to make sense ISIS's appeal to these people, we have to look at its ability to use extremist ideology encompassing a global network of scholars, websites, media outlets, and social media activities to reach and indoctrinate large numbers of people across the world.

ISIS is both weak and strong at creating loyalty. The group allowed too many people to join without proper vetting, attracting Saddam loyalists from the military and intelligence services, spies, gangsters, and criminals. Some believed in the cause, but many were corrupt and had divided loyalties (McCants 2015, p. 58). With its Wahhabi/jihadi ideology, ISIS is partly able to create strong group consciousness among its members. However, the implementation of the group's ideology through savage violence is a tactic approved by only a small portion of members. Even al-Qaeda denounced ISIS's brutality as extreme (Sherlock 2014). The group's use of violence and heavy-handedness in the application of Sharia eroded its base support among locals, which are central for ISIS' state-building efforts. There are reports that the most violent of the group are those foreign fighters coming from Western countries ("'They hate the West': Foreign IS fighters most violent to hostages, survivors say" 2016). In this sense, foreign fighters create long-term strife among group members at the ideological level. In terms of managing overstretch at the operational level, reports have also been made that these foreign fighters have become a liability rather than an asset (Mironova et al. 2016). The differences between local and foreign fighters in terms of aims, priorities, expectations, and methods have assumingly created tensions (Bradley 2016). Foreign fighters acting as mercenaries are generally less loyal to ISIS's core ideological cause. The research on VNSAs shows that foreign fighters generally join violent armed groups with their own external motivations that are mainly connected to the individual perception of large-scale events in world politics, while locals tend to act against internal happenings such as social and economic disadvantages, failing states, state-led torture and mass killings, etc. Foreign fighters that join ISIS are generally motivated by its propaganda of building Islamic States, while local forces join because it is generally the least bad option among others, especially in contrast to the Bashar al-Assad regime in Syria (Roy 2017). During the course of the wars in Iraq and Syria, local forces were motivated to fight against the Assad regime or US forces in Iraq, yet this motivation has shifted noticeably toward that of establishing the Islamic State (Berger and Stern 2015). This shift has also created friction among local forces, who have deep suspicions of foreign fighters and their will and capabilities ("Desperate ISIS fighters killing each other" 2016). ISIS's leaders attempt to reduce tensions among fractions by removing foreign fighters from administrative and political positions and relegating these fighters to IT-related intelligence work, IED factories, and technical tasks (Mironova et al. 2016).

4 Influence: Ability of Being Sustainable and Impact on Local, Regional, and International Politics

The third layer in the ARI framework is influence, through which VNSAs employ policy instruments, implement decisions, or simply show capacity and capabilities. Influence is made up of two dimensions. The first dimension addresses sustainability, asking if groups have deterrent-resistant motivations such as ideology and if they are flexible/adaptable enough to cope with the fast-changing environment on the ground. At the second level, influence refers to impact. Are groups able to force a state response that acknowledges their autonomy? Are they able to make transformative changes leading to major changes in states' policies, practices, and understanding? Success for a VNSA is to be able to make significant changes in government policies that could attain recognition and legitimacy. Violent means may be more effective than non-violent means in gaining recognition or legitimacy or vice versa. However, transformative capacities, those capacities that lead to major change in states' policies and affect state-centric systems, major alignments, or distribution of capabilities, are key ways VNSAs can exert influence (Aydinli 2016, pp. 17–19) (Table 3).

ISIS is highly adaptable to the changing environment on the ground in the military sense, (Wali 2015) as evidenced by long and hard battles fought against the group by a coalition of forces. Yet, ISIS has been largely weakened and contained over the last years. ISIS's endurance and sustainability as a state-like organization are on a downslide. The group's prospects for establishing a territorial proto-state are not promising as military campaigns waged against it have begun to make tangible progress in Iraq and Syria. However, the history of ISIS and other splinter groups shows that these VNSAs are relatively flexible and have the ability to go underground and regroup at a later phase of the conflict, even sometimes with another name. A post-territorial ISIS is highly possible (Revin and Olidort 2016). The most important factor making ISIS resistant is its ideological roots and the social/political context that create them in the first place. As long as the social/political context remains, ISIS will not be politically or ideologically defeated. As Shafi (2016) noted, "while national, regional and international actors are mainly focused on the military battle, there is an urgent need to address the aftermath of ISIS in Iraq and Syria, as well as the structural failures and societal grievances that have allowed the rise of ISIS in the first place." In a similar vein, Orton (2017) argues that ISIS will revive as long as the campaign against the group is handled largely by demographically inappropriate forces such as al-Hashd al-Shabi, the

Table 3 Influence

Sustainability	Deterrent-resistant motivations	As the origin of the group lies at the sectarian division in the region, ISIS has an ideologically powerful cause, establishing a caliphate. Therefore, even if the group is defeated militarily, it will not die politically or ideologically. The destruction of the caliphate will not guarantee its end because military defeats do not constitute political defeats
	Flexibility adaptability	It has shown military and strategic adaptability, yet has been contained and weakened by the war against the group waged by a coalition of 60 nations. However, the group is extremely adaptable and will likely go underground and regroup
Impact	Compellence	The group has used its asymmetrical coercive edge over the course of events in Iraq and Syria but has not achieved compellence. Some state and non-state actors avoid fighting directly against the group as long as it has not threatened them militarily
	Transformative capacity	It has brought a number of transformative changes both at regional and international level and has been one of the main drivers of the changing nature of the balance of power/threat in the region. It has also had a spectacular impact on international politics directly and indirectly. It has created (1) a strategic distraction among great powers, (2) tense relations among allies such as Turkey and the USA, (3) tense relations among regional countries, and (4) an environment where Iraq and Syria can stay united and an environment in which European political stability and strategic capabilities are tarnished

conglomeration of Shi'i militias backed by Iranian proxies, or the Kurdish Peshmerga in Iraq and the YPG/YPJ in Syria. These groups may be able to militarily defeat ISIS but will not be able to politically or ideologically eradicate ISIS and will instead harden its brand.

The second facet of influence is impact. No matter how powerful ISIS is politically, ideologically, or militarily, its autonomy in Iraq and Syria will never be recognized by any of the existing states. However, ISIS has engendered transformative changes in states' policies, practices, and understanding as one of the fundamental drivers shaking the geopolitics of the entire Middle East. ISIS' rise has directly threatened the survival of Syria, Iraq, and Libya, and Yemen, at its height, posed an ominous threat to Jordan and even Saudi Arabia. ISIS also hugely affected, directly or indirectly, the redistribution of power in the entire region (Panayiotides 2015). From Russia's involvement in Syria to the USA's difficult position between its NATO ally Turkey and its operational partner the YPG/YPJ, from the Iran-Saudi Arabia rivalry in the region to European disintegration, ISIS has played an important role. Foreign fighters pose a national security threat when they return to their home countries. ISIS-inspired lone wolf attacks, such as those in Istanbul and Manchester, are a direct threat to countries who fight against the group.

By intensifying the refugee flow from Syria and Iraq, ISIS also threatens the political unity and stability of the Middle East, Europe, and even beyond. Such events have played a large role in the recent rise of nationalism and Islamophobia in European cities, tarnishing Europe's strategic capabilities. In addition, ISIS has caused unimaginable destruction and suffering in the region. In this sense, ISIS has had a far greater influence in the region than any other terror networks in history.

5 Conclusion

Originating in Iraq in the 2000s and evolving into an insurgency group, ISIS went from near obscurity to an organized army aiming at the establishment and expansion of a caliphate in the Middle East. The group is a prime example of a hybrid of terror network and insurgent traits. Despite op-eds, articles, monographs, reports, and many other forms of nonscientific and scientific studies dealing with the group from different perspectives, research on the group's agency as a VNSA is far less comprehensive. The aim of the chapter is to summarize, synthesize, and analyze ISIS's territoriality by applying the ARI framework, which allows us to trace ISIS's agency through its levels of autonomy, representation, and influence.

In the autonomy dimension, contrary to general assumption, the group depends ideologically more on Sunni disenfranchisement and local tribes' support than Salafi/jihadi elements. Other factors that strengthen the group autonomy are its (1) organizational capacity, (2) fundraising capacity, and (3) regeneration capacity. The biggest challenge the group has faced in all of these is that states' opposition, especially from international states. The increasing momentum in the fight against the group has already crippled and reduced ISIS' autonomy. Also at the autonomy level lie claims of having a superior political legitimacy by rejecting the international system of states, existing borders, and legitimacy of regional states. On the one hand, this provides the group with an area where it can politically and ideologically create a "non-state complex" by generating an alternative imagined community (umma under a caliph) and providing new forms of security and welfare in a civil-war context. On the other hand, as the group became more successful at doing this, local and international opposition gained momentum. Thus, for ISIS, being sovereignty-free plays out both in their favor and as a hindrance to its success.

In the evaluation of the representation layer, the group's territories and corresponding aims must be examined. ISIS has aimed at (1) defending and expanding missions in the first-tier area, namely, Iraq and Syria; (2) establishing alliances and creating disorder and conflict to build a pre-territorial control in the second-tier area, namely, Libya, Afghanistan, Egypt, Yemen, and Mali; and (3) generating alliances and inflicting lone-wolf attacks in the third-tier area, areas beyond the first two. Hence, ISIS' representation is interlinked with the group's aims within these different parts of the world. In the first-tier area, the group must recruit new members and create loyalty among its existing members to support its political structure and fighting capacities. Officers and soldiers from the old regime, the

Sunni majority population, foreign fighters coming from a Sunni background, and local tribes are the most important and effective recruitment base for the group. Indeed, until 2015, the group managed to show stunning successes in both recruiting and generating loyalty among existing members in the first- and second-tier areas. However, this capacity has significantly slowed as the fight against the group has gained momentum, Turkey sealed off its border crossing and local forces encircled the group. Still, ISIS' most fundamental setback stems from its expansion into new areas with non-Sunni local populations or Sunni opposition. Yet, while the group's ability to regenerate has slowed in the first-tier area due to changing local dynamics, its ability has significantly expanded in the second- and third-tier areas, helping the group become a global phenomenon and endure as an ideological and political organization.

In the influence layer, the group has shown both strong resistance and flexibility in military battles. ISIS has significantly changed the dynamics in the region and created tense relations among allies, regional countries, and different political/religious sects and has served as a distraction to the great powers from the overreaching Syrian conflict. It has also been a major factor in dividing local nation states, especially Iraq and Syria. ISIS' role in creating major disruption and political instability from Europe to far East Asia either by creating refugee flows or generating a deadly wave of terror attacks and ultra-national, Islamophobic feeling, especially in Europe.

As a conclusion, this analytical survey shows that the military aspect of the fight against the group is necessary and has indeed been impactful. Yet, through the ARI framework, it becomes clear that the fight against the group must also focus on local dynamics to engender long-term success. ISIS's rise depended on the deep historical divisions and the complex local and regional dynamics. Along the way, ISIS manipulated Sunni disenfranchisement to create an ideological base for its autonomy, representation, and influence in Iraq and Syria while using its violent and extreme ideology to boost its regeneration capacity by enticing foreign fighters and other violent jihadi groups to join. The very history of ISIS reveals a pattern of transformation. While the group may weaken to the point that it is no longer targetable as a state-like organization, without the emergence of a legitimate and capable governance system to fill the vacuum in the region, it will continue as a terror network and seek to return.

Bibliography

Al-Ali, Z. (2014, June 19). How Maliki ruined Iraq. *Foreign Policy*. Accessed April 16, 2017, from http://atfp.co/1H4iLF0

Aliyev, H. (2017). Precipitating state failure: Do civil wars and violent non-state actors create failed states? *Third World Quarterly*, 1–17. https://doi.org/10.1080/01436597.2017.1319276

Almukhtar, S. (2015, May 19). ISIS finances are strong. *The New York Times*. Accessed April 24, 2017, from http://nyti.ms/2sagZCp

Anderson, J. (2016, June 21). ISIS: State or terror group? *Small Wars Journal*. Accessed May 14, 2017, from http://bit.ly/2sa0CW7
Aydinli, E. (2016). *Violent non-state actors: From Anarchists to Jihadists*. Abingdon: Routledge.
Baker, A. (2015, February 26). Why Bashar Assad won't fight ISIS. *Time*. Accessed May 1, 2017, from http://time.com/3719129/assad-isis-asset/
Batchelor, J. (2015, April 27). *ISIL is more than just a police state*. Accessed May 2, 2017, from http://bit.ly/2sa4yWV
Berger, J. M., & Stern, J. (2015, March 8). ISIS and the foreign-fighter phenomenon. *The Atlantic*. Accessed May 1, 2017, from http://theatln.tc/2sa2HBp
Bill, P. (2016). As ISIS's Caliphate crumbles, Jihadist tactics are evolving. *Newsweek, 167*(15). Accessed May 1, 2017, from http://bit.ly/2rbukgl
Bolton, J. R. (2015, November 24). John Bolton: To defeat ISIS, create a Sunni State. *The New York Times*. Accessed April 30, 2017, from https://goo.gl/HQjnnU
Boyle, J. (2015, January 6). Islamic State and the idea of statehood. *BBC News*. Accessed May 1, 2017, from http://bbc.in/2saalfl
Bradley, M. (2016, March 25). Rift grows in Islamic State between foreign, local fighters. *Wall Street Journal*. Accessed May 1, 2017, from http://on.wsj.com/2s9X8my
Brands, H., & Feaver, P. (2017). Was the rise of ISIS inevitable? *Survival, 59*(3), 7–54. https://doi.org/10.1080/00396338.2017.1325595
Bremmer, I. (2017, April 14). The top 5 countries where ISIS gets its foreign recruits. *Time*. Accessed April 17, 2017, from http://ti.me/2sa4tTh
Bunzel, C. (2014). From paper state to Caliphate: The ideology of the Islamic State. *Brookings Institute*. Accessed April 17, 2017, from http://brook.gs/2sa5YRt
Cali, C. (2014, August 21). The Islamic State's challenge to the international system. *E-International Relations*. Accessed April 24, 2017, from http://www.e-ir.info/?p=51685
Celso, A. N. (2015). The Islamic State and Boko Haram: Fifth wave Jihadist terror groups. *Orbis, 59*(2), 249–268. https://doi.org/10.1016/j.orbis.2015.02.010
Cigar, N. (2012). *Al-Qaida, the tribes, and the government: Lessons and prospects for Iraq's unstable triangle*. Washington, DC: Government Printing Office.
Coles, I., & Parker, N. (2015, December 11). How Saddam's fighters help Islamic State rule. *Reuters*. Accessed May 1, 2017, from http://reut.rs/2sa2vlH
Connable, B., Lander, N., & Jackson, K. (2017). *Beating the Islamic State (No. RR-1562-OSD)*. Washington, DC: Rand Cooperation. Accessed May 17, 2017, from http://amzn.to/2s9FejV
Crane, K. (2015). *The role of oil in ISIL finances: Testimony presented before the Senate Energy and Natural Resources Committee*. Washington, DC: Rand Cooperation. Accessed April 24, 2017, from https://goo.gl/WvhsdB
Cronin, A. K. (2015). ISIS is not a terrorist group: Why counterterrorism won't stop the latest Jihadist threat. *Foreign Affairs, 94*, 87.
Daragahi, B., & Solomon, E. (2014, September 21). Fuelling Isis Inc. *Financial Times*. Accessed April 16, 2017, from http://on.ft.com/2s9RsZS
Davis, D. E. (2009). Non-state armed actors, new imagined communities, and shifting patterns of sovereignty and insecurity in the modern world. *Contemporary Security Policy, 30*(2), 221–245. https://doi.org/10.1080/13523260903059757
Department of Defense. (2015). *Operation inherent resolve: Quarterly report to the United States Congress*. Washington, DC. Accessed May 10, 2017, from http://bit.ly/2s9OAwc
Desperate ISIS fighters killing each other. (2016, June 6). *The Horn News*. Accessed May 1, 2017, from http://bit.ly/2sa81EZ
Dobbins, J., & Jones, S. G. (2017). The end of a Caliphate. *Survival, 59*(3), 55–72. https://doi.org/10.1080/00396338.2017.1325596
Falk, R. (2015, December 11). ISIS's challenge to the statist world order. *Middle East Eye*. Accessed April 24, 2017, from http://bit.ly/2sakhVU
Fishman, B. (2007). *Fourth Generation Governance–Sheikh Tamimi defends the Islamic State of Iraq*. DTIC Document. Accessed April 17, 2017, from http://bit.ly/2s9MVqk

Gartenstein, D. R. (2015, February 9). How many fighters does the Islamic State really have? *War on the Rocks*. Accessed April 18, 2017, from http://bit.ly/2s9XMRf

Gerges, F. A. (2016). *ISIS: A history*. Princeton, NJ: Princeton University Press.

Hashim, A. S. (2014). The Islamic State: From al-Qaeda affiliate to Caliphate. *Middle East Policy, 21*(4), 69–83. https://doi.org/10.1111/mepo.12096

Hassan, H. (2016, June). The sectarianism of the Islamic State: Ideological roots and political context. *Carnegie Endowment for International Peace*. Accessed May 27, 2017, from https://goo.gl/KSoI0B

Hassan, H. (2017, May 9). Despite heavy losses, ISIL's structures remain resilient. *The National Interest*. Accessed May 10, 2017, from http://bit.ly/2s9SBAz

Itani, F. (2014). *Losing Syria and Iraq to jihadists*. Rafik Hariri Center for the Middle East, Atlantic Council. Accessed May 1, 2017, from http://bit.ly/2s9WQwd

Katagiri, N. (2015). ISIL, insurgent strategies for statehood, and the challenge for security studies. *Small Wars and Insurgencies, 26*(3), 542–556. https://doi.org/10.1080/09592318.2014.989672

Lia, B. (2015). Understanding jihadi proto-states. *Perspectives on Terrorism, 9*(4). Accessed May 2, 2017

Lister, T. (2016, June 29). Is ISIS going broke? *CNN*. Accessed April 24, 2017, from http://cnn.it/2sa7enK

Lister, T. (2017, March 27). ISIS 2.0: As the Caliphate crumbles, ISIS evolves. *CNN.com*. Accessed May 28, 2017, from http://cnn.it/2s9Sh4P

Lister, T., Sanchez, R., Bixler, M., O'key, S., Hogenmiller, M., & Tawfeeq, M. (2017, February 13). ISIS goes global: Mapping ISIS attacks around the world. *CNN*. Accessed April 17, 2017, from http://edition.cnn.com/2015/12/17/world/mapping-isis-attacks-around-the-world/

Malet, D. (2010). Why foreign fighters?: Historical perspectives and solutions. *Orbis, 54*(1), 97–114.

Martin, M., & Solomon, H. (2017). Islamic State: Understanding the nature of the beast and its funding. *Contemporary Review of the Middle East, 4*(1), 18–49. https://doi.org/10.1177/2347798916681319

McCants, W. (2015). *The ISIS apocalypse: The history, strategy, and doomsday vision of the Islamic State*. New York: Macmillan.

Miller, D. L. (2017, April 18). Double threat? ISIS and Al Qaeda are in talks to join forces, Iraq's VP says. *Fox News*. Accessed May 10, 2017, from http://fxn.ws/2s9Vxx4

Mironova, V., Hussein, M., Mironova, V., & Hussein, M. (2016, September 26). The downfall of ISIS. *Foreign Affairs*. Accessed April 17, 2017.

Oktav, Ö. Z., Parlar Dal, E., & Kursun, A. M. (2017). Reframing and reassessing the VNSAs in Syrian conflict: An introduction. In O. Z. Oktav, E. Parlar Dal, & A. M. Kursun (Eds.), *Violent non state actors and the Syrian civil war: The ISIS and YPG cases*. Cham: Springer.

Orton, K. (2017, April 22). Analysis: "Signs of recovery for the Islamic State." *Henry Jackson Society*. Accessed May 17, 2017, from http://bit.ly/2sacuHK

Panayiotides, N. (2015). The Islamic State and the redistribution of power in the Middle East. *International Journal on World Peace, 32*(3), 11.

Podder, S. (2014). Mainstreaming the non-state in bottom-up state-building: linkages between rebel governance and post-conflict legitimacy. *Conflict, Security and Development, 14*(2), 213–243. https://doi.org/10.1080/14678802.2014.889878

Revin, M., & Olidort, J. (2016, October 21). Does ISIS need territory to survive? *The New York Times*. Accessed May 17, 2017, from http://nyti.ms/2s9QhcU

Roy, O. (2017, March). Who are the new jihadis? *The Guardian*. Accessed May 28, 2017, from http://bit.ly/2sa7Eui

Saddam Hussein's officer drew up ISIS master plan. (2015, April 20). *Al Arabiya English*. Accessed May 1, 2017, from http://bit.ly/2s9SDs8

Shafi, W.-A. (2016, November 22). Post-ISIS Iraq and Syria: Stability through regional cooperation. *East-West Institute*. Accessed May 1, 2017, from http://bit.ly/2s9Qlti

Sherlock, R. (2014, February 3). Al-Qaeda cuts links with Syrian group too extreme even for them. *The Independent*. Accessed May 10, 2017, from http://bit.ly/2s9TCZp

Speckhard, A., & Yayla, A. S. (2017). The ISIS Emni: The origins and inner workings of ISIS's intelligence apparatus. *Perspectives on Terrorism, 11*(1). Accessed May 15, 2017.

"They hate the West": Foreign IS fighters most violent to hostages, survivors say. (2016, September 8). *ABC News*. Accessed May 10, 2017, from http://ab.co/2sa2crc

Unver, A. (2017). Contested geographies: How ISIS and YPG rule 'No-Go' areas in Northern Syria. In O. Z. Oktav, E. Parlar Dal, & A. M. Kursun (Eds.), *Violent non state actors and the Syrian civil war: The ISIS and YPG cases*. Switzerland: Springer.

Wali, Z. Z. (2015, October 22). US joint chiefs: ISIS is "adaptable and flexible." *Rudaw*. Accessed May 1, 2017, from http://bit.ly/2s9ZcLz

Wallace, T., Fairfield, H., & Watkins, D. (2015, May 21). How ISIS expands. *The New York Times*. Accessed May 10, 2017, from https://goo.gl/FxyFnz

Walt, S. M. (2015). ISIS as revolutionary state. *Foreign Affairs, 94*, 42.

Watkins, D., Yourish, K., & Giratikanon, T. (2015, June 17). Where ISIS has directed and inspired attacks around the world. *The New York Times*. Accessed May 10, 2017, from http://nyti.ms/2s9TuZV

Wright, R. (2016, April 30). How the curse of Sykes-Picot still haunts the Middle East. *The New Yorker*. Accessed April 30, 2017, from http://bit.ly/2s9RnFq

Zelin, A. Y. (2016). *The Islamic State's territorial methodology* (No. 29). The Washington Institute for Near East Policy.

How to Profile PYD/YPG as an Actor in the Syrian Civil War: Policy Implications for the Region and Beyond

Özlem Kayhan Pusane

1 Introduction

Since the Israel-Hezbollah confrontation in 2006, concepts such as "hybrid war," "hybrid threat," and "hybrid adversary" have been on the rise. These terms are part of the ongoing debate about the contemporary threat actors who effectively combine conventional and unconventional forces and capabilities in conflict situations. In fact, the end of the Cold War had already initiated both an academic and a policy-oriented debate about the changing security threats in the 1990s in the face of the increasing number of internal armed (ethnic, religious, communal, etc.) conflicts. However, we are going through a more radical change today with the "rising importance and centrality of nonstate actors and transnational relations" (Aydınlı 2015, p. 424). This transformation not only refers to a shift of actors in the international system but also signifies a major change in the traditional concepts of the Westphalian interstate system and its relationship patterns (Aydınlı 2015, p. 425).

Although more attention is paid to the role of nonstate actors in international politics today, research on this issue, so far, has focused primarily on benign agents and their liberal agendas, such as transnational activists, advocacy networks, and nongovernmental organizations (Aydınlı 2015, p. 426). However, *violent* nonstate actors (VNSAs), including insurgents, militias, terrorists, and groups of organized crime, still remain an understudied phenomenon in the current scholarship. This is an important gap considering the tremendous increase in the number and changing nature of the VNSAs, especially in the Syrian civil war.

The Democratic Union Party (*Partiya Yekîtiya Demokrat-PYD*) with its armed wing People's Protection Units (*Yekîneyên Parastina Gel-YPG*), constitutes one of these VNSAs. After the Syrian regime withdrew its forces from the Kurdish areas in

Ö.K. Pusane (✉)
Işık University, Şile, Turkey
e-mail: ozlem.pusane@isikun.edu.tr

Ö.Z. Oktav et al. (eds.), *Violent Non-state Actors and the Syrian Civil War*,
DOI 10.1007/978-3-319-67528-2_4

northern Syria in 2012, the PYD/YPG seized control of several towns and enclaves in this region and emerged as one of the most influential actors of the Syrian civil war. This chapter provides an analysis of the reasons why VNSAs in general and the PYD/YPG in particular have gained so much influence in regional and international politics with a special emphasis on the concepts of "hybrid war," "hybrid threat," and "hybrid adversary." It then looks into the policy implications of varying perceptions about the PYD/YPG as a complex nonstate actor and presents a discussion of how the Syrian regime, Kurdish actors in Syria and Iraq other than the PYD/YPG, regional actors such as Turkey, Iran, and Israel and international actors such as the USA and Russia have approached the PYD/YPG within the context of the Syrian civil war.

2 The Rise of VNSAs in the International System

VNSAs are not a new phenomenon. From the pirates of the ancient Mediterranean to the anarchists of the nineteenth century, VNSAs have mainly emerged out of failures of governance in different parts of the world. In the words of Phil Williams:

> [S]tates that are low in legitimacy and high in repressiveness, relying on coercion rather than consent, typically provoke opposition. . .Moreover, where states with low capacity are unable to meet the demands of the citizenry for security and other public goods, other actors fill the gap. When there is a security deficit in particular, VNSAs come into existence to provide security or, where they already exist, become more important in the provision of security (Williams 2008, p. 6)

Although governance-related problems often contribute to the emergence of VNSAs, the number and influence of these actors have increased tremendously since the end of the Cold War. There are two major reasons for this. The first one is the end of the bipolar confrontation. During the Cold War, international interactions were mostly state centric, which kept VNSAs under control (Zhidkova 2015, pp. 6–7). Aydınlı states that transnational activity tends to increase when interstate confrontation eases, such as the times of the Concert of Europe or the interwar years. Thus, the aftermath of the Cold War, which marked the end of the political and ideological confrontation between the USA and the Soviet Union, gave way to a tremendous increase in the transnational activities of nonstate actors, both peaceful and violent (Aydınlı 2008, p. 904). The second reason is the growing pace of globalization in the past couple of decades. With the improvement in transportation and communication technologies, it is now easier for nonstate actors to get a hold of weapons from the transnational market of illicit arms, have access to know-how and funding sources, or engage in transnational alliances with other state and nonstate actors (Williams 2008, p. 6). With the changes in technology, it is also much easier for a small group of people to kill a large number of people and cause a tremendous level of damage (Dutka 2006, p. 5). While mass killing was limited to state actors in the past—since this capacity required advanced infrastructure and large numbers of people to carry it out—this is not the case anymore, as seen in the September 11 attacks (Dutka 2006, p. 5). These two developments have empowered VNSAs and enhanced their capacity to challenge the international system.

The Syrian civil war provides a perfect example where alternative forms of governance have emerged vis-à-vis a state which has failed in its capacity to govern and which eventually lost monopoly on the use of force. Especially the PYD/YPG emerged out of this context as an actor, which possesses quasi-state features and both conventional and nonconventional fighting capacities. The following sections provide an analysis of the PYD/YPG as a complex VNSA of the Syrian civil war.

3 PYD/YPG as a Hybrid Nonstate Actor

In 2009, former US Secretary of Defense Robert Gates noted that:

> the categories of warfare are blurring and no longer fit into neat, tidy boxes. One can expect to see more tools and tactics of destruction—from the sophisticated to the simple—being employed simultaneously in hybrid and more complex forms of warfare (Gates 2009).

The concepts of hybrid threat/opponent/adversary and hybrid conflicts/wars have their roots in Hezbollah's defense against the Israeli Defense Forces in their armed conflict between July 12 and August 14, 2006. During this confrontation, despite their small size, Hezbollah forces acted in an organized fashion with the fusion of various units and with sophisticated arms, including antitank guided missiles, operational and tactical rockets, and unmanned aerial vehicles (Hoffman 2009; RAND 2011). Based on this experience and similar cases, Hoffman (2009) defines a hybrid threat as "any adversary that simultaneously and adaptively employs a fused mix of conventional weapons, irregular tactics, terrorism, and criminal behavior in the battle space to obtain their political objectives." Although recent debates about hybridity have mainly taken place within the framework of military studies and the issue of battlefield effectiveness, there is also a political side to these discussions. Organizations such as Hamas and Hezbollah are not only armed organizations but they also have a strong political, economic, and social dimension since they manage to establish a complex system of governance in the territories they control (Berti 2016, p. 1). Thus, scholars and policymakers assess hybrid nonstate actors today both as organizations that can integrate regular and irregular forces, tactics, and strategies in armed confrontations and as entities that carry state-like features and challenge those states that they are placed in.

The PYD/YPG is such an actor for which the demarcation between the state and nonstate actorness is blurred. The PYD was established in 2003, a few years after the now-jailed PKK leader Abdullah Öcalan's expulsion from Syria in response to Turkey's threat to use force otherwise and the Syrian regime's subsequent closure of the PKK camps in accordance with the agreement reached between Turkey and Syria. Organizationally, the PYD is a member of the Kurdistan Communities Union (*Koma Civakên Kurdistan-KCK*), which is an umbrella organization founded with the PKK leadership and where both the PKK and PJAK are also members. The YPG is widely considered as the armed wing of the PYD, and it was established after the 2004 Kurdish uprising in Qamishli, Syria, which was met with a strong crackdown of the Syrian regime (Global Security).

When the popular uprisings in Syria turned into a civil war from 2011 onward, the PYD/YPG emerged as the most influential Kurdish actor both institutionally and in terms of the organization's outreach among the Syrian Kurds. Especially when the Syrian regime withdrew its forces from the Kurdish areas in northern Syria in July 2012, the PYD/YPG filled the power vacuum and established a local self-administration in the form of three cantons, namely, Afrin, Kobane, and Jazira in the Turkish-Syrian border region. The PYD/YPG's role in the Syrian civil war was enhanced further when the YPG became the main local fighting force in the struggle against the Islamic State of Iraq and al-Sham (ISIS) from 2014 onward.

As mentioned above, hybrid actors can be assessed according to both their military capabilities and their political achievements. From a military perspective, YPG has so far presented itself in Syria as a well-organized local ground force, which uses a combination of conventional and guerrilla tactics. The group has played an important role in several occasions, including the defense of Kobane—a small Syrian Kurdish town in the Turkish-Syrian border—against ISIS between September 2014 and March 2015 and rescuing the Yazidi community in Sinjar, Iraq, when the town was occupied by ISIS in August 2014. The YPG is also expected to play a key role in the international coalition's upcoming offensive against ISIS' self-declared capital Raqqa.[1] According to an *Economist* article, the Syrian Democratic Forces (SDF), which is a multiethnic alliance struggling with the ISIS, but which is dominated by the YPG units, was composed of approximately 20,000 YPG fighters and 10,000 Sunni Arabs in 2016 (Economist 2016). This alliance also includes Christians and Turkmen units. A more recent *Reuters* article puts the number of YPG fighters at 60,000 including the 24,000 all-female Women's Protection Units (*Yekîneyên Parastina Jin-YPJ*). "[T]he YPG has a military intelligence branch that gathers information about ISIS, a 'special forces' unit tasked with operating behind enemy lines, and an anti-terror unit" (Barfi 2015).

The YPG has become the main US ally in the fight against ISIS. The US officials and YPG members are in direct contact in Kobane and Jazira, and they have been coordinating their military activities with regard to air and ground operations via a joint command center in the Iraqi Kurdistan Regional Government (KRG) (Bradley and Parkinson 2015). The US Special Operations Forces have been on the ground for some time in support of the SDF units. Hundreds of US Marines and Army Rangers have also been recently deployed in Syria as temporary personnel for the Raqqa operation (Perry 2017b). The YPG is also closely working with Russia in the Syrian context. A YPG member recently declared that Russia was in the process of establishing a new military base in northwestern Syria, where it would train YPG

[1]The anti-ISIS coalition is composed of 69 countries today. See http://theglobalcoalition.org/en/partners/

fighters (Perry 2017a). Although this is denied by Russian authorities, there is no doubt that the Russian military presence has been increasing in the Kurdish regions of Syria.

As for the PYD/YPG's domestic political establishment,[2] since July 2012, "the group has drafted a constitution, held elections, and installed numerous local councils" (Stein 2016). In September 2013, the PYD first established an "interim committee" aimed to prepare an administration plan. Then in November 2013, it created a "joint interim administration" with local and legislative assemblies and governments in the three cantons of Afrin, Kobane, and Jazira. Finally, in early 2014, the group announced the first "social contract of Rojava," which was regarded as a "provisional constitutional charter" (ICG 2014, p. 15). Thus, the PYD gradually created a system of local governance in northern Syria. This local governance structure also has a significant level of recognition at the international level. For example, since the early days of the Syrian civil war, the PYD Co-Chair Salih Muslim has been officially received by several countries. In February 2015, French President François Hollande invited two YPJ members to the Élysée Palace, which constitutes an important sign for the PYD/YPG's international legitimacy (Bradley and Parkinson 2015). Key US officials like the special envoy to the anti-ISIS international coalition Brett McGurk and Senator John McCain visited the PYD-controlled areas at different phases of the Syrian civil war (Perry and Mohammed 2016; Nissenbaum 2017).

However, the PYD's political establishment has also been widely criticized. An Amnesty International report presented various human rights abuses in PYD-controlled regions. These cases include arbitrary arrests of the PYD's rivals, arbitrary detentions, due process violations, and unsolved disappearances and killings (HRW 2014). The PYD denies these allegations.

The YPG's role in the struggle against ISIS as a key ground force, the administrative structure that the PYD created in northern Syria, and the extent of the group's international recognition show that the PYD/YPG has emerged as a sophisticated nonstate military and political actor. However, as is the case with almost all hybrid actors, the PYD/YPG has a complicated relationship with various domestic, regional, and international actors. The following sections provide an analysis of these connections.

3.1 *PYD/YPG's Relations with the Syrian Regime*

Since the PYD/YPG began to establish control in northern Syria, it has faced allegations about having a dubious relationship with the Bashar Al-Assad regime. Although VNSAs are often considered as actors that challenge the states in which

[2]For a more detailed discussion of the PYD's administrative structure in northern Syria, see Ünver (2017).

they emerge and flourish, the PYD/YPG's relationship with the Syrian regime is a more complicated one.

Suspicions about a shady relationship between the PYD/YPG and the Syrian regime have their roots in the latter's withdrawal of its forces from the Kurdish-populated areas of northern Syria and the subsequent PYD/YPG control of these regions without resistance on the part of the Syrian regime. This perception was combined with PYD Co-Chair Salih Muslim's unexpected return to Syria from his years-long exile in Qandil. It was argued that the Syrian regime, from time to time, provided material support to the PYD/YPG in its struggle with the opposition forces (ICG 2014, p. 8). Bashar Al-Assad even stated that he had provided arms to the YPG (Barfi 2016). After the Assad forces' military withdrawal from northern Syria (except in a small area in Qamishli) in 2012, the regime continued "to pay salaries to state employees and run administrative offices" (ICG 2014, p. 9). Thus, it was alleged that the PYD/YPG engaged in a deal with the Syrian regime, which allowed the former to establish itself as an autonomous actor in Kurdish-populated areas in return for preventing the acts of anti-Assad forces (ICG 2014). In their statements, PYD members have always described their group as a "third current" between the regime and the opposition (Salih 2016; ICG 2014, p. 7). As a result, since the beginning of the Syrian civil war, the Assad regime has avoided attacking the PYD/YPG-held areas, and the PYD/YPG has not directly confronted the Syrian regime forces except in minor confrontations.

However, analysts argue that the interaction between the PYD/YPG and the Assad regime constitutes a "marriage of convenience." In other words, it is the circumstances of the civil war that forced these two unlikely actors to arrive at a common understanding in their actions. The PYD perceives a significant portion of the anti-Assad opposition as too conservative with close links to the Nusra Front—the Al Qaeda affiliate in Syria[3]—and as closely allied with Turkey (Stein 2016). Ghadi Sary argues that what brought together the PYD and the regime is their common threat perception of the Salafist groups. Salih Muslim once stated that "if the regime collapses because of the Salafis [fundamentalist Islamic militants] it would be a disaster for everyone" (cited in Cockburn 2015). Muslim added that although he would want the Assad regime to end, he considered ISIS as the main enemy (Cockburn 2015). In sum, the future of the PYD/YPG's relationship with the Syrian regime is uncertain, and it seems that the fate of this relationship will be determined in line with the evolution of the Syrian civil war.

[3]In July 2016, Jabhat al-Nusra ended all its ties to al-Qaeda and changed its name to Jabhad Fatah al-Sham.

3.2 PYD/YPG's Relations with Other Kurdish Actors in the Region

The PYD/YPG's most controversial relationship is the one with the Kurdistan Workers' Party (*Partiya Karkerên Kurdistanê, PKK*). This is mainly because the PKK is recognized as a terrorist organization not only by Turkey, which has been struggling with the PKK insurgency since the early 1980s, but also by some of the major international actors such as the USA and the EU. Due to its connection to the PKK, Turkey considers the PYD/YPG as a terrorist organization. In fact, in November 2016, Turkey even issued an arrest warrant for Salih Muslim, claiming that a YPG member was linked to the bombing of a military convoy in Ankara on February 17, 2016 (Al Jazeera 2016).

The PYD was established in 2003 as an offshoot of the PKK. The PYD argues that the latter presents an ideological inspiration for the group, and its members acknowledge the PKK leader Öcalan as their leader (ICG 2014, p. 5). Öcalan portraits appear in PYD-controlled areas of Syria, including in government buildings, police stations, and classrooms (Enzinna 2015), and the PYD promotes the idea of "democratic autonomy," a concept developed by Öcalan. However, the PYD denies any direct links with the PKK.

In practice, the PYD/YPG and the PKK connection is a complicated one. The YPG's leadership cadres have been dominated by Syrian PKK militants who received military and ideological training at the PKK's Qandil base in northern Iraq. Additional PKK and PJAK members joined the PYD/YPG as the latter acquired further control over the Kurdish-populated areas in Syria and engaged in a fight against ISIS (ICG 2014, p. 5). A YPG militant, named Zind Ruken, states that "[i]t's all PKK but different branches. . .Sometimes I'm a PKK, sometimes I'm a PJAK, sometimes I'm a YPG. It doesn't really matter. They are all members of the PKK" (Bradley and Parkinson 2015).

The PYD/YPG's relations with other Kurdish groups in Syria and Iraq are also controversial due to the political divisions among the Kurds. Most importantly, the historical rivalry between Massoud Barzani's Kurdistan Democratic Party (KDP) and Öcalan's PKK as different representatives of Kurdish nationalism has serious reflections in the Syrian context. Alarmed by the rise of the PYD, KRG President Massoud Barzani promoted the creation of the Kurdish National Council (KNC, or *Encûmena Niştimanî ya Kurdî li Sûriyê, ENKS*) as early as October 2011, which brought together 11 different Syrian Kurdish political parties other than the PYD.[4]

[4] The KNC comprises the following Syrian Kurdish groups: The Kurdish Union Party in Syria (Yekîtî), The Kurdistan Democratic Party-Syria (PDK-S), The Kurdish Reform Movement-Syria, The Kurdish Democratic Equality Party in Syria, The Kurdish Democratic Patriotic Party in Syria, The Kurdish Democratic Party in Syria (el-Partî), The Kurdish Democratic Union Party in Syria (Democratic Yekîtî), The Kurdistan Democratic Union Party, The Kurdish Democratic Left Party in Syria, The Kurdistan Left Party-Syria, and the Kurdish Future Movement in Syria (See http://knc-geneva.org/?page_id=49&lang=en).

As the PYD focused on building a local autonomous structure during this period, the KNC joined the anti-Assad Syrian National Council (later Syrian National Coalition-SNC) and made an effort to gain "international legitimacy, visibility, and gravitas" (ICG 2014, p. 15). Barzani also played a key role in the Erbil Declaration of July 2012, which created the Kurdish Supreme Committee (KSC), a partnership of the PYD and KNC. According to the Erbil Declaration, KSC would establish a power-sharing framework between the KNC and PYD, in which these actors would be jointly responsible for the governance of Syria's Kurdish-populated areas, while the YPG and Peshmerga forces would protect this region's military security. However, the Erbil Declaration was never implemented, because while the KNC expected the PYD to give up half of its power, the PYD was only open to allowing the KNC to participate in its institutions (cited in ICG 2014, p. 2).

The relationship between the KNC and the PYD was further strained in the subsequent months. First, the PYD denied entry of the KNC's Peshmerga fighters into Syria under their own leadership. Instead, it offered to merge KNC forces into the YPG under the latter's command (ICG 2014, p. 2). In response, Barzani closed the Iraqi-Syrian border, preventing the movement of humanitarian aid into Syria. In 2014, the KRG even dug a 17-km-long trench between the Kurdish regions of Iraq and Syria in order to cut the connection between PYD-controlled areas and the KRG (Taştekin 2014; Thornton 2015, p. 872). Although Massoud Barzani stated that the trench aimed at stopping illegal crossings, the PYD perceived this as a move to weaken its local administrative structure. (Taştekin 2014).

The tensions between the PYD and the KNC are still present despite several attempts to establish a well-functioning power-sharing arrangement. The latest of these efforts is the Duhok Agreement (October 2014) which aimed for a KNC-PYD rapprochement. However, the Duhok Agreement has not been fully implemented, either due to the KNC claims about the PYD's authoritarian behaviors and abuses of power or the PYD's unilateral approach toward the administration of Rojava. (Gunes and Lowe 2015, p. 5). Reports about "raids on offices of KNC parties, arrests of activists and blocking protests" are noteworthy examples, showing that the tension between the KNC and the PYD rises to serious levels from time to time (Allsop 2016). In March 2017, the PYD even detained several KNC members in northern Syria (Etilaf 2017).

This does not mean that the influential role of the PYD/YPG in local administration and the struggle against ISIS has made the KNC irrelevant. Despite its uneasy relationship with the PYD/YPG, the KNC still plays an important role in representing the interests of the Syrian Kurds within the broader anti-Assad opposition (Allsop 2016).[5] For example, KNC representatives participated in the Syria-related Astana and Geneva peace talks.

[5]Here, it must be mentioned that the KNC withdrew from the latest round of Geneva talks, arguing that "the High Negotiations Committee has continuously ignored the Kurdish problem" (Sputnik 2017).

However, the PYD/YPG's links to the PKK and its uneasy relationship with the rest of the Syrian Kurdish groups pose the most important challenge to the PYD's position in the Syrian civil war. For, while its connections to a terrorist organization decrease the legitimacy of the PYD/YPG in its external relations, its adverse relations with the rest of the Syrian Kurds weaken its political power in the Syrian context.

3.3 *PYD/YPG's Relations with the Regional Powers: Turkey, Iran, and Israel*

3.3.1 Turkey

The PYD/YPG's most problematic relationship in the region is with Turkey. The emergence of the PYD/YPG as a key factor in the Syrian civil war, especially from 2012 onward, raised significant concerns in the minds of the Turkish policymakers due to two major reasons. First, after the consolidation of the KRG as an autonomous Kurdish entity along the Turkish-Iraqi border, Turkey was concerned about the repercussions of a new Kurdish entity this time along the Turkish-Syrian border. In addition to Turkey's "northern Iraq" problem since the early 1990s, Turkey was now facing a "northern Syria" problem (Bila 2013). Second, the newly emerging Kurdish de facto autonomous entity in northern Syria and its administration by the PYD/YPG, PKK's Syrian offshoot, have been automatically seen by Ankara as an existential threat to Turkey's national security. Thus, Turkey labeled the PYD as a terrorist organization and formulated its policies toward the Syrian crisis, primarily aiming at preventing the PYD/YPG from increasing its gains regionally and internationally.

When looking retrospectively, two important occasions showed signs of a warming relationship between Turkey and the PYD/YPG. The first one was from July 2013, when the then Minister of Foreign Affairs Ahmet Davutoğlu invited Salih Muslim to İstanbul for official meetings (Eldem 2013). These meetings took place approximately 7 months after Turkey's Justice and Development Party government initiated a peace process to end the PKK violence in Turkey and resolve the Kurdish question. As part of this process, the PKK units had begun to withdraw from Turkey into northern Iraq from May 2013 onward (Çandar 2013). Thus, Muslim's visit took place when there was a new political approach toward the Kurdish question in Turkey. In the aftermath of his visit, Salih Muslim declared that Turkey gave a green light to the Kurdish autonomy in Syria (Çandar 2013) as long as there was no prospect for independence. In response, Muslim promised that "the PYD would not declare autonomy or threaten Turkey's borders." He also agreed to take out the PYD flags from official buildings along the Turkish-Syrian border (Eldem 2013).

Another sign of a warming relationship was related to the PYD's support for Turkey's efforts to relocate Suleyman Shah's tomb in Syria in February 2015 because of the ISIS threat.[6] Turkey evacuated the Turkish soldiers guarding the tomb by carrying out an operation in an unexpected cooperation with the PYD/YPG units. Before the operation, Enver Muslim, Co-Chair of the Kobane canton, and a high level YPG figure visited Ankara to discuss the planning of the operation. Furthermore, Salih Muslim was in İstanbul closely following the developments during the operation. YPG fighters accompanied the Turkish military forces on the ground to the tomb's new location, Eshme, a village near the Turkish border. Although this unusual cooperation was dubbed the "Spirit of Eshme," the relationship between Turkey and the PYD/YPG once again turned into enmity as Turkey's Kurdish peace process ended in the summer of 2015 (Taştekin 2016).

In sum, except for a brief period of time, Turkey's policy toward the PYD/YPG has strongly emphasized the latter's connections to the PKK. Turkish policymakers often expressed their recognition of ISIS, PKK, PYD, and the YPG as terrorist organizations (DW Türkçe 2015; Reuters 2016; The Telegraph 2016). Thus, Turkey has pressured the major actors of the Syrian civil war, particularly the USA and Russia, about preventing the PYD's participation in the political negotiations about the future of Syria. Although Turkey has been successful in its effort to exclude the PYD/YPG from the political processes in Geneva and Astana due to its close relations with the USA and Russia, as well as its close association with the anti-Assad opposition forces, the PYD/YPG continues to be a key political and military actor of the Syrian civil war, and its interests are taken into account by these major actors.

3.3.2 Iran

Iran has been another important regional power involved in the Syrian civil war with a special place in the history of the Kurds. The first experience of Kurdish independence in the modern Middle East was the Mahabad Republic, which was established in northwest Iran in 1946 with Soviet backing (Vali 2011). Although the Mahabad Republic collapsed within less than a year when the Soviet forces withdrew from the region, this experience put Iran at a historical juncture with regard to the Kurdish history.

However, Iran's position vis-à-vis the Kurdish actors in the region has been a problematic one. On one hand, Iran has its own Kurdish citizens, who have pursued cultural and sociopolitical rights. Especially during the 1979 Islamic Revolution, Iranian Kurds were overwhelmingly part of the anti-Shah opposition, and they actively participated in the revolutionary process. However, once the Islamic Republic was formed, the new regime did not embrace the Kurdish demands and instead focused on creating a centralized Islamic state (Entessar 2014, p. 213). Over the years, Kurdish expectations for reform in Iran increased from time to time,

---

[6]The Suleyman Shah's tomb in Syria is considered the only Turkish enclave abroad according to a 1921 agreement with France (BBC 2015; Taştekin 2016).

particularly under the reformist presidents of Mohammad Khatami and Hassan Rouhani. Although there were improvements in the Kurds' position under these administrations, such as the election of the Kurds to the Iranian Majlis or the permission of the first Kurdish peaceful rally "in solidarity with the Syrian Kurds," Iran's unwillingness to grant wide cultural and sociopolitical rights to its Kurdish citizens have persisted to a great extent (Zaman 2015).

On the other hand, Iran has always pursued an instrumental approach toward Kurdish groups in the region to further its national interests. For example, since the 1980–1988 Iran-Iraq war, Iran has established close connections with the Iraqi Kurds, particularly the Patriotic Union of Kurdistan (PUK). Turkey also accused Iran throughout the 1990s of providing material support for the PKK in its insurgency campaign. While Iran developed close ties with the PUK-PKK axis in order to exert its influence in the regional Kurdish politics, this is also a long-term strategy for Iran to prevent the emergence of an independent Kurdistan.

It is possible to see the direct reflections of this Iranian policy in the current Iraqi and Syrian contexts (See Oktav 2017). When ISIS advanced toward northern Iraq in 2014, Iran was the first country to provide support to the Iraqi Kurds, particularly the PUK (Tanchum 2015; Mustafa 2016, p. 5). Micha'el Tanchum attracts attention to Salih Muslim's statement that the weapons airdropped by the anti-ISIS international coalition for the defense of Kobane in 2014 were paid for by the PUK, pointing to the Iranian connection (Tanchum 2015). Thus, Iran currently seems to be in a tactical engagement with the PUK, PKK, and the PYD/YPG in the struggle against ISIS. Iran also needs the cooperation of the PKK in Sinjar and the PYD/YPG in Kobane and Qamishli to maintain its smooth access to the Mediterranean, particularly to the Syrian port of Latakia (Tremblay 2016). Furthermore, it needs to maintain its close relationship with the Kurds in order to hinder the Kurdish efforts for an independent Kurdistan in the region (Mustafa 2016).

3.3.3 Israel

In contrast to Turkey and Iran, Israel is a regional actor which holds a positive attitude toward the possibility of an independent Kurdish state (Bengio 2016). Israel has been pursuing a policy of establishing connections to the non-Arab minorities in the region with the goal of alleviating the country's regional isolation (Lindenstrauss and Eran 2014, p. 87). The Israeli policymakers' efforts to maintain close relations with the region's Kurdish actors are rooted in this understanding. "[A]ny competitor or adversary of the Arabs" is regarded as a natural ally of Israel (Bengio 2016).

Israel particularly has a history of good relations with the Iraqi Kurds. In the 1970s, Israeli officials cooperated with the Iraqi Kurds in helping around 5000 Jews in Iraq to leave the country through its northern border, due to Saddam Hussein's persecution of the Kurdish Jews (Lindenstrauss and Eran 2014, p. 88; Neurink 2015). These relations were further enhanced in the aftermath of first, the 1991 Gulf War and then the 2003 Iraq War, which helped the Iraqi Kurds emerge as an autonomous political actor in northern Iraq. An important sign of this was Israel's willingness to buy oil directly from the KRG in 2015 at the expense of its relations with Baghdad. (Bengio 2016).

However, Israeli-Kurdish relations have not developed without problems. First, the KRG has preferred to keep its interactions with Israel behind closed doors since the former has been reluctant to alienate Iran as well as its Arab allies in the region (Bengio 2016). Second, it is also not easy for Israel to pursue close contacts with all Kurdish groups in the KRG, particularly the PUK and the Gorran, which have developed relations with Iran (Malik 2017). Finally, Israeli relations with the PKK have also been problematic due to the country's close relationship with Turkey and the Turkish-Israeli cooperation against the PKK in the 1990s. Although the Turkish-Israeli alliance has weakened since the 2008 Gaza War, this situation has not completely changed, yet.

Nevertheless, the YPG's effective fight against ISIS from 2014 onward strengthened the Israeli approach toward the Kurds and the idea of Kurdish self-administration. In fact, from the Israeli perspective, there does not seem to be a significant difference between Kurds as potentially an independent regional political entity or Kurds acting in the form of nonstate actors. Yet, the PYD/YPG's links to the PKK on one hand, and its dubious relationship with the Assad regime on the other, have created a difficult situation for Israel.

Despite this background, Bengio (2016) argues that Israel has sent humanitarian aid to the Syrian Kurds and "reportedly gathered intelligence" from them. ISIS is a common concern for the Syrian Kurds and Israel (Bengio 2016). This has created a common ground for Israel and the PYD/YPG to develop closer relations despite Israel's uneasiness about the PYD/YPG's links to Iran and the former's problematic relationship with Turkey.

4 PYD/YPG's Relations with the USA and Russia

The USA is an actor in the Syrian context, which most strongly feels the tension of the PYD/YPG's identity as a hybrid nonstate actor. On one hand, the PYD/YPG has turned into a key US ally in the struggle against ISIS since 2014, when ISIS forces besieged Kobane. The USA has been providing material and training support to the YPG since then, as well as air support for the ground campaign against ISIS. From October 2015 onward, the US Special Forces also have been on the ground in northeastern Syria (Clawson 2016, p. 53). A number of important US officials have visited PYD-controlled territories in the past few years and met with leading PYD figures (Stein 2016; Clawson 2016, p. 54). Furthermore, there are reports about the USA building a base in Manbij to train the forces which will take part in the Raqqa offensive (Taştekin 2017). On the other hand, the USA is in favor of maintaining Syria's territorial integrity, and it has declared that "it will not recognize a self-ruled Kurdish zone in Syria" (Stein 2016). Although the US officials' statements treated the PKK, which Turkey recognizes as a terrorist organization, and the PYD/YPG as separate organizations for some time, they have recently begun to acknowledge the links between these two. For example, former US Secretary of Defense Ashton Carter acknowledged that the PYD/YPG and the PKK were linked (Hurriyet Daily News 2016). Likewise, former CIA Chief David Petraeus identified the PYD as the cousin of the PKK at Munich Security Conference (Göksedef 2017). Although, under the Obama administration, the USA avoided officially appearing in contact with the PKK, it directly interacted with the PYD/YPG on the ground.

The USA wants to maintain its alliance with both Turkey and the PYD/YPG in the struggle against ISIS. While the YPG constitutes an effective local fighting force, there are a number of important reasons why the USA wants to avoid alienating Turkey—a close US ally since the second half of the 1940s—in the Syrian context. First, Turkey possesses a key geographical position that could stop ISIS' access to its external environment (Clawson 2016, p. 52). Second, Turkey's İncirlik Air Base constitutes an important base for the US military operations in Syria. However, it is difficult to keep these two actors together in the game. The US cooperation with the PYD/YPG is anathema to the Turkish policymakers' perception of the country's national interests. Thus, when the US special envoy to the anti-ISIS international coalition, Brett McGurk, visited Kobane in early 2016, President Tayyip Erdoğan asked the US "who is your partner, the terrorists in Kobane or me?" (Pecquet 2016). Although Turkey expects the new Trump administration to end the US support for the PYD/YPG in the struggle against ISIS, this does not seem likely as of early 2017.

Russia is another major power, which has been trying to handle the tensions of cooperating simultaneously with the Assad regime, PYD/YPG, and Turkey in the Syrian context. While Russia entered the Syrian civil war in support of the Assad regime, it also developed a political and military relationship with the PYD/YPG. From a military perspective, Russia has been providing air support to the SDF forces in the fight against ISIS. There are also recent reports about the increasing Russian military presence in the Kurdish areas of northern Syria. From a political point of view, Russia has not hesitated to meet with PYD officials in Moscow, and the PYD opened a representative office in this city in February 2016 (Drwish 2016). Also, in contrast to the USA, the Assad regime, and Turkey, Russia has been in favor of a federal Syria.

However, Russia's relations with the Assad regime and Turkey complicate this relationship. Russian officials have, so far, made explicit proposals to the Syrian regime about formulating an autonomous Kurdish region in Syria. However, these proposals have not been accepted by the Assad regime, yet (Bozarslan 2016). Furthermore, although Russia (as well as the USA) has promoted the inclusion of the PYD/YPG in the Syrian peace negotiations in Geneva, this has not happened due to a strong Turkish reaction to this idea. Russian officials once again put forth the idea of Kurdish autonomy in the future of Syria in the 2017 Astana meetings between Russia, Iran, and Turkey (Araabi 2017). However, PYD representatives were not present in these meetings, either, because of a similar pressure from Turkey. Thus, despite Russian efforts to promote the PYD/YPG as an important actor of the Syrian civil war, which needs to be represented in the peace table and as a possible autonomous actor in the future of Syria, its relationship with the Syrian regime and Turkey has been interfering with this policy.

Yet, Russia continues to pursue its complex relationship with the PYD/YPG. For example, although Russia deferred to the Turkish pressures with regard to not inviting the PYD to the Astana talks, Minister of Foreign Affairs Sergey Lavrov later met with the PYD representatives in Moscow "for further discussion of a Russian draft of a new Syrian constitution that had been offered in Astana" (Al-Monitor 2017).

Furthermore, although Turkey initiated its Operation Euphrates Shield in Syria with Russian backing in August 2015, when it liberated al-Bab from ISIS and was determined to move toward Manbij and Raqqa, this policy was hindered by the Russian agreement with the PYD/YPG, which stipulated the transfer of the western Manbij to the Assad regime. This was a clear sign of Russian disapproval of Turkey's ambitions in Syria.

5 Conclusion

In his article in *The Atlantic*, Steven cook asks with regard to the Syrian Kurds: "Are the Kurds terrorists, allies in the war against the Islamic State, or a nation in need of a state?" His answer is "yes to all of these" (Cook 2016). This statement very well describes the current tensions that are experienced with regard to the identity of the PYD/YPG as a complex hybrid nonstate actor.

This chapter provides an overview of the PYD/YPG as a VNSA in the Syrian context and discusses the implications of this complicated actorness for the policies of a number of domestic, regional, and international powers. On one hand, the PYD/YPG is a nonstate actor with sophisticated state-like political features, particularly a local administrative capacity. On the other hand, it is an effective local military force on the ground, which combines conventional and irregular capabilities. This complex identity of the PYD/YPG poses serious dilemmas for the actors with which it is interacting in the Syrian context.

First, the PYD/YPG has a dubious relationship with the Syrian regime. The PYD/YPG has reportedly engaged in an arrangement with the Assad regime, which allowed for the former's control over the Kurdish-populated areas of northern Syria in return for hindering the opposition's anti-regime acts. However, with a local governance structure, the PYD currently possesses the potential to challenge the political unity of the Syrian state in the future. Second, the PYD/YPG's hostile relations with some of the Kurdish groups in the region, such as the KNC and the KDP of northern Iraq, impose limits to its future ambitions. If the PYD/YPG aims to create a Kurdish autonomous region in the future of Syria, it needs to expand its support base among the Syrian Kurds from different political movements. Finally, the regional countries such as Turkey, Israel, and Iran, as well as other major international actors such as the USA and Russia, have been experiencing problems in their relations with the PYD/YPG because of the complex identity of the group.

On one hand, several countries perceive the YPG as an effective local force in the struggle against ISIS. However, the PYD/YPG's relations with a number of actors in the region and especially its close affiliation with the PKK pose a significant dilemma for these actors. Several countries involved in the Syrian civil war feel the need to strike a fine balance between their connections to this key nonstate actor and their existing interstate alliances. It remains to be seen whether the continuing evolution of the PYD/YPG in accordance with the realities of the Syrian civil war will help alleviate these dilemmas and restrictions once the civil war in Syria ends.

The Syrian civil war constitutes a perfect environment to have a better understanding of hybrid nonstate actors. Particularly, the PYD/YPG presents a key case to explain different dimensions and characteristics of this category. The international developments since the end of the Cold War show that the scholarship in International Relations needs to pay closer attention to the actors like PYD/YPG, their complex interactions in, and their challenges to the international system.

References

Al Jazeera. (2016, November 22). Turkey issues arrest warrant for Syrian Kurdish leader. *Al Jazeera*. Accessed March 16, 2017, from http://www.aljazeera.com/news/2016/11/turkey-issues-arrest-warrant-syrian-kurdish-leader-161122143148528.html

Al-Monitor (2017, January 29). Why did Russia offer autonomy for Syria's Kurds? *Al-Monitor*. Accessed September 11, 2017, from http://www.al-monitor.com/pulse/originals/2017/01/russia-offer-kurds-syria-autonomyturkey-islamic-state.html

Allsop, H. (2016, August 30). Are the old Syrian Kurdish parties relevant anymore? *Middle East Centre Blog*. The London School of Economics and Political Science. Accessed March 16, 2017, from http://blogs.lse.ac.uk/mec/2016/08/30/are-the-old-syrian-kurdish-parties-relevant-anymore/

Araabi, S. (2017, March 23). *Syria's decentralization roadmap. Carnegie Endowment for International Peace*. Accessed May 20, 2017, from http://carnegieendowment.org/sada/68372?mkt_tok=eyJpIjoiT1RVNE5HVTBNelF4T1RreSIsInQiOiIwSHM4Q0FJTUY4MDNjYzJ6RFdORjVFN0tValI3d2t2Y0ZTUTlkMWc1dXNIS3pYUTB1bXRWZlBUa1RXV0JyU3ZERE9ndXNGOXA2ME1kSENHNzRVZUtheUVLSUQ2c203XC9TeGtReTJ1UUhvdWFQY0NNSlhvb2RjQ0JFQzhERXVZaHEifQ%3D%3D

Aydınlı, E. (2008). Before jihadists there were anarchists: A failed case of transnational violence. *Studies in Conflict and Terrorism, 31*(10), 903–923.

Aydınlı, E. (2015). Assessing violent nonstate actorness in global politics: A framework for analysis. *Cambridge Review of International Affairs, 28*(3), 424–444.

Barfi, B. (2015, October 9). *Kurds now our best ally against ISIS in Syria. Policy analysis*. The Washington Institute for Near East Policy. Accessed March 25, 2017, from http://www.washingtoninstitute.org/policy-analysis/view/kurds-now-our-best-ally-against-isis-in-syria

Barfi, B. (2016, August 23). *Assad bombs the Kurds: Implications for U.S. strategy in Syria* (Policy Watch 2678). Accessed March 25, 2017, from http://www.washingtoninstitute.org/policy-analysis/view/assad-bombs-the-kurds-implications-for-u.s.-strategy-in-syria

BBC. (2015, February 22). Turkey enters Syria to remove precious Suleyman Shah tomb. *BBC News*. Accessed May 20, 2017, from http://www.bbc.com/news/world-middle-east-31572257

Bengio, O. (2016, March 18). Israel and the Kurds: Love by Proxy. *The American Interest*. Accessed March 16, 2017, from http://www.the-american-interest.com/2016/03/18/israel-and-the-kurds-love-by-proxy/

Berti, B. (2016, November 29). *What's in a Name? Re-conceptualizing non-state armed groups in the Middle East*. Palgrave Communications.

Bila, F. (2013, July 19). Kuzey Suriye Sorunu [The problem of Northern Syria]. *Milliyet*. Accessed March 16, 2017, from http://www.milliyet.com.tr/kuzey-suriye-sorunu/siyaset/ydetay/1738640/default.htm

Bozarslan, M. (2016, October 24). Syria rejects Russian proposal for Kurdish federation. *Al-Monitor*. Accessed May 18, 2017, from http://www.al-monitor.com/pulse/originals/2016/10/turkey-russia-mediates-between-kurds-and-assad.html

Bradley, M., & Parkinson, J. (2015, July 24). America's Marxist allies against ISIS. *Wall Street Journal*. Accessed March 25, 2017, from https://www.wsj.com/articles/americas-marxist-allies-against-isis-1437747949

Çandar, C. (2013, July 20). Has Turkey made U-turn on Syria's Kurds? *Al-Monitor*. Accessed March 25, 2017, from http://www.al-monitor.com/pulse/originals/2013/07/turkey-changes-position-on-syrian-kurds.html

Clawson, P. (2016). U.S. policy and the PYD. In P. Clawson (Ed.), *Syrian Kurds as a U.S. ally: Cooperation § complications* (pp. 52–59). Washington DC: The Washington Institute for Near East Policy.

Cockburn, P. (2015, September 24). Syria civil war: Kurdish leader says collapse of Assad regime "would be a disaster" despite its treatment of his people. *The Independent*. Accessed March 21, 2017, from http://www.independent.co.uk/news/world/middle-east/syria-civil-war-kurdish-leader-says-collapse-of-assad-regime-would-be-a-disaster-despite-its-10515922.html

Cook, S. A. (2016, February 25). Who exactly are the "Kurds"? *The Atlantic*. Accessed March 21, 2017, from https://www.theatlantic.com/international/archive/2016/02/kurds-turkey-pkk-ypg/470991/

Deutsche Welle Türkçe. (2015, October 16). Erdoğan'dan PYD Çıkışı. *Deutsche Welle Türkçe*. Accessed March 28, 2017, from http://www.dw.com/tr/erdoğandan-pyd-çıkışı/a-18786482

Drwish, S. M. (2016, June 22). Why Syria's Kurds are cooperating with Russia. *Al-Monitor*. Accessed March 28, 2017, from http://www.al-monitor.com/pulse/originals/2016/06/syria-kurds-accusation-cooperation-regime-russia.html

Dutka, D. L. (2006). *Violent non-state actors in world politics: Their formation, actions, and effects*. Dissertation. The Pennsylvania State University.

Economist. (2016, November 10). Islamic State in Syria: Anyone for Raqqa? *The Economist*. Accessed March 28, 2017, from http://www.economist.com/news/middle-east-and-africa/21709967-there-less-offensive-islamic-states-capital-meets-eye-anyone

Eldem, T. (2013). Turkey: Trapped at the gates of Syria? *Eurasia Daily Monitor, 10*(147). Accessed March 21, 2017, from https://jamestown.org/program/turkey-trapped-at-the-gates-of-syria/

Entessar, N. (2014). Between a rock and a hard place: The Kurdish Dilemma in Iran. In D. Romano & M. Gurses (Eds.), *Conflict, democratization and the Kurds in the Middle East* (pp. 211–224). New York: Palgrave Macmillan.

Enzinna, W. (2015, November 24). A dream of secular utopia in ISIS' backyard. *The New Your Times Magazine*. Accessed March 21, 2017, from https://www.nytimes.com/2015/11/29/magazine/a-dream-of-utopia-in-hell.html

Gates, R. M. (2009). A Balanced Strategy: Reprogramming the Pentagon for a New Age. *Foreign Affairs, 88*(1), 28–40.

Global Security. *Kurdish people's protection unit YPG*. Accessed March 16, 2017., from http://www.globalsecurity.org/military/world/para/ypg.htm

Göksedef, E. (2017, February 19). Petraeus: PYD, PKK'nın Kuzeni [PYD: PKK's Cousin]. *Al Jazeera Turk*. Accessed March 16, 2017, from http://www.aljazeera.com.tr/al-jazeera-ozel/petraeus-pyd-pkknin-kuzeni

Gunes, C., Lowe, R. (2015). *The impact of the Syrian war on Kurdish politics across the Middle East*. Research Paper. Middle East and North Africa Programme. Chatham house: The Royal Institute of International Affairs.

Hoffman, F. G. (2009). Hybrid vs compound war: The Janus choice: Defining today's multifaceted conflict. *Armed Forces Journal*. http://indianstrategicknowledgeonline.com/web/4198658.pdf

Human Rights Watch. (2014, June 19). *Under Kurdish rule: Abuses in PYD-run enclaves in Syria*. Accessed March 16, 2017, from https://www.hrw.org/report/2014/06/19/under-kurdish-rule/abuses-pyd-run-enclaves-syria

Hurriyet Daily News. (2016, April 29). US defense chief admits links among PYD, YPG, PKK. *Hurriyet Daily News*. Accessed May 28, 2017, from http://www.hurriyetdailynews.com/us-defense-chief-admits-links-among-pyd-ypg-pkk-.aspx?pageID=238&nID=98499&NewsCatID=358

International Crisis Group. (2014, May 8). *Flight of Icarus? The PYD's precarious rise in Syria* (Crisis Group Middle East Report 151).

Lindenstrauss, G., & Eran, O. (2014). The Kurdish awakening and the implications for Israel. *Strategic Assessment, 17*(1), 83–93.

Malik, H. (2017, April 20). Can Iran stop Iraqi Kurdistan independence? *Al-Monitor*. Accessed May 28, 2017, from http://www.al-monitor.com/pulse/originals/2017/04/iran-iraq-kurdistan-independence-qasem-soleimani.html

Mustafa, M. S. (2016, April 20). *Iran's role in the Kurdistan region*. Report. Al Jazeera Center for Studies. Accessed May 25, 2017, from http://studies.aljazeera.net/en/reports/2016/04/160420105055207.html

National Coalition of Syrian Revolution and Opposition Forces. (2017, March 8). *PYD Militia Detain 42 Kurdish National Council Members in Northern Syria*. Accessed June 14, 2017, from http://en.etilaf.org/all-news/news/pyd-militia-detain-42-kurdish-national-council-members-in-northern-syria.html

Neurink, J. (2015, October 21). A land with no Jews names Jewish affairs rep. *Haaretz*. Accessed May 25, 2017, from http://www.haaretz.com/middle-east-news/1.681660

Nissenbaum, D. (2017, February 22). John McCain makes secret trip to Syria in midst of U.S. assessment. *The Wall Street Journal*. Accessed May 28, 2017, from https://www.wsj.com/articles/mccain-makes-secret-trip-to-syria-in-midst-of-u-s-assessment-1487795458

Oktav, Ö. Z. (2017). Understanding Iran's approach to violent non-state actors: ISIS and YPG cases. In Ö. Z. Oktav, E. Parlar Dal, & A. M. Kurşun (Eds.), *Violent nonstate actors and the Syrian civil war: The ISIS and YPG cases*. Cham: Springer.

Pecquet, J. (2016, April 12) Will congress rein in US support for Syrian Kurds? *Al-Monitor*. Accessed May 25, 2017, from http://www.al-monitor.com/pulse/originals/2016/04/congress-syria-kurds-support-turkey-ypg-pkk-isis.html

Perry, T. (2017a, March 20). U.S.-allied Kurdish Militia says struck Syria base deal with Russia. *Reuters*. Accessed April 21, 2017, from http://www.reuters.com/article/us-mideast-crisis-syria-russia-idUSKBN16R1H4

Perry, T. (2017b, March 9). Syrian force a "few weeks" from Raqqa, U.S. marines deployed. *Reuters*. Accessed April 21, 2017, from http://www.reuters.com/article/us-mideast-crisis-syria-raqqa-idUSKBN16G1CB

Perry, T., & Mohammed, A. (2016, February 1). U.S. envoy visits Kurdish-held Northern Syria. *Reuters*. Accessed May 25, 2017. http://www.reuters.com/article/us-mideast-crisis-syria-visit-idUSKCN0VA2TR

RAND. (2011). *Preparing for "hybrid" opponents: Israeli experiences in Lebanon and Gaza* (Research Brief). RAND Arroyo Center.

Reuters. (2016, December 27). Erdogan says U.S.-led coalition gives support to terrorist groups in Syria. *Reuters*. Accessed March 21, 2017, from http://www.reuters.com/article/us-mideast-crisis-syria-turkey-idUSKBN14G1EU

Salih, A. S. (2016, February 10). Syrian Kurds: Left out. *Newsweek Middle East*. http://newsweekme.com/syrian-kurds-left-out/

Sputnik. (2017, March 30). *Representatives of Syrian Kurds say withdrawing from Intra-Syria talks round*. Accessed May 28, 2017, from https://sputniknews.com/politics/201703301052134772-syrian-kurds-talks/

Stein, A. (2016, March 17). The intentions of Syrian Kurds with self-administration. *Al Jazeera*. Accessed March 21, 2017, from http://www.aljazeera.com/indepth/opinion/2016/03/intentions-syrian-kurds-administration-160317080922855.html

Tanchum, M. (2015, August 18). To counter Iran, Ankara must accommodate the Kurds. *Turkish Policy Quarterly*. Accessed March 28, 2017, from http://turkishpolicy.com/blog/4/to-counter-iran-ankara-must-accommodate-the-kurds

Taştekin, F. (2014, April 21). KRG trench divides Syrian, Iraqi Kurds. *Al-Monitor*. Accessed May 25, 2017, from http://www.al-monitor.com/pulse/originals/2014/04/krg-trench-divides-syrian-iraqi-kurds.html

Taştekin, F. (2016, 27 November). Why Turkey issued arrest Warrant for this Kurdish leader. *Al-Monitor*. Accessed March 21, 2017, from http://www.al-monitor.com/pulse/originals/2016/11/turkey-syria-issue-arrest-warrant-for-pyd-chief-muslim.html

Taştekin, F. (2017, March 1). Will Turkey attack Kurds in Manbij or move to Raqqa. *Al-Monitor*. Accessed March 28, 2017, from http://www.al-monitor.com/pulse/originals/2017/03/turkey-syria-ankara-manbij-calculations-all-muddled.html

The Telegraph. (2016, January 22). Turkey alarmed by Russian troop build up in Northern Syria. *The Telegraph*. http://www.telegraph.co.uk/news/worldnews/europe/turkey/12116807/Turkey-alarmed-by-Russian-troop-build-up-in-northern-Syria.html

Thornton, R. (2015). Problems with the Kurds as Proxies against Islamic State: Insights from the Siege of Kobane. *Small Wars and Insurgencies, 26*(6), 865–885.

Tremblay, P. (2016, December 13). Iranian-Turkish Tug-of-War over Kurds. *Al-Monitor*. Accessed September 11, 2017, from http://www.al-monitor.com/pulse/originals/2016/12/turkey-iran-become-latest-surrogate-of-pkk.html

Ünver, A. (2017). Contested geographies: How ISIS and YPG rule 'No-Go' areas in Northern Syria. In Ö. Z. Oktav, E. Parlar Dal, & A. M. Kurşun (Eds.), *Violent nonstate actors and the Syrian civil war: The ISIS and YPG cases*. Cham: Springer.

Vali, A. (2011). *Kurds and the state in Iran: The making of Kurdish identity*. New York: I.B. Tauris.

Williams, P. (2008). *Violent non-state actors and national and international security*. Zurich: International Relations and Security Network, ETH.

Zaman, A. (2015, 11 May). Iran's Kurds rise up as their leaders remain divided. *Al-Monitor*. Accessed March 21, 2017, from http://www.al-monitor.com/pulse/originals/2015/05/iran-turkey-syria-kurds-iranian-kurds-rise-up.html

Zhidkova, T. (2015). Globalization and the emergence of violent non-state actors: The case of human trafficking. *New Global Studies, 9*(1), 1–25.

The Assistance Front Versus the Popular Protection Units Versus the Islamic State: Reciprocal Mobilization and the Ascendance of Violent Non-state Actors in the Syrian Civil War

Fred H. Lawson

1 Introduction

Recent scholarship on civil wars demonstrates the importance of the security dilemma as a source of heightened mistrust, rivalry, and belligerence among ethno-sectarian communities (Posen 1993; Melander 1999; Roe 1999; Rose 2000; Tang 2011). Less well understood is the ancillary dynamic known as the conflict spiral, that is, the marked escalation in bellicosity that occurs as antagonistic actors take reciprocal steps to protect themselves against one another by implementing increasingly assertive and coercive measures (Jervis 1976; Kydd 1997). Conflict spirals do not always grow out of security dilemmas, but whenever they do take shape, they sharply raise the stakes of the contest at hand and make conflict management substantially harder to accomplish.

Scholarship in international relations tends to conflate the concept of the security dilemma with that of the conflict spiral (Jervis 1976; Tang 2009). Yet these terms denote two analytically distinct components of the interaction that takes place between protagonists in a dispute. The security dilemma focuses on the initial phase of the confrontation: Faced with a situation in which an adversary poses a serious threat to one's security under anarchic circumstances, one can either choose to carry out hostile and provocative security-producing programs or decide instead to wait and see what happens. Both courses of action are highly problematic, and there is a strong tendency for all parties to adopt belligerent policies that end up leaving them worse off than they had been at the outset. Conflict spirals occur whenever adversaries choose to carry out hostile and provocative security-producing programs and then steadily increase the degree, level, or extent of combat against one another. Such escalation generally results from what Robert

F.H. Lawson (✉)
Centre for Syrian Studies at the University of St. Andrews, St. Andrews, UK
e-mail: lawson@mills.edu

Ö.Z. Oktav et al. (eds.), *Violent Non-state Actors and the Syrian Civil War*,
DOI 10.1007/978-3-319-67528-2_5

Jervis (1976, p. 63) calls "the fact that most means of self-protection simultaneously menace others," and it becomes more pronounced whenever actors "that seek security believe that the best, if not the only, route to that goal is to attack and expand."

Insight into the impact of conflict spirals in the context of civil wars can be gained from an exploration of the popular uprising that broke out in Syria in the first quarter of 2011. During the third phase of this uprising, which took shape in the winter of 2012–2013, radical Islamist forces battled not only against one another but also against Free Syrian Army units for influence within the anti-regime camp, in the course of which Islamist militants carried out sustained and indiscriminate attacks on minority communities all across the northern and northeastern provinces. Such attacks prompted Syria's Kurds, Turkmens, Christians, and Shi'is to mobilize to protect themselves, culminating in the emergence of a sizable armed formation affiliated with the radical wing of the Kurdish national movement, along with an assortment of other militias whose ranks consisted of members of the country's ethno-sectarian minorities. Subsequent fighting among radical Islamists, the Free Syrian Army and the newly emergent ethno-sectarian militias led to the rise of the Islamic State, an innovative type of militant Islamist formation whose ascendance marked the zenith of violent non-state actors in the Syrian civil war.

2 Early Phases of the Syrian Uprising

Syria's uprising has gone through several distinct phases since it broke out in February 2011 (Lawson 2013; Lister 2015). The initial phase consisted of nonviolent demonstrations by civil rights activists in the capital city of Damascus, the northern metropolis of Aleppo, and predominantly Kurdish towns situated in the northeastern provinces. These public protests elicited modest proposals for political reform from the authorities, which were flatly rejected by the leaders of the nascent opposition movement. A second phase of the uprising—all-out civil war between opponents and supporters of the Ba'th Party-led regime—was firmly in place by November 2011. Fighting at first clustered along the Mediterranean coast, in the rugged hill country of the northwest and around the northeastern city of Dair al-Zur. Anti-regime militants organized a variety of armed formations, some of which affiliated with the Free Syrian Army (Jaish al-Suri al-Hurr, FSA) but most of which jealously guarded their operational autonomy. Cadres of the Iraq-based Kurdistan Workers' Party (Partiya Karkeren Kurdistan, PKK) collaborated with radical activists of the Democratic Union Party (Partiya Yekitiya Demokrat, PYD) to set up a local militia, the Popular Protection Units (Yekineyen Parastina Gel, YPG), in Kurdish areas of the northeast. Turkmens residing in the hills adjacent to the coastal city of Latakia created a parallel formation, the Brigade of the Turkmen Mountain (Liwa Jabal al-Turkman), while Turkmen activists in Aleppo and Idlib provinces formed an assortment of local defense companies.

Late 2012 marked the beginning of the third phase of the Syrian uprising with the appearance of a reconfigured opposition grouping that took the name the National Coalition of Syrian Revolutionary and Opposition Forces (NCSROF). Like its predecessor, the Syrian National Council, the NCSROF exercised no authority over the disparate militias that were fighting inside the country and had only tenuous connections to the externally based FSA. The organization's leadership tried to create a unified military structure that December, but operational commanders rejected the scheme on the grounds that it would inhibit their ability to respond effectively to rapidly changing battlefield circumstances. Also like the Syrian National Council, the NCSROF enjoyed poor—if not actually antagonistic—relations with Syria's Kurdish, Turkmen, Syriac, Assyrian, 'Alawi, and Shi'i communities, since the coalition's leaders refused to commit themselves to guarantee comprehensive citizenship rights to the members of linguistic and sectarian minorities.

By the time that the third phase of the uprising got underway, a collection of radical Islamist militias had become the predominant forces inside the anti-regime camp (Holliday 2012; Lund 2012). Several such militant Islamist formations stood out: The Assistance Front for the People of Syria (Jabhah al-Nusrah li Ahl al-Sham) was notorious for its routine use of suicide bombings and expressed antagonism toward the country's 'Alawi, Shi'i, and Isma'ili minorities. Larger but less prominent was the Battalions of the Free of Syria (Kataib Ahrar al-Sham), which combined calls for the replacement of Ba'thi rule by some form of Islamic government with patriotic rhetoric and symbols and thus constituted a patriotic alternative to the globalist ambitions harbored by the Assistance Front. Equally patriotic in character was the Hawks of Syria Brigade (Liwa Suqur al-Sham) based in the countryside around the northwestern city of Idlib, whose leaders indicated a willingness to work with dissident 'Alawis and Ba'th Party members to effect fundamental political change. In addition, there existed several dozen formations whose ranks were filled with foreign nationals, such as the Dawn of Islam Movement (Harakah Fajr al-Islam), whose cadres consisted largely of Chechens, Uzbeks, and Britons. Most of the foreigner-staffed militias operated in the northwestern and north-central provinces, although the Islam Brigade (Liwa al-Islam) concentrated its activities in the towns outside Damascus.

At the end of 2012, the Battalions of the Free announced that it had forged an alliance with the Dawn of Islam Movement, the Truth Brigade (Liwa al-Haqq) of Homs, the Unity Army (Jaish al-Tawhid) of Dair al-Zur, and a handful of other radical Islamist militias that together adopted the name the Syrian Islamic Front (Jabhah al-Islamiyyah al-Suriyyah). This grouping explicitly rejected the transnational project advocated by the Assistance Front and focused its efforts on prosecuting armed struggle against the Ba'thi regime in Damascus. The Hawks of Syria had already joined the Islam Brigade and the al-Faruq Battalions of the north-central town of al-Rastan to form a rival Syrian Islamic Liberation Front (Jabhah Tahrir Suriya al-Islamiyyah). The two antagonistic blocs competed with one another throughout the winter of 2012–2013 by staking out territory and by currying popular support by distributing bread, heating oil, and other staples to the beleaguered residents of embattled districts across the north-central and northern provinces.

Despite such social welfare initiatives, the radical Islamists had started to alienate important segments of the Syrian populace by early 2013. Militant Islamist formations frequently engaged in armed confrontations with other anti-regime militias. Fighters of the Assistance Front repeatedly attacked units of the Free Syrian Army and devoted special attention to the largest FSA affiliate in Aleppo province, the Unity Brigade (Liwa al-Tawhid). Assistance Front cadres orchestrated public protests against both the NCSROF and the FSA in the districts that fell into their hands. At the same time, radical Islamist fighters targeted Syria's minority religious communities, routinely vandalizing and looting Christian churches and destroying Shi'i meeting houses (husainiyyahs). In February to March 2013, the Assistance Front, the Battalions of the Free, and the FSA-affiliated Descendants of the Prophet Brigades (Alwiya Ahfad al-Rasul) seized control of the northeastern city of al-Raqqah, ransacked its Shi'i pilgrimage mosques, and forced residents to adhere to practices that reflected the Assistance Front's stringent interpretation of Islam. Islamist militants on occasion assaulted members of the mainstream Sunni community as well: The Assistance Front desecrated the tombs of prominent Sunnis outside the northern town of A'zaz, for instance, on the grounds that they were "too pretentious for Islamic traditions."

3 Rise of the YPG

Under these circumstances, Syria's Kurdish community took more forceful steps to protect itself (International Crisis Group 2013, 2014; Federici 2015). The PYD had during the summer of 2012 assumed responsibility for day-to-day administration in a string of cities and towns across the north and northeast, along with the predominantly Kurdish districts of Shaikh Maqsud and Ashrafiyyah outside Aleppo. PYD officials assigned the task of patrolling these far-flung territories to the YPG and the PYD's internal security force, the Asayish. Friction between YPG contingents on one hand and local FSA units and radical Islamist formations on the other flared into violent confrontations in the towns of 'Afrin, 'Ain al-'Arab, Ras al-'Ain, 'Amudah, and al-Malikiyyah; in Ashrafiyyah fighting erupted that October between the YPG, the FSA-affiliated Salah al-Din Brigade, and the Assistance Front. Armed clashes between the YPG and the FSA also took place in the oil-producing areas of al-Hasakah and Dair al-Zur provinces.

At the same time, Christians in the northeast mobilized to defend their respective communities from the depradations of the militant Islamists. The Syriac Union Party set up a local defense company, called the SuToRo, to guard the Christian villages of al-Hasakah province and the predominantly Christian districts of the northeastern city of al-Qamishli (Al-Tamimi 2012, 2014; Drott 2013a, b). Members of the Syriac and Assyrian minorities residing in the Khabur River valley of al-Hasakah province at the same time filled the ranks of the Syriac Military Council and the Khabur Council of Guardians, respectively.

Fighting among the YPG, radical Islamist formations, FSA units, and the SuToRo became more frequent and intense as 2012 drew to a close. The steady escalation of armed conflict among these disparate forces compelled YPG commanders to expand their tactical operations outside the handful of cities and towns that had constituted the PYD's original domain. This trend became evident in the drawn-out struggle for control of the northern border town of Ras al-'Ain, during the course of which militant Islamists and FSA fighters first defeated the remaining government troops and then started to expel the town's Kurdish, Christian, and 'Alawi inhabitants. YPG cadres retaliated against the expulsions, only to find themselves attacked by the Assistance Front, the Descendants of the Prophet Brigades, the al-Faruq Battalions, and the radical Islamist Strange Ones of Syria (Ghuraba al-Sham).

After fending off this combined assault, the YPG in February 2013 negotiated a ceasefire agreement with the local FSA militia, according to whose terms YPG and FSA personnel were to set up joint checkpoints and work together to restore and maintain order—not only in Ras al-'Ain but also in the nearby towns of 'Amudah, al-Darbasiyyah, Tal Tamr, and al-Malikiyyah. The accord failed to gain the acceptance of the Assistance Front and the Strange Ones of Syria, nor did it win the acquiescence of the Descendants of the Prophet Brigades, the al-Faruq Battalions, and the armed tribespeople of the FSA-affiliated al-Jazirah and Euphrates Front for the Liberation of Syria (Jabhah al-Jazirah wal-Furat li-Tahrir Suriya). More important, the ceasefire was rejected by the head of the FSA, Colonel Salim Idris. It was therefore uncertain whether or not the YPG's disparate adversaries would actually carry out the terms of the agreement.

Kurdish commanders recognized how exposed their position at Ras al-'Ain had become and took steps to diminish the YPG's vulnerability by enlarging the territory under its control. In early March 2013, YPG fighters captured a number of oil facilities located around the towns of Rumailan and al-Qahtaniyyah in al-Hasakah province; they then attacked parts of al-Qamishli that continued to be garrisoned by Syrian government troops. Early June brought renewed skirmishes between Kurdish fighters and FSA units around Ras al-'Ain and Tal Tamr, in whose wake the YPG cultivated closer ties to the anti-regime faction of the SuToRo. By mid-July, when a collection of militant Islamists and FSA forces (including the largely Turkmen Yavuz Sultan Selim Brigade) once again advanced against Ras al-'Ain, the YPG had buttressed its position sufficiently not only to repel the assault but also to seize full control of the town. YPG fighters then overran a string of Islamist- and FSA-held villages situated between Ras al-'Ain and Tal Abyad and at the same time launched a drive to dislodge the Assistance Front from the crossing station at Ya'arabiyyah on the Iraqi border. The Assistance Front responded by carrying out mortar strikes and suicide bombings against YPG and Asayish positions in Rumailan and the village of Bab al-Hadid, east of al-Qamishli.

At the end of July 2013, the Assistance Front, the Battalions of the Free (now known as the Islamic Movement of the Free of Syria, Harakah Ahrar al-Sham al-Islamiyyah), the al-Jazirah and Euphrates Front, and an assortment of FSA units launched coordinated attacks against YPG positions at Ras al-‘Ain and in the oil fields around Rumailan. The two-pronged offensive led the PYD to call on all residents of the northeast “to step forward . . . anyone fit to bear arms should join the ranks of the YPG and face the assaults of these armed groups” (Hurriyet Daily News 2013). One prominent Kurdish figure told reporters that “We did not want the war and we did not attack. At the moment we are using our right of legitimate self-defense. If they don’t attack us, we won’t attack anyone. But the nature of our defense is gradually changing as all parts of Rojava are under attack and we have to expand the battles to defend ourselves” (al-monitor.com 2013). Several militias sponsored by Kurdish parties opposed to the PYD at that point aligned themselves openly with the YPG, as did some components of the SuToRo (van Wilgenburg 2013; Glioti 2014; Drott 2014a, b). Bolstered by these reinforcements, YPG commanders drew up plans to extend the PYD’s purview over the entirety of the territory stretching from ‘Afrin to ‘Amudah, including towns with predominantly Arab and Turkmen populations like A’zaz and Tal Abyad.

4 Rise of ISIL

In a comparatively obscure encounter in March 2013, Syrian government troops clashed with FSA units on the border with Iraq (Lister 2015; Weiss and Hassan 2016; Fishman 2016). The soldiers ended up inside Iraqi territory, were taken into custody by Iraqi border guards, and loaded into trucks to be escorted back to Syria. On the way, the convoy was ambushed by cadres of an Iraq-based radical Islamist formation called the Islamic State of Iraq (Dawlah al-‘Iraq al-Islamiyyah, ISI). The operation heralded the resurgence of ISI, which had suffered years of setbacks at the hands of the United States and Iraqi government forces. In carrying out the ambush, ISI forged tactical links to the Assistance Front, whose fighters had seized the key crossing station in the area. ISI in early April declared that it had amalgamated with the Assistance Front to form the Islamic State in Iraq and the Levant (al-Dawlah al-Islamiyyah fil-‘Iraq wal-Sham, ISIL). The head of the global al-Qa’idah network immediately ordered ISI to abandon the merger, but ISIL’s leader, Abu Bakr al-Baghdadi, pointedly refused to obey the directive.

Small contingents of fighters loyal to ISIL appeared in several locales across Syria during April and May of 2013. The largest concentrations of ISIL cadres could be found in the countryside surrounding the cities of Aleppo, al-Raqqah and Dair al-Zur, and in the northeastern towns of Tal Abyad and al-Mayadin (Lister 2015, p. 135). Over the following weeks, fighting flared between these ISIL cells and other radical Islamist formations, most notably the components of the Assistance Front that had refused to merge with ISI. Escalating conflict between ISIL and the Assistance Front led the former to attack Islamist militants that might align themselves with the latter, in particular, the Movement of the Free. These intramural clashes led ISIL to extend its activities into the area around the northern towns of

A'zaz, al-Bab, Minbij, and Jarabulus. In Dair al-Zur province, by contrast, ISIL cadres tended to coordinate operations with the Assistance Front and the Front's local affiliate, the Battalions of the Soldiers of Truth (Kataib Junud al-Haqq).

Matters came to a head when government troops advanced against the town of al-Qusair, on the Lebanese border northwest of Damascus. A fierce battle in early June 2013, in which the Syrian armed forces collaborated openly with the Lebanon-based, radical Shi'i movement the Party of God (Hizbullah), returned the town to government hands. Pro-regime forces then set out in the direction of the opposition-held towns of al-Rastan and Talbisah in Homs province and prepared to launch a large-scale offensive against the northern metropolis of Aleppo. Radical Islamist commanders threatened to carry out a wave of suicide bombings in response to the defeat at al-Qusair, and FSA units mounted unprecedented attacks against isolated Shi'i villages situated west of Aleppo.

Victory by pro-regime forces at al-Qusair marked the beginning of the fourth phase of the Syrian uprising. In the wake of the battle, government troops took steps to drive radical Islamists out of the districts next to the shrine of al-Sayyidah Zainab on the southern edge of Damascus. Regular army soldiers fought alongside the Abu Fadl al-Abbas Brigade, a pro-regime militia whose ranks were filled by Shi'is from Iraq, Iran, and Afghanistan. The sectarian-tinged campaign to regain control of the capital's southern suburbs sparked a surge of indiscriminate violence against 'Alawis and Shi'is on the part of Islamist militants. One radical Islamist formation swept through the Shi'i village of Hatla outside Dair al-Zur, slaughtering six dozen residents and torching the local mosque. Other Islamist radicals targeted YPG units in the countryside around 'Afrin, reportedly after the Kurds had tried to prevent Islamists from attacking Shi'i villages in the vicinity. Faced with a general upsurge in ethno-sectarian violence across the northeast, accompanied by renewed attacks against Ras al-'Ain and stepped up operations by militant Islamists around Dair al-Zur and the eastern border town of Al Bu Kamal, the PYD announced plans that July to create an autonomous administrative zone in the parts of Aleppo, al-Raqqah, and al-Hasakah provinces over which it had taken charge.

Fighting continued to escalate among radical Islamist formations, the FSA and the YPG, as the summer of 2013 turned to autumn. ISIL fighters shouldered FSA units aside in early August and seized the government air base at Minagh north of Aleppo city, confiscating its stockpile of heavy weaponry. This operation was followed by an offensive in the hills of northern Latakia province, which involved ISIL, the Assistance Front, the Movement of the Free, and a handful of smaller radical Islamist formations (Lister 2015, p. 160). Jockeying between militant Islamists and FSA fighters pushed the FSA-affiliated Kurds' Front (Jabhah al-Akrad) out of its home territory in Aleppo province. ISIL cadres then drove the last FSA units out of al-Raqqah city; the drive opened with a massive car bombing that killed two senior officers of the Descendants of the Prophet Brigades, in the wake of which that unit's surviving personnel decamped across the border into Turkey. ISIL went on to assassinate the Assistance Front's tactical commander (amir) in al-Raqqah and seize control of the city.

Shortly afterwards, ISIL launched an offensive to expel the FSA from the crossroads town of al-Bab northeast of Aleppo. The assault came in response to an attempt by the al-Faruq Battalions to root out ISIL supporters from districts surrounding the town. ISIL fighters at the same time wrested control of A'zaz from the Northern Storm Brigade (Liwa 'Asifah al-Shammal), a band of local toughs loosely connected to the FSA. Elements of the Unity Brigade hurried up from Aleppo to preserve FSA control over the crucial Bab al-Salam border station just north of A'zaz.

By early September 2013, ISIL's energetic initiatives had brought it into conflict with the Movement of the Free in al-Raqqah and Dair al-Zur provinces, as well as with the FSA's God is Greatest Brigade (Liwa Allahu Akbar) outside Dair al-Zur city. ISIL fighters concurrently assaulted the town of al-Shaddadah in al-Hasakah province, not far from a cluster of oil-producing facilities occupied by the Assistance Front. After that, ISIL pushed the Movement of the Free and FSA out of the towns of Harim and Sarmada in Idlib province. In carrying out these operations, the organization exhibited a marked shift in the direction of self-interested, unilateralist action, which in Charles Lister's (2015, p. 182) words "meant that it was increasingly devoting its resources towards acquiring and consolidating control over territory [that had] already [been] captured by the opposition."

5 Reciprocal Mobilization and the Ascendance of Violent Non-state Actors

In late September 2013, a half-dozen FSA-affiliated militias defected to the ranks of the Assistance Front, the Hawks of Syria, and the Unity Brigade. The Islam Brigade subsequently joined four dozen smaller radical Islamist formations to create the Army of Islam (Jaish al-Islam); the new coalition pledged to carry out operations both in the suburbs of Damascus and in the rugged Qalamun mountains northwest of the capital. The emergence of the Army of Islam set off a kaleidoscopic restructuring of opposition alliances, which culminated in the November 2013 announcement that the Movement of the Free had joined the Hawks of Syria, the Unity Brigade, the Islam Brigade, and the Truth Brigade to form a reconfigured Islamic Front (al-Jabhah al-Islamiyyah). Other radical Islamist formations operating around Aleppo, including the al-Faruq Battalions, then set up a rival Syrian Revolutionaries' Front (Jabhah al-Thuwwar al-Suriyyah). The Islamic Front and the Syrian Revolutionaries' Front carried out a succession of assassinations and bombings against ISIL and the Assistance Front throughout northern Syria during the winter of 2013–2014. Both alliances also made overtures to the Kurds' Front, which set the stage for a series of joint operations against ISIL in the environs of 'Afrin.

Radical Islamist formations at the same time battled Kurdish forces in the northern suburbs of Aleppo city. Mutual animosity between the YPG and Islamist militants on one hand and between the YPG and FSA-aligned militias on the other opened the door to a tentative rapprochement between the Kurdish National Council and the NCSROF, but the prospective reconciliation was quickly quashed by the PYD. Instead, the party's leadership implemented the plan to establish an autonomous administrative apparatus, which would include members of the Kurdish National Council. A Constitutive Assembly of the Temporary Administration of Western Kurdistan (Kurdistana Rojava) formally convened on 12 November 2013; three weeks later, the Rojava Constitutive Assembly declared that it had established a federated entity made up of three separate cantons, with provincial capitals in 'Afrin, 'Ain al-'Arab, and al-Hasakah. The YPG was directed to consolidate the three cantons into a coherent territorial unit and to form a new brigade recruited from Arabic speakers in the northeast called the Brigade of the Free of the Homeland (Liwa Ahrar al-Watan). Early January 2014 brought news that the Legislative Assembly of the Democratic Autonomous Administration of Rojava had promulgated a Charter of the Social Contract for the new zone, which guaranteed the civil rights of all linguistic and religious communities residing within its borders by means of what it called "unity in diversity."

So as 2014 began, sizable chunks of Syrian territory no longer rested within the purview of the central government in Damascus. The PYD exercised command over large parts of northern Aleppo, al-Raqqah, and al-Hasakah provinces, along with isolated oil fields in Dair al-Zur province. ISIL dominated al-Raqqah city and a ribbon of territory along the Euphrates River, stretching from al-Bab in the west to Al Bu Kamal in the east. Extensive areas of the Qalamun mountains lay in the hands of a variety of anti-regime forces, including the Assistance Front, the Islamic Movement of the Free of Syria, the Army of Islam, and an assortment of FSA units, even as scattered districts in the western and northern marches of Aleppo province were controlled by local Islamist and FSA formations, most notably the Unity Brigade.

In early January 2014, eight Aleppo-based militias coalesced into the Warriors' Army (Jaish al-Mujahidin), whose fighters immediately attacked ISIL and the Syrian Revolutionaries' Front in Aleppo and Idlib provinces. ISIL retaliated by striking positions occupied by the Warriors' Army, the Unity Brigade, the Movement of the Free, and the Hawks of Syria across the northern and eastern parts of Aleppo province. By early February radical Islamist and FSA militias in northern Syria had started to align themselves either with ISIL or with one of its primary rivals (Lister 2015, p. 194). This sorting-out process left ISIL in an exposed position in the region north of Aleppo city but bolstered by new partnerships with tribespeople in al-Hasakah province and former Assistance Front fighters based at Tal Halaf. ISIL consequently withdrew its cadres from A'zaz and redistributed them among the strongholds of al-Bab, Minbij, and Jarabulus, even as it attacked Assistance Front-held oil facilities in Dair al-Zur province.

Meanwhile, ISIL, the Movement of the Free, and a militant Islamist formation called the Supporters of the Caliphate Brigade (Liwa Ansar al-Khilafah) expelled YPG cadres from the towns of Tal Brak, Tal Hamis, and al-Markadah on the border between al-Hasakah and Dair al-Zur provinces. This campaign prompted several components of the Islamic Front to announce that they would coordinate operations with ISIL to block any further expansion of the Kurdish autonomous zone. Another radical Islamist formation broadly aligned with ISIL, the Levant Army Group (Jama'ah Jund al-Sham), appeared in the western marches of Homs province and started to harass the Melkite and Greek Orthodox villages that made up the Valley of the Christians (Wadi al-Nasara).

With the arrival of spring, government troops launched a large-scale offensive against opposition forces in the Qalamun mountains. Acting in concert with Hizbullah, the Syrian army gradually regained control of the hill town of Yabrud and the crossroads town of al-Nabak on the main north-south highway. These advances accompanied intense clashes between ISIL cadres and Kurdish forces along the border with Turkey. ISIL responded to the growing threat from the YPG by pulling its fighters out of all districts west of Aleppo city and redeploying them along the eastern fringes of Aleppo province. Despite this move, the YPG, working together with the FSA's al-Raqqah Revolutionaries' Brigade (Liwa al-Thuwwar al-Raqqah), succeeded that May in expelling ISIL from a string of towns in northern and eastern al-Raqqah province. ISIL commanders retaliated by mounting raids against Kurdish villages outside al-Bab and Islamic Front positions in eastern Homs province.

Heightened pressure on ISIL positions in Aleppo and al-Raqqah provinces exerted by the YPG and the al-Raqqah Revolutionaries' Brigade accompanied a sharp increase in skirmishing between the Assistance Front and ISIL in the Qalamun region. The convergence of challenges in these two theaters of the civil war prompted ISIL in early June 2014 to initiate a broad flanking maneuver in the direction of Dair al-Zur and Al Bu Kamal, which soon expanded into a major offensive in western and northern Iraq. ISIL's blitzkrieg against the Iraqi cities of Musil, Tikrit, Ba'qubah, and Fallujah provided the YPG with the opportunity to dislodge the last ISIL fighters around A'zaz, although ISIL cadres remained firmly entrenched at al-Bab, Minbij, Jarabulus, and Tal Abyad. Meanwhile, the Assistance Front captured the towns of Harim, Sarmada, Salqin, and Binnish in Idlib province, thereby consolidating its position along the border with the Turkish province of Hatay. ISIL, now rechristened the Islamic State (al-Dawlah al-Islamiyyah), responded to these developments by seizing a major natural gas facility in eastern Homs province and then overrunning a collection of government military bases in Dair al-Zur, al-Hasakah, al-Raqqah, and Aleppo provinces and confiscating the heavy weaponry and ammunition stockpiled there.

As warfare raged across the north and northeast, Syrian government forces regained control over the countryside around Homs. The spring and summer of 2014 saw sustained military operations against opposition-held suburbs of Damascus as well; by mid-September, a number of anti-regime bastions had fallen, including the towns of 'Adra and Duma. At the same time, the Islamic Front started to break apart, due to disputes among its diverse components over the internal distribution of foreign funds. The Unity Brigade disengaged from the Islamic Front and allied with six dozen smaller FSA-affiliated and independent Islamist militias to create the Command Council of the Syrian Revolution (Majlis Qiyyadah al-Thawrah al-Suriyyah). In late July a competing coalition took shape, which called itself the Supporters of the Religion Front (Jabhah Ansar al-Din); it consisted largely of expatriate militias, such as the Islamic Levant Movement (Harakah Sham al-Islam), the Islamic Dawn of the Levant Movement (Harakah Fajr al-Sham al-Islamiyyah), and the Army of Emigrants and Supporters (Jaish al-Muhajirin wal-Ansar).

As the Islamic Front fragmented, the Syrian Revolutionaries' Front gathered momentum. In mid-August 2014, the latter ordered the Assistance Front to pull its fighters out of Idlib province. The vacuum created by the abrupt departure of the Assistance Front generated a new outburst of internecine violence across the northwest. A key figure in the Hawks of Syria was assassinated by the Islamic State, and two commanders of the Movement of the Free were killed in a suicide bombing that was also attributed to the Islamic State. Local fighters affiliated with the Islamic State took advantage of the chaotic situation to capture the town of Akhtarin north of Aleppo, along with the nearby village of Dabiq—the site of the apocalyptic battle that was prophesied to usher in the Last Days. The YPG responded by forming an alliance with the Unity Brigade and a half-dozen FSA-affiliated militias, which launched a coordinated offensive to drive the Islamic State out of its newly acquired areas of Aleppo and al-Raqqah provinces. The opening of the so-called Euphrates Volcano (Burkan al-Furat) operation prompted the Islamic State to mount a counterattack against the YPG stronghold of 'Ain al-'Arab, which after a fast start bogged down into stalemate.

Brutal infighting among rival anti-regime militias enabled pro-regime forces to gain additional territory that autumn. In mid-September 2014, Syrian troops reoccupied strategically located villages around Hamah city, while a team of commandos destroyed a bridge across the Euphrates River outside Dair al-Zur that had connected the Islamic State's heartland in al-Raqqah to its domain in northern and western Iraq. The countryside around Dair al-Zur city also saw the emergence of a shadowy band of anti-Islamic State vigilantes that called itself the White Shroud (al-Kafn al-Abyad). Threats arising concurrently from the margins of al-Raqqah province prompted the Islamic State to redouble its attack against the Kurdish garrison at 'Ain al-'Arab. The assault was stopped due to furious resistance on the part of the town's YPG defenders, then reversed in the face of air strikes carried out by French, Saudi, Emirati, and US warplanes.

While the Islamic State remained stymied at 'Ain al-'Arab, the Assistance Front returned to Idlib province and drove the Syrian Revolutionaries' Front out of several villages adjacent to Idlib city. Fighters affiliated with the Assistance Front carried out these activities in conjunction with an assortment of radical Islamist formations, most notably the Levant Division (Failaq al-Sham) and a contingent of foreign militants called the Utmost Army (Jund al-Aqsa). The new alignment's battlefield successes inspired its leaders to announce that they intended to proclaim the existence of an "Islamic amirate" in Idlib. Stung by the overt challenge to its own declared "caliphate" in al-Raqqah, the Islamic State stepped up attacks around the predominantly Isma'ili city of al-Salamiyyah in eastern Hamah province and seized several natural gas-producing facilities in eastern Homs province.

Cadres of the Assistance Front routed a handful of local FSA units in Hamah and Idlib provinces in late November 2014, thereby weakening the Command Council of the Syrian Revolution. The Assistance Front then overran a pair of government military bases outside al-Ma'arrah al-Nu'man and forged a partnership with the Movement of the Free and the Army of Islam in the Qalamun mountains. The combined forces of the Assistance Front, the Movement of the Free, and the Army of Islam attacked groups of fighters in Qalamun loyal to the Islamic State, whose leaders had intimated that they were going to extend the al-Raqqah-centered caliphate to the western border region in early 2015.

Fierce fighting among radical Islamist forces enabled Syrian troops to advance into contested areas around Dair al-Zur and in the northern marches of Aleppo province. Gains by government forces prompted the Warriors' Army to merge with four smaller Aleppo-based militias to form the Levant Front (al-Jabhah al-Shamiyyah). This development spurred independent FSA units in northern Latakia province to create the Second Coastal Division (Failaq al-Sahil al-Thani), made up primarily of Turkmen battalions. Tribespeople in southern al-Hasakah province at the same time created an armed formation called the Commandos (al-Maghawir) with the assistance of Hizbullah. The appearance of the Commandos sparked a round of intense clashes between YPG fighters and pro-regime forces across the northeast in early January 2015.

Islamic State cadres abandoned their positions around 'Ain al-'Arab at the end of January and retreated to the western bank of the Euphrates River. YPG commanders then set their sights on the Islamic State-held towns of Tal Abyad to the east and Jarabulus and Minbij to the west. At the same time, Kurdish fighters at 'Afrin formed an alliance with the Levant Front and struck pockets of territory north of Aleppo occupied by the Islamic State and the Assistance Front. To reinforce its defenses around Jarabulus and al-Raqqah city, the Islamic State withdrew its remaining personnel from northern Aleppo province, thereby opening the door to a multipronged offensive on the part of government troops, Hizbullah, and pro-regime militias west and north of Aleppo city. In mid-February, the YPG captured more than a dozen villages in northern al-Raqqah province, after which its fighters advanced in the direction of Tal Hamis.

Islamic State cadres riposted by kidnapping a hundred Assyrian Christians from villages in the western marches of al-Hasakah province. The abductions failed to prevent Tal Hamis from falling to the YPG at the end of February 2015. Shortly afterward, a dozen Islamic State fighters were killed by vigilantes in the eastern town of al-Mayadin. While the Islamic State was losing ground across the northeast, the Assistance Front stepped up attacks against local FSA units in the environs of Idlib and Aleppo. The FSA-affiliated Steadfastness Movement (Harakah al-Hazm) crumbled in the face of simultaneous attacks by pro-government forces and Assistance Front cadres, and its survivors joined the ranks of the Levant Front. Rumors subsequently circulated that the Assistance Front was planning to merge with the Army of Emigrants and Supporters to create a force that might be capable of precluding any resurgence of the Islamic State around Aleppo.

On 10 March 2015, the Islamic State mounted a large-scale raid against Ras al-'Ain in an attempt to blunt the YPG's advance on Tal Abyad. Kurdish forces beat back the attack, and in the wake of the battle the Movement of the Free announced that it had merged with the Hawks of Syria. The amalgamated formation aligned with the Assistance Front, the Utmost Army, the Levant Division, the Truth Brigade, the Turkestan Battalion (Katibah Turkistan), the predominantly Chechen Soldiers of the Levant (Junud al-Sham), and the Uzbek Unity and Struggle Battalion (Katibah al-Tawhid wal-Jihad) to form the Army of Conquest (Jaish al-Fath), which seized control of Idlib city at the end of March and moved against a major government air base located south of that city. The Islamic State riposted by assaulting a cluster of Isma'ili villages east of Hamah and carrying out suicide bombings against outposts held by the Movement of the Free and the Unity Brigade.

As the Assistance Front and the Islamic State battled one another in far-flung parts of the country, the Aleppo-centered Levant Front imploded. Cadres of the Army of Conquest moved into the town of Jisr al-Shughur just west of Idlib city in late April, after it was abruptly abandoned by government troops. The Assistance Front then seized the government base at al-Qarmid in eastern Idlib province and dispatched units into the nearby al-Ghab valley in northern Hamah province. The Army of Conquest went on to capture the town of Ariha in northern Idlib province. Despite these setbacks, regular army soldiers and Hizbullah fighters resumed their northward advance in the Qalamun mountains at the beginning of May 2015. Initial resistance by the Assistance Front, the Movement of the Free, and the Army of Islam was quickly undermined by skirmishing between those forces and contingents of the Islamic State. Meanwhile, the Islamic State overran the desert towns of al-Sukhnah and Tadmur in the eastern marches of Homs province and attacked the crossroads village of Mari' north of Aleppo. These operations coincided with a coordinated offensive by the YPG and an assortment of militias based in the northeast against Islamic State-held areas west and south of Ras al-'Ain, which succeeded in expelling Islamic State fighters from Tal Abyad in mid-June.

Late May 2015 therefore marks the high point of the prominence of violent non-state actors in the Syrian civil war. The Assistance Front and its partners in the Army of Conquest exercised control over most of Idlib province and dominated the collection of armed formations that was fighting government troops, Hizbullah, and pro-regime militias in and around Aleppo city. The Islamic State ruled central al-Raqqah province with an iron fist and commanded large areas of Dair al-Zur province and the eastern half of Homs province. At the same time, the Popular Protection Units had created sizable pockets of Kurdish-administered territory around 'Afrin in the northwest and along the Turkish border from 'Ain al-'Arab to al-Qamishli.

From June 2015 onward, the Army of Conquest would find its sphere of influence steadily diminished at the hands of pro-government forces, backed that September by Russian military aircraft. The Islamic State would at the same time lose ground to the Assistance Front-led Army of Conquest on the west and the YPG-led Democratic Forces of Syria (Quwwat Suriya al-Dimuqratiyyah) on the north and northeast. The convergence of these trends would mark the opening of a fifth phase of the Syrian uprising, in which the central administration in Damascus started to reassert its authority.

6 Conclusion

Violent non-state actors appeared all across Syria during the summer and fall of 2011, as anti-regime militants organized to protect the residents of particular localities from the indiscriminate retaliatory measures that the authorities inflicted on unarmed protesters and their suspected supporters. Most of these armed formations exhibited no distinctive ethno-sectarian complexion, although in those parts of the northern and northeastern provinces where Kurds, Turkmens, and Christians predominated, the ranks of the defense companies tended to be filled by fighters whose ethno-sectarian makeup reflected the social composition of the local populace. Furthermore, the radical activists of the Democratic Union Party took advantage of the situation to advance the organization's long-standing demand that the authorities in Damascus recognize the political and cultural interests of Syria's Kurdish community and accord it some capacity to promote those communal interests. Turkmen leaders adopted a similar course of action. Consequently, by the winter of 2012–2013, a variety of violent non-state actors confronted one another in the northern and northeastern provinces, each one profoundly mistrustful of the others and each one fearing that any tactical advantage that might accrue to its adversaries would jeopardize the security of its own constituency.

Radical Islamist militias jockeyed with one another and battled against units of the Free Syrian Army for a predominant position in many parts of the north. The rivalry inflicted severe damage on noncombatants and increasingly accompanied deliberate attacks against the members of Syria's ethno-sectarian minorities. These negative externalities induced the largest Kurdish militia, the Popular Protection Units, to fight back against both the militant Islamists and the FSA. Finding itself initially at a tactical disadvantage, the YPG took steps to enlarge its area of operations, not only along the Turkish border but also in Aleppo, al-Raqqah, and Dair al-Zur provinces. Escalating conflict across the northeast gave other local militias a strong incentive to align themselves with the YPG, which ended up augmenting the latter's ability to shape the course of regional affairs.

Armed struggle between radical Islamists and the YPG became more intense after a new armed Islamist formation, the Islamic State in Iraq and the Levant, gained a foothold in Syria in the spring of 2013. Fighting between such older Islamist forces as the Assistance Front, the Battalions of the Free, and the Hawks of Syria on one side and ISIL on the other took place in, or soon spilled over into, territories guarded by the YPG. Furthermore, in the aftermath of the June 2013 battle for al-Qusair, the civil war became markedly more ethno-sectarian in nature, putting the members of minority communities in significantly greater danger. ISIL at the same time started to focus its attention and energies on those parts of the country that had fallen out of the hands of the central administration in Damascus.

From the fall of 2013 to the late spring of 2015, interaction among violent non-state actors in Syria exhibited the dynamics of a conflict spiral, in which each party did its best to gain a tactical advantage that might enhance its security, but found any momentary improvement in its position negated by countermeasures undertaken by its adversaries. The largely unintended consequence of this escalating conflict spiral was the steady expansion of the territorial domains captured and held by the Assistance Front-led Army of Conquest, the YPG-led Democratic Forces of Syria and the Islamic State. Exercising exclusive control over land constituted an integral component of the overall project pursued by the Islamic State (McCants 2015) and represented a high priority for the Democratic Union Party and the Army of Conquest as well. Yet none of these three violent non-state actors would have become so ascendant, had they all not engaged in the sort of reciprocal mobilization that characterized the fourth phase of the Syrian civil war.

References

al-monitor.com. (2013, August 4). Is an Arab-Kurdish War in the making in Syria?

Al-Tamimi, A. (2012, December 7). Syria's Assyrians, caught in the middle. *Daily Star* (*Beirut*).

Al-Tamimi, A. (2014, February 23). Christian militia and political dynamics in Syria. *syriacomment.com*.

Drott, C. (2013a, December 3). *Christians under pressure in Qamishli*. Beirut: Carnegie Middle East Center.

Drott, C. (2013b, December 4). *Christian militia politics in Qamishli*. Beirut: Carnegie Middle East Center.

Drott, C. (2014a, March 6). *A Christian militia splits in Qamishli*. Beirut: Carnegie Middle East Center.

Drott, C. (2014b, March 7). *Syriac-Kurdish cooperation in Northeast Syria*. Beirut: Carnegie Middle East Center.

Federici, V. (2015). The rise of Rojava: Kurdish autonomy in the Syrian conflict. *SAIS Review, 35* (2), 81–90.

Fishman, B. (2016). *The master plan: ISIS, al-Qaeda and the Jihadi strategy for final victory*. New Haven, CT: Yale University Press.

Glioti, A. (2014, February 13). Syrian Kurds recruit regime loyalists to fight Jihadis. *al-monitor.com*.

Holliday, J. (2012). *Syria's armed opposition* (Middle East Security Report No. 3). Washington, DC: Institute for the Study of War.

Hurriyet Daily News. (2013, July 31). Syrian Kurds urged to rise up against Jihadists.

International Crisis Group. (2013). *Syria's Kurds: A struggle within a struggle* (Middle East Report No. 136). Brussels: International Crisis Group.

International Crisis Group. (2014). *Flight of Icarus? The PYD's precarious rise in Syria* (Middle East Report No. 151). Brussels: International Crisis Group.

Jervis, R. (1976). *Perception and misperception in international politics*. Princeton, NJ: Princeton University Press.

Kydd, A. (1997). Game theory and the spiral model. *World Politics, 49*(3), 371–400.

Lawson, F. (2013). *Global security watch Syria*. Santa Barbara, CA: Praeger.

Lister, C. (2015). *The Syrian Jihad*. London: Hurst.

Lund, A. (2012). *Divided they stand: An overview of Syria's political opposition factions*. Uppsala: European Foundation for Progressive Studies.
McCants, W. (2015). *The ISIS Apocalypse*. New York, NY: St Martin's Press.
Melander, E. (1999). *Anarchy within: The security dilemma between ethnic groups in emerging anarchy*. Uppsala: Uppsala University Press.
Posen, B. (1993). The security dilemma and ethnic conflict. *Survival, 35*(1), 27–47.
Roe, P. (1999). The intrastate security dilemma: Ethnic conflict as a "tragedy"? *Journal of Peace Research, 36*(2), 183–202.
Rose, W. (2000). The security dilemma and ethnic conflict: Some new hypotheses. *Security Studies, 9*(4), 1–51.
Tang, S. (2009). The security dilemma: A conceptual analysis. *Security Studies, 18*(3), 587–623.
Tang, S. (2011). The security dilemma and ethnic conflict: Toward a dynamic and integrative theory of ethnic conflict. *Review of International Studies, 37*(2), 511–536.
van Wilgenburg, W. (2013, October 25). Syrian Kurds win support in battle with al-Qaeda forces. *al-monitor.com*.
Weiss, M., & Hassan, H. (2016). *ISIS: Inside the army of terror* (2nd ed.). New York, NY: Regan Arts.

Part II
Powerfulness

ISIS as an Actor Controlling Water Resources in Syria and Iraq

İbrahim Mazlum

1 Introduction

Since the 1990s, a growing literature has developed analyzing the use of natural resources as tools or weapons in violent conflicts and their instrumentalization as elements of broader strategies. Belligerent actors in a conflict may capture strategic natural resources to accomplish their political and economic aims or to establish control on the ground. They may also employ those natural resources as weapons of war to harm other parties militarily and/or economically. As Russet et al. (2000, p. 96) argue, natural resources not only give states the ability to develop but also provide “a greater degree of autarky or self-sufficiency.”

The civil war in Syria and the crisis in Iraq are the most recent violent conflicts of the twenty-first century in which capturing strategic natural resources and weaponizing them to accomplish political, economic, and military aims are among primary strategies of the belligerent parties. While the Syrian and Iraqi regimes are trying to protect their own natural resources, violent non-state actors (VNSAs) fighting against these states have tried to seize, control, and use them to accomplish their broader goals. Oil and water resources are critically important in this respect. For instance, Islamic State of Iraq and Syria (ISIS), the militarily strongest VNSA in these countries, has tried to capture and extract oil resources to finance its fight against the other belligerent state and non-state actors.

Regarding water resources, since the beginning of the civil war in Syria and its fight in Iraq, ISIS has tried to capture and control especially large dams and water facilities as both weapons in their fight in those countries and as strategic elements for achieving the political and economic objectives of its self-proclaimed state. Le Billion’s (2001, p. 580) argument, in which control of local resources influences

İ. Mazlum (✉)
Marmara University, Istanbul, Turkey
e-mail: imazlum@marmara.edu.tr

Ö.Z. Oktav et al. (eds.), *Violent Non-state Actors and the Syrian Civil War*,
DOI 10.1007/978-3-319-67528-2_6

belligerent actors' strategies according to various political and identity factors, can also be observed in the case of ISIS.

It can be argued that, compared to previous cases, we face a new situation since no violent non-state actor before ISIS had acquired such level of political, economic, and military capacity in capturing and controlling vast water resources and infrastructure. It has deliberately and continuously instrumentalized water resources to achieve its various objectives. For instance, according to King (2016, p. 162), ISIS' "systematic and sustained deployment of the water weapon is unprecedented in the history of modern conflict."

This chapter analyzes the main dynamics of ISIS' usage of water resources and systems for its own goals. After referring to some important recent examples of the weaponization of water resources in the region, it is argued that, even before the beginning of the civil war in Syria, economic and social problems due to the diminishing availability of water because of the recent drought had acted as aggravating factors contributing to the rise of the political and economic crises that led to the outbreak of civil war in the country. ISIS' appearance as an actor using water resources in Syria and Iraq is then analyzed in two main parts: its usage of water as a tool of political and economic objectives and its weaponization of water for offensive and defensive military purposes. Obviously, ISIS is not alone in weaponizing water in those countries so the chapter ends by briefly discussing the strategic and military use of water by various other actors.

2 Water as a Tool and Weapon of Conflict

From the border conflict between the city-states of Umma and Lagash around 2500 BC to the present, water resources have been used as military tools or as weapons of terrorism. More recently, they have even become a target of cyberterrorism (Pacific Institute 2017). In a pioneering study more than two decades ago, Gleick et al. (1994, p. 7) argued that "history reveals that water has frequently provided a justification for going to war," either as an object and tool of military conquest or a target of violent conflict. When political conflicts escalate into wars, capturing water resources and systems is often a key goal of military expansionism (Gleick 1993, p. 83). Especially in arid or semiarid regions like the Middle East where water is already scarce, it gains big value as a military target that provides strong leverage to the belligerent actors controlling it. Similarly to what has been going on recently in the Syrian civil war or the crisis in Iraq, the belligerent actors in the 1990–1991 Persian Gulf War used water as a weapon of war by targeting water supply systems and facilities, such as the Iraqi forces' destruction of most of Kuwait's desalination capacity or international coalition forces' bombing of Baghdad, which severely damaged the city's water and sewage infrastructure (Gleick et al. 1994, p. 15).

Saddam Hussein regime's use of water as a weapon in another instance had negative effects lasting for decades. In 1992, after the 1990–1991 Persian Gulf War, the Iraqi government drained the flow of Euphrates and Tigris rivers in

Mesopotamian marshes by constructing canals. One of the aims of this diversion was preventing Shiite regime dissidents from taking refuge in the marshes by using its natural structure as shield (Winnefeld and Morris 1994, p. 28).

Water infrastructure and systems were also targeted during the 2003 Iraq War, leading to much more severe destruction of Iraq's water supply and sewage infrastructure than during the 1990–1991 Persian Gulf War, from which it has still not completely recovered (Smith 2013). Indeed, the situation has deteriorated further during the last couple of years because of the struggle against ISIS.

Before analyzing ISIS' direct usage of water as a weapon of war, the indirect involvement of water resources in the outbreak of Syria's civil war should be considered first. More specifically, one factor bringing Syria to its current dire situation was water scarcity as a result of drought between 2006 and 2010, coupled with problems due to mismanagement of water and land resources since the 1950s. Thus, issues related to water scarcity aggravated other political and economic problems, leading to the outbreak of the uprisings in 2011.

3 Role of Water in the Syrian Uprisings in 2011

As with other Arab countries, the uprising in Syria in 2011 occurred as a result of the interaction of complex dynamics, including political, economic, and social factors. Among the primary issues triggering Syria's crisis were widespread corruption of state mechanisms, lack of democracy, increasing economic problems, and unemployment. However, as outlined above, another key factor was the effect of severe drought between 2006 and 2010, especially on the rural population in the agricultural sector.

Whereas Syria had already experienced six significant droughts between 1900 and 2005, with five lasting only one season and one lasting two, its seventh drought, from 2006 to 2010, was an extreme multiyear, multi-seasonal one. The average level of precipitation during this period was lower than all the previous twentieth-century droughts (Mohtadi 2012), with approximately 60% of the country's land experiencing severe drought (Femia and Werrell 2013, p. 25), although it hit hardest in the northeast, which is Syria's breadbasket and oil production region. It is also the most "impoverished and neglected" area, containing almost 60% of Syria's poor people (de Châtel 2014, pp. 522–525). Among the most affected places were the governorates of Deir al-Zor, Hassakeh, and Raqqa. Worth (2010) notes that, according to a UN survey of October 2010, the drought drove two to three million people into extreme poverty. Additionally, vulnerability to drought "dramatically increased" throughout the country because of reduced groundwater supplies (Kelley et al. 2015, p. 3241).

Many academic studies and news reports have argued that one of the main reasons for the drought was the climate change in the region. According to Hoerling et al. (2012, p. 2146), for example, the Middle East has experienced its 12 driest winters since 1902, of which 10 have occurred in the last 20 years, with climate change being one of the "key attributable factors for this increased drying."

Regarding its effect on the crisis, Femia and Werrell (2013, p. 32) argue that climate change "may have acted as a stress multiplier exacerbating environmental and social stresses," which in return contributed to the outbreak of the Syrian crisis. Media reports have also concentrated on the role of the climate change in the crisis. For instance, *The New York Times* columnist, Friedman (2013), called the "interplay between climate change, food prices ... and politics a hidden stressor that helped to fuel the revolutions."

In Syria, the decline of agricultural output, loss of livelihoods, and extreme poverty led to a large-scale migration of rural population to urban areas, especially to the outskirts of the cities like Damascus, Hama, Homs, Aleppo, and Dara'a—the city where the first significant protests against the Assad regime began in March 2011. It is estimated that more than 1.5 million people moved from the rural areas to the cities (Gleick 2014, p. 334). Since then these displaced people have been living in unfavorable conditions lacking adequate water, electricity, and sanitation. They have faced high rates of unemployment, and those finding jobs in agriculture, construction, or small businesses have been earning around five to ten US dollars a day (de Châtel 2014, p. 527). While competing with the host population for limited jobs in these cities, they have also been competing for access to water resources, which have been also limited because of Syria's infrastructure problems (Femia and Werrell 2013, p. 27). The regime itself lacked the necessary capacity or willingness to deal with the problems of the displaced communities (Sowers et al. 2013), which further marginalized the country's key rural population in the face of the drought, leading to the "Syrian social contract's unraveling" (Saleeby 2012). Thus, the regime's failure to provide for the needs of these people "arguably contributed to the outbreak of the civil war" (Feitelson and Tubi 2017, p. 47). In Parlar Dal's chapter (2017) in this book, economic and social factors have been analyzed among the conditioning factors of the Syrian civil war. Related to this, King (2016, p. 154) argues that "these environmental effects created a context of deprivation" that enabled ISIS' branch in Syria to recruit 60–70% of its fighters from the Syrian people at that time by referring to al-Tamimi's (2013) estimates from figures at the end of 2013. ISIS' financial capacity and its ability to provide public services in Aleppo was another factor (al-Tamimi 2013). The situation in Iraq was similar. According to King (2016, p. 154), both ISIS and the al-Nusra Front initially recruited fighters largely from Sunni Iraqis.

It could be asked why the drought's consequences were so much more serious for Syria, given that it also affected southeastern Turkey, northern Iraq, and other Eastern Mediterranean countries. According to de Châtel (2014, p. 522), the grave economic and social crises in Syria can be seen as the "culmination of 50 years of sustained mismanagement of water and land resources, and the dead end of the Syrian government's water and agricultural policies." She argues that Syria's water management system is particularly inefficient, corrupt, and rigid, which has led to large-scale over-exploitation of water and land resources (de Châtel 2014, p. 529).

Ultimately, while it was not the only major cause, the drought was one of triggers of the Syrian uprising in 2011, aggravated by the mismanagement of water resources, unsustainable agricultural policies, increased poverty of rural communities, and the failure of the Syrian government in addressing the demands of its displaced people.

Once the uprisings had turned into civil war, as the most powerful VNSA in the resulting conflict, ISIS began to use the country's limited water resources and systems, especially large dams and water supply facilities, deliberately to achieve political, economic, and military goals. It adopted similar tactics in Iraq as well.

4 ISIS' Control of Water Resources in Iraq and Syria

Control of water resources and infrastructures in Syria and Iraq have given the belligerent actors strategic control over vast territories, including cities. It has therefore become one of the major objectives of all groups fighting in both countries. During an interview about clashes around the Iraq's major dams, Machowski (quoted in Vidal 2014) stated that "controlling water resources in Iraq is even more important than controlling the oil refineries, especially in summer. ... Cut it [water] off and you create great sanitation and health crises."

Recognizing the strategic importance of water, ISIS has concentrated on controlling water resources and capturing water systems as an integral part of its military strategy from the beginning. von Lossow (2016, p. 82) argues that "gaining control over the large dams on the Euphrates and Tigris, which makes it possible to manipulate the region's most important water resources, has been a central pillar of IS'[1] expansionist strategy." Accordingly, for a considerable period since late 2012, ISIS has retained control over Syria's Tishrin, Tabqa, and Baath Dams. From 2014 until 2016, ISIS exerted similar control in Iraq over the upper reaches of the Euphrates and Tigris rivers, including Mosul Dam for a very brief period and the Samarra, Ramadi, and Fallujah Dams.

von Lossow (2016, p. 87) argues that ISIS' deployment of water as a weapon has been "more targeted, systematic and consistent" than other VNSAs in Syria and Iraq. As King (2016, p. 159, Fig. 3) reports, between August 2012 and July 2015, ISIS alone used water as a weapon in 21 incidents, whereas all the other major belligerent parties did so 25 times in total. Those parties include the Iraqi security forces (4), the Syrian regime (3), al-Nusrah Front (3), Free Syrian Army (2), Islamist Sharia Council (2), Iraqi Kurds (1), and other smaller groups (4). In six other incidents, the actors are unknown. Thus, ISIS was by far the greatest individual user of water as a weapon among the other belligerents during this period.

Although ISIS had already been using water as a weapon and controlling large dams on the Euphrates River in Syria, the international community became

[1] ISIS changed its name to Islamic State (IS) after the declaration of its caliphate in June 2014.

particularly alarmed after its capture of Mosul Dam on the Tigris River on August 7, 2014. In fact, ISIS was only able to control the dam for 10 days until August 18, when Iraqi forces and Kurdish peshmerga fighters retook the dam with the help of US airstrikes. It caused such strong concern because of the dam's significance for Iraq's national water infrastructure and its fragile character. The dam, which is the largest in Iraq and fourth largest in the Middle East, is located nearly 50 km north of Mosul. It was constructed in 1984, generates 45% of the country's electricity (310 MW a day), and holds over 11 billion cubic meters of water in its reservoir. In addition to electricity generation, it is mainly used for irrigation in the northern Ninevah province, flood control, and municipal water needs. Since the dam was constructed on highly soluble gypsum, anhydrite, and karstic limestone, it requires constant maintenance and repair because of soil dissolution, with cement (i.e., grouting) being continuously injected under its foundations since its construction. It was one of the primary objectives of US forces during the 2003 invasion because of its fragile character, the potential risk of failure, and the fear that the Saddam Hussein regime would use it as a weapon against US forces. In 2006, the US Army Corps of Engineers described it as "the most dangerous dam in the world" (quoted in Harrington and Null 2014), although Iraq's Water Resources Ministry argues that there is no imminent danger of collapse. If the dam ever collapsed, it has been estimated that a 20-m-high flood would devastate Mosul within 1–4 h before reaching Baghdad (350 km downstream) in 36 h with 4–5 m of water, causing the death of half a million people and the displacement of millions. It is estimated that—in the worst case scenario—over 6 million people, 16% of Iraq's population, would be affected by flood (Annunziato et al. 2016, p. 14).

The dam's condition worsened after it was captured by ISIS because no grouting had been done for 6 weeks. Even after that it has not reached its full level. In a new report in 2016, the US Army Corps of Engineers stated that "Mosul Dam is at a significantly higher risk of failure than originally understood and is at a higher risk of failure today than it was a year ago" (The Japan Times 2016). Although the Italian engineering firm, the Trevi Group, signed a contract of 300 million US dollars with the Iraqi government to repair the dam with hundreds of workers protected by 450 Italian troops and Kurdish peshmerga fighters, it is still questionable whether this repair effort can permanently solve the problem (BBC 2016a; Filkins 2017).

Examining ISIS' consistent strategy of controlling water since the beginning of their fight in Syria and Iraq clearly shows that the organization has instrumentalized water resources and infrastructures for two main goals. First, controlling water and providing water services is a tool to assist in achieving the political and economic objectives of the organization's self-proclaimed state. Second, it has used water systems for offensive and defensive purposes as part of its broader military strategy.

4.1 Water as a Tool of ISIS' Political and Economic Objectives

Since establishing its caliphate, one of ISIS' main objectives has been building a governing structure to provide major state functions "including static control of territory and providing municipal services" (King 2016, p. 159) throughout its territory. However, in their chapter, Mehmetcik and Kursun (2017) argue that claiming ISIS' similarity to current territorial states is misleading since ISIS opposes the current state system by aiming a single nation of all Sunni Muslims.

Even if they argue for another form of nation, al-Tamimi (2015, p. 123) mentions that in its "ambition to develop public services" as part of efforts in achieving statehood, ISIS created Islamic Services Committees to manage public services, including electricity, water, and "Diwans" (corresponding to government departments) after the declaration of its caliphate. Among these are departments responsible for carrying out public services (including electricity and water), managing valuable resources (including oil), agriculture, and environment (al-Tamimi 2015, p. 123; Table-1). At an operational level, in 2014, ISIS turned the Credit Bank in Raqqa into its taxation authority to collect $20 bimonthly from business owners for electricity, water, and security services (Hubbard 2014). Zelin (2014) argues that ISIS invested in everyday public services to win the people's acceptance and support, including monitoring electricity usage levels and installing new power lines among others. One of the advantages that ISIS possessed in this respect was that, by capturing already installed infrastructure and facilities, they were able to continue providing these services to the population under their control.

However, it can also be observed that ISIS might find it harder than anticipated to win people's acceptance and support because it lacked the capacity to develop expertise and a sophisticated organization to meet the residents' needs and allocate enough funding to carry out these functions. According to Knights (quoted in Johnson 2014), "They've gone from being the world's richest terrorist organization to the world's poorest state." For instance, after taking Mosul in June 2014, the first city that ISIS captured in Iraq, the residents fled when ISIS cut off water and electricity. It is reported that they have later returned shortly after ISIS "switched supplies back on, in a bid to engender support among the local population" (Massih 2014). In another instance in December 2014, Mosul's water had become undrinkable because supplies of chlorine were finished, which also caused the spread of hepatitis. Meanwhile, in Raqqa, ISIS' de facto capital city, water and electricity were unavailable for more than 3 or 4 h a day in addition to with problems in other public services, mainly because of fighting, bombardments, and lack of expertise (Sly 2014). However, the risk of losing legitimacy in the eyes of the people under their rule was one of ISIS' concerns. Therefore, to prevent this risk and avoid harming its own fighters by cutting water, ISIS usually only used the water weapon for a couple of days (von Lossow 2016, p. 95).

In addition to achieving political objectives, controlling water was also economically important for two main reasons. The first one was oil production, which had provided the bulk of ISIS' revenues. The oil fields that ISIS captured in Syria and Iraq required large amounts of water for various production stages so capturing water resources and infrastructure enabled ISIS to extract oil and profit from its sale (Strategic Foresight Group 2014, p. 17).

The second economic reason relates to agricultural production. ISIS has considered agriculture as a strategic sector because continuing agricultural production was important for ensuring food security in the territories it controls and providing tax income for the organization, especially since its revenues have been decreasing from sales of other natural resources like oil and other activities (Jaafar and Woertz 2016, p. 14). Jaafar and Woertz (2016, p. 14) report that, despite the ongoing conflicts, agricultural output in ISIS-controlled areas of Syria and Iraq was sustained during 2014–2015, while their preliminary findings suggest that the winter grain harvest for 2016 was above the mean level for the pre-conflict period in the organization's Iraqi territories, although below pre-conflict levels in its Syrian territories. They argued that, although continued agricultural production has given ISIS a degree of resilience, this was not sustainable in the long run.

According to the study, two-thirds of Syria's total agriculture was concentrated in ISIS-controlled territories in 2015. Despite only a small area of farmland had been irrigated, the Tabqa Dam and Lake Assad, controlled by ISIS between February 2013 and May 2017, were important for irrigated agriculture downstream (Jaafar and Woertz 2016: 17–20). From their analysis from satellite imagery of declining water levels in Lake Assad, Jaafar and Woertz conclude that ISIS was largely able to maintain agricultural production levels, particularly in Deir al-Zor and Raqqa during the 2013/2014 and 2014/2015 seasons, by relying on irrigation water from Lake Assad. Referring to Pearce (2014), they argue that the reservoir's declining water levels were also related to ISIS' maximizing water release to raise more revenues by increasing electricity production (Jaafar and Woertz 2016: 20–21). However, the decline in the water level due to this sharp increase in electricity production caused severe water cuts in Aleppo in early May 2014 because the reservoir's water pumps were unable to function properly at such low water levels. This forced residents in Aleppo and Raqqa to consume water from unreliable sources with risks to health (Chudacoff 2014; for a different side of the story, also see, The National 2014).

ISIS' second goal, its usage of water resources and systems as part of its broader military strategy, is as important as the first one because it gives us clues about how the organization weaponizes water in its military activities.

4.2 *Weaponization of Water by ISIS*

King (2016, p. 160) argues that, without ready access to water resources, ISIS would lack the capability to fight effectively since "water enables IS to create an economy of force to exercise strategic and virtual control over disproportionate amounts of territory with a relatively small attacking force." In addition, because

Syria's facilities supply water and electricity to distant areas, ISIS has been able to control those areas without invading them physically (Strategic Foresight Group 2014, p. 17).

As stated above, ISIS uses water for both offensive and defensive purposes. It can be argued that they weaponize water for offensive purposes in various forms: cutting water as a military tactic, depriving water from people they are in conflict with, and contaminating water. They also use water for defensive aims, particularly flooding territories to prevent other belligerent parties from advancing against them.

In this respect, Syria's Tishrin and Tabqa Dams have been very important for ISIS since they are the most upstream dams controlling the Euphrates River's water flow to other regions in both Syria and Iraq. The Tishrin Dam, located 90 km east of Aleppo, was first captured by Free Syrian Army rebels at the end of November 2012, cutting the Syrian government's supply lines to Aleppo (CTV News 2012). The dam fell under ISIS' control in 2014 (Sümer 2016). The dam was very strategic for ISIS because one of the primary supply lines connecting ISIS-occupied parts of Aleppo to its de facto capital Raqqa passed through the dam. Therefore, fierce battles occurred in the last week of December 2015 during the efforts of US-backed Syrian Democratic Forces (an opposition alliance including Kurdish YPG units and Arab rebel forces) to retake the dam from ISIS.

Tabqa Dam, located 40 km from the city of Raqqa, was another strategic facility for ISIS since it provides water to Raqqa and electricity to both ISIS-controlled territories and other parts of Syria. The dam was completed in 1973 while its reservoir, Lake Assad, is the country's largest reservoir. As mentioned above, it is a strategic water resource for regional agricultural production. The dam was reportedly being used as one of ISIS' headquarters lately, especially for hiding important prisoners and sheltering senior officials out of conviction that the USA would not bomb it for fear of causing a giant flood (Paletta 2016).

The Tabqa Dam was retaken from ISIS by US-backed Syrian Democratic Forces on May 10, 2017. This was also one of the major objectives of the Syrian militias in their preparations to launch an attack on Raqqa (Reuters 2017a). However, there are doubts about the dam's stability since both Russia and ISIS have claimed that US-led airstrikes have weakened the dam (Blanche 2017).

A couple of weeks later, in June 2017, the last dam along Syrian sections of the Euphrates in ISIS' hands was retaken by Syrian Democratic Forces. The Baath Dam, located 20 km west of Raqqa, had been captured by ISIS in February 2013. It was one of the organization's key strongholds (Reuters 2017b).

One of the most important examples of cutting water as a military tactic is the case of the Ramadi Dam, located on the Iraqi part of the Euphrates River, which ISIS captured in May 2015. In June 2015, it closed the dam's gates and diverted the flow of water into a tributary running to Lake Habbaniyah in order to reduce water levels to gain greater freedom of maneuver to attack Iraqi forces by making the river fordable. In fact, ISIS could not close all the gates, which would have been even more disastrous, because it had to leave two gates open to avoid flooding upstream areas under its control. In order to prevent water shortages and environmental damage from the decreased water flow, the Iraqi government released water from another dam to channel water from Lake Habbaniyah back into the lower reaches of the Euphrates (Reuters 2015a).

This case also involved depriving water from people that ISIS was in conflict with because the diversion left four southern provinces at risk of drought. These provinces were Babel, Karbala, Najaf, and Qadisiyah, mainly populated by Shiite Muslims opposed by ISIS. They are also important agricultural centers. Furat al-Tamimi, the head of the Committee on Agriculture and Water at the Iraqi Parliament, described the situation as critical because of the risk of extending into other provinces since the flow of the Euphrates was decreased by about 50%, the lowest for years (Middle East Monitor 2015). Similarly, in July 2014, ISIS captured Samarra Dam on the Tigris River, which controls electricity generation and the volume of water in Lake Thartar, Iraq's biggest lake (Massih 2014). This gave ISIS another tool for controlling Baghdad's water supply and threatening the city with flooding. In addition to Baghdad, the southern Iraq has been also become vulnerable as a result of this capture (Strategic Foresight Group 2014, p. 21–23).

ISIS had not been able to capture another militarily critically important dam in Iraq: Haditha Dam, located on the upper part of the Euphrates River in Iraqi territories. The dam is the second largest after Mosul Dam, producing 30% of the country's electricity, particularly for Baghdad. It is critical strategically because, if ISIS captured the dam, it could fully control the Euphrates' downstream water flow into central and southern parts of Iraq. Experts were anxious that its capture would represent "a huge symbolic and practical victory" (quoted in Massih 2014).

Another tactic ISIS has used for offensive purposes is chemically contaminating water to make it undrinkable or poisoning it. According to von Lossow (2016, p. 88), this tactic has mostly been applied locally. For instance, after ISIS destroyed an oil pipeline on April 16, 2014 the spill contaminated the Tigris River and western half of Baghdad's water supply (Bender 2014; Enzer 2014). Poisoning water resources is not only useable in Syria and Iraq as a part of warfare but may also be applied globally as an act of terrorism through ISIS recruits. For instance, in July 2015, Kosovan police arrested five people following claims that the water supply from an artificial lake that supplies the capital city Pristina with 40% of its water was being poisoned as part of an ISIS terror plot, although tests found no toxins (The Guardian 2015; Piggott 2015). In February 2016, Indonesian authorities were alarmed against ISIS threats to poison the food and water supply with cyanide, which might specifically target police and military personnel (Marshall 2016). In August 2016, an ISIS-backed hacking group posted a mobile app manual, "The Mujahideen Poisons Handbook," explaining how to make poisons (Ryan 2016).

In addition to the weaponization of water for offensive purposes, ISIS has also used water resources for defensive purposes, such as flooding. In April 2014, they closed the gates of Fallujah Dam to prevent Iraqi forces from advancing against them. After ISIS took control of the dam in February, Iraqi forces surrounded and shelled Fallujah. In order to force the Iraqi troops to lift the siege and retreat, ISIS flooded upstream areas by closing the dam's gates. A couple of days later, ISIS reopened five gates to relieve some water fearing that their strategy would harm themselves by flooding Fallujah due to increasing water levels more than intended (Al-Akhbar English 2014). Apart from these military goals, it was reported that ISIS also intended to disrupt Iraq's parliamentary election on April 30, which they did successfully since only a third of polling stations in Anbar province opened because of floods (Svensson 2014). In addition, ISIS also succeeded in depriving downstream areas of water, mainly Baghdad and southern provinces (MacKenzie 2014).

In terms of the civilian costs, the flood affected Abu Ghraib and 49 villages in surrounding areas, damaging more than 10,000 homes, leading to lost harvests and creating disease risks for the residents. At the height of the flood, it reached just a few kilometers short of Baghdad International Airport, forcing 12,000–20,000 families to leave their homes, according to UN estimates (IRIN News 2014).

Such civilian costs are not only confined to ISIS' weaponization of water since other belligerent actors in Syria and Iraq have been also responsible for imposing such costs on the people. For instance, in September 2012, Syrian government forces targeted water and electricity infrastructure in Aleppo, mainly, to put pressure on rebel groups, such as the Free Syrian Army and the al-Nusrah Front, who had been competing with ISIS to control the dams on the Euphrates River mentioned above that provide water and electricity to Aleppo and other cities, including Raqqa (BBC 2012; Scheumann 2014). On November 26, 2015, an air strike on the al-Khafsa water treatment facility in Aleppo cut water supplies for 3.5 million people. It was one of Syria's most important facilities with people across Aleppo governorate dependent on it as the only source of safe drinking water. The Syrian Network for Human Rights blamed the Syrian regime for the airstrike, while the Syrian state news agency SANA claimed that the US-led coalition had bombed the facility (Reuters 2015b). The UNICEF representative in Syria described the bombing as particularly alarming, noting that "in Syria, the rules of war, including those meant to protect vital civilian infrastructure, continue to be broken on a daily basis" (UNICEF 2015).

In another incident, UNICEF spokesman, Kieran Dwyer, reported that water was being used as a weapon of war by all sides. The reason for this statement was that, on September 23, 2016, a pumping station supplying water to rebel-held parts of Aleppo was damaged by Syrian army strikes while subsequent strikes made repairs impossible. At least 200,000 affected people had to resort to using contaminated water. In retaliation for that attack, a nearby pumping station that supplied water to the entire western part of the city was switched off, affecting nearly 1.5 million people (BBC 2016b).

The situation was similar in other parts of the country as well. For instance, from December 22, 2016, to the first weeks of 2017, clashes in the area of Ain al-Fijah springs between the Syrian army and rebels led to water cuts in the city and surrounding areas due to deliberate targeting of the water infrastructure. The springs are among the most important water supplies for Damascus, and it was not clear which side had targeted them (Fares 2017). The UN estimated that nearly four million inhabitants were affected by the water supply cut while suggesting that almost 15 million people need water assistance across the country (United Nations in Syria 2016).

The situation in Iraq was also similar. In November 2016, residents of Mosul experienced water cuts due to clashes during campaign to retake Mosul. Iraqi soldiers hit one of the three major water channels in eastern Mosul, while ISIS disabled water pipelines in neighborhoods close to areas of fighting. According to UN estimates, at least a half million people had no access to water in the city at that time (Ang 2016).

5 Conclusions

In late 2012 in Syria and 2014 in Iraq, ISIS began consistently controlling water resources and systems, both as a part of its broader political and economic goals and in order to weaponize water to achieve its military strategies. Geopolitically, it can be argued that, as a VNSA, ISIS had managed to access water resources in some cases to accomplish its goals compared to other belligerent actors. Even the Syrian and Iraqi regimes experienced difficulties preventing ISIS' use of water as weapon. When the geopolitical lenses are put aside, ISIS' capture and control of water during the last years have produced disastrous consequences.

First, the weaponization of water by ISIS and other belligerent actors has imposed humanitarian costs. Obviously, water is a critical element of human security in both countries and for the survival of displaced people, especially in Syria (Oktav 2017, p. 248). Depriving people of water—either by cutting supplies or destroying water supply facilities and their power lines or flooding them has jeopardized their security in these countries. These actions threaten people's physical security, their economic welfare, and health. It can be argued that, in each case of the weaponization of water, the first actor whose security to be threatened are always human beings before the states.

Solving these humanitarian problems requires regional and international cooperation. As Kibaroğlu and Gürsoy (2015, p. 834) argue, it is needed "concerted efforts of regional governments and the international organizations." They should take responsibility and increase their efforts in providing humanitarian aid to the people of these countries.

The second negative consequence is the environmental costs of ISIS' weaponization of water. The cases analyzed in this chapter show us that in each incident of weaponization, there may incur negative environmental consequences. In the case of deprivation or diversion of water, water scarcity downstream can directly place at risk the population, agricultural production, other services, and the entire ecosystem in the affected area. Flooding has similar consequences, primarily adding forced displacement to the chain of problems. It should be noted here that ISIS' capture of oil wells—another strategic natural resource in the region—and its use of oil resources as a weapon of war have caused another set of environmental disasters. Just as Saddam Hussein regime burned oil wells while retreating from

Kuwait, leading to severe environmental consequences including air and water pollution, ISIS has also set oil wells on fire during the recent battle for Mosul. Its main aim was to obscure the view of Iraqi and coalition warplanes to prevent air strikes. It is estimated that 5000 barrels of oil were burning each day during this incident (Wedeman and Alkhshali 2016).

In addition to the territories of Syria and Iraq, the ongoing civil war and fight with ISIS in both countries have also basin-wide effects. It can be argued that particularly while the Syrian regime is in no position to manage the waters of the Euphrates River efficiently, ISIS clearly had no interest in sound management of the water resources it captured in both Syria and Iraq. This situation and the deterioration of relations among the riparian countries hinder efficient management of water throughout the Euphrates-Tigris basin (Kibaroğlu and Maden 2014, p. 351).

In short, the civil war in Syria, the ongoing crisis in Iraq, and difficulties in the military, political, and economic measures taken against ISIS have further exacerbated the situation by worsening the humanitarian and environmental problems caused by the weaponization of water resources. There is an urgent need to prevent conditions deteriorating further, and it is imperative for all belligerent parties to abstain from using water as weapon.

References

Al-Akhbar English. (2014, April 11). *ISIS captures Iraqi dam, floods areas*. Accessed February 25, 2017, from http://english.alakhbar.com/node/19385

al-Tamimi, A. (2013, December 24). The Syrian rebel groups pulling in foreign fighters. *BBC*. Accessed February 26, 2017, from http://www.bbc.com/news/world-middle-east-25460397

al-Tamimi, A. (2015, August). The evolution in Islamic State administration: The documentary evidence. *Perspectives on Terrorism, 9*(4), 117–129.

Ang, B. (2016, December 1). *ISIS uses water as weapon in Mosul conflict*. Accessed February 17, 2017, from http://www.hngn.com/articles/219558/20161201/water-becomes-troubling-weapon-isis-mosul-clash.htm

Annunziato, A., Andredakis, I. & Probst, P. (2016). *Impact of flood by a possible failure of the Mosul dam*. European Commission JRC Technical Report. https://doi.org/10.2788/689469

BBC. (2012, September 8). *Aleppo water supply cut as Syria fighting rages*. Accessed February 14, 2017, from http://www.bbc.com/news/worldmiddle-east-19533112

BBC. (2016a, February 29). *US warns of Mosul dam collapse in Northern Iraq*. Accessed March 5, 2017, from http://www.bbc.com/news/world-middle-east-35690616

BBC. (2016b, September 24). *Syria conflict: Air strikes leave Aleppo 'without water'*. Accessed January 21, 2017, from http://www.bbc.com/news/world-middle-east-37460849

Bender, J. (2014, June 10). A Jihadist group that's too radical for Al Qaeda is threatening Iraq's water supply. *Business Insider*. Accessed February 27, 2017, from http://www.businessinsider.com/al-qaeda-offshoot-now-effectively-controls-iraqs-water-supply-2014-6

Blanche, E. (2017, April 2). In Syria, everyone uses water as a weapon of war. *The Arab Weekly*. Accessed April 14, 2017, from http://www.thearabweekly.com/?id=8127

Chudacoff, D. (2014, July 7). 'Water War' threatens Syria lifeline. *Al Jazeera*. Accessed March 9, 2017, from http://www.aljazeera.com/news/middleeast/2014/07/water-war-syria-euphrates-2014757640320663.html

CTV News. (2012, November 26). *Rebels seize strategic Tishrin dam in North Syria, activists say*. Accessed February 26, 2017, from http://www.ctvnews.ca/world/rebels-seize-strategic-tishrin-dam-in-north-syria-activists-say-1.1053600

De Châtel, F. (2014). The role of drought and climate change in the Syrian uprising: Untangling the triggers of the revolution. *Middle Eastern Studies, 50*(4), 521–535. https://doi.org/10.1080/00263206.2013.850076

Enzer, G. (2014, April 24). *Tigris oil spill pollutes Iraq water supply*. Accessed March 9, 2017, from http://www.arabianoilandgas.com/article-12343-tigris-oil-spill-pollutes-iraq-water-supply/

Fares, M. (2017, January 7). How my spring became a weapon in the Syrian civil war. *Newsweek*. Accessed February 18, 2017, from http://www.newsweek.com/damascus-water-shortage-syrian-civil-war-barada-valley-538441

Feitelson, E., & Tubi, A. (2017). A main driver or an intermediate variable? Climate change, water and security in the Middle East. *Global Environmental Change, 44*, 39–48. https://doi.org/10.1016/j.gloenvcha.2017.003.001

Femia, F., & Werrell, C. E. (2013). Climate change before and after the Arab awakening: The cases of Syria and Libya. In C. E. Werrell & F. Femia (Eds.), *The Arab Spring and climate change: A climate and security correlations series* (pp. 23–32). Washington: Center for American Progress, Stimson, The Center for Climate and Security.

Filkins, D. (2017, January 2). A bigger problem than ISIS? *The New Yorker*. Accessed March 9, 2017, from http://www.newyorker.com/magazine/2017/01/02/a-bigger-problem-than-isis

Friedman, T. (2013, March 2). The scary hidden stressor. *The New York Times*. Accessed December 26, 2016, from http://www.nytimes.com/2013/03/03/opinion/sunday/friedman-the-scary-hidden-stressor.html

Gleick, P. H. (1993). Water and conflict: Fresh water resources and international security. *International Security, 18*(1), 79–112.

Gleick, P. H. (2014). Water, drought, climate change, and conflict in Syria. *Weather, Climate and Society, 6*(3), 331–340. https://doi.org/10.1175/WCAS-D-13-00059.1

Gleick, P. H., Yolles, P. & Hatami, H. (1994). Water, war & peace in the Middle East. *Environment, 36*(3), 6–15; 35-42.

Harrington, C. & Null, S. (2014, August 20). What can Iraq's fight over the Mosul dam tell us about water security? *New Security Beat*. Accessed February 16, 2017, from https://www.newsecuritybeat.org/2014/08/iraqs-fight-mosul-dam-water-security/

Hoerling, M. et al. (2012, March 15). On the increased frequency of mediterranean drought. *Journal of Climate, 25*, 2146–2161. https://doi.org/10.1175/JCLI-D-11-00296.1.

Hubbard, B., & An Employee of the NYT. (2014, July 23). Life in a Jihadist capital: Order with a darker side. *The New York Times*. Accessed March 7, 2017, from https://www.nytimes.com/2014/07/24/world/middleeast/islamic-state-controls-raqqa-syria.html

IRIN News. (2014, May 27). *Threat of disease in Iraq villages flooded by militants*. Accessed February 24, 2017, from http://www.irinnews.org/feature/2014/05/27

Jaafar, H. H., & Woertz, E. (2016). Agriculture as a funding source of ISIS: A GIS and remote sensing analysis. *Food Policy, 64*, 14–25.

Johnson, K. (2014, July 28). The Islamic State is the newest Petrostate. *Foreign Policy*. Accessed February 15, 2017, from http://foreignpolicy.com/2014/07/28/the-islamic-state-is-the-newest-petrostate/

Kelley, C. P. et al. (2015, March 17). Climate change in the fertile crescent and implications of the recent Syrian drought. *Proceedings of the National Academy of Sciences, 112*(11), 3241–3246. https://doi.org/10.1073/pnas.1421533112

Kibaroğlu, A., & Gürsoy, S. I. (2015). Water-energy-food nexus in a transboundary context: The Euphrates-Tigris river basin as a case study. *Water International, 40*(5–6), 824–838. https://doi.org/10.1080/02508060.2015.1078577

Kibaroğlu, A., & Maden, T. E. (2014). An analysis of the causes of water crisis in the Euphrates-Tigris river basin. *Journal of Environmental Studies and Sciences, 4*(4), 347–353. https://doi.org/10.1007/s13412-014-0185-9

King, M. D. (2016). The weaponization of water in Syria and Iraq. *The Washington Quarterly, 38* (4), 153–169.

Le Billon, P. (2001). The political ecology of war: Natural resources and armed conflicts. *Political Geography, 20*, 561–584.

MacKenzie, D. (2014, June 12). Extremists in Iraq now control the country's rivers. *New Scientist*. Accessed February 6, 2017, from https://www.newscientist.com/article/dn25722-extremists-in-iraq-now-control-the-countrys-rivers/

Marshall, W. (2016, February 19). ISIS is threatening to poison Indonesia's food and water supply. *Munchies*. Accessed March 4, 2017, from https://munchies.vice.com/en_us/article/78mjge/isis-is-threatening-to-poison-indonesias-food-and-water-supply

Massih, N. (2014, July 21). ISIS gains highlight 'aggressive' use of water as weapon of war. *The Daily Star*. Accessed March 7, 2017, from http://www.dailystar.com.lb/News/Middle-East/2014/Jul-21/264554-isis-gains-highlight-aggressive-use-of-water-as-weapon-of-war.ashx

Mehmetcik, H., & Kursun, A. M. (2017). Making sense of the territorial aspirations of ISIS: Autonomy, representation and influence. In O. Z. Oktav, E. Parlar Dal & A. M. Kursun (Eds.), *Violent non state actors and the Syrian civil war: The ISIS and YPG cases*. Springer.

Middle East Monitor. (2015, June 19). *ISIS 'causing drought' by cutting water supplies in four Iraqi provinces*. Accessed February 16, 2017, from https://www.middleeastmonitor.com/20150619-isis-causing-drought-by-cutting-water-supplies-in-four-iraqi-provinces/

Mohtadi, S. (2012, August 16). Climate change and the Syrian uprising. *Bulletin of the Atomic Scientists*. Accessed February 19, 2017, from http://thebulletin.org/climate-change-and-syrian-uprising

Oktav, Ö. Z. (2017). Turkey's water policy in the Euphrates-Tigris basin. In M. Behnassi & K. McGlade (Eds.), *Environmental change and human security in Africa and the Middle East* (pp. 239–255). Cham: Springer.

Pacific Institute. (2017). *Water conflict chronology list*. Accessed May 26, 2017, from http://www2.worldwater.org/conflict/list/

Paletta, D. (2016, January 20). Islamic state uses Syria's biggest dam as refuge and potential weapon. *The Wall Street Journal*. Accessed March 14, 2017, from https://www.wsj.com/articles/islamic-state-uses-syrias-biggest-dam-as-rampart-and-potential-weapon-1453333531

Parlar Dal, E. (2017). The contagion of the Syrian civil war into Turkey under the impact of ISIS and YPG cases: Conditioning factors and diffusion mechanism. In O. Z. Oktav, E. Parlar Dal & A. M. Kursun (Eds.), *Violent non state actors and the Syrian civil war: The ISIS and YPG cases*. Springer.

Pearce, F. (2014, August 25). Mideast water wars: In Iraq, a battle for control of water. *Yale Environment 360*. Accessed April 9, 2017, from http://e360.yale.edu/features/mideast_water_wars_in_iraq_a_battle_for_control_of_water

Piggott, M. (2015, July 12). ISIS: authorities cut water supply to Pristina after threat to poison reservoir. *International Business Times*. Accessed March 3, 2017, from http://www.ibtimes.co.uk/isis-authorities-cut-water-supply-pristina-after-threat-poison-reservoir-1510487

Reuters. (2015a, June 3). *Islamic State militants use water as weapon in Western Iraq*. Accessed February 26, 2017, from http://www.reuters.com/article/us-mideast-crisis-iraq-water-idUSKBN0OJ1TN20150603

Reuters. (2015b, December 1). *U.N. condemns air strike that cut water supplies to Syria's Aleppo*. Accessed January 18, 2017, from http://www.reuters.com/article/us-syria-crisis-aleppo-water-idUSKBN0TK4F020151201

Reuters. (2017a, May 10). *U.S.-backed Syria militias say Tabqa, dam captured from Islamic State*. Accessed May 12, 2017, from http://www.reuters.com/article/us-mideast-crisis-syria-tabqa-idUSKBN1862E4

Reuters. (2017b, June 4). U.S.-backed Syrian forces seize dam west of Raqqa from Islamic State: SDF. Accessed June 5, 2017, from http://www.reuters.com/article/us-mideast-crisis-syria-raqqa-idUSKBN18V0EX

Russet, B., Star, H., & Kinsella, D. (2000). *World politics: The menu for choice*. Boston: Bedford/St. Martin's.

Ryan J. (2016, August 23). ISIS Jihadist has published a guide on 'how to poison westerners' on encrypted mobile app. *The Sun*. Accessed March 4, 2017, from https://www.thesun.co.uk/news/1660902/isis-jihadist-has-published-a-guide-on-how-to-poison-westerners-on-encrypted-mobile-app/

Saleeby, S. (2012, February 16). Sowing the seeds of dissent: Economic grievances and the Syrian social contract's unraveling. *Jadaliyya*. Accessed March 23, 2017, from http://www.jadaliyya.com/pages/index/4383/sowing-the-seeds-of-dissent_economic-grievances-an

Scheumann, W. (2014, June 30). Water and electricity—Weapons in the Syrian conflict. *The Current Column*. Accessed February 20, 2017, from https://www.die-gdi.de/uploads/media/German_Development_Institute_Scheumann_30.06.2014.pdf

Sly, L. (2014, December 25). The Islamic state is failing at being a state. *The Washington Post*. Accessed February 27, 2017, from https://www.washingtonpost.com/world/middle_east/the-islamic-state-is-failing-at-being-a-state/2014/12/24/bfbf8962-8092-11e4-b936-f3afab0155a7_story.html?utm_term=.b7e91c19e191

Smith, R. J. (2013, March 15). The failed reconstruction of Iraq. *The Atlantic*. Accessed March 4, 2017, from https://www.theatlantic.com/international/archive/2013/03/the-failed-reconstruction-of-iraq/274041/

Sowers, J., Waterbury J., & Woertz E. (2013, September 12). Did drought trigger the crisis in Syria? *Footnote*. Accessed March 14, 2017, from http://footnote.co/did-drought-trigger-the-crisis-in-syria/

Strategic Foresight Group. (2014). *Water and Violence: Crisis of Survival in the Middle East*. Mumbai: Strategic Foresight Group. http://www.strategicforesight.com/publication_pdf/63948150123-web.pdf

Sümer, V. (2016, January 12). *War over Tishreen dam: Growing significance of hydraulic structures in the Middle East*. Accessed February 14, 2017, from http://www.orsam.org.tr/index.php/Content/Analiz/4546?s=orsam%7Cenglish

Svensson, B. (2014, June 13). Water as an instrument of war. *Qantara.de*. Accessed 16 February 16, 2017, from https://en.qantara.de/content/flood-disaster-in-iraq-water-as-an-instrument-of-war

The Guardian. (2015, July 11). *Kosovo cuts Pristina water supply over alleged ISIS plot to poison reservoir*. Accessed March 11, 2017, from https://www.theguardian.com/world/2015/jul/11/kosovo-cuts-pristina-water-supply-over-alleged-isis-plot-to-poison-reservoir

The Japan Times. (2016, February 10). *'Most dangerous dam' facing collapse, threatens half million in Mosul: U.S. army*. Accessed March 2, 2017, from http://www.japantimes.co.jp/news/2016/02/10/world/dangerous-dam-facing-collapse-threatens-half-million-mosul-u-sarmy/#.WGmD27YrLVr

The National. (2014, May 11). *Syrian rebels cut off water supply to both halves of Aleppo*. Accessed February 25, 2017, from https://www.thenational.ae/world/syrian-rebels-cut-off-water-supply-to-both-halves-of-aleppo-1.243612

UNICEF. (2015, December 1). *Statement by Hanaa singer, UNICEF representative in Syria on airstrikes against the Al-Khafsa water treatment facility in Aleppo*. Accessed January 20, 2017, from http://www.unicef.org/media/media_86402.html

United Nations in Syria. (2016, December 29). *Four million in Damascus have no access to water*. Accessed March 3, 2017, from http://reliefweb.int/sites/reliefweb.int/files/resources/UN%20Statement%20Water%20Crisis%20in%20Damascus%2029.12.2016.pdf

Vidal, J. (2014, July 2). Water supply key to outcome of conflicts in Iraq and Syria, Experts warn. *The Guardian*. Accessed February 23, 2017, from https://www.theguardian.com/environment/2014/jul/02/water-key-conflict-iraq-syria-isis

von Lossow, T. (2016). The rebirth of water as a weapon: IS in Syria and Iraq. *The International Spectator, 51*(3), 82–99. https://doi.org/10.1080/03932729.2016.1213063

Wedeman, B. & Alkhshali, H. (2016, October 13). Life under ISIS: Iraqis choke as sabotaged oil wells blaze. *CNN*. Accessed April 7, 2017, from http://edition.cnn.com/2016/10/12/world/burning-oil-wells-isis-iraq/index.html

Winnefeld, J. A., & Morris, M. E. (1994). *Where environmental concerns and security strategies meet: Green conflict in Asia and the Middle East*. Santa Monica: RAND.

Worth, R. F. (2010, October 13). Earth is parched where Syrian farms thrived. *The New York Times*. Accessed March 14, 2017, from http://www.nytimes.com/2010/10/14/world/middleeast/14syria.html?_r=2&adxnnl=1&adxnnlx=1330449407-yAiPXrD1kQsKbG2Bb5A61A&pagewanted=1

Zelin, A. (2014, June 13). The Islamic state of Iraq and Syria has a consumer protection office. *The Atlantic*. Accessed February 6, 2017, from https://www.theatlantic.com/international/archive/2014/06/the-isis-guide-to-building-an-islamic-state/372769/

Part III
Effectiveness

Surrogate Warfare in Syria and the Pitfalls of Diverging US Attitudes Toward ISIS and PYD/YPG

Helin Sarı Ertem

1 Introduction

Today's international system is far from preserving the characteristics of the Westphalian world order based on equal sovereignty and territorial integrity of the nation-states. Facing the increasing number of non-state actors, nation-states have long stopped being the only determinants of international politics. In fact, the biggest challenge to them comes from violent non-state actors (VNSAs), which target the existing territorial borders and the legitimacy of the nation-states that they exist in or are surrounded by.[1] Contrary to Max Weber, the monopoly of the use of physical force within a given territory is no longer held only by the nation-states. VNSAs are everywhere, using all kinds of force to achieve their political aims and it is not an easy task for the classical actors of the international system, namely the states, to overcome this challenge.

[1]VNSAs are considered as a distinct form of non-state actors, resorting not only to random or opportunistic aggression but to collective violence as a tool to achieve certain goals. Their non-state character distinguishes them from police forces and military. "VNSAs, such as terrorist organizations, play an increasingly important role in the international security environment" (Bartolomei et al. 2004, p. 1). VNSAs are also known as armed non-state actors (ANSAs). The Geneva Call uses the concept of ANSAs to refer to "armed entities that are primarily motivated by political goals and operate outside effective state control. They include armed groups, de facto authorities, and non or partially internationally recognised states" (Geneva Call's Report 2011, p. 9). Pointing out the link between fragile statehood and ANSAs, Schneckener underlines that ANSAs, ranging from rebels or guerrilla fighters to militias or paramilitaries, from clans chiefs and warlords to terrorists and criminals and from mercenaries and private security companies to marauders, may formally or informally be supported by state actors (Schneckener 2006, pp. 25–27).

H. Sarı Ertem (✉)
Istanbul Medeniyet University, Istanbul, Turkey
e-mail: helin.sariertem@medeniyet.edu.tr

Ö.Z. Oktav et al. (eds.), *Violent Non-state Actors and the Syrian Civil War*,
DOI 10.1007/978-3-319-67528-2_7

Despite this "coercive transition" era which is hard to resist (Davis 2009, p. 241), the recent rise of VNSAs obliges the great powers, as well as the regional states, to establish a counterstrategy against this new type of threat, which break the routine regarding the current balance of power in certain geographies such as the Middle East. The United States (US) is one of the great powers claiming to be in search of an effective method to fight against/weaken/eliminate VNSAs, some of which target American national interests as well. However, as this chapter argues, the country has long been suffering from a lack of a credible counterstrategy against VNSAs due to several internal and external reasons. First of all, the USA itself has been the direct or indirect founder or consolidator of some VNSAs with the strategies it applies usually for temporary solutions with limited engagements. Second, there is a strong pragmatic tendency in Washington to apply different policies toward each one of these VNSAs due to their diverging meanings for the US national interests. This creates confusion in the region and causes a lack of trust with some regional allies, which try to minimize the damage they might face due to the transboundary nature of the VNSAs. Therefore in this chapter, I claim that the US policy to minimize its risks and maximize its interests through the help of some VNSAs might actually create new threats and damage regional alliances, especially when certain sensitivities of regional countries regarding their national security priorities are not pursued. Possible consequences include an unintended rise of rival actors, state or non-state, which might necessitate a huge and costly US military intervention in the future although Washington's initial aim was to refrain from such involvement.

This is what we observed in the Middle East generally and in Syria specifically during the Obama era. Former US President Barack Obama tried to manage a shift from his predecessor George W. Bush's interventionist approach to a "surrogate war," allowing Washington to preserve a limited engagement in the Syria crisis. With the enormous loss of financial and human resources as well as worldwide anti-Americanism, the Iraqi occupation in 2003 reminded Americans of the Vietnam quagmire and that is why the Obama administration refrained from getting excessively involved in Syria. Applying the idea that "regional problems should mainly be solved by regional actors," Obama pursued a limited military engagement in the Middle East and left the arena to the local forces (states and non-state ones) to cope with the emerging crises. As vital US national interests were not felt to be under direct threat, the mobilization of partners and allies in accordance with the American vision would allow Washington to "outsource" the Syrian crisis, thus minimize and share the possible costs that might discomfort the American public.

The name of this strategy can be defined as "surrogate warfare," which, stated briefly, is the externalization of the strategic, operational, and tactical burden of warfare to surrogates to minimize the expected cost (Krieg 2016a, p. 99). However, this specific tactic, which has long been pursued by the USA under the general title of proxy warfare, has satisfied neither regional allies nor liberal interventionists in Washington. Moreover, it has turned the USA into an indirect cause for the emergence and/or strengthening of some VNSAs, including Al-Qaida, ISIS (al-Dawla al-Islamiya al-Iraq al-Sham/Islamic State of Iraq and Syria), PYD (Partiya Yekîtiya Demokrat/Democratic Union Party), Lebanese Hezbollah, Jabhat Al-Nusra, Jabhat Fatah Al-Sham, etc. while making these organizations significant political actors that are hard to ignore. In addition, the US preference of using YPG (Yekitina Parastine Gel/People's Protection Units)—the military wing of the secular and pro-Kurdish PYD—to defeat ISIS in Syria (in other words using one VNSA against another) has been one of the most significant shortcomings of the US surrogate warfare. Another problem of this strategy is the resulting tension with Turkey, a significant regional ally which has been asking for a greater US involvement in Syria to end the Assad regime but has felt frustrated with the heavy US reliance on PYD/YPG, which in Ankara's eyes is clearly the Syrian branch of its archenemy PKK (Partiya Karkerané Kurdistané/Kurdistan Workers' Party). This US pragmatism increases the possibility of a greater Turkish military involvement, which would not contribute to the solution of the Syrian crisis but rather worsen the situation in the region.

For a detailed analysis of these arguments and to elaborate what the prospects and pitfalls of American reliance on PYD/YPG as a surrogate in the Syrian war are, the chapter will first explain the main characteristics of "surrogate warfare" and its differences from the highly popular "proxy warfare," supporting them with evidence from previous US practices in various foreign issues that sheds light on the pros and cons of using surrogates as a military/political strategy. Second, it will focus on how the Obama administration performed this strategy in Syria, using PYD/YPG forces as a surrogate against ISIS, the motivations behind this preference and the pitfalls of it, such as the US' loss of credit in Turkey due to Washington's diverging national security priorities. In this section, the chapter will also examine the first 6 months of the Donald Trump era with regard to the continuing surrogate warfare of the USA in Syria.

2 "Surrogate Warfare" in an Apolar World

At the core of the international relations (IR) discipline, which was found in 1919 under the hubris of World War I, there lies the traditional dilemma between war and peace. As the international system could not get rid of the war phenomenon, actors have always been in a quest to maximize their interests and minimize their risks when facing wars. Parallel to this, a huge literature on the nature of war and its possible strategies came out in order to enable actors to survive and achieve their best possible outcome (Tzu 2003; Thucydides 2009; Machiavelli 2006; Clausewitz 1976). Modern war literature, however, has especially expanded when the major players of war were multiplied by the inclusion of non-state actors and the nature of conflict changed by shifts from interstate to intrastate, symmetric to asymmetric, and regular to irregular warfare.

Being aware of this, American intellectuals have been in search of an appropriate grand strategy, which will best serve US national interests regarding their relations with the outside world. Especially at times of crisis, which might lead to a war, having no clearly defined grand strategy is almost put on par with losing senses and going astray. For that reason it is not an easy task for the US administrations to determine and announce a comprehensive road map, usually summarized by the national security strategies or presidential doctrines. As Art argues, a correct formulation of proper means and ends is the key factor that determines the success of the strategy that will be performed. For that reason, understanding American interests correctly and using military power effectively to protect them are vitally important (Art 1998/1999, p. 79). However, it is a well-known fact that no single foreign policy doctrine is likely to receive widespread popular support due to various internal and external reasons.

2.1 Understanding Surrogate Warfare

Every single day, the world is getting more complicated, and this increases the hesitancy of the US presidents in determining their grand strategies and explaining them to the public. In fact, since the end of the Cold War, we have witnessed a quick shift from a bipolar to an apolar world, where the anarchic character of the international system is much more visible and the lines between state and non-state actors are blurred (Krieg 2016a, pp. 97–98). Due to the bitter memories of the G. W. Bush era, which had to go through two foreign interventions (Afghanistan in 2001 and Iraq in 2003) and faced the challenges brought out by Taliban and Al-Qaida (two other examples of VNSAs), Obama found himself obliged to remove the war fatigue felt by the American society and ease the relations with the outside world where anti-Americanism had reached its peak levels. In order to do that, finding a proper means to end long and costly military engagements in the Middle East, while not giving up, American interests became his number one priority.

The means Obama chose to protect American interests while redefining his country's assertive international role was "surrogate warfare," which Krieg defines as "a patron's externalization, partially or wholly, of the strategic, operational and tactical burden of warfare to a human or technological surrogate with the principal intent of minimizing the burden of warfare for its own taxpayers, policy-makers and military" (Krieg 2016a, p. 99). The word "surrogate" underlines a substitution of one for another, implying that the surrogate, which is usually distinct from the source of its authority, acts on behalf of the interests of another while being able to pursue its own interests as well (Smith 2006, p. 24). A surrogate force, on the other hand, is defined as "an indigenous, non-national force" (Day 2002, p. 4).

Under the light of these explanations, surrogate warfare is the fulfillment of a specific actor's national interests through manipulation of one or more substitute actors, who act on behalf of the former's own forces (such as the ground ones) but not totally replace its entire military capability. Acting as power maximizers, the surrogates can be both state and non-state actors, which might include third countries, partner nations, alliances, coalitions, insurgency groups, terrorist organizations, private military companies, and ethnic diasporas. They can be used not only by military but also by intelligence organs for plausible deniability. The table below explains this complex nature of surrogate warfare where a patron country, such as the USA, too can get involved by using special operation forces as well as conventional ones depending on the surrogate environment and the type of the operation (Smith, p. 29).

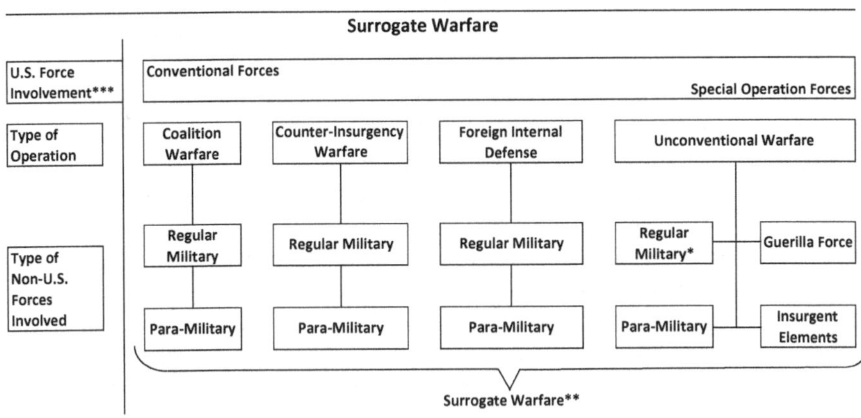

* Translates a type of operation to a type of force

** Surrogate warfare provides a framework for all the options for employing indigenous forces of all types (regular and irregular)

*** The level of involvement between conventional and special operation forces varies based on each particular operational situation

According to this table, the type of surrogate operations can be a coalition, a counterinsurgency warfare, or a foreign internal defense, where regular or paramilitary forces can take part as the non-US forces that are involved. In addition, it can also be an unconventional warfare, where guerrilla forces and insurgent elements as well as regular and paramilitary forces can take roles. As seen, it is possible to place a wide range of operation and force types under the general title of surrogate warfare. However, as Day underlines, surrogate warfare is often defined under the roof of unconventional warfare as a method that special operation forces can use to achieve their targets. For that reason, despite the comprehensive definition of Smith above, surrogate warfare in practice isolates itself from the wars made with the support of formal members of an alliance or a coalition, which tend to act almost as equal partners. In addition, the ad hoc relationship between a nation-state and a surrogate (Day 2002, p. 3) is worth underlining, as this is one of the most visible characteristics of such cases being practiced.

2.2 Surrogate or Proxy Warfare?

War by surrogates has certain convergences with "proxy warfare," which is also used to define various manipulative foreign policy activities of global and regional actors trying to "lead from behind" so as to limit involvement in a military engagement. In fact for Smith "a surrogate is also a proxy for a particular function or set of functions" (Smith, p. 24). For that reason, surrogate warfare can be considered as a more specialized and target-oriented version of proxy warfare that we often come across while dealing with various foreign policy strategies and intervention tactics.

Compared to the surrogate warfare, proxy warfare is defined more simplistically. According to the Oxford Dictionary, proxy warfare is "a war instigated by a major power, which does not itself become involved." It is also known as the "indirect engagement in a conflict by third parties wishing to influence its outcome" (Mumford 2013, p. 1). As seen, the definitions made for proxy warfare are quite general and can easily cover surrogate warfare as well. However, we can claim that some proxies (other than surrogates) tend to substitute the entire military capability of the patron and have a more autonomous character. Despite the money and arms they receive from the patron, these proxies can set their own agenda and conduct their own operations. The surrogates, as more specific versions of proxies, on the other hand, usually receive orders from the patron and have a submissive character. Facing highly complex, globalized, privatized, securitized, and mediatized conflicts in today's sociopolitical atmosphere (Krieg 2016b), surrogate warfare is a product of deeper expertise compared to the narrow Cold War method of proxy warfare. While proxy warfare usually means a "strategic" partnership of a state with other states or non-state actors, surrogate warfare contains operational and tactical relations as well as the strategic ones.[2]

With the abovementioned characteristics, proxy wars have been one of the main military/strategic tactics of the USA and the Soviets during the Cold War to protect their national interests in faraway lands while avoiding a close combat between each other. Under the fear of a mutually assured destruction, the two nuclear powers performed various such wars especially in the Third World countries. Provision or training of man power, supplying of material equipment or money, and sharing or dissemination of information such as spreading propaganda were among various means to conduct such warfare (Mumford, p. 6). The post-Cold War era and the 9/11 atmosphere of the new century did not curtail the use of proxy warfare due to the extended meaning of security, multi-actor character of the new global order, and changing military/economic capacities of great powers. This indirect way of warfare has become a popular concept especially with the spread of the Arab uprisings

[2] I would like to thank Dr. Andreas Krieg for his useful insights above, on how to distinguish surrogate warfare from the widely used concept of proxy warfare. (Information exchange through e-mail on 5 May 2017). Krieg's and Jean Marc Rickli's coming book, *Surrogate Warfare—A Mode of War for the 21st Century* will cover many interesting details on this war concept.

and the rise of the VNSAs in the Middle East under the negative legacy of G. W. Bush's famous "War on Terror."

As a more specialized method of proxy wars, surrogate warfare too is highly popular in the post-Cold War era. According to Krieg, in addition to the increasingly apolar nature of the international system, the shift from a threat-based to a risk-based perception of security and fundamental changes in the operating environment are the main reasons behind the current popularity of surrogate warfare (Krieg 2016a, p. 100). As known, in today's world there is an ongoing competition between the nation-states and non-states over the existing sovereignties and territorial borders. In this radically changing atmosphere, states need to find extra means to minimize risks other than getting into traditional state to state combats aiming to remove perceived threats. Intervening directly in foreign problem areas is a costly adventure that might cause loss of human and financial resources as well as public support, which is a great concern of vote-sensitive policy-makers.

However, states are not willing to give up their interests in other parts of the world either due to geostrategic calculations. Balancing or eliminating a rising threat continues to be the main motivation of the states (regional or global) and urges them to think about transferring risks to local surrogates. In addition to that, the changing nature of the operation field due to various VNSAs also obliges the states to find new ways of dealing with these unconventional players in the conflict/crisis zones. However, depending on their ideological inclinations and political/military targets, VNSAs are being perceived either as unusual sources of threat or local power maximizers. Within this context the "terrorist or freedom fighter" dilemma continues to survive due to diverging national interests of the global and regional actors in their relations with the VNSAs.

2.3 *Former Examples of American Surrogate Warfare*

Looking at how surrogates have been used by the US, we should consider its extensive history, starting from the end of the nineteenth century. In the Philippine War of 1899–1902, for instance, the USA used Macabebe Scouts, an anti-independence ethnic minority group, to overcome the US inability to defeat the pro-independence Filipino guerrillas (Boot 2002, p. 118). Macabebes were the descendants of Mexican Yaqui Indians, brought to the Philippines by Spain, and the US army officers used their ethnic and cultural difference to manipulate them against the native Filipinos' quest for independence.

In the beginning of the twentieth century, the USA also applied surrogate warfare in various Latin American countries. In 1927, for example, the Nicaraguan National Guards, a native militia group, served the USA as surrogate forces against Augusto Sandino's guerrillas asking for stronger national sovereignty by ending the American presence in the country. Although this did not bring a US victory and the American forces had to withdraw by 1934, the use of surrogates decreased the casualties on the US side and distracted the attention of the national and international society by making the case look like an intrastate conflict. The US-supported commander of the National Guards, Anastasio Somoza, founded a dictatorship that lasted for more than 40 years and eased American intervention in the region.[3]

Such examples can be multiplied considering the Cold War era and afterwards. The famous Iran-Contra affair was one of these examples. As revealed in 1986, the senior officials of the Reagan administration allowed arms sale to Iran, which was in fact under a US embargo. Through this secret sale, the Reagan administration tried to kill two birds with one stone. The first US target was to receive Iranian support to persuade Lebanese Hezbollah, another significant VNSA in the Middle East, to release the American hostages in Lebanon. The second target was to create a fund through this arms sale to strengthen the Contras in Nicaragua to enable them to topple the communist regime in this country. This was a perfect case showing how the USA might actually turn the VNSAs into credible addressees in its quest to achieve stronger political purposes. It is interesting to see that the US official reports on the scandal at that time simply defined covert actions and paramilitary wars as a necessity to achieve US foreign policy objectives instead of denying them (Kornbluh 1987/1988, pp. 138–139).

After the Soviet occupation in 1979, the USA supported the local Mujahideen forces in Afghanistan with the same logic while bringing about a heavier cost for future US interests. From 1980 to 1992, the USA is claimed to have spent 4–5 billion dollars to help this armed political group to eradicate the Soviets from Afghanistan, and a similar amount is believed to have been transferred to them by countries such as Saudi Arabia to support the American cause (Rasid 2000, pp. 26–27). This was a part of Operation Cyclone, which is claimed to have been formulated by then—US National Security Advisor Zbigniew Brzezinski—and allowed the CIA to help Mujahideen forces in Afghanistan financially and militarily. Through this operation, the USA manipulated the Muslim fundamentalists in Afghanistan to end or at least contain the influence of the Soviets and its communist ideology in the region.

With the USA's efforts to detach itself from Afghanistan when the Taliban among the Mujahideen took over Kabul in 1992, the relationship between this surrogate force and Washington gradually deteriorated. Rasid claims that the problems which occurred were actually a result of having no US grand strategy in this region but temporary policies. According to him, considering the Taliban to be anti-Shite and anti-Iran, the USA ignored the fundamentalist and inhuman agenda of this organization (Rasid, pp. 290–291). Brzezinski's famous words asking, "What is more important in world history? The Taliban or the collapse of the Soviet Empire? Some agitated Muslims or liberation of central Europe and the end of the Cold War?" are quite important to explain this pragmatic but tainted US approach of that time (Le Nouvel Observateur 1998). Soon after the collapse of the

[3]For a chronology of the events during the US intervention in Nicaragua, see: "Timeline: Nicaragua", https://web.stanford.edu/group/arts/nicaragua/discovery_eng/timeline/

Soviets, Washington too would understand the deficiencies of its policy when the Taliban project gradually backfired and turned into a serious headache for the USA.

The problem was mainly because of the rise of Al-Qaida, which would commit the 9/11 attacks in the USA in 2001. As a former surrogate in Afghanistan, like the Taliban, Al-Qaida forces were also used by the USA to end the Soviet influence in the region. As former British Secretary of Foreign Affairs Robin Cook pointed out: "Al-Qaida...was originally the computer file of the thousands of Mujahideen, who were recruited and trained with help from the CIA to defeat the Russians. Inexplicably, and with disastrous consequences, it never appears to have occurred to Washington that once Russia was out of the way, Bin Laden's organisation would turn its attention to the west" (Cook 2005). Regarding the Taliban and Al-Qaida problems, as former US Secretary of State Hillary Clinton underlined, the USA harvested what it sowed. In a statement to the US Congress in 2009, H. Clinton confessed that the people they were fighting today were actually funded by them 20 years ago (Ganji 2014).

Although being significant, Clinton's statements were far from explaining the details on how Al-Qaida was funded and consolidated by the USA. In actuality the financial, military, and human support to this VNSA were mainly coming from Saudi Arabia and Pakistan, the two regional allies of the USA. Saudi Arabia was especially substantial in Al-Qaida's rise, as it encouraged its citizens to go and fight in Afghanistan (Ganji 2014). The Al-Qaida leader, Osama bin Laden, was among these citizens who went to Afghanistan to fight against communism but backfired on the USA after the withdrawal of the Soviets, the then common enemy of jihadists and the West.

Despite such negative consequences, surrogate warfare continues to be a practicable military strategy for the USA. The main idea behind it is to make the surrogates perform certain actions to assist the fulfillment of US military/strategic objectives by substituting the capabilities that either the USA does not have or does not want to activate (Smith, p. 26). Surrogates are usually significant within the environments where the US military forces do not have as much information as the locals and/or where local forces might have superior capabilities. However, the use of surrogates might also be desired because of former traumatic experiences such as Vietnam (1965–1973), Afghanistan (2001–...), and Iraq (2003–2011). As an American army member, Smith also favors surrogate warfare summarizing the expected benefits of it as follows (Smith, p. 27):

(a) The chance to gain a stronger international legitimacy (although the level of this legitimacy depends on the type of the surrogate that is being benefited from): Using the NATO alliance as a surrogate cannot be equal to using a local military/political organization, especially a VNSA to achieve national interests.
(b) The need to use a relatively smaller number of military equipment and personnel: This would allow the USA save extra financial, military, and human resources either to use them entirely for internal policy choices or for other outside interventions.

(c) The provision of certain capabilities that the USA does not have: Here, one should not think of only the military capabilities as the USA is assumed to be one of the greatest military powers of the world. A surrogate's best contribution can in fact be its ethnic, linguistic, and cultural characteristics, which might ease the job of the USA, as a foreign force, in a completely unknown environment.

In addition to the above, quick response capability and convenient contract are also considered among the advantages of surrogate warfare (Day 2002, pp. 4–8). A correct surrogate support is believed to strengthen the US capability to organize a quick and decisive response to the necessary target, involving land, air, and naval assets. A convenient contract, on the other hand, allows both sides to end the arrangement whenever they want.

All these characteristics, however, contain potential problems as well as opportunities. The USA often tends to define its partnerships with surrogates as "temporary marriages," rather than permanent strategic commitments. However, the surrogates might often be disappointed with this temporary, pragmatic US approach if their own interests are not equally satisfied or if they believe that they were let down. Consequently, under the changing circumstances, the USA, international organizations, or the regional allies might consider these former surrogates as "destabilizing forces" and ask for their disbandment. If those surrogates resist doing that, both the region and the USA should get ready to face further problems in the future.

The latest example of this might be observed in Syria, as the USA has been practicing surrogate warfare there, especially since 2014. The following section will focus on the details of the Obama administration's implementation of surrogate warfare in Syria, which also seems to be being followed by the newly elected Trump administration when this chapter was written.

3 US Surrogate Warfare in Syria

In today's world, it is almost impossible for Washington to fully refrain from intervening in external affairs. In fact, it often suffers from being the only center of attention, to which the international society turns, when it expects something to be done in prominent interstate or intrastate crises. The USA can limit the number of its interventions while not being able to eliminate them totally. But especially under the influences of global economic turmoil, it should carefully evaluate every single idea of intervention. Where and how to intervene are the basic questions that should be answered by the US decision-makers.

3.1 Reasons of Obama's Limited Involvement

Facing the escalation of the Syrian civil war under the influence of the Arab uprisings, the Obama administration had to make careful calculations. One of the problems was about determining to what extent this crisis was a concern of the US national interests. In fact, national interest has become such an elastic and vague concept that one can easily question its guiding role for foreign policy-making (Keohane and George 1980, p. 142). Possible answers of "where do national interests begin and where do they end?" are quite subjective, often being shaped by the personal beliefs and worldviews of the politicians. This is the reason why American foreign policy-makers as well as the public have the difficulty of deciding whether the use of force is appropriate only in defense of vital "national interests" and the homeland or whether it should also be used to end humanitarian disasters and promote regional security in remote lands with limited US interests (Garofano 2002, p. iii).

Being aware of these shortcomings, Obama and his close circle pursued a highly cautious policy in Syria through which the USA would neither pay a heavy price with a massive intervention nor leave the region and the allies fully alone. In fact, this was a way of muddling through the Syrian crisis while trying to find a "via media" between the two extremes of the traditional US foreign policy dilemma, isolation or commitment. For that reason, despite the heavy suffering of the civilians, the USA tried to "lead the Syrian crisis from behind" and chose a limited engagement (Sarı Ertem 2013).

With respect to this, Obama first of all took some diplomatic steps. On 18 August 2011, he called Assad to leave power while resisting the increasing Republican pressure on him to provide arms to Syrian rebels. On 20 August 2012, he gave a relatively stronger message and underlined that any use of chemical weapons by the Assad regime would cross the "red line" for Washington. On 11 December 2012, he recognized the Syrian National Coalition (SNC) as the "legitimate representative of the Syrian people" (*Wall Street Journal* 2012), and in his State of the Union address on 13 February 2013, he declared that the USA would "keep pressure on the Syrian regime that has murdered its own people" (*State of the Union Address* 2013). The signs of a broader US support for the SNC came by the end of February 2013. At the "Friends of Syria" Summit in Rome on 28 February 2013, then US Secretary of State John Kerry announced a 60 million dollars worth of financial and humanitarian aid (namely medical and food supplies) to the Syrian rebels (*New York Times* 2013).

Washington was still far from any military engagement to Syria in order to not alienate the American public, which was suffering from Iraqi war fatigue. Even the Assad regime's allegedly crossing the US red line with the August 2013 chemical attack near Damascus did not bring an American military intervention to Syria. Once again, the use of military power was proven to be the most contentious issue of the American public. Obama rather chose to agree with Russia, a strong Assad ally, on dismantling of the Syrian chemical weapons, which would turn out to be a failure in a couple of years with a new chemical attack again allegedly committed by the Assad regime.

The US inaction in Syria especially in military terms was a part of the Obama Doctrine, which favored noninterventionism and was directed more toward domestic issues. When the subject is the Middle East, Obama was often called a "minimalist" (Beinart 2014). Gerges, who believes that the end of American involvement in the Middle East has already begun, summarizes Obama's approach to the region in two steps: (1) Military action had to be limited to the defense of vital US interests and (2) it should be carried out by a leaner, more flexible military force acting not unilaterally but multilaterally in cooperation with local allies (Gerges 2013, p. 301). The second step in particular is sufficient enough to understand why the Obama administration chose surrogate warfare as a means to deal with the Syrian crisis, as it would allow the USA to establish a multilateral policy supported by the local allies.

3.2 *The Use of PYD/YPG as a Surrogate*

Under increasing domestic and foreign pressure, the Obama administration finally realized that it could not totally isolate itself from the civil war in Syria and decided to gradually increase its military aid to the opponents while refraining from activating a no-fly zone that would require extra US commitments. Knowing that the wars in Afghanistan and Iraq caused the death of 6000 Americans and cost more than 1.5 trillion dollars, the Obama administration was focused on looking before leaping into Syria. For that reason, it was determined to share the burden with partners through a policy of "multilateral retrenchment" (Drezner 2011). This was in harmony with the then demands of the American public[4] and consequently brought about the questioning of the utility of a great military power while pushing Washington to improve the skills of special operation forces and new technologies of warfare such as unmanned systems.

The "2015 National Security Strategy" was a part of that approach, underlining the need for burden sharing especially when the US national interests were not directly threatened. Seeing failed or vulnerable states as the major cause of rising terrorism, the Obama administration declared that it would train and equip local partners and provide operational support to gain ground against terrorist groups,

[4]A public survey made in the USA on 14–19 November 2014 showed that 57% of Americans were against sending US ground troops to fight ISIS. Among those who favor to send ground troops, the Republicans were the majority, although both Democrats and Republicans perceived ISIS as a threat by 70–72%. In the same survey, it was also revealed that 43% of the Americans saw ISIS as an extension of Al-Qaida, while only 16% of them considered ISIS as a threat against vital US interests. The survey also points out that ISIS will return even if the US intervenes (56%) and that it is better not to fight Assad's army to allow them to fight ISIS instead (60%). (Brookings Institute's Survey on American Public Attitudes toward ISIS and Syria, 2015, January 8).

adding that this would include efforts to better fuse and share information and technology (*National Security Strategy* 2015, p. 9). This has again been influential on the preference of surrogate warfare, prioritizing the externalization of the burden to human and technological surrogates. The "train and equip" strategy came to the agenda under these circumstances. This kind of a support had long been asked for by the regional allies, such as Turkey, which took sides with the Free Syrian Army (FSA), an umbrella organization founded on 29 July 2011, gathering together dozens of different armed opposition groups in Syria.[5] In February 2015, Turkey and the USA signed a "train and equip" support deal under which 300 Syrian opponents were chosen and brought to Turkey for training. The same type of training was also given by the US experts in Saudi Arabia, Qatar, and Jordan to the groups taking part particularly in the FSA.

Behind this US decision, there lay the rising danger of ISIS, which gained enormous ground in Iraq by mid-2014 while causing a humanitarian disaster that captured the attention of the international media. In June 2014, ISIS militants took control of Mosul, the strategically important oil town of Iraq, and in August 2014 they occupied the Sinjar region, causing the death of thousands of Yazidis including women and children. The rest of the Sinjar residents escaped to the mountains mainly toward Duhok and Irbil in northern Iraq, looking for refuge. This created a huge reaction in the West, especially in the USA, and increased the military support given to the Iraqi forces, including the Kurdish Peshmerga, to fight against ISIS. The support given to the FSA was also multiplied with the devastating ISIS advance in Iraq and Syria. 2014 was also the year when ISIS committed its first terror attacks in the West and killed two American journalists in the Middle East. After these shocking terror incidents, the Obama administration felt obliged to develop much more effective strategies to eliminate ISIS.

However, the biggest problem was the complex nature of the Syrian opposition groups, some of which were considered to be linked with Al-Qaida-like jihadist organizations. This was the reason why the credibility of the FSA decreased in the eyes of Washington, whose nerves have been quite sensitive about the extremist ideas targeting Western values. For that reason, despite the existing ISIS threat, in October 2015, the Obama administration abandoned the 500 million dollar train and equip program, designed for 5400 Syrian opponents, claiming that the US vehicles and ammunition were actually being handed over to the extremists (*BBC News* 2015). From then on, the USA has preferred to focus its support mainly on the secular, Kurdish PYD and its armed wing YPG, which have been controlling the majority of northern Syria, performing as a hybrid actor combining conventional and unconventional fighting capabilities and possessing quasi-state characteristics (Kayhan Pusane 2017). Applying the aforementioned surrogate warfare methods,

[5]Although it was designed to be a centrally commanded organization, FSA soon became decentralized, and this decreased the chance of its success against the regime forces. Lister claims that this might well be a result of the late and insufficient support of the USA (Lister 2016, pp. 3–6).

the USA has been giving YPG comprehensive military training and equipment as well as supporting it with airstrikes. In return, the YPG would provide the USA with strategic and logistical support, be sacrificed instead of Americans if necessary, and decrease the risks/costs that would anger the American public. In addition, it would get into an ad hoc relationship with the USA rather than requiring permanent commitments through official agreements that can be the subject of international law. Consequently, losing the US support has deepened the hostility between the FSA, which is being supported mainly by Turkey, and the YPG, which has turned into the most favored anti-ISIS partner of the USA in Syria.[6] This has happened despite the concerns on the future political agenda of the PYD and its ambiguous relationship with the Assad regime (Lister 2016, p. 32). Turkish military intervention in Syria by August 2016 was a clear sign of the increasing lack of trust between Ankara and Washington over possible Kurdish achievements.

3.3 Tension with Turkey

One of the negative impacts of the US surrogate warfare in Syria has been the worsening of relations with Turkey as a significant regional ally. This was mainly because of the differentiating priorities of Washington and Ankara regarding their national interests. With the failure of the Kurdish peace process in 2013–2014, clashes between the PKK and Turkish armed forces escalated. After a couple of unsuccessful talks with PYD leader Saleh Muslim in 2014 and 2015, Ankara hardened its stance against this Kurdish organization as well, claiming that it has direct links with the PKK. The PKK has fought a Kurdish insurgency in southeastern Turkey since 1984 and is considered a "terrorist" organization by the USA as well as the EU. Although Turkey equates PYD/YPG with the PKK, Washington denies the claims that PYD/YPG is a terrorist group like the PKK. Senior US diplomat Brett McGurk, special envoy to the international coalition fighting ISIS, for example, came together with the YPG fighters in Kurdish controlled Kobane in Syria several times. Fearing the establishment of a Kurdish autonomy in Syria, which might unite with the Iraqi one in the future and embolden Turkey's own Kurdish minority, Turkey undertakes a tough stance against the negligence of the USA. Ankara believes that as a NATO ally and a strategic partner, Washington should determine common enemies and fight against them together with Turkey.

Under these circumstances the Turkish army entered Syria on 24 August 2016 and started "Operation Euphrates Shield," which is the biggest cross-border operation of Turkey since its 1974 intervention in Cyprus. With this operation, Turkey aimed both to clear Turkey's 900-km border with Syria of ISIS and prevent the

[6]Lawson gives the details of the gradually increasing rivalry between the main opposition groups in Syria, including the FSA and the PYD/YPG (Lawson 2017).

PYD/YPG from uniting the Kobani and Jazeera cantons with the Afrin canton in the west of the Euphrates River. Turkey is well aware of the possible strategic consequences of the Syrian civil war, which include the establishment of a Kurdish land, extending from the Iranian border in the East to the Mediterranean Sea in the West either in federative or unitary form (Ünver 2016, p. 81). Due to the rising ISIS and PKK attacks in Turkey, some of which were directly committed from Syrian territories, Turkey legitimized this military move relying on UN Charter's article number 51 for self-defense. Although this operation could not bring to an end the US cooperation with the PYD/YPG, it certainly made Turkey gain a bargaining power in Syria where it has taken the de facto control of the Jarablus and El Bab towns, strategically significant for Syrian Kurds.

Turkey finalized the Operation Euphrates Shield on 29 March 2017, with 67 losses from the Turkish army and more than 600 from the FSA. The number of deaths from ISIS was declared to be 2705 and from YPG 322 (*Milliyet* 2017). In cooperation with the FSA forces, Turkish army was able to secure an area of 2015 km^2 beyond its border with Syria. In addition to that, on 25 April 2017, Turkey launched a series of strikes against Kurdish positions in Hassakeh, a northeast province of Syria, and against Sinjar region of northern Iraq, near the Syrian border. These surprise Turkish strikes fueled the contentious atmosphere between Turkey and the USA and once again proved the multidimensional character of the fight against ISIS. Turkey has been fighting against ISIS but also against YPG, while the YPG has been seen by the USA as the most effective and reliable anti-ISIS force in the region. Thus, contrary to the traditional belief, the enemy (YPG) of Turkey's enemy (ISIS) was not its friend but its foe. This dilemma continues to be one of the basic obstacles before Washington's surrogate war in Syria despite the presidential change from Democrats to Republicans.

Contrary to his critiques against Obama's Middle East policy during the election campaign, the new US President Donald Trump seems to be continuing his predecessor's surrogate warfare in Syria. Even his surprising US missile attack on the Assad regime's Shayrat airfield to punish the Sarin gas attack on civilians was far from pointing out a policy change in Washington. Consequently, on 10 May 2017, the Trump administration officially approved supplying arms to the YPG fighters to support an operation to retake the Syrian city of Raqqa, which is considered to be one of the de facto capitals of ISIS along with Mosul in Iraq. It was interesting to see that this approval came just before Turkish President Recep Tayyip Erdogan's visit to Washington on 16 May 2017. By the beginning of May 2017, there were around 900 American advisors in northern Syria for the training of Syrian Democratic Forces (SDF), an umbrella organization consisting of Arab opponents as well as Kurdish YPG forces (Snow 2017). With the US administration's approval of providing more arms to YPG, Kurdish fighters are claimed to have received sophisticated American combat equipment including US-manufactured night vision goggles, rifles, and advanced optics used by American Special Operation forces (Snow 2017). The USA promise to inform Turkey about the content of the arms; it is going to deliver to the YPG forces and to collect these arms back once ISIS is defeated has been far from satisfying Turkey's concerns.[7]

Holding the second largest army in NATO, Turkey tried to persuade the USA to give up its cooperation with the YPG and offered to provide full support to the offensive on Raqqa strongholds of ISIS, which has started by 6 June 2017 (*Guardian* 2017). However, the USA did not show any interest in that offer as dealing with the YPG as a successful surrogate would be easier than coming to terms with Turkey, a strong regional ally eager to stay at the post-ISIS table. To decrease the tension with Turkey, however, the USA claims that its relations with the Kurds are on an ad hoc basis and the final aim is to build an Arab force capable of ruling the cities like Raqqa when ISIS falls. According to the US officials, this would automatically limit the Kurdish influence in the region. However, the presence of 27,000–50,000 YPG fighters in the SDF complicates Washington's materialization of the abovementioned post-ISIS plans. Will the USA be able to limit the PYD/YPG plans for the region? Will the PYD/YPG be willing to listen to Washington? These are tough questions to answer as the PYD/YPG is believed to have its own Syria and Middle East plans based on the idea of "democratic confederalism" pioneered by PKK's imprisoned leader Abdullah Ocalan as a way of developing alternative power forms based on self-organization of the peoples, rather than capitalist modes of nation-state (*Al Monitor* 2017; Jongerden and Akkaya 2013, pp. 172–174). PYD/YPG's oppression of other Kurdish political groups, such as "Kurdistan Democratic Party of Syria" (KDP-S) and "Kurdish National Council in Syria" (ENKS), increases concerns on the future of the relations with this surrogate, which might risk further American interests in the region (*BasNews* 2016; *Amnesty International* 2017).

Despite that, as a group that has most benefitted from the US support and which has been consolidated with romantic media coverage of the West, the PYD/YPG has achieved at least two significant advantages: (1) stronger international legitimacy that is turning it from a local force into an international player and (2) boosted self-confidence which allows it to extend to the Arab areas in northern Syria. These advantages might potentially have huge impacts not only on Syria but also on the neighboring countries, such as Turkey (Sly 2017). Washington's ignoring this fact, building temporary alliances, and focusing on short-term priorities such as elimination of ISIS, while forgetting about the possible harmful effects of its policies in the long run is the biggest handicaps of the US surrogate warfare in Syria. In fact, the use of PYD/YPG as a surrogate might in fact cause a snowball effect of further destabilization of the region, ruin traditional alliances, and even threaten future American interests in the Middle East.

[7]Soon after returning from Washington, President Erdogan mentioned that Turkey was ready to retaliate if they faced any threat from the YPG at their border (*Reuters* 2017). In response to this, US Secretary of Defense Jim Mattis sent a letter to Ankara noting that the alliance with Turkey was permanent and strategic, while the cooperation with the YPG-dominated Syrian Democratic Forces (SDF) was just tactical (*Middle East Observer* 2017).

4 In Lieu of Conclusion

The catastrophic civil war, which has been going on in Syria for more than 6 years, sped up the changes that we have been observing in the current international system. The Westphalian sovereignty and territoriality of the nation-states are rapidly being challenged by violent non-state actors (VNSAs), which threaten the existing status of the traditional players of international politics. However, neither the global powers such as the USA and Russia nor the regional powers such as Turkey, Iran and Saudi Arabia are willing to come against each other directly, to remove this vague atmosphere. Instead they all pursue a proxy war by using local forces to achieve their aims. Suffering from the symptoms of a failed state, Syria hosts tens of different armed factions, many of whom have diverging regional interests that can easily be manipulated by outside forces.

Trying to remove the bitter memories of the long-lasting and costly Afghanistan and Iraq operations, the Obama administration paid extra attention not to get involved in the Syrian crisis. Instead, in an effort to harmonize the American values with interests, it chose to practice a surrogate war in Syria, through which the USA would externalize the strategic, operational, and tactical burden of the warfare to local forces in order to minimize the expected human and financial cost. The increasingly apolar nature of the international system, as well as the changing operational environment in the twenty-first century, pushed the USA to move from a threat-based to a risk-based perception of security and avoid involving itself in further Iraq-like direct combats. As a more specific and target-oriented way of proxy warfare, surrogate warfare has become quite popular among the American military/bureaucratic elite who favor a "multilateral retrenchment," rather than a "deep military and political involvement" in external conflicts, especially when vital American national interests are not under direct threat.

As a part of Obama's Middle East strategy, based on core principles summarized above, surrogate warfare has been put into practice in Syria to increase the internal and external legitimacy/approval of Washington's actions in the region, required smaller American footprint on the ground, and fulfilled the lack of certain capabilities that either the USA does not have or does not want to consume in this remote geography. The USA also believes that through surrogate warfare, it can speed up the process of achieving certain targets, among which defeating ISIS has number one priority. In addition, the ad hoc character of this warfare leads the USA to believe that it can end this patron-surrogate relationship whenever it wants.

The surprising advance of ISIS in 2014 pushed the USA to focus much more on this strategy and choose PYD/YPG as the most effective surrogate in the fight against ISIS. However, the heavy US reliance on YPG and the increasing American military support to it added one more problem to the already existing crisis between Ankara and Washington. As known, the two NATO allies have long been suffering from the aftershocks of 1 March Motion Crisis in 2003, which prevented the passage of US troops from southeast Turkey to northern Iraq to start the military campaign against Saddam Hussein. Already full of anti-American sentiments nourished by hostile treatments, such as the Hook Event in 4 July 2003, where Turkish Special Forces were caught up by US forces in northern Iraq, the Turkish ruling elite as well as public have huge concerns on whether the USA is actually helping Kurds to establish a Kurdish zone right beneath Turkey, which might turn into an independent state in the future by uniting with northern Iraq. Such a possibility triggers Turkey's traditional anxiety about an independent Kurdish state and increases its desire to become involved in the Syrian conflict.

As a matter of fact, the surrogate warfare, which the USA has been favoring to lead the Syrian civil war from behind, has the potential of turning into a disadvantage both for Washington and the region. The US-supported YPG's current success in the fight against ISIS might easily target future American interests, ruin traditional alliances, and destabilize the region in the long run. For that reason, the USA might soon find itself dealing with the costly side effects of the surrogate warfare in Syria, of which it cannot easily wash its hands. Considering the previous US practices of surrogate warfare, Washington's use of one VNSA against another has long proved to be a policy equal to holding a powder barrel ready to explode.

References

Amnesty International. (2017, June 9). Syrian Kurdish activists arbitrarily detained. Accessed June 12, 2017, from https://www.amnesty.org/download/Documents/MDE2463812017ENGLISH.pdf

Art, R. J. (1998/1999, Winter). Geopolitics updated: The strategy of selective engagement. *International Security, 23*(3), 79–113.

Bartolomei, J., Casebeer, W., &Thomas, T. (2004, November). *Modelling violent non-state actors: A summary of concepts and methods*. Research Paper for the Institute for Information Technology Applications. Colarado: United States Air Force Academy.

BasNews. (2016, August 30). PYD-affiliated forces detain rival people in Afrin: KDP-S. Accessed June 20, 2017, http://www.basnews.com/index.php/en/news/middle-east/296381

BBC News. (2015, October 9). US to abandon training new Syria rebel groups. Accessed May 23, 2017, http://www.bbc.com/news/world-middle-east-34486572

Beinart, P. (2014, August 28). Actually, Obama does have a strategy in the Middle East. *The Atlantic*. Accessed May 27, 2017, from https://www.theatlantic.com/international/archive/2014/08/actually-obama-does-have-a-strategy-in-the-middle-east/379368/

Boot, M. (2002). *The savage wars of peace: Small wars and the rise of American power*. New York: Basic Books.

Brookings Institute's Survey on American Public Attitudes toward ISIS and Syria. (2015, January 8). *Principal Investigator: Shibley Telhami*. Washington, DC: Brookings Institute. Full Report. Accessed February 28, 2017, from Available Online: www.brookings.edu/ISISopinionpoll

Clausewitz, C. V. (1976). *On war* (M. Howard & P. Paret, Ed. & Trans.). Princeton, NJ: Princeton.

Cook, R. (2005, July 8). The Struggle against terrorism cannot be won by military means. *The Guardian*. Accessed May 12, 2017, from https://www.theguardian.com/uk/2005/jul/08/july7.development

Davis, D. E. (2009). Non-state armed actors, new imagined communities, and shifting patterns of sovereignty and insecurity in the modern world. *Contemporary Security Policy, 30*(2), 221–245.

Day, A. E. (2002, February 4). *Implications of surrogate warfare*. Paper submitted to the Faculty of the Naval War College in partial satisfaction of the requirements of the department of Joint Military Operations. Accessed February 10, 2017, from https://www.researchgate.net/publication/235129598_Implications_of_Surrogate_Warfare

Drezner, D. W. (2011, July/August). Does Obama have a grand strategy? *Foreign Affairs, 90*(4), 57.
Ganji, A. (2014, August 31). US-Jihadist relations—Part 1: Creating the Mujahideen in Afghanistan. *Huffington Post.* Accessed May 10, 2017, from http://www.huffingtonpost.com/akbar-ganji/us-jihadist-relations_b_5542757.html
Garofano, J. (2002). *The intervention debate: Towards a posture of principled judgment.* Carlisle, PA: Strategic Studies Institute, U.S. Army War College.
Geneva Call's Conference Report on Armed Non-State Actors and Protection of Internally Displaced People. (2011, March 23–24). Geneva. Accessed April 23, 2017, from https://genevacall.org/wp-content/uploads/dlm_uploads/2013/11/20110324_protection_-of_internally_displaced_people.pdf
Gerges, F. A. (2013, March). The Obama approach to the Middle East: The end of America's moment? *International Affairs, 89*(2), 299–323.
Guardian. (2017, June 6). US-Backed Syrian forces launch offensive to retake Raqqa from Isis. Accessed June 20, 2017, from https://www.theguardian.com/world/2017/jun/06/syrian-forces-launch-offensive-to-recapture-raqqa-from-islamic-state
Jongerden, J., & Akkaya, A. H. (2013). Democratic confederalism as a Kurdish Spring: The PKK and the quest for radical democracy. In M. Ahmed & M. M. Gunter (Eds.), *The Kurdish Spring: Geopolitical changes and the Kurds* (pp. 163–185). Costa Mesa, CA: Mazda.
Kayhan Pusane, Ö. (2017). How to profile PYD/YPG as an actor in the Syrian Civil War: Policy implications for the region and beyond. In O. Z. Oktav, E. Parlar Dal, & A. M. Kursun (Eds.), *Violent non state actors and the Syrian Civil War: The ISIS and YPG* cases. New York: Springer.
Keohane, R. O., & George, A. L. (1980). The concepts of national interests: Uses and limitations. In A. L. George (Ed.), *Presidential decision making in foreign policy* (pp. 217–237). Boulder, CO: Westview.
Kornbluh, P. (1987/1988, Winter). The Iran-Contra scandal: A postmortem. *World Policy Journal, 5*(1), 129–150.
Krieg, A. (2016a). Externalizing the burden of war: The Obama Doctrine and US Foreign Policy in the Middle East. *International Affairs, 92*(1), 97–113.
Krieg, A. (2016b, December 12). Surrogate war and the illusion of state-centrism. *Defence-In-Depth.* https://defenceindepth.co/tag/surrogate-warfare/
Lawson, F. H. (2017). The assistance front versus the popular protection units versus the Islamic state: Reciprocal mobilization and the ascendance of violent non-state actors in the Syrian Civil War. In O. Z. Oktav, E. Parlar Dal, & A. M. Kursun (Eds.), *Violent non state actors and the Syrian Civil War: The ISIS and YPG* cases. New York: Springer.
Le Nouvel Observateur. (1998, January 15–21). The Brzezinski interview. Accessed May 12, 2017, from http://dgibbs.faculty.arizona.edu/brzezinski_interview
Lister, C. (2016, November). The free Syrian army: A decentralized insurgent brand. Analysis Paper (Brookings Institution No.26).
Machiavelli, N. (2006). *The art of war* (H. Neville, Trans.). Mineola, NY: Dover.
Middle East Observer. (2017, June 22). US to take back weapons from PKK/YPG when Daesh defeated: Mattis. Accessed June 23, 2017, from https://www.middleeastobserver.org/2017/06/22/37662/
Milliyet. (2017, March 30). Fırat Kalkanı Harekâtının 216 günlük bilançosu. Accessed May 29, 2017, from http://www.milliyet.com.tr/firat-kalkani-harekatinin-216-gundem-2423279/
Mumford, A. (2013). *Proxy warfare.* Cambridge: Polity.
National Security Strategy. (2015). p. 9. Accessed May 27, 2017, from https://obamawhitehouse.archives.gov/sites/default/files/docs/2015_ national_security_strategy.pdf
New York Times. (2013, February 28). U.S. steps up aid to Syrian opposition, pledging $60 million. Accessed May 22, 2017, from http://www.nytimes.com/2013/03/01/world/middleeast/us-pledges-60-million-to-syrian-opposition.html?pagewanted=all&_r=0
Rasid, A. (2000). *Taliban* (Published in Turkish). Istanbul: Everest.

Reuters. (2017, May 18). Turkey ready to retaliate against any threats, Erdogan warns. Accessed June 23, 2017, from http://www.reuters.com/article/us-usa-turkey-erdogan-idUSKCN18E0H6

Sarı Ertem, H. (2013, May 15). *Assessing the U.S. inaction in Syria: The limits of 'leading from behind' in the Arab Spring* (Revue Française EurOrient, Syria Special Issue. No:41-42). Paris: l'Harmattan, pp. 305–330.

Schneckener, U. (2006). Fragile statehood, armed non-state actors and security governance. In A. Bryden & M. Caparini (Eds.), *Private actors and security governance* (pp. 23–40). Berlin: Lit-Verlag.

Sly, L. (2017, January 7). U.S. military aid is fueling big ambitions for Syria's leftist Kurdish militia. *The Washington Post*. Accessed May 29, 2017, from https://www.washingtonpost.com/world/middle_east/us-military-aid-is-fueling-big-ambitions-for-syrias-leftist-kurdish-militia/2017/01/07/6e457866-c79f-11e6-acda-59924caa2450_story.html?utm_term=.dfb7fcb7cc6b

Smith, K. H. (2006, May). *Surrogate warfare for the 21st Century*. Monography prepared for the School of Advanced Military Studies. Fort Leavenworth, KS: United States Army Command and General Staff College. Accessed February 10, 2017, from https://www.researchgate.net/publication/37163034_Surrogate_warfare_for_the_21st_century

Snow, S. (2017, May 7). Syrian Kurds are now armed with sensitive US weaponry, and the Pentagon denies supplying it. *Military Times*. Accessed May 29, 2017, from http://www.militarytimes.com/articles/syrian-kurds-ypg-us-military-weapons

The State of the Union. (2013). The White House. Accessed April 20, 2017, from http://www.whitehouse.gov/state-of-the-union-2013

Thucydides. (2009). *The Peloponnesian War* (M. Hammond, Trans.). Oxford: Oxford University Press.

Timeline: Nicaragua. Accessed May 11, 2017, from https://web.stanford.edu/group/arts/nicaragua/discovery_eng/timeline/

Tzu, S. (2003). *The art of war* (L. Wusun, Trans.). San Francisco, CA: Long River.

Ünver, A. H. (2016, Spring/Summer). Schrödinger's Kurds: Transnational Kurdish geopolitics in the age of shifting borders. *Journal of International Affairs, 69*(2), 65–98.

Wall Street Journal. (2012, December 12). U.S. formally recognizes Syria's main rebel group. Accessed May 22, 2017, from http://online.wsj.com/article/SB10001424127887324339204578173272657834096.html

External Actors and VNSAs: An Analysis of the United States, Russia, ISIS, and PYD/YPG

Doruk Ergun

1 Introduction

The Syrian civil war, in its sixth year as of 2017, has resembled Pandora's box, unleashing terrors for the Syrian people, the Middle East, and across the globe. An effect of the war, and a cause of its prolongation, has been the proliferation of many different violent non-state actors (VNSAs) on the one hand and the involvement of various states in the conflict to further their interests on the other. Among these VNSAs, the Islamic State of Iraq and al-Sham (ISIS, also ISIL, IS, or DAESH) and the Democratic Union Party (Partiya Yekîtiya Demokrat-PYD) and its armed wing People's Protection Units have been especially prominent in their ability to influence regional and international dynamics. Whereas the former became the first VNSA in modern history to exclusively rule over territory amounting to nearly half of Iraqi and Syrian landmass combined, the latter represents a rare example of a VNSA that has managed to gain international recognition to an extent unparalleled in recent memory. From a theoretical standpoint, the two VNSAs operate in uncharted territory in many ways (for a detailed discussion, see Oktav et al. 2017), necessitating a more practical analysis to understand existing currents and complement the analysis provided elsewhere in this volume.

The war has also attracted the interest and, later, military involvement of the two "superpowers," the United States and Russia. On the surface, the fact that both Moscow and Washington cooperate with the PYD/YPG and combat ISIS suggests that they may have similar goals and positions. This manuscript aims to dig deeper to unearth the dynamics of the interaction of the two countries with the two VNSAs. With this, the author aims to contribute to the literature by displaying the differentiated interactions of the two external state actors with two VNSAs operating in the

D. Ergun (✉)
Centre for Economics and Foreign Policy Studies, Istanbul, Turkey
e-mail: dergun@edam.org.tr

Ö.Z. Oktav et al. (eds.), *Violent Non-state Actors and the Syrian Civil War*,
DOI 10.1007/978-3-319-67528-2_8

same context and timeframe. It sets out by providing a background on VNSAs in the context of the Middle East and distinguishes key characteristics of ISIS and PYD/YPG. After providing a brief background on the past of Moscow and Washington's interaction with VNSAs, it analyzes the rationales for becoming entangled in the Syrian civil war of both sides and their outlook toward and interaction with the PYD/YPG and ISIS. The paper concludes by comparing how the United States and Russia viewed and interacted with the PYD/YPG and ISIS.

2 VNSAs and State Engagement: A Brief Background

VNSAs have existed for centuries, from slaves that rebelled against the Roman Empire in 73–71 BC (Strauss 2010) to the Nizaris that posed a threat to Seljuks, Mongols, and Crusaders alike between the eleventh and thirteenth centuries (Stanton and Ramsamy 2012). Yet one can hardly find any reference to VNSAs in classical international relations theory. Seeing the world through the lens of power dynamics and competition for survival, the realist theory assumes that states are the most powerful and hence the most significant players. In turn, while the liberal theory recognizes non-state actors to some extent, it is primarily focused on their economic interests and roles. In time, both camps readjusted to the new dynamics surrounding VNSAs by offering alternative theoretical frameworks to accommodate the rising role of VNSAs (see Geeraerts (1995) for an outlook and Pierman (2015) for a recent attempt). Yet, they continue to have shortcomings in explaining rapidly changing systems, such as the Middle East today, as they assume the continuity of actors and their approaches and practices in the context in which they operate (Valensi 2015). Whereas constructivism offers more to explain VNSAs, it is better equipped to understand past interactions rather than to predict the future (Walt 1998) and cannot fully account for the complexity of VNSAs.

The lack of a theoretical framework has certainly not prevented states from engaging VNSAs, and states have interacted with them at varying capacities and with differing motivations for as long as VNSAs have existed. Some have engaged non-state actors to provoke rebellion in order to weaken their rivals. A prominent example for this is that of the British Empire's interaction with Arab tribal leaders to incite rebellion and weaken the Ottoman Empire during WWI—T.E. Lawrence being an iconic example of British officers tasked with this duty. Others utilized paramilitary groups to push for regime change. An example of this is the Bay of Pigs—the United States's failed attempt against the Cuban leadership through a CIA-sponsored VNSA in 1961. Some states have even shared authority, control, service delivery, and, thus, legitimacy with VNSAs, whether voluntarily or involuntarily. One such example in the Middle Eastern context is the case of Lebanon, where Hezbollah has become much more than a VNSA, playing a substantial role in the society and occupying a legitimate position within the Lebanese government (Early 2006).

In other cases, states warred without direct military engagement but through using VNSAs as proxies in a third-party host nation. Though it remained "cold," one of the reasons that made the Cold War a "war" was the violent competition that the two primary actors played out by relying on VNSAs as their proxies. In two famous examples, the Soviet Union provided support to the Viet Cong to undermine South Vietnam backed by the United States, whereas the United States later delivered aid to Afghan mujahideen to counter the Soviet Union's invasion of Afghanistan.

In time, VNSAs have evolved and become more capable in changing the course of global affairs. Today, most armed conflicts take place within states and are characterized by VNSAs fighting among one another or with a state (DCAF and Geneva Call 2015). Compared to a few decades ago, a small number of people can now conduct more lethal attacks, owing to advances in technology, the growing concentration of civilians in urban settings, and increasing complexity of infrastructure that societies rely upon (Dutka 2006). The most shocking example of this has been al-Qaeda's attack on the World Trade Center on September 11, 2001, which claimed close to 3000 lives and ushered in a new era in international affairs, shaping national security policies, foreign policy interests, and domestic and global political currents, and creating new societal conditions. Furthermore, the increasing capacity and accessibility of communications technologies, notably the Internet, has given VNSAs unprecedented exposure to recruit individuals globally or inspire them to conduct attacks in their home states, as well as giving VNSAs the ability to exchange information and knowledge, and coordinate with other VNSAs, adding to the transnationality and lethality of conflict.

As such, while proxy/surrogate wars persist as trends, some VNSAs have gained the ability to influence regional and global affairs. Indeed in general, VNSAs that are able to attract foreign terrorist fighters (FTFs) are more successful, and FTFs themselves are found to be responsible for more violence when compared to local recruits (Malet 2010). In fact, the power vacuums created by the failure of states to fully or partially exercise control over their territory have presented conditions conducive for VNSAs to proliferate and expand their influence, without necessarily having the backing of state actors.

2.1 VNSAs in the Middle East

The Middle East is no stranger to VNSAs. In the north, Turkey has been host to VNSAs throughout the ideological spectrum, most notably to the Kurdistan Workers' Party (Partiya Karkeren Kurdistane (PKK)). To the east, Iran has been the target of VNSAs such as Jundallah and Kurdistan Free Life Party (Partiya Jiyana Azad a Kurdistane (PJAK))—an affiliate of the PKK. In the Levant, Hezbollah in Lebanon has been a notable example of a VNSA exercising control and quasi-state functions over a territory, whereas Hamas in Israel has also found itself in a similar position. To the west, Egypt has dealt with Egyptian Islamic Jihad for decades even before the VNSA joined the al-Qaeda in 2001. Likewise, jihadist VNSAs have plagued Yemen in the south.

More recently, Libya, Iraq, Yemen, and Syria have found themselves embroiled in civil, sectarian, and tribal conflict and are the hosts to numerous VNSAs. Indeed, today a number of states in the Middle East are incapacitated to fully or partially control their formal territorial borders. When coupled with the colonial past of the region that feeds the perceived artificiality and illegitimacy of nation-state borders, this results in primordial identities, such as ethnic, tribal, sectarian, and religious ones, to gain prominence (Soltan 1997). In this context, VNSAs are rising to prominence across the region. For example, Iraq is de facto divided into Sunni, Shia, and Kurdish spheres of influence after the deposition of the Saddam regime in 2003, whereas pockets of Syrian territory are controlled by various state and non-state entities. By the first half of the Syrian civil war that began in 2011, over 1000 distinct VNSAs were operating in the country (Dews 2014).

Out of that 1000, two actors have risen to prominence in terms of their ability to have an impact on regional and global affairs, as well as in the way that states acknowledged them as "actors" and engaged with them using military, diplomatic, and economic means. The most notable is ISIS, which managed to establish de facto control over a significant amount of territory and erode the border between Iraq and Syria. ISIS expanded even further, claiming attacks in 29 countries (CNN 2017) and becoming "fully operational" in 18 countries (Hoffman 2017). The second VNSA is the Democratic Union Party (PYD), along with its military wing the People's Protection Units (YPG) and affiliated Syrian Democratic Forces (SDF) (the dynamics will be mentioned below). The PYD, with its affiliates, has gained international acknowledgment and established partnerships with both the United States and Russia, by leveraging its position as the most capable VNSA fighting against ISIS.

2.1.1 The Distinctive Features of the Islamic State of Iraq and al-Sham (ISIS)

While it has been in the international spotlight for the past few years, ISIS' roots go back to Jama'at al-Tawhid wal-Jihad, a jihadist VNSA founded in 1999. The group led by Abu Musab al-Zarqawi eventually pledged allegiance to al-Qaeda and adopted the name Islamic State in Iraq (ISI) in 2006. Even during the Iraq insurgency, ISI's willingness to target civilians and focus on the Shia drew criticism from al-Qaeda leadership (Tønnessen 2015). ISI was crippled after the US Surge and Sunni Awakening in Iraq but managed to survive. After the outbreak of the Syrian civil war, the VNSA first focused on expanding its control over strategic territories such as Raqqa—which would become its "capital" in the future (Rabil 2014). In 2013, it announced a merger with the Nusra Front, al-Qaeda's branch in Syria, under the name Islamic State of Iraq and al-Sham. This merger did not materialize, and in mid-2014, ISIS broke off from al-Qaeda, adopted the name the Islamic State, and declared its leader, Abu Bakr al-Baghdadi, as Caliph—the leader of the Islamic world.

What sets ISIS apart from other VNSAs has not only been its brutality but also its ability to establish exclusive control over an unprecedented amount of territory. By 2015, ISIS controlled over half of the Syrian territory (The Guardian 2015) and 40% of the Iraqi territory (Moore 2017). By eroding the Iraqi–Syria border, ISIS did something that "no other country has been able to do with one exception over the past century—redraw the map [of] the Middle East and dissolve at least one of the Western-imposed geographical boundaries created after World War I" (Hoffman 2017).

ISIS' ambitions do not stop at controlling territory in Iraq and Syria. The organization's propaganda suggests a willingness to expand its territory as much as possible, encompassing the Muslim world and beyond. The VNSA has already presented itself as a successful alternative to the al-Qaeda brand, receiving pledges of allegiance and recruits from across the globe.

As ISI's ability to survive against heavy losses in Iraq rested on its adaptability, so has ISIS' expansion in Iraq and Syria, where the group adopted and successfully implemented a hybridized understanding of conventional and asymmetric war—hybrid war. The model that al-Qaeda followed rested on latching itself to Taliban in Afghanistan, and after the US-led intervention, it formed a loose network across the globe. ISIS, on the other hand, has been intent on military conquest and becoming the only power to hold exclusive control over the territories under its de facto control (for further discussion, see Mehmetçik and Kurşun 2017). In addition to military means, ISIS has used trade relations, marriages, propaganda, and coercion to draw numerous Sunni tribes into its allegiance across Syria and Iraq, relationships which ISIS was already cultivating before the Syrian civil war broke out.

Beyond territorial conquest, ISIS has also been interested in providing governance structures for the people under its control, comparable to many other VNSAs operating in Syria. Yet, an issue that sets ISIS apart from many other VNSAs operating in the Middle East is that unlike Hezbollah or Hamas, ISIS does not work within an established state framework and does not attempt to replicate it. It instead represents the complete dissolution of the modern nation-state structure. In this sense, Valensi (2015, p. 66) argues, "ISIS is a supra-national and 'a-national' organization." What ISIS attempts to replicate is a state structure based on an understanding of how the Islamic society was in its "golden ages" using a verbatim interpretation of religious texts. In the territories that it controls, ISIS appoints governors, public administrators, legal councils, and sharia judges in a very centralistic fashion. In addition to these structures, its security, intelligence, and military apparatuses enable it to remain entrenched. In 2014, ISIS even claimed that it will be issuing its own currency, though this appears to have been more propaganda than reality.

VNSAs that aim to assert themselves as major political actors over a given territory, such as secessionist groups, often strive for international recognition as a means of legitimizing their existence. What sets ISIS apart from such groups is that the organization does not seek any formal international recognition aside from inciting fear and inspiration across the globe, as it finds legitimization through the religious aura surrounding its ideology, practices, and leadership. In this regard, it is important to note that ISIS has attempted to exist not only as more than a state but also as an ideal. In an audio message released in 2014, ISIS leader al-Baghdadi claimed that it was a duty for Muslims worldwide to immigrate to the "Islamic State" and made a special call for judges, doctors, engineers, and people with administrative expertise to help build the "Islamic State" (BBC 2014). ISIS exists as a quasi-state, a transnational terrorist organization, an armed rebel group, an alternative governance and rule of law model, among others, making it a unique VNSA in many regards.

ISIS' doctrine also aims to delegitimize the international system and international actors, notably the United States and Russia. Analogous to al-Qaeda and other militant jihadist organizations, these two powers are seen as natural enemies. The VNSA has gained international notoriety, being the subject of two United Nations Security Council resolutions (UNSC Res. 2249 [2015] and UNSC Res. 2253 [2015]). As a transnational terrorist organization, it presents direct security challenges across borders, most notably to countries with a sizeable Muslim population or majority, or countries of symbolic importance, such as the United States. It aims to take advantage of civil wars, failed states, and ungoverned spaces to seize territory and establish branches of the caliphate, as is the case in Libya, Egypt, Yemen, and Afghanistan. Moreover, it serves as a radicalization challenge, drawing more individuals to its ranks or ideology and inspiring "lone-wolf" attacks in the absence of any organic links between the perpetrator and ISIS cells. ISIS has managed to attract foreign fighters of an unprecedented variety—over 30,000 recruits from at least 85 countries poured into Syria and Iraq by 2015, most of which joined ISIS (Benmelech and Klor 2016)—and the eventual return of these FTFs is a source of concern for states. For Muslim majority states, especially secular ones, ISIS also presents an ideological challenge. In many ways, the challenges ISIS presents across the globe are novel and hard to predict.

2.1.2 Democratic Union Party (PYD) and People's Protection Units (YPG)

One of the biggest challenges that ISIS continues to face on the Syrian battlefield has come from the PYD and its affiliated military forces, People's Protection Units (YPG), and YPG-dominated Syrian Democratic Forces (SDF). The VNSA was founded in 2003 as an offshoot of the PKK, a left-wing terrorist organization that has led an insurgency against the Turkish state for almost four decades. The two organizations exist as part of a network of Kurdish political and militant non-state actors across Turkey, Iran, Iraq, and Syria, which follow the ideology of Abdullah Öcalan, the imprisoned leader of the PKK. While this ideology and associated militant and terrorist organizations have existed since 1974, no part of this movement has ever been as prominent as the PYD/YPG and managed to establish control over and govern territory (Drott 2014).

In 2012, PYD/YPG took over Kurdish majority areas in Syria after government forces withdrew, and gradually expanded its territorial control throughout the civil war clashing with other VNSAs, including ISIS. Over time, the organization managed to amass territories beyond traditionally Kurdish inhabited areas, coexist with Syrian regime forces, receive the support of Russia and the United States, and strengthen its bid to gain international recognition and autonomy.

PYD/YPG began to gain acknowledgment when it assisted Iraqi Kurdish Peshmerga forces and PKK forces in defending Yazidis based in Iraq facing genocide and enslavement at the hands of ISIS in August 2014 (Reuter 2014) (Tharoor 2014). The VNSA later came under the international spotlight during its defense of Kobanî/Ayn al-Arab against ISIS beginning in September 2014 (O'Driscoll 2015). In time, it would assert itself as the primary ground force fighting against ISIS. Compared with other VNSAs operating in Syria, the PYD/YPG managed to gain a uniquely positive image in international media—positive representations of PYD/YPG such as praising female PYD/YPG fighters fighting against ISIS have continued to surface in international media outlets (for some examples, see The Independent 2017; Huffington Post 2016; Sputnik News 2015).

In a similar fashion to ISIS, PYD/YPG has also been interested in expanding its territorial control. Indeed, territorial control is among the means of rating the "success" of a VNSA (DCAF and Geneva Call 2015), but the PYD/YPG has had a rather more contained set of goals compared to the almost cancerous growth patterns of ISIS. From a political standpoint, the PYD/YPG's primary aim is to ensure autonomy through becoming the primary actor providing security and governance in its areas of control and ensuring international and local legitimacy. As such, from a territorial standpoint, PYD/YPG's primary aim has been to link its three self-declared autonomous territories and create a contiguous territorial presence to strengthen its bid for autonomy (Wahab 2016). To this end, in March 2016, the PYD/YPG declared an autonomous federation that remains unrecognized. More recently, the PYD/YPG has also shown an interest in reaching the Mediterranean Sea to ensure sustainability and access to the outside world (The Guardian 2017). Initially, the PYD/YPG was reluctant to expand beyond its core territory but later capitalized on the opportunity of being the main coalition partner with the United States on the ground and now leads the incursion into the ISIS stronghold Raqqa.

In the context of VNSAs, provision of services, security, and justice usually come as a means of justifying their authority (Idler and Forest 2015). As far as service provision goes, the PYD/YPG has been exemplary due to its institutional preparedness through the umbrella of the pro-Öcalan Kurdish movement. Not only has PYD/YPG quickly created service provision mechanisms, but in some areas under joint PYD/YPG and Syrian regime presence, the sides have even established complementary and sometimes contradictory governance mechanisms—while in some areas there reportedly is a division of labor in service provision, there are also accounts of double taxation and parallel justice mechanisms (Khalaf 2016). Akin to ISIS, PYD/YPG has also devoted significant effort and attention into providing security and services in the territories that it controls. On the former point, the

PYD/YPG has presented itself as the protector of the local populace from ISIS. Furthermore, its nonaggression pact with the Syrian regime, and ability to leverage a partnership with the United States and Russia, has ensured that there is more stability in PYD/YPG-held areas than almost every other territory embroiled in the civil war. To back this point, Khalaf (2016) notes that the approval for PYD/YPG and its internal security apparatus is higher in areas under PYD/YPG control that witness a specific security threat and lower in areas that are further away from the line of conflict.

Like other ideologically inclined VNSAs, the PYD/YPG also perpetuates its ideology in territories under its control. While the PYD/YPG has certainly been less coercive compared to ISIS, there have been accusations that PYD/YPG violated human rights and international norms on a number of occasions. According to one such allegation, the PYD/YPG has conducted ethnic cleansing of Arabs in order to change demographics in favor of ethnic Kurds (Pollock 2016). Other reports suggest that it has harassed political opposition groups (Congressional Research Service 2016), that it recruits child soldiers, and that it indoctrinates children through schools (Human Rights Watch 2014).

While such allegations continue to be a liability for the PYD/YPG and its international partners, the VNSA uses its ability to provide security and services as sources of legitimization internally, while it relies on a comprehensive diplomacy and image management campaign externally. The PYD has opened diplomatic offices across Europe, including in Germany, Russia, and Sweden, and has met with US representatives on a number of occasions. Furthermore, it adopts a discourse tailored to appeal to different audiences; arguing its governance is "a revolution anchored on women's rights, democracy, pluralism, diversity, economic justice and even environmental sustainability" (Khalaf 2016, s. 22). The PYD/YPG also presents itself as the most viable alternative to the authoritarian Syrian regime that is responsible for countless atrocities and a fragmented opposition that is mostly dominated by Islamist groups.

Most importantly, the PYD/YPG presents itself as the bulwark against ISIS. Neither the PYD/YPG nor ISIS is evaluated solely by their political and military characteristics—identity-/norm-based perceptions of the two VNSAs are also significant in determining the international approach toward them. ISIS has been a cause to rally against for the international community, inspiring election campaigns throughout Europe and the United States. World leaders and international media have attributed mainly negative characteristics for the VNSA, such as "evil" and "barbaric" (see, e.g., remarks by former President Barack Obama at Obama White House Archives 2014; and Russian Foreign Minister Sergei Lavrov RT 2015a, b). Hence, the PYD/YPG has also built a positive image by portraying itself as the opposite of what ISIS stands for.

Against its strength as a VNSA, its embroilment in some human rights abuses, and its ties to the PKK, the PYD/YPG is not perceived as a direct threat by most actors engaged in the Syrian civil war—Turkey being the biggest exception. This is due to the fact that the PYD/YPG has limited and territorially bound ambitions compared to ISIS which aims to spread globally. In contrast to ISIS' brutality and cataclysmic nature that aims to beset and undermine not just states but also the values that the international system is based upon, the PYD/YPG strives to carve itself a space within the "establishment" and gain international recognition (for further discussion, see Kayhan Pusane 2017); and for many observers, its human rights violations pale in comparison to many actors engaged in the Syrian civil war. Furthermore, its effectiveness as a VNSA, willingness to prioritize fighting against ISIS, openness to cooperating with international actors, and amiable relationship with the Syrian regime have made the PYD/YPG an appealing partner for numerous external actors—most notably the United States and Russia. In this context, it is not surprising that while governments and international media perceive threats from "radicalized" foreign fighters that join ISIS, foreign fighters that join PYD/YPG ranks are largely viewed as "volunteers" and are not perceived, at least openly, as threats (for an example, see PBS Newshour 2015; for a discussion on the "spectrum of private violence," see Percy 2003).

3 Historical Background of the Relations Between Violent Non-state Actors and the Two Global Actors (Russian Federation and the United States)

Though perhaps the most daunting aspect of competition between the Soviet Union and the United States was in the realm of nuclear weapons, the two actors have also relied on non-state actors as a means of furthering their foreign policy goals. The Cold War has witnessed both actors supporting (or fighting against) primarily ideologically driven VNSAs—right-wing in the case of the United States and left-wing groups for the USSR—as a means of pushing for regime change (or preserving it) throughout Latin America, Africa, Asia, and the Middle East. For the most part, pragmatism guided the two global powers, and their primary motivation for relying on VNSAs was counteracting the other's influence globally without directly becoming a party to open conflict. In some cases, such as the US support to Afghan mujahideen, or the Iran–Contra affair,[1] such use of VNSAs has even ended up harming the interests of the two superpowers instead of bolstering them (Myre 2014).

After the Cold War, while Russia receded from the power struggle for over a decade, the United States continued to engage with VNSAs as a means of furthering its interests. The breakup of Yugoslavia, which became a source of contention among Russia and the United States, was one such example of US engagement. The

[1]The Afghan mujahideen which the United States supported to undermine the USSR's invasion in Afghanistan in 1980–1988 ended up forming the backbone of the al-Qaeda and the global jihadist movement. Meanwhile, the Iran-Contra affair refers to the clandestine sale of US weapons to Iran (which was illegal according to US law) to secure the release of American hostages held by Hezbollah, the proceeds of which were then funneled to Nicaragua to support the Contra rebels.

US engagement with VNSAs intensified after 9/11 when Washington declared a "Global War on Terror" and targeted jihadist VNSAs and their affiliates across Asia, Africa, and the Middle East. In Iraq, the United States also engaged with VNSAs as part of its military strategy, both to limit its commitment and to avoid self-defeating military action. Washington's cooperation with Iraqi Kurdish Peshmerga forces, which eventually formed the backbone of the Kurdish Regional Government, and with different Sunni tribes and militias in what became the Sunni Awakening are two examples of such interactions (Petraeus 2013). Washington's interaction with VNSAs, especially after 9/11, has primarily been driven with broadly defined national security interests in mind and with a pragmatic mindset that prioritizes achieving US core interests in the short term. In this regard, it can be argued that after the Cold War, and especially after 9/11, Washington's interactions with VNSAs have been pragmatic, context driven, and less characterized by ideological outlook.

In turn, after the Cold War, the newly founded Russian Federation primarily clashed with VNSAs that it perceived as direct national security threats—most notably with Chechen rebels on two occasions. Moscow also colluded with VNSAs in breakaway regions in response to the dissolution of the USSR, such as the case of Moldova and Transnistria. Moscow's interaction with VNSAs intensified after the second half of the 2000s, coinciding with a strengthening Russian economy and increasing Russian assertiveness on the international stage and its military modernization and doctrine shift. Akin to its involvements with VNSAs during the dissolution of the Soviet Union, Russia once again engaged with VNSAs in its hinterland, utilizing ethnic, linguistic, and ideological ties, or simply seized the opportunity to back separatist movements to increase its regional standing at the expense of former Soviet countries. In 2008, Russia warred with Georgia in favor of separatist groups in Abkhazia and South Ossetia. Later, in 2014, Russia intervened in Ukraine, annexing Crimea and engaging in a prolonged campaign in Eastern Ukraine. Indeed, the so-called little green men (Reeves and Wallace 2015) played a central role in assisting local rebel groups and appeared to reflect Russia's new "hybrid" understanding of warfare (Chivvis 2017), commonly referred to as the Gerasimov doctrine after the Russian General Chief of Staff Valery Gerasimov. Therefore, the majority of Russia's interactions with VNSAs after the Cold War focused on those within its perceived hinterland, utilizing ethnic and nationalistic ties.

3.1 The Russian Federation and Its Interaction with VNSAs in Syria

3.1.1 Russian Motives, Goals, and Interests in Syria

Russia's engagement in Syria presents a rather new phenomenon, marking Russia's first significant military presence in the Middle East since it was expelled from

Egypt in 1972 (Hannah 2016) and its first military operation beyond its immediate neighborhood since the end of the Cold War (Khlebnikov 2016). While Russia was engaged in the Syrian civil war since its beginning, closely supporting the Assad regime, its direct intervention only came in late 2015 and altered the rules of the game for everyone involved.

In his address at the United Nations General Assembly in September 2015, shortly after the Russian intervention in Syria began, Russian President Vladimir Putin argued that the intervention was aimed at defeating ISIS and other terrorist organizations and called for a joint front similar to the "anti-Hitler coalition" (The Washington Post 2015). Indeed, Russia justified its support to the Syrian regime on similar grounds, arguing that the Syrian army is the "most effective and powerful ground force to fight Islamic State" (RT 2015a, b).

Yet this was just one of the rationales for Russia's intervention in Syria. Briefly put, Russian intervention aimed to ensure that the Assad government or any government that would be amenable to Moscow survived, whether in the form of a unitary state covering the entire Syrian territory or as a microstate encompassing Russian military bases, notably Tartus naval base and Khmeimim air base (Kasapoglu and Ergun 2015). Especially through its air defenses, Russia ensured that external actors, notably the United States and Turkey, could not impose military eventualities in Syria. Russia significantly improved its military and naval bases in Syria, gaining a long-term foothold in the region. In the diplomatic stage, Moscow also wanted to break its Western-imposed isolation after the annexation of Crimea by forcing the US-led coalition to communicate, if not cooperate, with Russia while also challenging NATO's freedom of movement in Syria in particular and in the Middle East in general. In sum, Russia aimed to achieve a favorable outcome to the Syrian civil war, gain a military foothold in the Eastern Mediterranean, and establish itself as a military and political player in the Middle East as an alternative to NATO and the United States. Furthermore, as a by-product, Russia's involvement also allowed it to display its power projection capabilities and to test its military equipment and capabilities. Some analysts argue that this allowed Russia to advertise its weapon systems and as such, Russian weapon exports may receive an increase of up to $7 billion due to this "marketing effect" (Khlebnikov 2016).

3.1.2 Russia's Approach Toward ISIS

Conversely, it is true that Moscow perceives and may genuinely face threats from ISIS, perhaps much more so than the United States. Russia is among the top three "exporters" of fighters to ISIS and other jihadist groups in Syria and Iraq. For example, by the end of 2015, around 2400 Russian nationals had traveled to Syria and Iraq, mostly to join ISIS (The Soufan Group 2015). Russia is specifically sensitive about the Chechen/Dagestan connection. Moderate and secular elements of Chechen and, in broader terms, North Caucasian opposition to Moscow have gradually eroded, and Salafi jihadist ideologies have increasingly characterized the opposition in the region (Souleimanov and Petrtylova 2015). While the outflow of jihadists from the region into Syria and Iraq may have alleviated Russia's internal threat perceptions, the prospect for their return is a source of concern. This is especially true given that Chechens present a significant bloc within ISIS, as exemplified by Tarkhan Batirashvili or in his nom de guerre Abu Omar al-Shishani, who served as the "Commander of the North" before he was killed in a US airstrike in 2016 (McFate 2015).

Meanwhile, Moscow also sees the rise of radicalization in Central Asia as a threat to both its national security and the stability of its neighborhood. Official Russian estimates put the amount of people that joined ISIS and other jihadist organizations from former Soviet countries between 5000 and 7000 (Bremmer 2017). This statistic becomes even starker, given that Central Asian recruits have risen to prominent positions in a number of jihadist organizations, including ISIS, and several terror attacks across Europe (including the İstanbul New Year's Eve shooting, Stockholm attacks in April 2017, and St. Petersburg attack in April 2017) had Central Asian perpetrators in common.

Yet against the declared Russian rationale for its Syrian intervention, the reality of Russia's involvement has painted a different picture. In the first month after the Russian intervention, the vast majority of Russian airstrikes focused on rebel groups that posed a threat to the Syrian regime instead of ISIS (Business Insider 2015). This trend has continued for the majority of Russia's intervention (see the Institute for the Study of War's monthly reports on Russian airstrikes and Mautner 2017). Indeed, Russian military assets in Syria include advanced air defense systems, ballistic missile systems, interceptor aircraft, and naval assets, none of which have a use in counterinsurgency and counterterrorism operations (Casagrande and Weinberger 2017).

In a nutshell, combating ISIS has only been one of the many objectives that Russia had in Syria, and ISIS has served as the means for Russia to legitimize its intervention in Syria in the eyes of the international community. It is worth noting that a similar justification was used by Moscow after 9/11 in its counterterrorism operations in Chechnya, linking its efforts to the Global War on Terror (Notte 2015).

3.1.3 Russian Approach Toward the PYD/YPG

Russia's interaction with the Kurds is not a new phenomenon, as Moscow has continued to maintain relations with different factions of the ethnic group throughout Tsarist, Soviet, and post-Soviet times (Borshchevskaya 2016). With the PKK specifically, Russia has been engaged with varying degrees since the organization was founded in the 1970s (Stratfor 2015). A Marxist–Leninist organization, the PKK received overwhelming support from Syria, a staunch Soviet ally, and its leader Abdullah Öcalan was hosted in Syria until Turkey mobilized and threatened military action in 1998. After he was expelled from Syria, the Russian Duma granted him refuge, and Öcalan briefly resided in Odintsovo, Moscow (Milliyet

Daily 1998). While Öcalan was expelled from Moscow and eventually captured by Turkish authorities in Kenya in 1999, the PKK was allowed to retain a political office in Russia. Moscow still is one of the few capitals that does not recognize the PKK as a terrorist organization.

Thus, Russia had the ground to engage with the PYD/YPG. In addition to its previous interactions with the Kurds in the region, the PYD already had amicable relations with Moscow's ally Damascus. In 2013, PYD leader Salih Muslim visited Moscow upon the invitation of the Russian defense ministry, after which he argued that the PYD should be a part of international negotiations for the future of Syria. This call was repeated on a number of occasions by Russian authorities as well, who suggested including PYD representatives into both the Geneva process and, later, Astana talks.[2] Again in 2013, Russia began issuing visas to PYD leaders, after the US' refusal to do so (Borshchevskaya 2016). In his speech at the United Nations General Assembly on September 2015, President Putin also elevated the PYD/YPG's and the Syrian regime's image, by openly saying that, to the dismay of Turkish authorities, "we should finally acknowledge that no one but President Assad's armed forces and Kurdish militias are truly fighting the Islamic State and other terrorist organizations in Syria" (The Washington Post 2015).

Beyond its amiable relations with the Syrian regime and its role in fighting against ISIS, the PYD/YPG also presented Moscow with a foreign policy tool to pressure its "frenemy" Ankara. For one, Russia has engaged with pro-Kurdish political opposition in Turkey, hosting Selahattin Demirtaş, the coleader of the Peoples' Democratic Party along with Salih Muslim in December 2014. The second visit of Demirtaş to Moscow came shortly after Turkey downed a Russian warplane for violating Turkish airspace in November 2015, where the opposition figure criticized Ankara's position. Russia expedited its partnership with the PYD/YPG after the downing—and the PYD opened its first representative office in Europe in Moscow in February 2016 (Borshchevskaya 2016). Russia also provided air support to the PYD/YPG in its campaign against Turkey-backed rebel forces (Tabler and Cagaptay 2016). Although Ankara eventually mended its ties with Russia, this rapprochement did not prevent Russia from stationing its advisors and troops in support of the PYD/YPG against a Turkish military advance. Images of the Russian flag waving on top of flag posts across from the Turkish border in PYD/YPG-held territories are noteworthy with respect to understanding the diverging interests between the two countries. Should relations with Turkey sour again in the future, Russia can utilize its ties with the PYD/YPG and the PKK to support them in a diplomatic or potentially military capacity (Delanoe 2016).

[2]The Geneva process refers to United Nations-backed negotiations that began in 2012 with the aim of finding a peaceful resolution to the Syrian civil war and discuss the conditions for a transition government. The Astana talks refers to a process initiated by Russia and Turkey in 2015, later joined by Iran, that brings members of the opposition and the regime together in order to negotiate conditions for a ceasefire. Against Russian insistence, PYD representatives were excluded from both processes, mostly due to the resistance of Ankara.

Additionally, it should be noted that the PYD/YPG has strengthened its bid to become an autonomous actor in the Syrian context, akin to the Kurdish Regional Government in Iraq, with which Russia also enjoys warm ties. By maintaining its influence over the PYD/YPG, Russia ensures that the VNSA does not stray too far from Russian interests and fall into the US' sphere of influence. Therefore, beyond its utilities as a VNSA that can coexist with Russian allies and interests, fight ISIS, stabilize the areas under its control, and provide a tool to pressure the Turkish government, the PYD/YPG is emerging as a potential actor for Russia to engage with. To this end, Russia has even floated the idea of granting the PYD/YPG some level of autonomy in its draft constitution for Syria presented in early 2017 (Al-Monitor 2017), which was rejected both by the Syrian regime and the opposition. In this regard, the PYD/YPG is also a tool for Moscow to pressure Damascus. Yet Moscow is not fully committed to the PYD/YPG's bid for autonomy, nor is it vested too much into the cause of the VNSA. As such, the depth of Russia's future interaction with the VNSA will continue to depend on its utility for Moscow.

3.2 *The United States and Its Interaction with VNSAs in Syria*

3.2.1 Style and Substance of US Policies Toward Syria

Although the US government took a stance against the Assad government in the earlier stages of the Syrian civil war, its military support for VNSAs to shape the outcome of the war would begin in 2013. According to a report by the US Congressional Research Service, the United States began providing nonlethal assistance to opposition groups in 2012 and initiated covert weapon transfers to VNSAs beginning in June 2013 (Humud et al. 2017). According to the same report, the United States initiated its train and equip programs in 2014, spending around $1.25 billion up to May 2017, with an additional $430 million requested for 2017 and $500 million requested for 2018. Seeing that its initial train and equip program, which rested mainly on vetting and training local forces from scratch, produced very limited results, Washington switched to vetting and supporting existing forces on the Syrian battlefield in the second half of 2015. The two primary donors of this assistance have been the SDF/PYD/YPG and the New Syrian Army (NSA) operating in southeastern Syria along the Jordanian border.

Though the US position has been for Syrian President Bashar al-Assad to abdicate his seat since the outset of the war, Washington never took sufficient action to depose him of the leadership. The recent precedents of the US-led interventions against Saddam Hussein in 2003 and Muammar Gaddafi in 2011 as well as the chaos that ensued after their deposition compelled the Obama administration to have a lighter footprint in Syria. Hence, even though Washington drew multiple redlines, including the one against the use of chemical weapons, it took very limited coercive action to punish the Syrian regime for violating them. This would only come later with the Trump administration, which retaliated to a chemical attack conducted in April 2017 by striking a Syrian airfield. One month later, US forces targeted pro-Syrian regime forces in southeastern Syria in response to their maneuvers near the NSA and US forces.

Indeed, throughout the civil war, Washington's priority would not be to support VNSAs that fought against the Syrian regime (Clawson 2016). This was one of the pitfalls of the initial train and equip program, as Washington was challenged with finding VNSAs that would refrain from fighting against the Syrian regime (Welch and Bailey 2016). After the Russian intervention in 2015, Washington's position on the future of the Syrian regime wavered even more. Since then, Washington has continued to focus on its ultimate priority—defeating ISIS in Syria and Iraq—and played a more direct role in this endeavor while keeping its engagement in Syria limited.

3.2.2 US Approach Toward ISIS

Shortly after rebranding itself as the Islamic State of Iraq and al-Sham, the VNSA began targeting government forces and other rebel groups, notably other jihadist ones, in August 2013. In less than a year, by June 2014, ISIS captured major towns, including Fallujah, Ramada, Tikrit, and Mosul in Iraq and Raqqa and Deir ez-Zor in Syria, stunning all spectators (Glenn 2016). On June 18, 2014, the Iraqi government formally asked the United States to conduct airstrikes against ISIS, but it would not be until ISIS began conducting genocide against Yazidis in Kurdish-dominated areas of Iraq in August 2014 that the United States stepped up its support. Shortly after, ISIS retaliated by beheading American journalists James Foley and Steven Sotloff and British aid worker David Haines, shocking the international community. In September 2014, the United States expanded its airstrikes into Syria, notably to support the PYD/YPG in its defense of Kobanî against ISIS.

Yet, Washington's perception of ISIS goes beyond 2014. For one, ISIS is rooted in a global jihadist movement that conducted 9/11 and is a natural part of the Global War on Terror. More directly, the United States engaged with ISIS and its previous forms and manifestations throughout its campaign in Iraq that began in 2003. The VNSA proved its resilience by surviving the US Surge and Sunni Awakening, and its ability to regain its capabilities once a window of opportunity is presented makes it more menacing and more acute of a threat for the United States to address.

Furthermore, ISIS has moved beyond al-Qaeda by emerging as an alternative brand to the network. Yet in this competition for shepherding jihadist movements transnationally, ISIS did not simply "split the pie" with al-Qaeda; on the contrary, it expanded it further. The threat that ISIS poses and the ensuing US concern now extend from Manila and Canberra in the east to homegrown/lone-wolf terror attacks in the United States to the west and to pockets of conflict throughout the Middle East, Africa, and Asia, including in areas of US engagement such as Libya, Yemen, Afghanistan, and Somalia. While the backbone of this network was formed by existing jihadist VNSAs that merely pledged allegiance to ISIS, ISIS breathed life into many others and established new transnational links. Furthermore, ISIS has inspired thousands across the globe to join its cause more effectively than any other jihadist VNSA in Syria. The majority that was radicalized but has not joined its cause may serve to spread its ideology, provide funds and logistical assistance, and present a pool of recruits for ISIS or any future jihadist organization.

In this regard, countering ISIS has become the primary goal for the US involvement in Syria and Iraq. The most profound effect of Washington's counter-ISIS policy has been in Iraq, where the US' military assistance has supported the government forces' efforts to take back areas of strategic importance such as Mosul. Washington was also among those that pressured former Iraqi Prime Minister Nouri al-Maliki, who was seen as part of the problem due to his policies that antagonized Sunnis, to resign in 2014 (The Wall Street Journal 2014). In Syria, however, defeating ISIS trumped Washington's other objectives, some of which were eroding the Syrian regime, curbing Iran's rising outreach and Russia's increasing influence, preventing the use of WMD in the civil war context, and limiting spillovers. To this end, Washington adopted multifaceted and even sometimes contradictory policies in Syria, as will be expanded below. ISIS also had a profound influence on the US elections in 2016 and played a central role in President Donald Trump's campaign.

3.2.3 US Approach Toward the PYD/YPG

Looking for able partners to counter the rising ISIS threat and wary of deploying ground troops, the Obama administration eventually turned to the PYD/YPG, reminding spectators of its decision to collaborate with the Iraqi Kurds in the 2003 Iraq War. The US engagement with the PYD/YPG began in August 2014 amidst a mounting ISIS campaign on the PYD-held Kobanî. US airstrikes to assist PYD/YPG against ISIS elements that besieged the town began in September 2014 and gradually intensified until ISIS was pushed back in January 2015—which marked the first major defeat of ISIS on the battlefield (Lund, 2016). Over time, US-led coalition airstrikes would increasingly assist the PYD/YPG's advances, near al-Hasakah, Sarrin, and al-Haul (see Clawson 2016 for a detailed geographic distribution). Clawson further argues that it is likely that forward air controllers—covert operatives or members of US or coalition special forces—were based on the ground to assist the close air support at that time.

The relationship between the PYD/YPG and the United States intensified after October 2015 with the establishment of the Syrian Democratic Forces (SDF). The SDF was created through the combination of Kurdish YPG forces with Sunni Arab and Syriac Christian elements, with the aim of avoiding resentment from Arab populations in future operations against ISIS in largely Sunni Arab areas. Furthermore, it was also a way of diluting domestic and international concerns over the ethnic cleansing that YPG elements earlier engaged in and legitimizing future operations. Yet, this was nothing more than a rebranding, and the PYD/YPG has continued to have significant influence over the SDF. Most Arab elements that made up the SDF were either "long-standing PKK allies or proxies ... or more recent allies drawn from the Sunni Arab tribal landscape" (Lund 2016). Initially, Arab elements constituted less than 20% of the SDF (Pollock 2016), and according to official US sources, while this ratio may currently be more even, "YPG continues to play a leading role in SDF operations" (Humud et al. 2017, p. 13).

Nonetheless, shortly after the SDF was established, the United States began openly providing equipment, training, and military advisors to them. In addition to being one of the primary parties to the revamped train and equip program, the SDF also received assistance from US Special Forces, trainers, advisers, and explosive ordinance disposal personnel, currently amounting to 500–700 personnel according to official numbers and estimates (Humud et al. 2017). The arms that the SDF received allegedly included advanced weaponry such as FGM-148 Javelin antitank systems—one of the most capable man-portable antitank systems currently in use (Conflict News 2016).

In addition to materiel support, US public figures also met with members of SDF/PYD on a number of occasions and openly displayed their support for the VNSA. In 2016 alone, Brett McGurk, Special Envoy for the anti-ISIS coalition, made two visits in January and September, while US Central Command Commander General Joseph Votel visited the SDF in May (Clawson 2016). Therefore, in addition to military assistance, the United States also engaged with the YPG/PYD/SDF politically, to the dismay of the Turkish leadership which sees such moves as emboldening the PKK which it equates with the PYD/YPG. Indeed, Ankara conducted its own military intervention in Syria not only to purge ISIS from its borders but also to prevent the PYD from establishing a territorial link between its de facto territories and strengthening its bid for autonomy.

Yet against publicly expressed Turkish concerns, a year later, the United States stationed its forces across from the Turkish border to support the SDF/YPG and deter Turkish operations against the group. Indeed, at the time, US forces in Manbij were so close to Russian forces that they could "visually observe one another's movements" (Humud et al. 2017, s. 16), necessitating an increased use of deconfliction channels. On May 2017, President Trump approved overtly supplying weapons to Kurdish elements within the SDF for the first time to assist capturing Raqqa from ISIS. Worried that the weapons would be transferred to the PKK and would eventually be used against Turkey or limit Turkey's capacity to conduct counterterrorism operations, the Turkish leadership dreaded this decision (Reuters 2017).

Discussing the effects of Washington's support for the PYD in its relations with Turkey is beyond the scope of this paper (see Parlar Dal 2017). Still, it should be noted that even if Washington was more lenient to Turkish interests, it had little, if any, tangible alternatives to supporting the YPG/SDF forces. Looking for a local partner to bear the brunt of the ground operations in Syria, the United States partnered with the PYD/YPG. Yet over time, Washington's strategy has become dependent on the PYD/YPG. As a result, although its partnership with the PYD/YPG proved militarily beneficial for the United States, it also became a liability for Washington (for further discussion, see Sarı Ertem 2017), plaguing its relations with its ally Turkey. When coupled with Russia's inclusion into the Kurdish equation, this dependency has also hampered the US' ability to influence future decisions and actions of the PYD/YPG. These dependency and constrained influence are likely to persist as Washington lacks alternative actors on the ground. This dependency was highlighted recently when Washington downed a Syrian Air Force warplane for its strikes against SDF forces and risked a confrontation with the Syrian regime.

4 In Lieu of Conclusion: Comparing the US and Russian Stances Toward ISIS and PYD/YPG

Non-state actors, especially violent ones, are increasingly becoming more significant in the global stage. ISIS and PYD/YPG present two unique examples to this trend. While both strive for "statehood" in the general sense, ISIS has attempted to achieve this by presenting an antithesis to nation states and international borders. It succeeded in acquiring large swaths of territory in both Iraq and Syria, established itself in a number of countries, and inspired many followers and VNSAs across the globe. It also made enemies out of both Russia and the United States, making the Russian analogy for an anti-Hitler coalition possible, through the methods it used and the threat it poses to the international order. Contrariwise, the PYD/YPG has vied for its goal by seeking international legitimacy and recognition and has presented itself as an antithesis to ISIS, both in its military capabilities and in the image that it portrays to the international community. In doing so, it has managed to cooperate with both Russia and the United States—a very rare and perhaps transient privilege.

Yet the way in which Russia and the United States have viewed and interacted with ISIS and PYD/YPG has been different from one another. For the United States, fighting ISIS is grounded in recent history, both as part of its Global War on Terror and in its counterinsurgency and counterterrorism operations in Iraq, the base for ISIS' roots. Even though the United States has been involved in the Syrian civil war with a very limited capacity, ISIS' entry to the stage became a game changer for both Syria and Iraq. It was ISIS that compelled Washington to take military action in Syria. Defeating ISIS quickly became the primary security interest and foreign policy goal of Washington, dwarfing all other priorities. ISIS even shaped domestic politics in the United States and became the centerpiece of the Trump campaign especially after a number of ISIS-linked attacks targeted the country, notably the Orlando nightclub attack in June 2016.

Wary of a direct intervention after the Iraq War and the aftermath of the deposition of Gaddafi in Libya, Washington sought capable partners to take the brunt of fighting ISIS on the ground. It quickly turned to the PYD/YPG, reminding spectators of its decision to collaborate with Iraqi Kurds merely a decade ago. In addition to conducting airstrikes against ISIS to alleviate PYD/YPG/SDF operations, the United States also assisted the VNSA by providing extensive training and weapons and by deploying several hundreds of US military advisors and Special Forces elements to aid its operations. Furthermore, US officials have openly praised the PYD/YPG and sent a number of diplomatic representations to the VNSA. Although the PYD/YPG has been a notable asset for the United States, over time the US strategy against ISIS in Syria became so dependent on PYD/YPG that the VNSA also became a liability, plaguing Washington's relations with its ally Ankara and exposing the United States to allegations of abetting the PYD/YPG's violations of international norms. Furthermore, the dependency of US' Syria strategy on PYD/YPG constrains the United States' ability to influence the future actions of the VNSA. This dependency is likely to continue in the near term, as it is unclear (and unlikely) whether the United States will be able to forge bilateral relations with Arab elements of the SDF outside the auspices of PYD/YPG. Furthermore, recent maneuvers of the Syrian regime in southeastern Syria have shown that Damascus is attempting to impede the access of US-backed forces deeper into Syrian territory, limiting the prospect for Washington to substitute its relationship with the PYD/YPG with its VNSA partners elsewhere in Syria.

While Moscow certainly has reason to perceive threats from ISIS, especially given that it is one of the top countries of origin of foreign fighters among ISIS ranks, countering the VNSA has not been Moscow's primary motivation for intervening in Syria. This is exemplified by Russian military activity in Syria, the bulk of which has targeted rebel groups that posed a direct threat to the survival of the Syrian regime. Russia has a number of goals in Syria, including, but not limited to, ensuring the permanence of the Assad regime or any other pro-Russian entity in Syria, increasing its military and political presence in the Middle East as an alternative to the United States, and impeding US/NATO's freedom of movement in Syria and Syrian airspace. Combating ISIS has only been one of these goals. Overall, for Moscow, combating ISIS has been the "means" for justifying its intervention in Syria and obtaining US' acquiescence to accomplish a broad range of Russian political/military objectives.

In this context, what made the PYD/YPG attractive to Moscow was its ability to cooperate and coexist with the Assad regime. To give a concrete example, in February 2016, Russia provided air support to PYD/YPG operations launched from Afrin against rebel groups around Aleppo, which complemented regime efforts to cut the rebels' access to their lifeline in the Turkish border, and expedited the regime's offensive to retake Aleppo (Tabler and Cagaptay 2016). Through maintaining ties with the PYD/YPG, Moscow has also prevented the VNSA from becoming too dependent on the United States and falling into its sphere of influence. Furthermore, its links with the PYD/YPG have been a tool for Moscow to put pressure on both Ankara and Damascus. Yet Russia has not invested in its relations with the PYD/YPG as much as the United States has and hence does not have codependency with the VNSA. Moreover, while the PYD/YPG has benefitted from the United States the most in terms of military assistance, Russia may hold the key to its political goals, such as autonomy and access to the Mediterranean, by having access to most parties involved in the Syrian civil war, most notably the Syrian regime. Therefore, Moscow is in a much better position to leverage its partnership with the PYD/YPG compared to the United States, and its interaction with the VNSA has not come at the expense of its other foreign policy and security interests. Against its lighter footprint, Moscow's relations with the VNSA have more facets compared to the US-PYD/YPG relationship, which rests on countering ISIS. As such, compared to Washington, Moscow remains more flexible when it comes to the PYD/YPG and ISIS. Yet, as Moscow has other priorities, most notably those pertaining to the survival of the regime, it may be a matter of time before these many priorities become contradictory (such as the unity of the Syrian state and the autonomy requests of the PYD), forcing the capital to make uneasy decisions.

This manuscript has provided a comparison of how the United States and Russia view and interact with the PYD/YPG and ISIS. On the surface, the two capitals that had polar opposite takes on VNSAs throughout the Cold War have finally found something to agree upon—that ISIS is the enemy and PYD/YPG is a partner. Nonetheless, scratching that surface reveals significant differences on how the two countries perceive and engage with the two VNSAs. The author argues that the main difference in the engagement of the two countries with the VNSAs stems from the difference of their broader agenda vis-à-vis the Syrian civil war. The different priorities and mindsets of the two capitals have shaped the extent to which they were influenced by the VNSAs in turn. This interaction will continue to shape their policy in Syria and may even be a source of contention among the two states.

References

Al Monitor. (2017, January 29). Why did Russia offer autonomy for Syria's Kurds? *Al Monitor*. Retrieved from http://www.al-monitor.com/pulse/originals/2017/01/russia-offer-kurds-syria-autonomy-turkey-islamic-state.html

BBC. (2014, July 1). ISIS leader calls on Muslims to 'build Islamic state'. *BBC*. Retrieved from www.bbc.com/news/world-middle-east-28116846

Benmelech, E., & Klor, E. F. (2016, April). *What explains the flow of foreign fighters to ISIS?* The Kellogg School of Management, Northwestern University. Retrieved from http://www.kellogg.northwestern.edu/faculty/benmelech/html/BenmelechPapers/ISIS_April_13_2016_Effi_final.pdf

Borshchevskaya, A. (2016, November). Russia, Syrian Kurds, and the Assad regime. In P. Clawson (Ed.), *Syrian Kurds as a U.S. Ally: Cooperation & complications*. Washington, DC: The Washington Institute for Near East Policy.

Bremmer, I. (2017, April 14). The Top 5 countries where ISIS gets its foreign recruits. *Time*. Retrieved from http://time.com/4739488/isis-iraq-syria-tunisia-saudi-arabia-russia/

Business Insider. (2015, October 8). 90% of Russian airstrikes in Syria have not targeted ISIS. *Business Insider*. Retrieved from http://www.businessinsider.com/90-of-russian-airstrikes-have-not-targeted-isis-2015-10

Casagrande, G., & Weinberger, K. (2017). *Putin's real Syria agenda*. Washington, DC: Institute for the Study of War.

Chivvis, C. S. (2017). *Understanding Russian "hybrid warfare" and what can be done about it*. Santa Monica, CA: Rand Corporation.

Clawson, P. (2016). U.S. policy and the PYD. In P. Clawson (Ed.), *Syrian Kurds as a U.S. Ally: Cooperation & complications* (pp. 52–60). Washington, DC: Washington Institute for Near East Policy.
CNN. (2017, February 13). ISIS goes global: 143 attacks in 29 countries have killed 2043. *CNN*. Retrieved from http://edition.cnn.com/2015/12/17/world/mapping-isis-attacks-around-the-world/index.html
Conflict News. (2016, February 23). US Javelin missiles Seen with YPG in Syria. *Conflict News*. Retrieved from http://www.conflict-news.com/articles/the-us-are-supplying-javelin-anti-tank-missiles-to-the-ypg-in-syria
Congressional Research Service. (2016). *Kurds in Iraq and Syria: U.S. partners against the Islamic state*. Washington, DC: Congressional Research Service.
DCAF, & Geneva Call. (2015). *Armed non-state actors: Current trends & future challenges* (DCAF Horizon 2015 Working Paper No. 5), 1–24.
Delanoe, I. (2016, September 15). *Does Russia still have a "Kurdish card" to play in Syria?* Russian International Affairs Council. Retrieved from http://russiancouncil.ru/en/blogs/igor_delanoe-en/32649/
Dews, F. (2014, May 27). *A glossary of forces in the Syrian civil war*. Brookings. Retrieved from https://www.brookings.edu/blog/brookings-now/2014/05/27/a-glossary-of-forces-in-the-syrian-civil-war/
Drott, C. (2014, May 20). *The Syrian Experiment with "Apoism"*. Carnegie Middle East Center. Retrieved from http://carnegie-mec.org/diwan/55650
Dutka, D. L. (2006, May). *Violent non-state actors in world politics: Their formation, actions, and effects*. Doctoral thesis, The Pennsylvania State University, Pennsylvania.
Early, B. R. (2006). "Larger than a party, yet smaller than a state": Locating Hezbollah's place within Lebanon's state and society. *World Affairs, 168*(3), 115–128.
Geeraerts, G. (1995, October). *Analyzing non-state actors in world politics*. (Vol. 1, No. 5). Pole Paper Series. Vrije Universitiet Brussel. Retrieved from http://poli.vub.ac.be/publi/pole-papers/pole0104.htm
Glenn, C. (2016, July 5). *Timeline: Rise and spread of the Islamic state*. The Woodrow Wilson International Center for Scholars. Retrieved from https://www.wilsoncenter.org/article/timeline-rise-and-spread-the-islamic-state
Hannah, J. (2016, September 13). Russia's Middle East offensive. *Foreign Policy*. Retrieved from http://foreignpolicy.com/2016/09/13/russias-middle-east-offensive/
Hoffman, B. (2017, February 27). The battle against ISIS: The Trump administration's 30-day review. *The Cipher Brief*. Retrieved from https://www.thecipherbrief.com/column/network-take/battle-against-isis-trump-administrations-30-day-review-1089
Huffington Post. (2016, March 9). Meet the brave women fighting ISIS in Syria. *Huffington Post*. Retrieved from http://www.huffingtonpost.com/entry/kurdish-women-fighting-isis_us_56e05e98e4b065e2e3d46569
Human Rights Watch. (2014). *Under Kurdish rule: Abuses in PYD-run enclaves in Syria*. New York, NY: Human Rights Watch.
Humud, C. E., Blanchard, C. M., & Nikitin, M. B. (2017). *Armed conflict in Syria: Overview and U.S. response*. Washington, DC: Congressional Research Service.
Idler, A., & Forest, J. J. (2015). Behavioral patterns among (violent) non-state actors: A study of complementary governance. *Stability: International Journal of Security & Development, 4*, 1–19.
Kasapoglu, C., & Ergun, D. (2015). *Act of desperation or game changer? Russian deployments in Syria*. Istanbul: Centre for Economics and Foreign Policy Studies.
Kayhan Pusane, Ö. (2017). How to profile PYD/YPG as an actor in the Syrian civil war: Policy implications for the region and beyond. In O. Z. Oktav, E. P. Dal, & A. M. Kursun (Eds.), *Violent non state actors and the Syrian civil war: The ISIS and YPG cases*. Springer.
Khalaf, R. (2016). *Governing Rojava: Layers of legitimacy in Syria* (pp. 1–28). London: Chatham House.

Khlebnikov, A. (2016, October 11). *Russia's Syria campaign: Measuring costs and benefits*. Russian International Affairs Council. Retrieved from http://russiancouncil.ru/en/analytics-and-comments/analytics/chto-rossiya-vyigrala-v-sirii/?sphrase_id=174112

Lund, A. (2016, January 22). Origins of the Syrian democratic forces: A primer. *News Deeply: Syria Deeply*. Retrieved from https://www.newsdeeply.com/syria/articles/2016/01/22/origins-of-the-syrian-democratic-forces-a-primer

Malet, D. (2010). Why foreign fighters? Historical perspectives and solutions. *Orbis, 54*, 97–114.

Mautner, J. (2017, April 6). *Russian airstrikes in Syria: March 1–April 3, 2017*. Institute for the Study of War. Retrieved from http://iswresearch.blogspot.com.tr/2017/04/russian-airstrikes-in-syria-march-1.html

McFate, J. L. (2015). *The ISIS defense in Iraq & Syria: Countering an adaptive enemy*. Washington, DC: Institute for the Study of War.

Mehmetçik, H., & Kurşun, A. M. (2017). Making sense of the territorial aspirations of ISIS: Autonomy, representation and influence. In O. Z. Oktav, E. P. Dal, & A. M. Kursun (Eds.), *Violent non state actors and the Syrian civil war: The ISIS and YPG Cases*. Springer.

Milliyet Daily. (1998, November 14). Rusya Apo'yu Neden Barındırmadı? (Why didn't Russia Harbour Apo). *Milliyet Daily*. Retrieved from http://www.milliyet.com.tr/1998/11/14/dunya/dun01.html

Moore, J. (2017, November 4). After Mosul losses, ISIS now controls less than seven percent of Iraq. *Newsweek*. Retrieved from http://www.newsweek.com/mosul-isis-seven-percent-iraq-582160

Myre, G. (2014, September 20). When The U.S. backs rebels, it doesn't often go as planned. *NPR*. Retrieved from http://www.npr.org/sections/parallels/2014/09/20/349549267/when-the-u-s-backs-rebels-it-doesnt-often-go-as-planned

Notte, H. (2015). *Russia in Chechnya and Syria: Pursuit of strategic goals*. Middle East Policy Council. Retrieved from http://www.mepc.org/russia-chechnya-and-syria-pursuit-strategic-goals

O'Driscoll, D. (2015). *The YPG and the changing dynamics of the fight against IS* (pp. 1–6). The Polish Institute of International Affairs.

Obama White House Archives. (2014, September 10). President Obama: "We will degrade and ultimately destroy ISIL". *Obama White House Archives*. Retrieved from https://obamawhitehouse.archives.gov/blog/2014/09/10/president-obama-we-will-degrade-and-ultimately-destroy-isil

Oktav, Ö. Z., Parlar Dal, E., & Kurşun, A. M. (2017). Reframing and reassessing the VNSAs in Syrian conflict: An introduction. In O. Z. Oktav, E. P. Dal, & A. M. Kursun (Eds.), *Violent non state actors and the Syrian civil war: The ISIS and YPG cases*. Springer.

Parlar Dal, E. (2017). The contagion of the Syrian civil war into Turkey under the impact of ISIS and YPG cases: Conditioning factors and diffusion mechanisms. In O. Z. Oktav, E. P. Dal, & A. M. Kursun (Eds.), Violent non state actors and the Syrian civil war: The ISIS and YPG cases. Springer.

PBS Newshour. (2015, July 21). Why some Americans are volunteering to fight the Islamic State. *PBS*. Retrieved from http://www.pbs.org/newshour/bb/americans-volunteering-fight-islamic-state/

Percy, S. V. (2003). This gun's for hire: A new look at an old issue. *International Journal, 58*(4), 721–736.

Petraeus, D. (2013, October 29). How we won in Iraq. *Foreign Policy*. Retrieved from http://foreignpolicy.com/2013/10/29/how-we-won-in-iraq/

Pierman, G. (2015). The grand strategy of nonstate actors: Theory and implications. *Journal of Strategic Security, 8*(4), 69–78.

Pollock, D. (2016). Making Rojava more like KRG. In P. Clawson (Ed.), *Syrian Kurds as a U.S. Ally: Cooperation & complications* (pp. 1–11). Washington, DC: Washington Institute for Near East Policy.

Rabil, R. G. (2014, July 17). The ISIS chronicles: A History. *The National Interest*. Retrieved from http://nationalinterest.org/feature/the-isis-chronicles-history-10895?page=2

Reeves, S. R., & Wallace, D. (2015). The combatant status of the "little green men" and other participants in the Ukraine conflict. *International Law Studies, 91*(361), 360–401.

Reuter, C. (2014, August 18). The drama of Sinjar: Escaping the Islamic state in Iraq. *Spiegel Online*. Retrieved from http://www.spiegel.de/international/world/pkk-assistance-for-yazidis-escaping-the-jihadists-of-the-islamic-state-a-986648.html

Reuters. (2017, May 10). Turkey warns U.S. of blowback from decision to arm Kurdish fighters in Syria. *Reuters*. Retrieved from http://www.reuters.com/article/us-mideast-crisis-usa-turkey-idUSKBN1860SG

RT (2015a, September 17). Int'l anti-ISIS coalition flawed, you can't fight evil with illegal methods – Lavrov. *RT*. Retrieved from https://www.rt.com/news/315740-lavrov-isis-coalition-flawed/

RT (2015b, September 11). Russia backs Syria's fight against ISIS, not Assad's regime – Lavrov. *RT*. Retrieved from https://www.rt.com/news/315040-russia-support-syria-lavrov/

Sarı Ertem, H. (2017). Surrogate warfare in Syria and the pitfalls of diverging US attitudes towards ISIS and PYD/YPG. In O. Z. Oktav, E. P. Dal, & A. M. Kursun (Eds.), Violent non state actors and the Syrian civil war: The ISIS and YPG cases. Springer.

Soltan, G. A. (1997). State building, modernization and political Islam: The search for political community(s) in the Middle East. *Revista CIDOB d'Afers Internacionals, 37*, 29–38.

Souleimanov, E., & Petrtylova, K. (2015). *Russia's policy toward the Islamic state*. Middle East Policy Council. Retrieved from http://mepc.org/russias-policy-toward-islamic-state

Sputnik News. (2015, December 17). Why there are so many women among Kurds fighting Daesh. *Sputnik News*. Retrieved from https://sputniknews.com/middleeast/201512171031870319-kurdish-women/

Stanton, A. L., & Ramsamy, E. (2012). *Cultural sociology of the Middle East, Asia, and Africa: An encyclopedia*. Washington, DC: Sage.

Stratfor. (2015, December 23). *Why a pro-Kurdish Russia infuriates Turkey*. Stratfor. Retrieved from https://www.stratfor.com/geopolitical-diary/why-pro-kurdish-russia-infuriates-turkey

Strauss, B. (2010). Slave wars of Greece and Rome. In V. D. Hanson (Ed.), *Makers of ancient strategy: From the Persian wars to the fall of Rome* (pp. 185–205). Princeton, NJ: Princeton University Press.

Tabler, A. J., & Cagaptay, S. (2016, May 25). *The PKK could Spark Turkish-Russian military escalation*. The Washington Institute for Near East Policy. Retrieved from http://www.washingtoninstitute.org/policy-analysis/view/the-pkk-could-spark-turkish-russian-military-escalation

Tharoor, I. (2014, August 11). A U.S.-designated terrorist group is saving Yazidis and battling the Islamic state. *The Washington Post*. Retrieved from https://www.washingtonpost.com/news/worldviews/wp/2014/08/11/a-u-s-designated-terrorist-group-is-saving-yazidis-and-battling-the-islamic-state/

The Guardian. (2015, May 21). Isis 'controls 50% of Syria' after seizing historic city of Palmyra. *The Guardian*. Retrieved from https://www.theguardian.com/world/2015/may/21/isis-palmyra-syria-islamic-state

The Guardian. (2017, May 6). Syria's Kurds march on to Raqqa and the sea. *The Guardian*. Retrieved from https://www.theguardian.com/world/2017/may/06/syria-kurds-raqqa-mediterranen?utm_source=Sailthru&utm_medium=email&utm_campaign=EBB%2005.08.2017&utm_term=Editorial%20-%20Early%20Bird%20Brief

The Independent. (2017, January 5). The Kurdish woman building a feminist democracy and fighting Isis at the same time. *The Independent*. Retrieved from http://www.independent.co.uk/news/world/middle-east/kurdish-woman-building-feminist-democrac-fighting-isis-at-the-same-time-syria-kurdistan-rojava-new-a7487151.html

The Soufan Group. (2015). *Foreign fighters: An updated assessment of the flow of foreign fighters into Syria and Iraq*. New York, NY: The Soufan Group.

The Wall Street Journal. (2014, June 19). U.S. signals Iraq's Maliki should go. *The Wall Street Journal*. Retrieved from https://www.wsj.com/articles/u-s-signals-1403137521

The Washington Post. (2015, September 28). Read Putin's U.N. general assembly speech. *The Washington Post*. Retrieved from https://www.washingtonpost.com/news/worldviews/wp/2015/09/28/read-putins-u-n-general-assembly-speech/

Tønnessen, T. H. (2015). Heirs of Zarqawi or Saddam? The relationship between al-Qaida in Iraq and the Islamic state. *Perspectives on Terrorism, 9*(5). Retrieved from http://www.terrorismanalysts.com/pt/index.php/pot/article/view/443/html

Valensi, C. (2015). Non-state actors: A theoretical limitation in a changing Middle East. *Military and Strategic Affairs, 7*(1), 59–78.

Wahab, B. (2016). Iraqi Kurds and Syrian Kurds. In P. Clawson (Ed.), *Syrian Kurds as a U.S. Ally: Cooperation & complications* (pp. 39–45). Washington, DC: Washington Institute for Near East Policy.

Walt, S. M. (1998). International relations: One world, many theories. *Foreign Policy, 110* (29–32), 34–46.

Welch, S., & Bailey, K. (2016). *In pursuit of good ideas: The Syria train-and-equip program*. Washington, DC: Washington Institute for Near East Policy.

The EU's Stance Toward VNSAs During the Syrian Crisis: YPG and ISIS Cases

Yonca Özer and Fatmanur Kaçar

1 Introduction

More than 6 years since violence erupted in Syria, the EU is still striving to alleviate the impacts of the Syrian crisis, both at home and abroad. However, its actorness has become diluted as the diverging political expectations of its member states, the pressures exerted by other actors, including the USA and Iran, and the highly controversial existence of VNSAs in the region have complicated the situation, putting the EU's actorness and effectiveness into debate once more.

The EU, often presented as a peace project, began as an economic union in the aftermath of World War II before developing into an economic, political, and social union of 28 member states by 2013. Since 1957, its foreign and security policy has become one of the most challenging in terms of nature[1] and design. In the first decades, security policy was only concerned with the security within the European continent, while foreign policy only involved trade matters (common external tariffs). In the following decades, however, it expanded through consecutive treaties and was reshaped by each international crisis. Currently, as regulated by Articles 21–46 of the Treaty on the European Union (TEU) (European Union 1992), the EU Foreign and Security Policy encompasses peace and security issues, diplomacy and partnership, peace-keeping missions, the means to intervene, the European Neighborhood Policy, and counterterrorism measures. In addition to

[1]Foreign policy is one of the most challenging policy areas especially considering pooled sovereignty as in the case of the EU. According to Diez et al. (2011: 215) with a number of exceptions, such as the EU's supranational bodies, the state is not commanded by any superior international body. Although the EU envisages shared sovereignty in certain policy areas, foreign policy mostly remains the monopoly of member states.

Y. Özer (✉) • F. Kaçar
Marmara University, EU Institute, Istanbul, Turkey
e-mail: yoncaozer@marmara.edu.tr; fatmanur.kacar@marmara.edu.tr

Ö.Z. Oktav et al. (eds.), *Violent Non-state Actors and the Syrian Civil War*,
DOI 10.1007/978-3-319-67528-2_9

being regulated by treaties, EU foreign policy is also guided by strategy papers. In its search for direction and priorities to guide EU foreign policy, the high representative for the Common Foreign and Security Policy (CFSP) Solana released the EU's first European Security Strategy Paper in 2003 (European Council 2003). This paper articulated various strategic objectives in response to threats to European security. In its updated 2008 version, the document

- Listed terrorism, WMD proliferation, regional conflict, state failure, and organized crime as the main threats to EU security
- Emphasized that these security threats must be confronted at home and abroad
- Emphasized that the security of the EU must first be enhanced by stabilizing the Western Balkans and resolving the Israeli-Palestinian conflict
- Articulated the principle of effective multilateralism as the cornerstone of EU foreign policy (European Council 2008)

While EU anti-terrorism measures date back to the 1970s,[2] terrorism has become one of the EU's main focuses since then. The 2003 Strategy Paper neatly states that "terrorism puts lives at risk; it imposes large costs; it seeks to undermine the openness and tolerance of our societies and it poses a growing strategic threat to the whole of Europe" (European Council 2003: 3). Europol, Eurojust, and the EU Counterterrorism Coordinator are the main EU agencies associated with its counterterrorism policies, while the European Arrest Warrant and the EU's efforts to counter terrorist finances, namely, economic sanctions and embargoes, are among its key counterterrorism legal instruments (Bures 2011).

The latest strategy paper, the European Union Global Strategy (EUGS), was issued in June 2016. Like the abovementioned documents, the priorities for external action are EU security, security and defense, counterterrorism, cybersecurity, energy security, and strategic communications (European Council 2016). However, the EUGS has lowered expectations somewhat. Regarding the Middle East, Tocci (2016: 6) claims that unilaterally bringing peace, security, democracy, or prosperity is an illusion, as the EUGS acknowledges. Because, considering merely the EU, such a *grandiose* mission is impossible without the others. As Ginsberg puts it, "the end of the Cold War catapulted the EU into a position of leadership in Europe before the EU itself was ready" (Ginsberg 2010: 246). Nevertheless, expectations—both within and outside the union—have not diminished, making the EU's actorness even more contentious. Thus, Tocci argues that the West and the EU have played crucial roles "in the unravelling of the Middle East, often driven by the illusion that we could 'fix' the region. The EUGS attempts to move away from this dangerous myth, without however forgetting Europe's responsibilities towards the region" (Tocci 2016: 6). Hill had already acknowledged that illusion in 1993 with his capability-expectations gap argument, in which he argued that the EU's capabilities did not match the expectations from the EU in world affairs. Although the EU is acknowledged to

[2]For a meticulous historical background of EU counterterrorism policy, see the 3rd Chapter of Bures (2011).

be a soft[3] (Nye 1990) or civilian power[4] (Duchêne 1973), every international crisis has required a common EU voice in terms of hard power[5] (Nye 2003), which brings to mind Hill's argument. The Syrian crisis has been an exemplary case regarding this argument.

In reducing the expectations from the union, the Syrian crisis has also showed the EU that "their neighbors' and their partner's weaknesses are their own weaknesses" (European Council 2016: 4). For the EU, therefore, the crisis is not just a foreign policy issue related to pursuing foreign policy interests but also an international issue with crucial internal implications given enormous refugee flows to Europe and the direct and imminent security challenges within the EU borders posed by VNSAs, particularly ISIS-like factions. As EU Counterterrorism Coordinator (CTC) Gijs de Vries emphasized "the role of the union [EU] is not to supplant Member States but to support them in working internationally and the main thrust of Europe's defense against terrorism remains firmly at the level of national governments" (Laitner 2005). However, the terrorism developing out of the Syrian civil war requires a more effective and visible EU role given the rising death tolls in the region and within EU borders. In particular, in the areas where the Syrian state has lost control, VNSAs like the Islamic State of Iraq and the Levant (ISIS) and People's Protection Units (YPG) are struggling to expand their control, mainly in order to change borders in the region. This has increased the suffering of Syrian people in their disintegrating country and threatens both theirs and the EU's security. This has forced the EU to reconsider its foreign and counterterrorism policy, particularly once the threat of terrorist attacks became imminent in certain EU cities, like Berlin, Paris, Brussels, Nice, London, and Manchester. Within the broad spectrum of its foreign policy, the EU's counterterrorism policy includes prevention, protection, pursuing, and responding factors. However, the recent terrorist attacks and worldwide crisis show that the EU is far from dealing with terrorism effectively.

This chapter investigates the EU's actorness vis-à-vis its counterterrorism policy by analyzing its effectiveness in responding to the rising threats from the new

---

[3]Originally coined by Nye in 1990, soft power refers to the use of persuasion and diplomacy rather than military means (Nye 1990). This kind of power tends to "work indirectly by shaping the environment for policy and sometimes takes years to produce the desired outcomes" (Nye 2004: x). The strength of soft power lies in its ability to shape preferences via culture, values, and norms.

[4]Awarded the Nobel Peace Prize in 2012 for cooperation between countries, the EU exemplifies both soft power and civilian power. That is, the EU (then the EEC) should maintain itself as "a civilian group long on economic power and relatively short on armed force" (Duchêne 1973: 19). In contrast to the USA, which tends to resort to military instruments, the EU prefers civilian instruments, primarily humanitarian assistance, development aid, trade sanctions, and agreements with third countries. With this different understanding of actorness or foreign policies, the EU aims to contribute in the long run to the transforming of the international system through persuasion, legal agreements, dialogue, and positive incentives (Smith 2003: 108). However, the EU's ability to utilize these tools with the support of broader political steps also depends on the "others."

[5]The concept of hard power, according to Nye, is the "ability to use the carrots and sticks of economic and military might to make others to follow your will" (Nye 2003).

generation of VNSAs to the stability and security of both the EU and the region. It discusses the frameworks the EU uses to deal with VNSAs and considers whether it may contribute to building a new order in the Middle East in cooperation with other major powers and key regional countries. The chapter argues that the EU's foreign policy, especially regarding its priority of countering terrorism spreading out from the Syrian war, demonstrates again that the EU's actorness is highly contentious, while its engagement with the developing world is often described as inconsistent.

Obviously, the Syrian crisis represents direct and urgent challenges to the EU's internal interests, which has forced the EU to deal with VNSAs. The EU's stance, as understood from the EUGS, has been to acknowledge the instability and insecurity and the necessity to work with partners like Turkey to conduct negotiations. According to Akgün et al. (2017:11), the EU's focus in negotiations with Syria was

> to find a solution to decrease the violence on the ground, rather than to secure a political solution. The fight against terrorism has become the priority for the international community rather than the replacement of President Bashar al-Assad. Terrorist groups like the Islamic State of Iraq and Syria (ISIS) and al-Nusra has been the major concern both inside and outside Syria as the terror attacks hit different geographical regions from France to Turkey.

The EU thus faces a tricky balancing act while designing its strategies in terms of how this new generation of VNSAs has affected its policy and search for cooperation with other regional players in the region, particularly how the EU can take into consideration the security and sovereignty concerns of regional countries like Turkey. As Salih (2015: 1) notes to fight against ISIS in Syria, "Europe needs Turkish partnership, given that Turkey shares a 911-kilometre border with Syria that has been the key crossing point for ISIS fighters travelling to and from Europe." Accordingly, this chapter also closely examines the EU's relations and cooperation with Turkey regarding the fight against terrorism.

1.1 The EU's Contentious Actorness and the Syrian Crisis

From a classical perspective, actorness depends on statehood, although it can also be attributed to international organizations in specific matters. NATO is a concrete example in foreign policy matters. However, in NATO's case, despite being intergovernmental, relative US leadership is pivotal in providing a kind of leadership to give a common voice to the organization as an actor. In the EU's case, there is neither hegemony nor hierarchy among member states. This intergovernmentalism in certain areas makes it difficult to reach common decisions in foreign policy issues. Thus, the EU is not a state; yet neither is it a simple international organization, but regarded as a "fuzzy entity lying in between" (Tocci 2016: 3). Besides, its place in international affairs is still "new, unorthodox, sui generis, and counterintuitive to those who only see a world of Westphalian states" (Ginsberg 2010: 246). Therefore, the issue of its actorness has drawn special attention. Jupille and Caporaso (1998) attempted to conceptualize its actorness in terms of the recognition, authority, autonomy, and cohesion factors. Building on this, Bretherton and Vogler (1999) proposed a conceptualization of EU actorness based on criteria of opportunity, presence, and capability.

Bretherton and Vogler describe actorness in relation to international law, assuming that "[w]eak states may have full legal status but are insignificant as actors, while bodies such as the European Union can fulfil important functions without possessing legal personality" (Bretherton and Vogler 2006: 14). However, it should be noted that the EU gained legal personality in 2007 through the Lisbon Treaty. According to Bretherton and Vogler, law is crucial because it provides institutional context (Bretherton and Vogler 2006: 14). That is, legal context and recognition of actors are important dimensions of actorness. However, this is not a sufficient definition because an entity's actorness also requires "autonomy from its external environment and indeed from its internal constituents, and which is capable of volition or purpose." Thus, for Bretherton and Vogler, a global actor is "an entity that is capable of formulating purposes and making decisions, and thus engaging in some form of purposive action" (Bretherton and Vogler 2006: 15). As has been long discussed, the EU is unique, multifaceted, and a "multiperspectival polity" (Ruggie 1993: 172). Understanding the EU's role, limitations, and responsibilities is also crucial for understanding its actorness and the frameworks within which its actorness has been situated. Bretherton and Vogler define their criteria of actorness, opportunity, presence, and capability, as follows:

- Opportunity denotes factors in the external environment of ideas and events, which constrain or enable actorness. Opportunity signifies the structural context of action.
- Presence conceptualizes the ability of the EU, by virtue of its existence, to exert influence beyond its borders. An indication of the EU's structural power, presence combines understandings about the fundamental nature, or identity of the EU and the (often unintended) consequences of the Union's internal priorities and policies.
- Capability refers to the internal context of EU external action -the availability of policy instruments and understandings about the Union's ability to utilize these instruments, in response to opportunity and/or to capitalize on presence. (Bretherton and Vogler 2006: 22)

Article 25 of TEU (European Union 1992) lists general guidelines, decisions, joint actions, common positions, implementation of decisions, and systematic cooperation between EU member states as instruments for CFSP. However, these concepts lose their ground when applied to the EU's stance in actual international crises such as the Syrian civil war and to deal with VNSAs emerging from that crisis environment. Following uprisings in nearby countries, the Syrian crisis erupted in 2011 as an opportunity for the EU to demonstrate its actorness. However, it lacked a solid presence mainly because of its regional "capability shortfall," for example, a lack of air- and sealift, air-to-air refueling, attack helicopters, reconnaissance and liaison helicopter battalions, combat search and rescue, communication equipment, early warning and distant detection intelligence gathering satellites, cruise missiles, precision-guided munitions, force headquarters, and rapid deployment (Ginsberg 2010). Moreover, as the EUGS acknowledges, the EU "will strive for a strong UN as the bedrock of the multilateral rule-based order, and develop globally coordinated responses with international and regional organizations, states and non-state actors" (European Council 2016) thereby claiming its actorness in cooperation with its partners.

The issue of EU member states' diverse stances emerging from different interests, perceptions, and approaches should particularly be emphasized here as a crucial factor hampering the EU's actorness. As Smith (2003: 105) notes, the EU's "logic of diversity" also hinders its success as an effective actor in international issues. Between 2000 and 2002, the EU established European Security and Defense Policy (ESDP) institutions, while the EU and NATO established procedures for the EU's use of NATO assets whenever NATO did not wish itself to be involved in a security operation. Just as the EU was developing these new ESDP institutions, so increasing its capabilities, it gave a very divided response to the US-led operation to Iraq in 2003 with some members supporting the operation while others did not, which weakened its "common" foreign policy (Ginsberg 2010: 252). Similarly, EU's common voice was becoming hoarse when the US President George W. Bush insisted on NATO expansion. Unlike the support of the UK, France and Germany were opposed to expansion, which was perceived as a threat by Russia (Spiegel 2008). Despite the divergences in NATO expansion, Göral (2015: 168) argued that an obstinate advocacy of European Neighborhood Policy (ENP) was contradictory to the reasons why Chancellor Merkel and President Sarkozy object to NATO enlargement. Divergences among major European countries are also congruent with realist assumptions that "great powers always worry about the balance of power in their neighborhood" (Mearsheimer 2014: 176) and push back when other great powers gain influence against them.

Similar divisions have appeared over the Syrian crisis. Although the EU as a whole has tried to maintain transatlantic relations with the view that there cannot be a peaceful transition under Syria's current regime, individual member states are divided regarding Assad's role in the transitional period (European Parliament 2016: 8; The Guardian 2015a), with France prominent in declaring that any such role is unacceptable. According to François Hollande, the French president, "Assad is the source of the problem" who "cannot be part of the solution" (The Guardian 2015b). However, as the VNSAs increased their actions and intensified their terrorist attacks in Europe, France has changed its perspective, and French Foreign Minister Laurent Fabius stated that "France is prepared to accept a political transition in Syria that includes regime leader Bashar al Assad, indicating a softening stance towards Assad" (TRT World 2015). It makes clear that even a single member state depicts divergences when major national interests are under threat. The EU's foreign policy Chief, Federica Mogherini, has a similar view. On the other hand, the German Chancellor, Angela Merkel, has stated that "Assad must be included in Syria peace talks" (Aljazeera 2015). Germany and the UK support his involvement in the transitional period. Other EU member states—Austria and Spain—have been more explicit about the need for security cooperation and dialogue with the Syrian president, whom they claim is "best placed to fight ISIS" (Black 2015). Current approaches to the Democratic Union Party (PYD)/YPG also diverge across Europe. While Germany and Belgium have been relatively reluctant to engage officially and openly with the PYD/YPG, France has taken a very different approach, taking the unexpected step of meeting with PYD co-leader and commander of the YPG's women's unit in 2015 despite Turkey's sensitivity (Salih 2015: 9).

In evaluating EU performance, Vogler and Bretherton (2013) employed the interconnected concepts of presence, opportunity, and capability. They conclude that the achievement of the increased capability stipulated by the Lisbon Treaty, "together with resolution of the Eurozone crisis, with its deleterious effect upon the Union's presence, would not fully compensate for the loss of opportunity provided by the changing international structure" (Vogler and Bretherton 2013: 375). According to them, the EU is a global actor "past its peak," as can be observed from the situation that EU member states are more visible actors than the EU itself. The experience of the Syrian war, including the refugee deal with Turkey, has shown that neither a single member state—Germany—can become "an acceptable leader for the entire EU" (Pierini 2016) nor makes the EU a global actor. Some realists even go a step further and argue that there is no potential regional hegemon in Europe in a foreseeable future since the top contenders of the continent, Germany and Russia, lose relative power due to decreasing population (Mearsheimer and Walt 2016: 82). Instead, this new architecture produced either inaction and inertia or "confusion (as on the refugee deal with Turkey, whose key features were negotiated mainly by Germany instead of the EU institutions)" (Pierini 2016). Such initiatives by some member states bypassing the EU institutions demonstrate ineffectiveness of the latter, which lead to questioning the EU's actorness. Another example of the EU's challenges regarding its actorness is the structure of the European Counter Terrorism Centre. It was formed to provide a coordinated response to terrorist attacks in 2016 by Europol; but its experts are only temporarily seconded from the member states depending on the nature of the event (ECTC 2017), which prevents the EU from having an established structure for countering terrorism and therefore dilutes the EU's actorness in this respect.

Moreover, it is difficult for the EU to project a collective identity in global affairs with its intergovernmental decision-making processes in foreign policy especially with regard to military- and defense-related ones and without overcoming the differences between its member states. After highlighting the role of identity in the construction of actorness, which links the EU's presence and understandings about its capabilities in constructing expectations concerning EU practices, Bretherton and Vogler (2006) consider two dimensions of EU identity; one is inclusive and the other one is exclusive. The inclusive identity, which is based (primarily) on constructions of the union as a value-based community, seems irrelevant in the Syrian and VNSAs case as EU values and norms are not appropriate instruments for dealing with belligerent VNSAs. Regarding exclusive identity, Bretherton and Vogler (2006) consider constructions of the union as a "fortress" that reflects understandings of a range of practices centered on the concepts of "access and eligibility, which serve to restrict or exclude participation in the prosperity and security, which the Union itself claims to offer." An exclusive identity denotes processes of active othering, through which outsiders are characterized as alien, "non-European," and potential threats. As they claim, "exclusionary practices associated with the Union's identity as fortress can be found in relation to trade; immigration, asylum and border control; and accordance of candidate status to aspirant members" (Bretherton and Vogler 2006). They conclude that "the Union, through its practices, maintains links between the exclusive and inclusive facets of its identity—demonstrating, for example, a comprehensive approach to security and using its economic power to impose conditionalities in the spheres of human rights and environmental protection" (Bretherton and Vogler 2006). Thus, as Risse (2012: 91) argues, "creating a distinct foreign policy identity is the whole point about the EU's efforts in external affairs, representing the outward looking version of the EU's modern and enlightenment identity."

Niemann and Bretherton (2013) claim that the EU is at an important crossroad. On the one hand, its increased capacity via institutional reforms to involve itself in major international events has rendered the union a global actor to outside observers. On the other hand, Niemann and Bretherton (2013) list several factors clouding the EU's actorness, particularly its slow and often only modest internal reforms, an increasing politicization of formerly "low politics" issues, and the prolonged sovereign debt crisis in the Eurozone. In addition, there is a less favorable external environment, considering the change of US presidents from Obama to Trump, with the USA's shifting regional interests and emerging powers creating a more polycentric world order, along with a proactive Russian impact in Syria.

The idea of a role "assumes that an actor can and should find for itself something approximating to a part played on a stage, namely a distinctive, high-profile and coherent identity" (Hill 1993: 307). According to Hill, the EU has been expected to become a replacement for the USSR in the global balance of power, regional pacifier, global intervenor, mediator of conflicts, bridge between rich and poor, and joint supervisor of the world economy (Hill 1993: 312–314). Howorth (2009), quoting Shakespeare ("some are born great, some achieve greatness and some have greatness thrust upon them"), tries to show that the EU has achieved greatness. However, the third option is also open to debate. In addition to the EU's achievements, it has also had greatness attributed to it since it is perceived as an attraction center from outside. Despite failing to demonstrate greatness in certain events such as the crisis in the 1990s in the middle of Europe or the Syrian crisis, the EU is still perceived as a great power. This shows that it is benefiting from greatness thrust upon it as well. Yet, on the other hand, it also suffers from its vague foreign policy regarding the Syrian conflict.

1.2 ISIS and the YPG as the Focal Point in the EU's Fight Against Terrorism

The Arab Spring, or sporadically enunciated as Arab Awakening referring to a series of protests and demonstrations across the Middle East and North Africa, has been sparked by protests that occurred in Tunisia in 2010 in Sidi Bouzid following Mohamed Bouazizi's self-immolation. As have been widely acknowledged, these uprisings are caused by the dissatisfaction with the rule of local governments, wide gaps in income levels, political corruption, unemployment, poverty, dictatorship, and human rights violations. With the domino effect of the first demonstrations in Tunisia, a wave of popular discontent has shaken the Arab world, with people calling for dignity, democracy, and social justice, spreading to other countries like Jordan, Algeria, Egypt, and Syria. While the Middle East has been struggling with the turmoils, the EU has also been quick to recognize the challenges of the political and economic transition faced by the region as a whole. It recognized the need to adopt a new approach to relations with its southern neighbors engaging politically with a wide range of government, opposition, and parliamentary and civil society interlocutors in the region through visits from the president of the commission, the president of the European Parliament, the high representative, and several commissioners.

The EU's first strategic response to the Arab uprisings came as early as 8 March 2011, including a joint communication of High Representative Catherine Ashton, and the European Commission proposed "a partnership for democracy and shared prosperity with the southern Mediterranean" (European Commission 2011). This communication stressed the EU's support for the demand in these countries for political participation, dignity, freedom, and employment opportunities and the EU's approach based on the respect of universal values and shared interests. Indeed, it highlighted the EU's "more for more" principle under which increased financial assistance and enhanced access to the EU Single Market is made available to those partner countries most improved in consolidating reforms (European Commission 2011: 5–9). This principle represents an example for how the EU, through its practices, maintains links between the exclusive and inclusive facets of its identity. The EU's compromise was deep democracy and sustainable economic growth and development.

In Syria, however, the crisis and violent conflicts have turned out to be more complex than those in other countries experiencing the Arab Spring. This has left the EU with one of its biggest humanitarian crises since World War II. Unlike in Tunisia or Egypt, instead of alleviating discontent, the unrest turned into a full-blown civil war resulting in the spread of serious violence and VNSAs. Forming currently the largest refugee population in the world, 6.6 million Syrians have been displaced internally, while almost 5 million have sought safety in neighboring countries, and the rest of the war-torn population urgently needs help.[6] While the EU and other actors, including the UN, are providing humanitarian aid, security measures are also severely needed. Currently, VNSAs are trying to fill the clearly visible security vacuum in Syria, by striving to create their own sovereignty in the areas they control.

The VNSAs operating in Syria,[7] mostly against the government regime, have grown continuously. They are both diverse and fragmented in terms of ideologies, number of fighters, and their stance toward Europe. Because of their sporadic terrorist acts, most notable ones in Europe are ISIS and the YPG. Originating in 2002 from among Salafi jihadists, ISIS has sought to establish an Islamic caliphate based on its extreme interpretation of Islam and Sharia. As the armed wing of the PYD, the YPG is considered the counterpart of the People's Defense Forces (HPG) in Syria. The PYD/YPG has recently gained "a degree of international support, becoming a key ally" as an effective military force in the anti-ISIS coalition (Salih 2015: 1–4).

Regular terrorist attacks outside Syria have currently alarmed Europe. Because terrorist attacks under the guise of Islamism killed hundreds and injured many more in Europe for several years.[8] As the EU's counterterrorism agenda has been "crisis-driven" and the shocks it has experienced so far have been related to Islamic terrorism, the main focus of EU counterterrorism concerns has been Islamic terrorism. The vulnerability of individual European countries makes them so interdependent that none of them can effectively protect their citizens on their own (Dalgaard-Nielsen 2004: 172–173). The European Parliament (2017: 90–109)

---

[6]Over half of the prewar population of 21.4 million has been displaced: 6.6 million have been displaced within the country, there are almost 5 million UNHCR registered refugees in neighboring countries, mainly Turkey, Lebanon, and Jordan, and over 1 million Syrians have sought asylum in Europe (United Nations Office for the Coordination of Humanitarian Affairs [OCHA] 2017; United Nations High Commissioner for Refugees [UNHCR] 2017).

[7]For further information on the conceptualization and categorization of the VNSAs, see the "Introduction" chapter of this book (Oktav et al. 2018). As the war protracted, the VNSAs have consolidated their existences necessitating to make a distinction for comprehensive conceptualizations. The "Introduction" chapter of this book made a distinction between old and new generations of VNSAs and categorized ISIS and the YPG as the new generation of VNSAs. Table 3 succinctly lays out ISIS and YPG's distinguishing characteristics.

[8]On 13 November 2015, 11 members of ISIS killed 130 civilians and injured more than 400 in a series of attacks in Paris, France. 3 gunmen also opened fire at Bataclan concert hall and killed audience members. On 22 March 2016, ISIS coordinated 3 suicide attacks in Belgium, 2 at Brussels' Zaventem Airport, and 1 at Brussels' Maelbeek metro station killing 35 civilians and injuring more than 200. On 19 December 2016, 11 were killed when a hijacked truck plowed into a Christmas market in Berlin, Germany, injuring 48. On 22 March 2017, a Muslim man mowed down pedestrians on a bridge in London, killing 5 and injuring 29, including stabbing a police officer to death. On 7 April 2017, in Stockholm, Sweden, a "radicalized" Muslim stole a truck and crushed five pedestrians, including an 11-year-old girl, killing 5 and injuring 14. On 22 May 2015, 22 young people, mostly children, were killed at a concert by a Fedayeen suicide bomber in Manchester, England. On 3 June 2017, 3 terrorists plowed into pedestrians on London Bridge, then proceeded to a market, killing 7 people.

presents a comprehensive list of current EU policy documents and other international agreements and policy documents and gives an overview of measures that have been given in the context of counterterrorism (2017: 175).

The EU does not, and probably never will, run its own counterterrorist operations, so member states carry out anti-terrorist operations individually (Keohane 2005: 21). The EU's role in fighting terrorism, as defined by the Council, is to assist not to supplant member states. Although the EU has struggled to develop a coherent collective response to the civil war in Syria, it has been able to neither succeed this nor preclude the terrorist attacks. Six years on, the EU remains hesitant about how to respond to the Arab Spring and its aftermath, as well as to terrorist attacks. It established its approach to the crisis in Syria and its response to the ISIS threat in its regional strategy for Syria and Iraq, which is based on three main pillars: humanitarian assistance, prevention of regional spillovers, and fighting terrorism (Council of the EU 2015). However, the EU's fight against terrorism has stayed at an intergovernmental level between member states rather at the union level. Unlike the European Monetary Union, which is completely supranational, foreign and security policy has remained intergovernmental,[9] with decisions reached consensually or unanimously for most cases (Risse 2012: 89). Furthermore, highlighting its soft, diplomatic power, the EU has been unable to develop a clear solution for the Syrian refugee problem beyond providing humanitarian aid. According to Akgün et al.,

> The European Union is affected by the Syrian conflict, mainly the conundrum associated with the refugee crisis. Whilst it has played a distant role in political terms (due to divisions among its member states and the lack of diplomatic influence and despite determined efforts undertaken by the High Representative of the Union for Foreign Affairs and Security Policy, Federica Mogherini), it has constantly condemned the attacks on civilians and called for a peaceful political settlement, adopted consistent sanctions against the spoilers and has been a leading donor to the international response to the crisis. (Akgün et al. 2017: 20–21)

The only instruments that the EU has been able to deploy in the case of Syria are economic sanctions and an arms embargo. However, these were rendered futile in May after France and the UK objected to support them further and decided to arm the rebels (Whitman and Juncos 2014: 163). While it has engaged politically with the issues supporting the political process in Syria under UN auspices (European Parliament 2016), the EU has not been considered as an actor in its relations with Syria. Politically, the EU froze the draft Association Agreement as soon as the conflict broke out in 2011 and suspended bilateral cooperation programs under the European Neighborhood Policy between the EU and the Syrian government, while the European Investment Bank suspended loan operations and technical assistance to Syria (European Parliament 2016: 8). Syria itself asked to suspend its participation in the Union for the Mediterranean (European Parliament 2016: 8). As the Parliament briefing (2016: 8) states, the

[9]For further elaboration of the intergovernmental nature of foreign policy, see Howorth (2007).

EU has continuously stressed that the Syrian regime holds primary responsibility in the violent crisis. The regime has nurtured extremism and hampered any chance for a political transition. The EU has also made urgent calls for a stop to all violence against civilians. From a critical perspective, the EU may be evaluated as a unitary actor in so far as its authoritative discursive mode dominates the agenda and counterterrorism issues are constructed by a common language (Baker-Beall 2016: 11). However, these calls have been ineffective, while the EU's military presence and sanctions have been weak and dependent on individual member states. For example, the UK's parliament that rejected the possibility of military action in Syria in 2013 did approve airstrikes against Syrian targets a year later, in particular oilfields under ISIS control (BBC 2015). In a similar vein, Germany and France took initiative to fight ISIS in Syria. As for these two member states, the European Parliament briefing states that

> the German Bundestag approved the deployment of 1200 military personnel in the Middle East to support US, British, and French airstrikes against ISIS. The German contribution until the end of 2016 will consist of Tornado reconnaissance planes, refueling aircraft and a frigate, and complements German training operations in northern Iraq. For the first time in history, France also invoked the mutual defense clause enshrined in Article 42(7) of the Lisbon Treaty, requesting all EU partners to assist France in fighting ISIS. (European Parliament 2016: 10–11)

Tobias Schumacher (2011) advocated that because of its incapability in determining internal and external dynamics of the Egyptian crisis, the EU failed to play an effective role in this crisis. A similar situation is also relevant for the case of Syria. In the long run, to be able to fight successfully against ISIS, reiterating the role of local dynamics, Mehmetcik and Kurşun (2018) also contend that "one way or another ISIS has been able to generate autonomy, representation and influence on the ground" and this should be considered as well. Adopting a different vantage point, Tömmel (2013) argues there is a specific kind of the interaction between the Commission and the Council. And this interaction constructs a policy that "corresponds with the normative aspirations and realist interests of the EU," but he further argues that while accomplishing this, the EU rarely acts according to "the needs and expectations of the partner states." This division between the institutions might affect the union's actorness adversely. In line with that argument, it is also possible to state that rather than being an active power, the EU's ineffectiveness can be attributed to its being a "bystander, trapped in its internal institutional process and passively reacting to crisis events by proposing long-term solutions with little short-term impact" (Noutcheva 2015). The EU's engagement with the developing world is often described "as a policy patchwork" (Holland 2003) as it is effective in humanitarian aid and economic sanction, yet slow and relatively inactive in counterterrorism measures. Thus, counterterrorism[10] policy might serve as a solid

[10]For a comprehensive analysis of the EU's counterterrorism policy, see Lugna (2006) and Argomaniz (2012).

argument for that enunciation of patchwork. It is also possible to underline "how the internal-external division and the coordination gaps between the national and European level contribute to undermine a coherent approach" in considering the EU's relative weakness in that area (Argomaniz 2012: 10). Besides, it complicates the relations between the EU and its candidate state Turkey sharing its borders with Syria and compromising a strategic role.

1.3 Turkey and the EU: At the Cul-de-Sac of Terrorism

Turkey, which shares a 911 km border with Syria and currently hosts more than 3 million refugees, has become the most directly influenced actor from the Syrian crisis. It also perceives an important degree of security threat from VNSAs which try to expand the territory under their control and sphere of influence in Syria. The EU's relations with such a country which is both a candidate for full membership and a critical neighbor of Syria are particularly important. Their stances and policies are consistent particularly regarding ISIS, and they have currently developed their cooperation in fighting terrorism as their priority after both experienced large-scale deadly terrorist attacks in their territories. However, they still need to reconcile their stances regarding the PYD/YPG.

Turkey thinks that the exclusion of the Assad regime should be a priority. However, it refrained from any direct intervention in the Syrian conflict although it supported Syrian opposition groups both politically and militarily. Turkey first publicly considered military intervention in Syria after the partial withdrawal of regime forces from Kurdish majority areas in northeastern Syria near the border with Turkey and the PYD's take-over of several northeastern towns. This shows that Turkey's Syria policy is to a great extent tied to its Kurdish issue. According to Turkey, Kurdish autonomy inside Syria could become a major threat to its territorial integrity, provoking Kurdish separatism at home and offering the PKK new bases, in addition to those in Iran and northern Iraq, from which to hit Turkish targets. The idea of a "Greater Kurdistan" comprising Kurdish areas in Turkey, Iraq, Iran, and Syria might even become possible in the long term (Zalewski 2013: 187–188). For these reasons, Turkey supports a peaceful solution to the Syrian conflict that respects Syrian territorial integrity and rejects any proposals that include the PYD, the Syrian affiliate of the PKK, and/or the Syrian Democratic Council (SDC) in negotiations about Syria's future political settlement. Accordingly, Turkey also rejected the PYD's unilateral declaration of the Federal Democratic System of Rojava and northern Syria on 17 March 2016 (Akgün et al. 2017: 16–17). Because it has focused on the PKK in its efforts to fight terrorism, particularly following a severe surge of violence in the country since

July 2015, its major concern regarding the Syrian civil war and the VNSAs derived from that crisis environment has been dispelling increasing PKK influence over northern Syria through the PYD and its military wing, the YPG.

Unlike the PKK, which is at war with Turkey, the PYD/YPG is not recognized as a terrorist organization by the EU or the USA (Salih 2015: 2). Indeed, by complementing the anti-ISIS coalition's airstrikes as an effective military force, the YPG has become a key Western ally in taking territory from ISIS and containing it (Salih 2015: 1). Thus, the EU and the USA have so far refrained from acknowledging the well-established organic link between the PYD/YPG and the PKK (Akgün et al. 2017: 16). However, according to Salih (2015: 2, 9), EU member states have distanced themselves from the PYD/YPG due to their alleged ties to the Assad regime and the possibility that they may unilaterally advance into additional territories that are not predominantly Kurdish, thereby threatening Syria's territorial integrity. Turkey strongly shares these concerns, based on its view that the PYD/YPG and the PKK are equivalent. Turkey's partnership is necessary to combat ISIS and provide stability in Syria, considering that Turkey is a key crossing point for ISIS fighters travelling to and from Europe and also for Syrian refugees fleeing the war and arriving in Europe. Accordingly, some EU states, particularly Germany and Belgium, are reluctant to engage with the PYD openly or provide material support to the YPG with the worry of alienating Turkey. France, however, has taken a more supporting approach, which has angered Turkey. For example, François Hollande received the co-leader of the PYD and commander of the women's unit of the YPG at the Élysée Palace in February 2015 (Salih 2015: 9). These differences between EU member states regarding the PYD/YPG are another example of inconsistency in EU policy regarding the Syrian conflict that weakens the EU's actorness. Furthermore, "the PYD has repeatedly called for both the US and the UK to visit its territory and examine their operations directly; however, as of yet this offer has not been taken up, largely due to the fact that this autonomy is not supported in the first place" (O'Driscoll 2015: 3). This approach of PYD, namely, its resorting to the UK, also can be considered as a hallmark of the member states' actorness rather than the EU.

For the EU, both Turkey and the PYD/YPG are important to contain ISIS and to provide stability in northern Syria. Therefore, as Salih (2015) argues an effective anti-ISIS policy for the EU should target partnership and coordination with both by reconciling their interests. The YPG's expansion into additional territories would lead to territorial disintegration or additional conflicts since Turkey would retaliate in response to Kurdish overreach while Syrian Sunni Arabs would be isolated to the detriment of the anti-ISIS struggle. Therefore, on the one hand, the EU should encourage Turkey to revive the peace process with the PKK in order to eliminate the risk of a spillover of the Turkey-PKK conflict into northern Syria and not to distract Turkey and the YPG from the shared goal of containing ISIS. On the one hand, it should pressure the PYD/YPG to adopt a more constructive role in the areas it controls by avoiding further expansion into areas that are not predominantly

Kurdish and not displacing local Sunni inhabitants (Salih 2015: 2, 7, 8). Otherwise, supporting the PYD/YPG within the framework of the fight against ISIS will remain controversial in Turkey.

Turkey had been criticized, as a NATO member and Western ally, for not taking a more active role against the ISIS. Its reluctance had arisen partly from fear of retaliation by ISIS within Turkey (Yeginsu 2015). However, it has started to address the terrorist threat from ISIS more strongly, particularly after it directly suffered serious ISIS terror attacks in 2015. In response to these attacks, Turkey strengthened its involvement in the Global Coalition to Counter ISIS, which it had joined in September 2014, continued airstrikes against ISIS positions, allowed the coalition to use Incirlik Air Base in its operations against ISIS, joined coalition airstrikes, and took new measures to prevent cross-border activities by ISIS fighters. Finally, Turkey launched a cross-border military ground operation called Euphrates Shield together with the Free Syrian Army (European Commission 2016: 92). While the EU is one of the leading partners of the coalition regarding humanitarian aid, some member states have also been active in military terms like Denmark, France, the UK, Italy, the Netherlands, and Germany both in Iraq and Syria. Among these member states, just the UK and France joined the airstrikes against ISIS positions in Syria (European Parliament 2016: 9). Unlike Turkey, the EU member states reject to be involved in ground combat forces against ISIS. Obviously, the motivation behind Turkey's involvement in the military ground operation was not only to clear ISIS from its border areas but also to contain PKK influence over northern Syria.

The EU and Turkey held three summits between November 2015 and March 2016 in order to deal with the massive irregular and illegal refugee flow to Europe mainly arising from the war in Syria and the accompanying risk of ISIS fighters' travelling to Europe. At the first EU-Turkey Summit on 29 November 2015, which led to the adoption of the EU-Turkey statement, the parties agreed to hold regular summits, political dialogue meetings, and discussions on areas of common interest like countering terrorism beyond the existing framework of cooperation. Enhancing political dialogue and cooperation in areas of common concern was contemplated in order to re-energize the stalled accession process and to achieve progress in the negotiations.[11] Accordingly, they aimed at a structured and more frequent high-level dialogue through regular, twice-yearly summits to provide a platform to assess the development of Turkey-EU relations and discuss international issues. Turkey and the EU also recognized the fight against terrorism as a priority considering the rising threat of terrorism in all its forms. They therefore pointed out the necessity of enhancing regular discussions, dialogue, and cooperation on foreign and security policy, including counterterrorism as a key area of joint concern, considering the importance of overcoming existing threats in a coordinated manner. The two sides agreed to hold comprehensive regular political dialogue meetings at ministerial/

[11]In other words, this initiative was not planned as an alternative form of relations but to support and complement the accession negotiations.

high representative/commissioner level in addition to the regular Association Council meetings (European Council 2015).

Consistent with what was agreed at the EU-Turkey Summit of 29 November 2015, Turkey and the EU held two High-Level Political Dialogues on 25 January and 9 September 2016 on foreign and security policy, including counterterrorism, Syria, Libya, and Iraq. More specifically, they met for an EU-Turkey Dialogue on Counter-Terrorism in June 2016, which reaffirmed the fight against terrorism as a priority in view of the recent terrorist attacks in their territories. While the EU countries and citizens faced a grave threat from Islamic terrorism, Turkey was also struck by several large-scale deadly terrorist attacks attributed to the PKK and ISIS in 2015 and 2016 (European Commission 2016: 4). The EU and Turkey reiterated in this dialogue meeting their commitment to urgently increase efforts to deal with the threat particularly posed by ISIS, while specific attention was paid to the issue of restricting the flow of foreign terrorist fighters (EEAS 2016). Turkey has been seriously affected by foreign terrorist fighters transiting through the country, which unfortunately has turned it into a corridor for terrorist fighters travelling to and from Europe. Parlar Dal's statement of "Hosting such a high number of refugees, and becoming a transit route for the refugees seeking asylum from European countries and illegally passing to Europe, increases the risk of conflict violence for Turkey." Parlar-Dal (2017: 9) also supports that argument. Accordingly, as the European Commission (2016: 84) reported, Turkey had developed cooperation with member states on detecting foreign fighters attempting to cross Turkey to reach Syria or Iraq. In the dialogue meeting, the parties also agreed to explore ways of enhancing collaboration on information sharing, law enforcement, and judicial cooperation, including cooperation regarding terrorism related deportations and financing of terrorism (EEAS 2016).

In a nutshell, one may argue that Turkey might have both gains and loses concerning the Syrian crisis. Regarding the refugee deal between Turkey and the EU, Habets underlines "the millions of refugees that have come from Syria have caused problems in northern Turkey, but have simultaneously put Turkey in a position of power, especially vis-à-vis the EU" (Habets 2016: 81). Similarly, Turkey's strategic importance has increased for the EU as a partner in countering terrorism spreading out from the Syrian crisis and therefore in providing stability in northern Syria.

2 Concluding Remarks: Dealing with Effects of the Syrian Crisis—Facts, Fallacies, and Proposals

At the end of both World War II and the Cold War, the EU demonstrated its presence as a peace project in war-torn regions both within and beyond Europe. However, the parameters and effectiveness of its actorness were redefined by each crisis. On the one hand, it implemented institutional reforms, expanded its policy areas, and increased its power in foreign policy. On the other hand, faced with various severe crises, from economic (Euro-crisis) to social (refugee crisis and extreme right-wing populism), the EU has simultaneously had to struggle with internal issues, such as Brexit. Among those challenges, the probable UK's withdrawal from the EU is by far the most serious one, which requires institutional formatting for the EU. In addition to these multifaceted crises and challenges that require specific focus, the civil war in Syria has had important internal implications for the EU. This situation has highlighted the EU's lack of adequate institutional structures and mechanisms, which, in a way has reduced its influence regarding foreign policy and counterterrorism issues. The rapid growth of VNSAs means that the EU needs to develop its military capabilities, in addition to its civilian capacity, and to develop a more collectively conducted counterterrorism policy.

Given that the EU's claim to actorness mainly relies on individual member states regarding counterterrorism, the EU has to build a policy that also encompasses and regulates counterterrorism efforts vis-à-vis regional countries because the protracted Syrian civil war and its effects on the surrounding countries have been drastic as well. Turkey, a candidate country to the EU for the last 18 years, exemplifies that claim. Obviously, the EU needs partnership and coordination of Turkey as a regional country bordering northern Syria to develop an effective strategy against ISIS, given the governance vacuum that has allowed it to grow. Turkey has critical importance in controlling the vast number of illegal and irregular refugees fleeing the war, and more importantly, ISIS fighters travelling to and from Europe, and in providing the anti-ISIS coalition with military support. Accordingly, the EU should take Turkey's security and sovereignty concerns into account, particularly those related to Kurdish expansion in northern Syria while designing its policies toward the Syrian crisis in general and VNSAs in particular.

As declared in the Maastricht Treaty, the EU promises an area of freedom, security, and justice. However, recent terrorist attacks in Europe, mainly by ISIS, show that the current EU infrastructure cannot guarantee security. VNSAs pose a clear common threat that requires a common response (Monar 2007: 293), which the EU still lacks. Consequently, as Bures (2011: 247) argues, the EU counterterrorism policy remains a "paper-tiger" in many areas, while EU enforcement capabilities in counterterrorism remain rather weak with a lack of effective coordination between EU institutions, EU member states, and their national agencies tasked with counterterrorism. Regarding the Syrian crisis, the EU is somewhat more effective regarding humanitarian aid and economic sanctions, yet slow and inactive in counterterrorism measures. This chapter therefore concludes that the EU's foreign policy, especially regarding its priority of counterterrorism spreading out from the Syrian civil war, demonstrates again that the EU's actorness is highly contentious while its engagement with the developing world is often rightly described as inconsistently effective.

References

Akgün, M. et al. (2017, April). State-building: Political, structural and legal issues. In M. Akgün & S. Tiryaki (Eds.), *Future of Syria*. Euromesco Joint Policy Study 7, European Institute of the Mediterranean (IEMed). http://www.euromesco.net/images/joint_policy_studies/jps7-future%20of%20syria.pdf

Aljazeera. (2015, September 24). Merkel: Assad must be included in Syria peace talks. http://www.aljazeera.com/news/2015/09/merkel-assad-included-syria-peace-talks-150924080649644.html

Argomaniz, J. (2012). *The EU and counter-terrorism: Politics, polity and policies after 9/11*. London: Routledge.

Baker-Beall, C. (2016). *The European Union's fight against terrorism: Discourse, policies, identity*. Manchester: Manchester University Press.

Black, I. (2015, September 25). Syria crisis: where do the major countries stand? *The Guardian*.

Bretherton, C., & Vogler, J. (1999). *The European Union as global actor*. London: Routledge.

Bretherton, C., & Vogler, J. (2006). *The European Union as global actor* (2nd ed.). New York: Routledge.

Bures, O. (2011). *EU counter-terrorism policy: A paper Tiger?* Farnham: Ashgate.

Council of the EU. (2015). *Council conclusions on the EU Regional Strategy for Syria and Iraq as well as the ISIL/Da'esh threat*. Press release, 16 March. http://www.consilium.europa.eu/en/press/press-releases/2015/03/16-council-conclusions-eu-regional-strategy-for-syria-and-iraq-as-well-as-the-isil-daesh-threat/

Dalgaard-Nielsen, A. (2004). Homeland security American and European responses to September 11th. In J. Pilegaard (Ed.), *The politics of European security* (pp. 159–179). Copenhagen: Danish Institute for International Studies.

Diez, T., Bode, I., & Costa, A. (2011). *Key concepts in international relations*. India: Sage.

Duchêne, F. (1973). The European community and the uncertainties of interdependence. In M. Kohnstamm & W. Hager (Eds.), *A nation writ large? Foreign-policy problems before the European community* (pp. 19–20). London: Macmillan.

ECTC. (2017). *Operational support*. European Counter-Terrorism Center. https://www.europol.europa.eu/about-europol/european-counter-terrorism-centre-ectc

EEAS. (2016). *Turkey-EU Counter Terrorism Dialogue*. European External Action Service, Press Releases, 8 June, Brussels. https://eeas.europa.eu/headquarters/headquartershomepage_en/5018/Turkey-EU%20Counter%20Terrorism%20Dialogue

European Commission. (2011, March 8). *A partnership for democracy and shared prosperity with the Southern Mediterranean*. Brussells. https://ec.europa.eu/research/iscp/pdf/policy/com_2011_200_en.pdf

European Commission. (2016, November 9). *Turkey 2016 report*, Communication on EU Enlargement Policy, Commission Staff Working Document, COM (2016) 715 final, Brussels. https://ec.europa.eu/neighbourhood-enlargement/sites/near/files/pdf/key_documents/2016/20161109_report_turkey.pdf

European Council. (2003, December 12). *A secure Europe in a better world. European security strategy*. Brussels. https://www.consilium.europa.eu/uedocs/cmsUpload/78367.pdf

European Council. (2008, December 11). *Providing security in a changing world*. Report on the Implementation of the European Security Strategy. Brussels. https://www.consilium.europa.eu/uedocs/cms_data/docs/pressdata/en/reports/104630.pdf

European Council. (2015, November 29). *Meeting of heads of state or government with Turkey EU-Turkey statement*. Press releases and statement. http://www.consilium.europa.eu/en/press/press-releases/2015/11/29-eu-turkey-meeting-statement/

European Council. (2016). *A global strategy for the European Union's foreign and security policy*. https://europa.eu/globalstrategy/sites/globalstrategy/files/regions/files/eugs_review_web_0.pdf

European Parliament. (2016, January). *Conflict in Syria trigger factors and the EU response*. Briefing. http://www.europarl.europa.eu/RegData/etudes/BRIE/2016/573924/EPRS_BRI(2016)573924_EN.pdf

European Parliament. (2017). *The European Union's policies on counter-terrorism relevance, coherence and effectiveness*. http://www.europarl.europa.eu/RegData/etudes/STUD/2017/583124/IPOL_STU(2017)583124_EN.pdf

European Union. (1992, February 7). *Treaty on European Union (Consolidated Version), Treaty of Maastricht*. Official Journal of the European Communities C325/5. http://www.refworld.org/docid/3ae6b39218.html

Ginsberg, R. H. (2010). *Demystifying the European Union: The enduring logic of regional integration*. USA: Rowman&Littlefield.

Göral, E. (2015). A critique of European neighbourhood policy: The case of Russian intervention in Ukraine. *Marmara Journal of European Studies, 23*(1), 159–177.

Habets, I. (2016). Obstacles to a Syrian peace: The interference of interests. *European View, 15*, 77–85.

Hill, C. (1993). The capability-expectations gap or conceptualizing Europe's international role. *Journal of Common Market Studies, 31*(3), 305–328.

Holland, M. (2003). 20/20 vision? The EU's Cotonou partnership agreement. *The Brown Journal of World Affairs, 9*(2), 161–175.

Howorth, J. (2007). *Security and defence policy in the European Union*. Basingstoke: Palgrave Macmillan.

Howorth, J. (2009). The EU as a global actor: Grand strategy for a global grand bargain. *Journal of Common Market Studies, 48*(3), 455–474.

Jupille, J., & Caporaso, J. A. (1998). States, agency and rules: The European Union in global environmental politics. In C. Rhodes (Ed.), *The European Union in the world community* (pp. 213–229). Boulder, CO: Lynne Rienner.

Keohane, D. (2005). *The EU and counter-terrorism*. London: Centre for European Reform.

Laitner, S. (2005, March 7). Delays thwart EU chief's anti-terror fight. *Financial Times*.

Lugna, L. (2006). Institutional framework of the European Union counter-terrorism policy setting. *Baltic Security & Defence Review, 8*, 101–127.

Mearsheimer, J. J. (2014). Faulty powers (Mearsheimer Replies). *Foreign Affairs, 93*(6), 175–178.

Mearsheimer, J. J. and Walt, S. M. (2016, July–August). The case of offshore balancing: A superior U.S. grand strategy. *Foreign Affairs*, 70–8.

Mehmetcik, H., & Kurşun, A. M. (2018). Making sense of the territorial aspirations of ISIS: Autonomy, representation and influence. In Ö. Z. Oktav, E. Parlar-Dal, & A. M. Kurşun (Eds.), *Violent non-state actors and the Syrian civil war: The ISIS and YPG cases*. Cham: Springer.

Monar, J. (2007). Common threat and common response? The European Union's counter-terrorism strategy and its problems. *Government and Opposition, 42*(3), 292–313.

Niemann, A., & Bretherton, C. (2013). The EU external policy at crossroads: The challenge of actorness and effectiveness. *International Relation, 27*(3), 261–275.

Noutcheva, G. (2015). Institutional governance of European neighbourhood policy in the wake of the Arab spring. *Journal of European Integration, 37*(1), 19–36.

Nye, J. (1990). Soft power. *Foreign Policy, 80*, 153–171.

Nye, J. (2003, January 10). Propaganda isn't the way: Soft power. *International Herald Tribune*. http://www.belfercenter.org/publication/propaganda-isnt-way-soft-power

Nye, J. (2004). *Soft power: The means to success in world politics*. New York: Public Affairs.

OCHA. (2017). Syrian Arab Republic. https://www.unocha.org

O'Driscoll, D. (2015). The YPG and the changing dynamics of the fight against IS, D. policy paper. *The polish institute of international relations, 24*(126), 1–6.

Oktav, Ö. Z., Parlar-Dal, E., & Kurşun, A. M. (2018). Reframing and reassessing the VNSAs in Syrian conflict: An introduction. In Ö. Z. Oktav, E. Parlar-Dal, & A. M. Kurşun (Eds.), *Violent non-state actors and the Syrian civil war: The ISIS and YPG cases*. Cham: Springer.

Parlar-Dal, E. (2017). Impact of transnationalization of the Syrian civil war on Turkey: Conflict spill over cases of ISIS and PYD-YPG/PKK. *Cambrigde Review of International Affairs, 24* (4), 1–25.
Pierini, M. (2016, August 18). *In search of an EU role in the Syrian war.* http://carnegieeurope.eu/2016/08/18/in-search-of-eu-role-in-syrian-war-pub-64352
Risse, T. (2012). Identity matters: Exploring the ambivalence of EU foreign policy. *Global Policy, 3*(1), 87–95.
Ruggie, J. G. (1993). Territoriality and beyond: Problematizing modernity in international relations. *International Organization, 47*(1), 139–174.
Salih, C. (2015). *Turkey, the Kurds, and the fight against Islamic State.* European Council on Foreign Relations. ECFR/141. http://www.ecfr.eu/page/-/Turkey-theKurds-IslamicState.pdf
Schumacher, T. (2011). The EU and the Arab spring: Between spectatorship and actorness. *Insight Turkey, 13*(3), 107–119.
Smith, K. (2003). The European Union: A distinctive actor in international relations. *The Brown Journal of World Affair, 9*(2), 103–113.
Spiegel Online. (2008, April 3). *NATO expansion defeat: France and Germany thwart bush's plans.* http://www.spiegel.de/international/world/nato-expansion-defeat-france-and-germany-thwart-bush-s-plans-a-545078.html
The BBC. (2015, December 3). UK air strikes on IS in Syria. http://www.bbc.com/news/live/uk-34991344
The Guardian. (2015a, September 5). *Cheering German crowds greet refugees after long trek from Budapest to Munich.* https://www.theguardian.com/world/2015/sep/05/refugee-crisis-warm-welcome-for-people-bussed-from-budapest
The Guardian. (2015b, September 28). *UN general assembly: International community has failed Syrians, says Rouhani.* https://www.theguardian.com/world/live/2015/sep/28/united-nations-un-general-assembly-putin-obama-hollande-world-leaders
Tocci, N. (2016). Interview with Nathalie Tocci on the global strategy for the European Union's foreign and security policy. *The International Spectator, 51*(3), 1–8.
Tömmel, I. (2013). The new neighbourhood policy of the EU: An appropriate response to the Arab spring? *Democracy and Security, 9*, 19–39.
TRT World. (2015, December 6). *France to accept Syria transition with Assad.* http://www.trtworld.com/europe/france-to-accept-syria-transition-with-assad-12216
UNHCR. (2017). *Syria regional refugee response.* http://data.unhcr.org/syrianrefugees/regional.php
Vogler, J., & Bretherton, C. (2013). A global actor past its peak? *International Relations, 27*(3), 375–390.
Whitman, R. G., & Juncos, A. E. (2014). Challenging events, diminishing influence? Relations with the wider Europe. *Journal of Common Market Studies, 52*(S1), 157–169.
Yeginsu, C. (2015, August 18). Elections seem likely in Turkey as ISIS threat rises. *The New York Times.* https://www.nytimes.com/2015/08/19/world/europe/isis-video-urges-turks-to-revolt-against-their-president.html?mcubz=0&_r=0
Zalewski, P. (2013). Turkey, Syria and the Kurds: There goes the neighborhood. In S. Aydın-Düzgit, A. Duncker, D. Huber, E. F. Keyman and N. Tocci (Eds.), *Global Turkey in Europe: Political Economic and Foreign Policy Dimensions of Turkey's Evolving Relationship with the EU* (pp. 187–193). Roma: Istituto Affari Internazionali (IAI). http://www.iai.it/sites/default/files/iairp_09.pdf

Understanding Iran's Approach to Violent Non-state Actors: The ISIS and YPG Cases

Özden Zeynep Oktav

1 Introduction

From its inception, Iran has projected itself as a champion of the Muslim community and has stayed clear of sectarian disputes, accusing pro-Western Arab leaders of failing to protect oppressed Muslims, namely, the Palestinians. In following this policy, Iran created a network of both Shiite and Sunni violent non-state actors (VNSAs), including Hezbollah and Hamas. This network of VNSAs has had a twofold impact on Iranian foreign policy, the further isolation of Iran in international society and an increase in Iran's maneuvering capability vis-ἀ-vis global powers such as the United States and the European Union. Lacking a conventional military and power projection capabilities in the face of the US embargo on its program for conventional military modernization for many years, Iran focused its energy on building a nuclear deterrent and a VNSA network.

Two important developments changed Iranian policies concerning its efforts to build a nuclear weapon of mass destruction (WMD) and its relations with VNSAs. The first was the election of a moderate cleric, Hassan Rouhani, to the presidency in 2013 and the finalization of the historic nuclear deal with the P5 + 1 in 2015. The second was the rise of two VNSAs, the Islamic State of Iraq and Syria (ISIS, Daesh in Arabic and Persian), an Al-Qaeda breakaway group, and the PYD/YPG (Peoples Protection Units, the military wing of the Democratic Union Party, the PYD). This chapter offers a review of key milestones in Iran's response to the emergence of ISIS and the YPG throughout the Syrian crisis at a time when Tehran was initiating tectonic changes in its relations with international society, focusing on the impact of

Ö.Z. Oktav (✉)
Faculty of Political Sciences, International Relations Department, Istanbul Medeniyet University, Istanbul, Turkey
e-mail: ozoktav@yahoo.com

Ö.Z. Oktav et al. (eds.), *Violent Non-state Actors and the Syrian Civil War*,
DOI 10.1007/978-3-319-67528-2_10

ISIS and the YPG on Iran's evolving role in the international system and its relations with the United States.

In this context, after a brief overview of Iran's historical use of violent non-state actors (VNSAs) as an extension of its foreign policy, the first section will examine the reasons for Iranian involvement with Hezbollah and Hamas, two VNSAs labeled by international society as "terrorist." Another concern of this chapter will be to assess the extent to which Iran's use of VNSAs is "stigma rejection" and "counter stigmatization" due to Iran's long stigmatization by international society as a "rogue state" or part of the "axis of evil." In this context, the theoretical approach to stigma adopted by Erving Goffman in *Stigma: Notes on the Management of Spoiled Identity* will be used. The aim is to provide a macro context with which to examine the Iranian usage of VNSAs as a manifestation of its identity, norms, and Tehran's challenge to the boundaries of acceptable behavior imposed by the international order on itself.

The second section will explain how Iranian involvement with the VNSAs entered a different dimension when Tehran was forced to undertake the role of repelling the advances of another VNSA, ISIS, in Iraq and Syria. This has had manifold consequences, which will be analyzed in terms of Iran's shifting policies with a special emphasis on its transition from being a part of the "axis of evil" into "the last best hope" of Washington (Yazd 2014).

Last but not least, the chapter will focus on the Iranian approach to another VNSA, the YPG, throughout the Syrian crisis with a special concern on its impact on Iranian relations with Turkey.

2 A Brief History of Iranian Usage of Non-state Armed Groups

According to many analysts, Iran began employing VNSAs shortly after Khomeini came to power due to two developments: the 1980 invasion of Iran by Saddam Hussein and the hawkish policies of the Reagan administration in Washington. Leaving aside Iran's feelings of strategic encirclement, Khomeini's desire to reestablish ties with Shiite groups in order to incite a pan-Shiite movement brought about the adoption of a strategy that relied upon a network of VNSAs (O'brien 2006, p. 53). Speaking on the significance of maintaining the integrity of the state while simultaneously expanding the influence of Shiism and Iran, Khomeini described VNSAs as a network constructed upon his personal relationship with other Shiite leaders to weaken Iran's rivals, namely, the United States, Iraq, and Israel. As O'brien notes, "as the VNSAs were expanded, Iran created a large web of interconnected yet disassociated VNSAs. Initially this web was regional; ultimately, it spread to enjoy global capabilities" (2006, p. 59).

According to Tabarani, VNSAs were seen by Iran as a part of its state security. As the utility of these armed groups and the proficiency of the Iranian Revolutionary Armed Corps (IRGC) became more apparent, Christian and Sunni groups were equally able to draw support from Iran (Tabarani 2008, p. 71).

The Iranian style of security understanding has had far-reaching political and strategic ramifications. For example, as noted by IRGC commander Yahya Rahim Safavi, "the IRGC has no geographical border. The Islamic revolution is the border of the IRGC. It has an extensive network of contacts across the Muslim world, with a particular emphasis on Lebanon, Iraq, the Gulf region, and the wider Arab world in general" (Byman et al. 2001). Simply put, Iranian revisionism was related to status, not land. By touting the country's revolutionary credentials to impress sympathizers abroad, Iran aimed both to legitimize/validate its theocratic regime at home and to cope with the power asymmetry stemming from advanced weapons technology of the West. A war of ideas rather than technology by means of ideologically motivated VNSAs provided Iran with an inexpensive power projection capability. As O'brien explains, "Tehran can hit targets inside an enemy as distant as the United States without developing an intercontinental ballistic missile or an aircraft carrier" (O'brien 2006, p. 28).

The erosion of state supremacy and the gap in military means made the use of VNSAs a viable option, resulting in the proliferation of interstate and intrastate actors. It has been customary to portray Iran's exploitation of this proliferation of interstate and intrastate actors and its contribution to VNSAs only in militaristic terms. This portrayal, however, disregards the fact that the real motive behind Iran's commitment to VNSAs was its desire to lead the struggle between the "oppressor," namely, the United States and Israel, and the "oppressed," the Palestinians and Shiites. In order to achieve this goal, Tehran does not employ overt aggression. Instead, "it chooses to back groups that, if they ascend to power, will be indebted to Iran" (O'brien 2006, p. 53). For example, after the Israeli invasion of Lebanon in 1982, Ayatollah Khomeini did not send large forces to Syria and Lebanon but instead provided logistic support and trained the Shiite men there: thus, Hezbollah was born. The creation of Hezbollah according to Norton was "a realization of the revolutionary state's zealous campaign to spread the message of the self-styled Islamic revolution" (Norton 2007, p. 37). Hezbollah's importance as a non-state actor and a prominent figure in Iran's strategic calculus became most evident in Hezbollah's triumph over Israel in 2006. With Hezbollah's success, Tehran gave the message that its extensive involvement in the Shiite community in Lebanon and its championship of the Palestinian cause in cooperation with Hamas mainly aimed to rescue the "oppressed" (Shiites and the Palestinians). The 2006 July war was a turning point in the formation of the Shiite crescent of Hezbollah-Hamas-Iran-Syria as it not only helped the two "rogue" states (Iran and Syria) and two "terrorist" organizations (Hamas and Hezbollah) increase their popularity in the eyes of the Arabs on the street but also destroyed the image of Israel's invincibility (Wilkins 2013, p. 62). Put differently, Iran's broad intensification of resistance to the status quo throughout the Middle East by stimulating cultural and psychological forces in cooperation with Hezbollah and Hamas during the 2006 war illustrates and even epitomizes the counter stigmatization of Iran. Iranian supreme leaders who have labeled members of international society, principally the United States and Israel, as "evil forces" or the "great Satan," since the revolution, used counter stigmatization as a foreign policy tool. Thus, Iran has created a role for itself as an international leader of the disinherited, economically destitute, oppressed Muslim people of the Middle East.

3 Understanding "Counter Stigmatization" and Iran-Hezbollah-Hamas Alignment

In the aftermath of the 2003 Iraq war, Iran's two sworn enemies the Taliban and Saddam Hussein were removed. Some analysts conclude that these developments put Iran in a better strategic situation than it had been at any time since the revolution. From the perspective of the conservative Sunni elites, especially the Arab Gulf leaders who remained wary of Iran's expansionist ambitions, the grave danger to Arab national security stemming from Iran was at its peak during the overt success of the formation of a Shiite crescent with Hezbollah's unprecedented popularity in the aftermath of its victory in 2006. In addition to the United States' inability to maintain a balance of power with the aim of preventing any regional supremacy, failure to establish political stability and security in Iraq and Afghanistan set off alarm bells among Sunni Arab leaders. Their biggest fear was that the rise of Iranian influence would set into motion a process of polarization and axis building like that of the 1950s by according Iran a leading regional role with which it could declare superiority over Arabs by exploiting anti-American sentiments among the Arab masses, enhancing its nuclear efforts, challenging energy competition with its energy resources, boosting its significant soft power, and provoking the Arab masses against the pro-Western ruling elite of the Arab Sunni countries. Hosni Mubarak openly declared that the Shiites in the region were more loyal to Iran than their own countries.

Here, the crux of the issue is that it was this common strategic threat perception[1] (Oktav 2008, p. 77) rather than the Shiite ideology which brought Iran and Syria together in the 2006 war in Lebanon (Barzegar 2008, p. 93). Seen from a different angle, the creation of an anti-status quo alliance between Iran and Syria and their cooperation with Hamas and Hezbollah stood in opposition not only to Israel and the United States but also to the ruling elite of the regional pro-Western Sunni Arab countries. This best exemplifies why Syria and Iran are stigmatized as "rogue states." The abovementioned strategic/pragmatic anti-status quo alliance between Iran, Syria, and Hezbollah and Hamas illustrates Washington's failure to produce an understanding of "normality" that can mobilize the Arab masses rather than securing the loyalty of the ruling elite in the Middle East. This, according to Nissen, raises the question of who stigmatizes whom (Adler Nissen 2014, p. 172).

Conventional wisdom has it that the stigmatization of some states or groups as "failed," "pariah," "norm breakers," or "outlaws" bring about the formation of

[1]Iran and Syria have been threatened by the Bush administration equally as they were defined as the members of "axis of evil" "and, therefore, are the next to be attacked after Iraq."

counter stigmatization. Iran's siding with the oppressed masses by waging a proxy war and creating a network among Shiites and even Sunnis by means of VNSAs in Lebanon, Palestine, Iraq, etc. is, in a way, a manifestation of Tehran's counter stigmatization and a response to its exclusion from the Western-dominated international society. The backbone of Iran's counter stigmatization is anti-Zionism and the definition of Israel as a "cancerous tumor that should be cut" (The Telegraph 2012) and a country which should be wiped off the map so as to create a world without Zionism as uttered by leaders such as Khamanei and Ahmedinejad. Khamanei also accused the United States and Israel of creating Al-Qaeda and Daesh, sowing the seeds of discord among Muslims and opposing the Islamic Republic (Tasnim News 2014).

Noting that "modern international society was built on a dynamic of stigmatization" (Zarakol 2014, pp. 312–313), Zarakol defends the idea that "people who have grown up in countries whose modernity has never been in question may not fully understand how all-consuming the stigma of comparative backwardness may become for a society; how tiring it is to conduct all affairs under the gaze of an imaginary and imagined West, which is simultaneously idealized and suspected of the worst kind of designs" (Zarakol 2011a, b, p. 6). Here, unlike the countries explained by Zarakol and the ruling elite of the Arab countries, Iran and its partners, Hamas and Hezbollah, are not concerned much with approval by the West or conducting all affairs under the gaze of the West and, on the contrary, seek to gain legitimacy in the eyes of the masses on the Arab street. Iran and its allies not only reject an international society whose main driver is stigmatization but also ignore the "normative standard that defines their own attributes as discreditable" (Goffman 1963, p. 7). They, on the contrary, create their own normative standard which puts an end to, in Goffman's words, "a language of relationships" (Goffman 1963, p. 3) by creating their own language and putting it at the core of the relations with the outsiders/the West. For example, "resistance and martyrdom" have been two concepts providing Iran and Hezbollah with relative legitimacy in the eyes of the Arab masses as well as parts of a broad strategy shared by the Hamas-led Palestinian administration and Iran. During Ismail Haniyeh's visit to Iran in 2006, the two sides agreed on a course of resistance and perseverance for the return of the Palestinian lands to Palestinians as, according to them, "armed resistance is the only language the enemy understands" (Samii 2006). Three points should be once more stressed here. Iran, using VNSAs, primarily Hamas and Hezbollah, challenges the legitimacy of the state. Because it appeals to religious authority, the Iranian ruling elite is usually at odds with the Westphalian state system through which the long secularizing trend in international politics has started (Zarakol 2011a, b, p. 2317). Second, Tehran uses force rather than negotiations as its primary instrument. For example, the main reason behind Iran's thorny relations with the late Yassir Arafat and his successor Mahmoud Abbas was their recognition of Israel and protracted negotiations with the state rather than armed resistance. According to Iranian officials, negotiations would only result in greater concessions by the Palestinians and the Arabs to Israel and the West (Bahgat 2006, p. 369). Third, Iran, by undertaking the role of norm breaker, serves most as a reinforcer of the notion of normality (Adler Nissen 2014, p. 158). Iran's stigmatization as a deviant norm-breaker brings the world together, even countries such as Russia and Turkey who still struggle to be accepted by international society.

As noted by Nissen, "stigmatization may lead to empowerment, allowing the public mark of deviance to be transformed into an emblem of pride" (Adler Nissen 2014, p. 152). The 2006 war in Lebanon against Israel offered Iran an opportunity to transform its stigmatized status as a "deviant" country into an emblem of national pride. Two factors helped Iran further its strategy of counter stigmatization and strengthen the perception of the two stigmatizing countries, Israel and the United States, as transgressor states among the Arab masses. One is Iran's skillful strategy of siding with the oppressed Shiites not only by providing military and logistic aid but also expanding social services to the Shiite community together with Hezbollah. With Iran's support, Hezbollah provided the basic needs that the Lebanese government could not (Bahgat 2008, p. 145). Second is that the Iranian ruling elite's adoption of rhetoric uniting all Muslims against the oppressor rather than creating an inter-sectarian polarization furthered Hezbollah's legitimacy in the eyes of the Arabs on the street and Muslims in general. For example, during a visit to Lebanon, the Iranian foreign minister Kharazi described Hezbollah's victory over Israel which resulted in Israeli withdrawal from Southern Lebanon in 2000 as a victory for all Muslims (Allen-Mills 2000). This war, which was seen by many as Israel's Vietnam, was one of the most important achievements of Hezbollah, who engaged Israel in both a war of attrition and psychological warfare (Bahgat 2006, p. 370). The Israeli withdrawal from Southern Lebanon without the loss of a single life proved the significance of the Iranian role in Hezbollah's achievement and validated the Iranian argument that Hezbollah was not a terrorist group but a sub-state actor who challenged the two "transgressor" states, Israel and the United States. In the aftermath of the 2006 war in Lebanon, Iran and its prime supporter Hezbollah united all Muslims regardless of the sectarian difference against the abovementioned "transgressor" states so successfully that "even Ayman al-Zawahiri, deputy leader of al-Qaeda released a taped message endorsing Hezbollah's fight against Israel" (Bahgat 2008, p. 147).

All in all, Iran, with its soft power and message that the Iranian government "supports the just struggles of the oppressed against the oppressors in every corner of the globe,"[2] mainly rejects its stigma and aims to put its counter stigmatization strategy into practice. With this strategy of counter stigmatization, Tehran not only challenges the "audience of normal" (Adler Nissen 2014, p. 152) but also stands against "the standard of civilization which creates a pressure for conformity with Western values/practices and poses a demanding cultural challenge to the non-West" (Buzan 2014, p. 581). Tehran, thus, proves the deficiencies of the existing standard of civilization and wants to bring a higher morality standard to the existing international system to flout Western values and practices. This policy at the same time shows that there is "an ongoing legacy of problems for the

[2]The article 154 of the constitution of Iranian revolutionary regime.

legitimacy of international law that still persists and reflects the Western imperial values" (Gong 1984, pp. 7–24).

Nissen notes that "when counter-stigmatization succeeds it may even have a boomerang effect, resulting in the stigmatizer becoming perceived as the transgressor" (Adler Nissen 2014, p. 165). It is beyond the scope of this study to prove whether Iran has succeeded in turning its stigma into a badge of honor and to show the world that the stigmatizers are, at the same time, "transgressor" states. Suffice it to say that Iran's war by proxy in Lebanon and its alliance with Hezbollah and Hamas initiated a hot debate whether "the era of Western domination is coming to an end because in a world where the revolutions of modernity spread, it would be unlikely for one civilization to be able to set the standard for the rest" (Buzan 2014, p. 593).

The mass protests in the aftermath of the Arab Spring and the Syrian Civil war should be understood in this context as they were insurrections against the existing undemocratic rulers in the Middle East and their vested interests under Western domination. Iran's immediate reaction to the Arab Spring was positive at first hand. However, the context in which the Syrian revolution began was troubling for the Ayatollahs in Iran, and the Syrian crisis led to a dramatic change in style and substance of Iranian foreign policy and its traditional use of VNSAs.

4 Syrian Civil War and Iran

Iran regarded the mass protests on the Arab streets as an "Islamist awakening" against Western-backed autocrats. However, the Arab Spring, and specifically the Syrian crisis, crystallized the limits of Tehran's appeal to the Arab world due to several reasons. One is that Tehran was no more able to maintain its policy of championing the rights of oppressed Muslims regardless of the sectarian division as the Syrian crisis led to a sharp division between Sunnis and Shiites. Second, the duality and ambivalence of Iran's approach to the Arab uprisings also led to a loss of Iran's credibility when it failed to recognize the legitimacy, potency, and wide popular base of the Arab revolutions. Put differently, while supporting the insurgents in Bahrain, Yemen, and Tunisia, its policy of differentiating Syria's upheaval from that elsewhere in the Arab world and its portrayal of the Syrian revolution as the work of violent local actors manipulated by foreign powers (namely, the West, the Gulf states, and Israel), (Reuters 2011) "alienated a wide range of Islamist actors. These included not only predictably hostile groups, such as the Salafist movements that saw Shiites and Alawites as heretics, but also the Muslim Brotherhood and moderate Islamist movements with an affinity for Iran's style of governance" (Hokayem 2014, p. 71).

Beginning in May 2012, Iran conducted operations with Asad by sending Quds forces (an elite group within the Iran Revolutionary Guard Corps (IRGC)) to Syria and convinced Maliki to assist in the movement of goods and weapons through Iraqi territory and to facilitate Syrian trade and finance through Iraqi banks. This helped

Asad resist the sanctions imposed by the United States and regional countries such as Turkey and the GCC states.

Iran's overt support of Syria sharpened the Sunni-Shiite division and remolded its ties with the VNSAs, putting its network under pressure. For example, Hamas moved its office from Syria to Qatar in January 2012, and its $23 million in financial support from Shiite Iran soon began to dry up due to reports that Hamas's military wing was helping Sunni rebels fighting the Asad regime (The Guardian 2014). This also showed the limits of Iran's ambitious policy of uniting all Muslims. Moreover, Asad's survival was very costly as Tehran physically inserted itself in the Syrian and Iraqi conflicts. Iran "dispatched not just fuel and weapons but hundreds of 'advisers' from its elite Revolutionary Guards Corps (IRGC) as well as thousands of fighters from the Shiite militias that Iran has fostered, armed, trained and funded in Lebanon and Iraq" (Smyth 2014). It even recruited Shiite fighters from Afghanistan. Since 2012, Iran also lost at least three generals in Syria. Syrian opposition sources claim that Iran spent as much as $15 billion in aid, much of it in the form of fuel, to prop up the Syrian regime (The Economist 2015).

This policy had multiple effects on Iranian domestic politics, economics, and security. First of all, Iran's policy toward Syria led to its further isolation and alienation as its pro-Asad policies deepened the existing tension in its relations with the Gulf and the United States and led to a division among the Iranian elite who questioned the merit of supporting the Asad regime at the expense of détente with the West during the nuclear negotiations which might ease the heavy sanctions on the Iranian economy. Second, the Syrian crisis demonstrated "the overriding power of hardline elements within the country" (Hughes 2014) whose priority was to prevent Asad's downfall even though the principal responsibility for the bloodshed in Syria lies with Asad and his regime. Even the use of chemical weapons in August 2013 and the death of 1300 Syrian civilians did not deter Tehran from defending the idea that the Syrian civil war was the one manipulated by the foreigners and driven by sectarianism. However, Iran's stance nullified its previous counter stigmatization strategy of harshly criticizing Israeli usage of lethal weapons such as cluster bomb against Palestinian civilians.

Leaving aside few critiques of Iranian officials concerning Asad's inflexibility including his rejection of concession to loyal opposition groups, Tehran never ceased investing in the Asad regime and succeeded to secure his survival. This both enhanced the Sunni Arab ruling elite's threat perception concerning Iran's potential to destabilize their own domestic politics and proved Iran's centrality in the search for a solution to the Syrian crisis. Saudi foreign minister Prince Saud al-Faisal, for example, invited his Iranian counterpart Javad Zarifi to negotiate a settling of differences to the satisfaction of both countries (Al Arabiya News 2014). Hamas officials also spent much effort to renew contacts with Iran. For example, Hamas leader Meshal met Iranian representatives several times in Ankara and Doha (The Guardian 2014) and, as noted by Hezbollah leader Hassan Nasrallah, sought to rejoin the Iranian–Syrian axis (Khoury 2015).

In a nutshell, Tehran's investment in the Asad regime paid off by 2014. Iran succeeded in making Westerners accept that the Iranian support for Asad was a necessary cost of countering Al-Qaeda-affiliated Jihadist groups such as Jabhat al-Nusra and ISIS. If there is one single issue that has had an impact on Iran's achievement of securing Asad regime's survival so as to lead to a covert rapprochement between itself and the United States, it is the advance of ISIS in Syria and Iraq. Thus, the ouster of Asad was no longer the highest priority for Western powers (Hokayem 2014, p. 70).

5 ISIS and Iran's Evolving Role

Almost all of the regional states such as Turkey and the Gulf states saw the Jihadist groups Jabhat al-Nusra and ISIS as an unavoidable byproduct of the Syrian civil war and expected that Asad would fall quickly because of their efficient fight against Asad's forces. However, the brutal war waged by ISIS and its advance to Mosul in June 2014 led to an increasing paradox in the relationships between the United States/Sunni countries and Iran. On one hand, ISIS is perceived as a common threat by both Iran and the United States, while on the other, the United States has once again prioritized the elimination of radical Sunni groups in Syria and Iraq, weakening relations with its Sunni allies primarily Saudi Arabia.

In a nutshell, ISIS has served interests of the Asad regime and the Iranian administration by turning them into warriors against Sunni extremism, while Sunni countries such as Saudi Arabia, Turkey, and Qatar suffered damage to their credibility because, from the perspectives of Washington and Brussels, they prioritized the ouster of Asad rather than the elimination of Sunni extremism. The Arab countries' fear of Iran's new role is thus related to four major developments: (1) the election of the moderate, Rouhani, in June 2013, (2) the start of nuclear talks between Iran and the West, (3) Iran's rising influence in Iraq, and (4) the Iranian economy's increasing importance for Western investments in the Middle East.

When looking closely, ISIS advances in Iraq have led to a dramatic change in the style and substance of Iranian policies toward the West, primarily the United States. Since mid-July 2014, Tehran, while previously questioning the effectiveness and legitimacy of the US-led international coalition against ISIS in Iraq, has revoked its long-standing support for Maliki, made only minimal condemnations of American re-involvement in Iraq through air strikes on ISIS positions and began to engage with its regional rival, Saudi Arabia, on mitigating threats posed by ISIS (Esfandiary and Tabatabai 2015, (5). Seen from a different angle, Iran's stakes in Iraq appeared to be too high to be risked for the sake of bilateral relations with Iraq under Maliki considering his alienation of Kurds and Sunnis (Sharafedin 2014). Tehran saw that it was unlikely to be able to maintain its current level of engagement in Syria should the crisis in Iraq worsen due to competing priorities and resources with its adversaries. ISIS' substantial advance to Kermanshah in western Iran and the group's aim of the annihilation of Shiites and the partition of Iraq urged the Iranian ruling elite to build cooperative, albeit covert, relations with the United States. This became most evident in the liberation of Saddam Hussein's hometown of Tikrit with the joint efforts of the Iraqi army, Iranian-backed Shiite militias, and de facto US Air Force support. Thus, the liberation of the iconic Sunni city illustrated the tacit alliance between the United States and Iran (Jansen 2015).

From Iran's perspective, the ISIS threat appeared as an opportunity to create for itself a new image as the savior of regional religious minorities, such as the Shiites, Christians, and Yezidis. Therefore, in stark contrast with the Quds Force's shadowy involvement in Syria, Iran publicized its efforts to arm proxy groups in Iraq and to provide political, military, economic, and humanitarian aid to key stakeholders such as the Shiites and the Kurds. As Esfandiary and Tabatabai note, "the public relations campaign conducted by the Quds Force Commander General Qassem Soleimani on social media, including photos of him in Iraq engaging with various groups, is evidence of these efforts" (Esfandiary and Tabatabai 2015, p. 5).

Iran's ambition to play a new role in Iraq, Syria, and Lebanon, its perceived use of Lebanon's Hezbollah, Iraq's Asaib al-Haq and Kataib Hezbollah, and its military incursions into Iraq and Syria were all interpreted as a serious change in the balance of power between Iran and the Sunni Arab countries, including the non-Arab Sunni Turkey. Worse still, the April 2015 framework agreement on Iran's nuclear program and Rouhani's call for more economic liberalization in January 2015 set off alarm bells among Sunni countries as it was seen as a realization of "Tehran's international rehabilitation leaving it with much higher political/economic stakes" (Stevenson 2014, p. 137).

Therefore, the questions that are of concern at this point are the following: Is the fight against Sunni extremism an opportunity for Iran to get rid of its long-lasting stigma of being a "rogue," a "pariah," and a "failed" state? Will Iran sacrifice its relations with the Asad regime and Hezbollah for the sake of resetting its relations with the United States? What kind of an impact would Iran's fight against ISIS have on its strategic interests on the regional level considering the increasing cooperative relations among the Sunni Arab countries against the rise of Shiism?

Since the Islamic revolution, Iran has had three main foreign policy objectives: regime survival, national security, and regional influence. Iranian use of VNSAs has served their realization. However, for Iran to sustain an anti-American agenda, Tehran adopted a "look to the East" foreign policy orientation in parallel with the deterioration of its relations with the international community during President Ahmadinejad's terms in office. Accordingly, Tehran aimed to cope with economic stagnation by improving its relations with global actors such as China and Russia which would at the same time help Iran to project its identity in the international community based on anti-American Islamism. However, according to Akbarzadeh, Iran failed to continue this policy due to two reasons. First, unlike Tehran's expectations, expanding trade relations with the East did not prevent Eastern powers from siding with the United States either by choice or expediency. Second, Iran kept mum in the face of repressed Muslim minorities (Checens and Uygurs) in Russia and China for the sake of greater geostrategic gains (Akbarzadeh 2015, p. 100).

This pragmatism in Iranian foreign policy became most evident when ISIS threatened Iranian geostrategic interests. The threat posed by ISIS resulted in transformations in Iranian foreign policy. Iran ceased its zealous attempts to unite all Muslims and instead championed the rights of Shiites as it fought at its border against ISIS, which had vowed to eradicate Shiites and establish an Arab Sunni caliphate in the region. Second, despite its refusal of the Westphalian state system in the post-revolution period (after 1979) after the appearance of the ISIS threat, Tehran began to follow nation-state-like policies such as prioritizing its national economic and geostrategic interests rather than its ideologically driven revolutionary foreign policy. For example, Rouhani indicated a shift in priorities, saying "gone are the days when it was said if foreign investors come to Iran its independence will suffer" (Bloomberg Business 2015). Third, the Iranian proxy war in Syria and Iraq grew costlier with ISIS in the equation due to the overstretched Iranian military presence hoping to preserve its role of "architecture of the new Islamic Middle East." In a reversal of its previous "leading from behind" strategy, Tehran sent 100 Quds Force members to Iraq in mid-June 2014 (Esfandiary and Tabatabai 2015, p. 10) in the face of increasing danger stemming from the spread of ISIS. Fourth, Iran is caught between championing the rights of oppressed groups against ISIS/Al-Qaeda and preserving its national strategic and economic interests. Possible strategic gains in relations with international society and the Gulf states and the removal of sanctions are seen by the Iranian ruling elite as roads to the removal of stigmas. Last but not least, as Iranian threat perceptions have peaked due to the destabilization of Iraq along their 910-mile border and deteriorated relations with Saudi Arabia due to the Yemen crisis, the survival of Asad regime is of crucial importance for Tehran.

In short, the tacit alliance over battling ISIS and conciliation of the nuclear issue strengthened the bridges between Iran and members of the Western axis. However, conventional wisdom has it that alliances bring about the formation of counter-alliances. In the face of the Yemen crisis, a Saudi-led coalition was formed against the Houthis in Yemen "as a means of putting a check of Iranian expansion in the region, particularly by securing the strategic Suez Canal" (Meky 2015). Seen from a different angle, the evolving role of Iran in Iraq and Syria in the aftermath of the Arab Spring not only exacerbated the power struggles and geopolitical issues in the region under the guise of sectarian differences but also put the United States in an awkward situation. While flexing its maritime muscles against Iranian vessels near Yemen to prevent Iran from surreptitiously attempt to transfer weaponry to the Houthis, Washington has tried to build sustainable relations with Iran so as to give its Sunni allies the impression that the "U.S. formulates its foreign policy based on an unwritten commitment to certain religious groups and sects—especially Christians and Shiites—and an animus towards other ones; Muslims in general but especially Sunnis" (Nazer 2014). Washington's attitude not only elevated the Iranian position and converted it from the "axis of evil" to the "last best hope" for Washington but also made the United States a fickle super power with the potential to make a volte face toward its Sunni Arab allies in the region.

Three points should be stressed. First, the mutual trust between Iran and international society has not yet been restored, and solidarity with the United States in dealing with ISIS has not been translated into any tangible action capable of changing Iranian policies in the region making it a close ally of Washington, despite the certain thaw in Iran's relations with the West. This became evident in Tehran's boosting of its military presence in Syria[3] (Dagher and Fitch 2015) in the wake of Russian airstrikes inside Syria supporting Asad's regime. Iran took the risk of antagonizing the United States and its Persian Gulf allies who want to push aside President Bashar al-Asad (Wright 2015).

Second, Iran still has difficulty in getting rid of its stigmas and integrating into international society even though it has begun liberalization of its economy and reached an agreement over the nuclear issue. For example, Iran made two medium range ballistic missile tests in October 2015 and March 2017 at the expense of damaging its newly amended relations with the United States and the UN (The Guardian 2015; WSJ 2017). Thirdly, Iran's status alleviation came to an end with Trump's inauguration in January 2017 because Trump, unlike Obama, follows policies antagonizing Iran. According to the Trump administration, Iran has been increasingly threatening the allies of the United States with its potentiality to destabilize the region. For example, Iran has organized a massive paramilitary force made up of Hezbollah and Shiite militia in Syria, in Israel's backyard. Another US ally, Saudi Arabia, is also threatened by Tehran's backing of the Shia population in the Eastern Province of Saudi Arabia, home to Ghawar, the largest oil field in the world, and of the Houthis, the Zaidi Shia movement in Yemen.[4] A NATO ally, Turkey's threat perceptions concerning Iranian partnership with YPG also are quite high. That Iran has not ceased its support of the PYD/YPG since 2013 as a part of its strategy to prevent Turkey from mounting influence in Syria and Iraq is the main source of friction between the two neighboring countries.[5]

6 YPG and Iran

The PKK-affiliated PYD and its military wing YPG have appeared as the sole VNSA fighting against ISIS, the common foe of the Asad regime, the United States, Iran, and Russia. The proclamation of the establishment of a federal region named "Rojava and Northern Syria United Democratic System" on 16 March 2016 in Rimelan has had differing impacts on regional and global actors. While American Secretary of State Kerry and Russian Foreign Minister Lavrov made statements favoring the future formation of a probable federative system in Syria, Tehran continued to talk of preserving Syria's territorial integrity. However, as noted by

[3]"Experts believe Iran has some 7000 IRGC members and Iranian paramilitary volunteers operating in Syria already."

[4]Shahir Shahidsaless, Tump versus Iran: Three Flashpoints that could spark war, Middle East Eye, February 3, 2017, http://www.middleeasteye.net/columns/isolationist-trump-could-be-dragged-one-america-s-worst-wars-256134427

[5]Gazetevatan.com, İran PYD'ye Silah Taşıdı, 11 Kasım 2016, http://www.gazetevatan.com/iran-pyd-ye-silah-tasidi-1005778-dunya/

Sinkaya,[6] Tehran turned a blind eye to the PYD's declaration of an autonomous or federal region because its priority is the preservation of the Asad regime. It, therefore, brokered an agreement between the PYD/YPG and the Asad administration following the advance of the Turkish military-backed Free Syrian Army (FSA) fighters toward the ISIS stronghold Al-Bab in northern Syria.[7] For Iran "to sustain a safe route to the Mediterranean, ideally connecting Tehran to the Syrian port city of Latakia, the Kurds' cooperation is essential. Major towns such as Kobani and Qamishli in northern Syria and Sinjar in Iraq are crucial connecting points on this projected Iranian corridor."[8] Therefore, a stable Kurdish presence is of immense importance for Iranian national interests. According to Basnews, the "PKK is getting support from PUK the Patriotic Union of Kurdistan and Gorran (Change) Movement and Kurdistan Islamic Group (KIG)[9] to execute Iran's project of Shi'ite Crescent, a corridor extended from Iran through northern Iraq and Syria, all the way to Lebanon."[10]

While Turkey has had stable relations with the Kurdistan Regional Government (KRG) in northern Iraq and the Kurdish National Council (KNC or ENKS), Iran has allied itself with the YPG and the Iraqi Popular Mobilization Units/Hashd al-Shaabi. The KNC, which includes the 11 most heavily anti-regime Kurdish parties in the region, was founded in October 2011.[11] It was convened largely under the influence and sponsorship of the president of the Kurdish Regional Government (KRG) in Iraq, Massoud Barzani, who maintains good ties with the Turkish government to the extent that the KRG sells most of their oil extractions to Turkey.

The main reason for the current tension between the PYD/YPG and the KNC mainly stems from the KNC's skepticism of the PYD/YPG's relationship with the Asad regime.[12] During the Kobane crisis in October 2014, the PYD/YPG did not want the participation of the Rojava Peshmerga, the KNC's armed forces, in the defense of the city. Since then, the KNC has declined the PYD's invitation for the

---

[6]Bayram Sinkaya, Federalism in Syria, PYD and Ambivalent Position of Iran, ORSAM, April 4, 2017, http://www.orsam.org.tr/index.php/Content/Analiz/5094?c=orsam%7Cenglish

[7]Yenisafak.com, PYD, Assad, Iran reach secret deal as FSA advances toward al Bab, November 18, 2016, http://www.yenisafak.com/en/world/pyd-assad-iran-reach-secret-deal-as-fsa-advances-toward-al-bab-2566332

[8]Pınar Tremblay, Iranian-Turkish tug-of-war over Kurds, Al-Monitor, December 13, 2016

[9]For further information, see Hawre Hasan Hama & Arkan Ahmed Jaf, Double Standard, Inconsistent Policies of PUK, Kurdish Policy Foundation, January 30, 2017, https://kurdishpolicy.org/2017/01/30/double-standard-inconsistent-policies-of-puk/

[10]PKK Securing a Corridor Extending from Iran to Syria Through Iraq, basnews, March 16, 2017, http://www.basnews.com/index.php/en/news/kurdistan/336929

[11]International Crisis Group, Syria's Kurds: A Struggle Within a Struggle, Middle East Report N°136 | 22 January 2013, p. 3, https://www.acaps.org/sites/acaps/files/key-documents/files/136-syrias-kurds-a-struggle-within-a-struggle.pdf

[12]AraNews, Kurdish National Council calls on PYD to release political prisoners, April4, 2017, http://aranews.net/2017/04/kurdish-national-council-calls-pyd-release-political-prisoners/

Rojava Peshmerga to join the Syrian Democratic Forces project, accusing the YPG of being agents of the Asad regime and Iran. In a similar vein, the PYD/YPG accused the KNC of working with forces hostile to the region, most notably Turkey, where its leaders are based.[13] While the KNC sees the creation of a Kurdistan region of Syria as a solution to the crisis and its parties fly the flag of Kurdistan, the PYD rejects the traditional Kurdish desire for a nation-state, favors a multiethnic federation for the north of Syria, and insists on flying the flag of Rojava.[14]

When looked at closely, it can be seen that Iran uses the YPG as a proxy to bring Turkey to heel. For example, Iran's intensified logistical support to the YPG and PKK[15] after the Kurdistan Freedom Falcons (TAK), a PKK offshoot, claimed responsibility for attacks killing 38 and wounding 155 in Istanbul in December 2016 was perceived by many as a retaliation for Turkey's alleged support for Saudi- and Qatari-backed Islamists in Iraq and Syria: "the primary Iranian concern in this regard is Ankara's alleged links to Jabhat Fatah al-Sham [formerly Jabhat al-Nusra] and its support of Ahrar al-Sham, another militant Salafi group.[16]

Tehran also sees the PKK affiliated groups, primarily the YPG, as an asset in counterbalancing Turkish military presence in Bashiqa. As the tension between Ankara and Tehran over the future of Tal Afar climbed, both Iran and Hashd al-Shaabi became more willing to enter into tactical alliance with the YPG." Put differently,[17] Turkey and Iran have been in rivalry not only in Syria but also in Iraqi territory.

However, according to some analysts, when looking at the various areas of cooperation between Iran and Turkey, antagonizing Ankara would complicate things in the region for Tehran for two reasons. First, Iran is currently enormously skeptical about the PKK-affiliated YPG's attempts to carve a contiguous Kurdish-controlled territory, worrying that this entity could then provide a base for Western powers. Second, Tehran and Ankara have a shared interest in preventing greater Kurdish autonomy in the region, since it could potentially ignite sentiments among Kurdish communities within their own borders. In a similar vein, Ankara wants to continue cordial relations with Tehran and Russia for several reasons. Foremost are the increasingly strained relations with Washington, particularly after President Trump's approval of a plan to directly arm the YPG in Syria. Ankara's hopes that Turkish–American relations regarding Syria and the YPG-dominated Syrian Democratic Forces in particular would be more different under Trump than Obama were dashed. Second is the lack of a shared threat

[13]Kom News, KNC to take "PYD violations" to Geneva, February 22, 2017, https://komnews.org/knc-take-pyd-violations-geneva/

[14]AraNews, Washington invites Syrian Kurdish officials for first time: KNC, January 27, 2017, http://aranews.net/2017/01/washington-invites-syrian-kurds-for-first-time-knc/

[15]Sabah, İran'dan terör örgütü PKK'ya 3 kamp, November 3, 2016.

[16]Hamidreza Azizi, Is Iran following Russia's lead in Syria?, Al-Monitor, January 8, 2017, http://www.al-monitor.com/pulse/originals/2017/01/iran-turkey-russia-syria-cease-fire-kurds-raqqa-assad.html

[17]Moustapha Saadoun, Iran-Turkey Fight over Tal Afar, Al-Monitor, November 18, 2016, http://www.al-monitor.com/pulse/originals/2016/11/tal-afar-iraq-turkman-turkey-pmu-syria.html

perception among members of the NATO alliance and NATO's unwillingness to become involved in fighting against ISIS. Currently, Turkey sits uncomfortably between NATO and the Russia–Iran axis.

In a nutshell, the VNSAs YPG and ISIS both play a significant role in the redistribution of the balance of power in a Middle East with increasingly porous borders. This shared threat to border security brings the two neighboring non-Arab powers Iran and Turkey and their current strategies in Syria into both alliance and conflict.

7 Concluding Remarks

The rise of ISIS has led to tectonic changes in the style and substance of Iranian foreign policy as well as in its relations with global powers, especially the United States. While before the Syrian crisis Iran preferred methods other than the open use of force (Petty 2008, p. 193) such as "leading from behind," Iran has begun stepping up military operations in Iraq against the advance of ISIS. At the outset of the Syrian crisis, Iran did not want to give the impression that it was bolstering a sectarian-based war in the region which would lead to its further isolation by the West and thus denied its involvement in the fight against ISIS in Syria and Iraq until the end of 2014. The presence of the head of the Quds Force in the Islamic Revolutionary Guards Corp(IRGC), Qasem Soleimani, in Iraq (The Guardian 2014), however, revealed Iran's use of force and how seriously it viewed the worsening crisis in Syria and Iraq (Akbarzadeh 2015, p. 45). Secondly, because the presence of ISIS in Iraq enhanced Tehran's feeling of strategic encirclement, Iran, although not a member of the US-led coalition against ISIS, played a vital role in the opposition and cooperated covertly with Washington. This both sharpened the sectarian divide with its Sunni-Arab neighbors and strengthened the view that Iran would potentially attempt to dominate the region in countries like Bahrain and Yemen with a large Shiite population. Thirdly, Iran's tacit agreement with the United States in regard to ISIS proved that it put ideology aside and focused more on national strategic interests. This became most evident with the positive response of Iran's supreme leader, Ayatollah Ali Khamenei, to Obama's secret letter which suggested the possibility of US-Iranian cooperation in fighting against the Islamic State if a nuclear deal was secured (The Huffington Post 2015).

Last but not least, the rise of ISIS undermined the legitimacy of Iran's use of VNSAs to defend the rights of all "oppressed Muslims" in the Arab world regardless of their sectarian difference because Tehran openly sided with the Shiites against the Sunnis in cooperation with the West. Thus, Iran gave up resisting against its own stigmas such as "outlaw" and "rogue state" imposed by the West. Instead, Iran was paradoxically transformed from being stigmatized by the West into the stigmatizer of Sunni jihadism. In many ways, ISIS served as a unifier for Iran and the West, providing them with a common enemy and leading to an upgrade in Iran's relations with the Western axis.

The Iranian economy, which was severely damaged by a decade of international sanctions, was the primary reason for Iran's attempts at international rehabilitation. With expenditures in Syria exceeding 16 billion dollars by the end of 2013 (Wenig 2015), Iran has been consumed by simultaneously supporting the Baath regime militarily in Syria, Iraq in its war against ISIS, and the Houthis in Yemen in their war against a Saudi-led coalition of Arab nations.

In a nutshell, the United States and the European Union have become a port in the storm for an Iran that is increasingly alarmed by the rise of ISIS. However, this relative rapprochement has not yet been able to transform Iran into a "close ally" in the eye of Washington: despite their common foe in Iraq, Washington dispatched warships to waters off Yemen to block Iranian weapons shipments to Shiite Houthi rebels fighting in Yemen. This intervention has openly shown that American and Iranian strategic interests do not overlap in many areas. Most important, Tehran's strategy in Syria and Iraq, as noted by Bowen and McInnis, is focused more on containing and managing ISIS rather than defeating it completely, despite appearing as an effective ally in rolling back the group at a time when the United States is wary to commit to another ground war in the Middle East. In Syria, ISIS is seen by Tehran as an effective tool in both weakening US and the Gulf states, GCC-backed opposition militias and buttressing the argument that President Asad is the most amenable alternative in Syria (Bowen and McInnis 2015).

Currently, Iran has adopted a bifurcated diplomatic posture. While conciliation over the nuclear issue and fighting against ISIS brutality has necessitated strengthening ties with the United States and bringing Iran back to the Western fold, Khamenei also sent the commander of the Quds Force, Qassem Suleiman, to Moscow to plan a new Russian–Iranian offensive in the face of "the deteriorating situation in Syria, where the US backed rebel advances toward the coast were posing a danger to the heartland of Asad's Alawite sect, where Russia maintains its only Mediterranean naval base in Tartous" (Bassam and Perry 2015).

In a nutshell, the current impact of ISIS on Iranian-US relations is not positive and, on the contrary, has set a process of further polarization and axis building into motion in which Iran and the United States seem to be on opposite camps.

Another VNSA, the YPG, also has had a significant impact on Iranian policies toward the Syrian crisis both on the regional and global level, as the group has crystallized the limits of the cordial relationship between Turkey and Iran. Because the YPG is currently described as the elephant in the room in the Middle East that will resurface once the conflicts in Syria and Iraq are over, it is evident that the YPG, rather than ISIS, will be the main proxy of global actors and regional countries in the determination of the fate of Syria and Iraq in the future.

References

Adler Nissen, R. (2014). Stigma management in international relations: Transgressive identities, norms, and order in international society. *International Organization, 68*, 143–176.

Akbarzadeh, S. (2015). Iran and the Shanghai Cooperation Organization: Ideology and realpolitik in Iranian foreign policy. *Australian Journal of International Affairs, 69*(1), 88–103.

Al Arabiya News. (2014, May 13). Saudi ready to negotiate with Iran: FM. Accessed March 28, 2015, from http://english.alarabiya.net/en/News/middle-east/2014/05/13/Saudi-ready-to-negotiate-with-Iran-FM.html

Allen-Mills, T. (2000, June 4). Villagers braced for the first attack in Israeli border Limbo. *Sunday Times*.

Bahgat, G. (2006). Israel and Iran in the New Middle East. *Contemporary Security Policy, 27*(3), 363–375.

Bahgat, G. (2008). Iran and the United States: Reconcilable differences? *Iranian Studies, 41*(2), 139–154.

Barzegar, K. (2008). Iran and the Shiite Crescent: Myths and realities. *The Brown Journal of World Affairs, 15*(1), 87–99.

Bassam, L., & Perry, T. (2015, October 6). How Iranian general plotted out Syrian assault in Moscow. *Reuters*. Accessed October 28, 2015, from http://www.reuters.com/article/2015/10/06/us-mideast-crisis-syria-soleimani-insigh-idUSKCN0S02BV20151006

Bloomberg Business. (2015, January 4). Rouhani tells Iranians economy can't grow with nation isolated. Accessed April 14, 2015, from http://www.bloomberg.com/news/articles/2015-01-04/iran-s-economy-can-t-grow-while-nation-isolated-rouhani-says

Bowen, A. J., & McInnis, J. M. (2015, July 23). Sorry America: Iran won't defeat ISIS for you. *The National Interest*. Accessed October 14, 2015, from http://nationalinterest.org/blog/sorry-america-iran-wont-defeat-isis-you-13407

Buzan, B. (2014). The standard of civilization as an English concept. *Journal of International Studies, 42*(3), 576–594.

Byman, D., Chubin, S., Ehteshami, A., & Green, J. D. (2001). *Iran's security policy in the post-revolutionary era*. Santa Monica, CA: RAND Corporation. Accessed May 2, 2015, from http://www.rand.org/pubs/monograph_reports/MR1320

Dagher, S., & Fitch, S. (2015, October 2). Iran expands role in Syria in conjunction with Russia's airstrikes. *The Wall Street Journal*. Accessed October 28, 2015, from http://www.wsj.com/articles/iran-expands-role-in-syria-in-conjunction-with-russias-airstrikes-1443811030

Esfandiary, D., & Tabatabai, A. (2015). Iran's ISIS policy. *International Affairs, 91*(1), 1–15.

Goffman, E. (1963). *Stigma: Notes on the management of spoiled identity*. New York, NY: Simon & Schuster.

Gong, G. W. (1984). *The standard of 'civilization' in international society*. Oxford: Clarendon Press.

Hokayem, E. (2014). Iran, the Gulf States and the Syrian civil war. *Survival: Global Politics and Strategy, 56*(6), 59–86.

Hughes, G. A. (2014). Syria and the perils of proxy warfare. *Small Wars & Insurgencies, 25*(3), 523–535.

Jansen, M. (2015, March 30). Uneasy alliance between US and Iran must hold after Battle of Tikrit. *The Irish Times*. Accessed April 20, 2015, from http://www.irishtimes.com/news/world/middle-east/uneasy-alliance-between-us-and-iran-must-hold-after-battle-of-tikrit-1.2157850

Khoury, J. (2015, March 12). Hamas and Tehran boost ties as Meshal meets Iran's Larijani in Doha. *Haaretz*. Accessed April 27, 2015, from http://www.haaretz.com/news/diplomacy-defense/.premium-1.646624

Meky, S. (2015, March 30). Egypt eyes halting Iran expansion through Yemen war: Analysts. *Al-Arabiya*. Accessed April 28, 2015, from http://english.alarabiya.net/en/perspective/analysis/2015/03/30/Egypt-eyes-halting-Iran-expansion-through-Yemen-war-analysts.html

Nazer, F. (2014, August 14). How religion could complicate US ıntervention in Iraq. *CNN.com*. Accessed April 28, 2015, from http://edition.cnn.com/2014/08/14/opinion/iraq-intervention-religion/index.html

Norton, R. (2007). *Hezbollah*. Princeton, NJ: Princeton University Press.

O'brien, J. M. (2006). *'Exporting Jihad'*. Masters of Arts in law and diplomacy thesis, Tufts University.

Petty, K. A. (2008). Veiled impunity: Iran's use of non-state armed groups. *Denver Journal of International Law and Policy, 36*, 191–219.

Reuters. (2011, April 12). Iran calls Syrian protests a western plot. Accessed March 25, 2015, from http://www.reuters.com/article/2011/04/12/us-syria-iran-idUSTRE73B22V20110412

Samii, B. (2006, August 14). Iran: Is Tehran protecting its investment in Hezbollah? *Payvand*. Accessed March 28, 2015, from http://www.payvand.com/news/06/aug/1151.html

Sharafedin, B. (2014, August 13). Why Iran has finally let go of Maliki. *BBC News*. Accessed April 21, 2015, from http://www.bbc.com/news/world-middle-east-28777142

Smyth, P. (2014, September 18). All the Ayatollah's men, foreign policy. *Foreign Policy*. Accessed March 30, 2015, from http://foreignpolicy.com/2014/09/18/all-the-ayatollahs-men/

Stevenson, J. (2014). The Syrian tragedy and precedent. *Survival: Global Politics and Strategy, 56* (3), 121–140.

Tabarani, G. (2008). *How Iran plans to fight America and dominate the Middle East*. Indiana: Author House.

Tasnim News. (2014, October 13). http://tnews.ir/news/2DFD31724384.html. In Akbarzadeh, S. (2015). 'Iran and Daesh: The case of a reluctant Shia power', *Middle East Policy*, *22*(3), 53.

The Economist. (2015, January 3). Death of a general. Accessed March 30, 2015, from http://www.economist.com/news/middle-east-and-africa/21637416-wars-syria-and-iraq-are-sucking-iran-ever-more-tangled-conflicts-death

The Guardian. (2014, January 9). Hamas and Iran rebuild ties three years after falling out over Syria. Accessed March 30, 2015, from http://www.theguardian.com/world/2014/jan/09/hamas-iran-rebuild-ties-falling-out-syria

The Guardian. (2015, October 16). 'Iran's missile test was a clear violation of UN sanctions' says US AmbAsador'. Accessed October 31, 2015, from http://www.theguardian.com/world/2015/oct/16/iran-ballistic-missile-test-violation-un-sanctions

The Huffington Post. (2015, February 13). Iran Ayatollah Khamenei sent Obama secret letter: *WSJ*. Accessed October 30, 2015, from http://www.huffingtonpost.com/2015/02/13/iran-khamenei-obama-letter_n_6682002.html

The Telegraph. (2012, February 3). Iran: We will help cut out the cancer of Israel. Accessed October 30, 2015, from http://www.telegraph.co.uk/news/worldnews/middleeast/iran/9059179/Iran-We-will-help-cut-out-the-cancer-of-Israel.html

The Wall Street Journal. (2017, March 9). Iran test-fires medium-range ballistic missle. https://www.wsj.com/articles/iran-test-fires-medium-range-ballistic-missile-1489082919

The Washington Times. (2003). Syria and the new axis of Evil. 29 September in Oktav, Ö. Z. (2008). *Limits of relations with the west, Turkey, Syria and Iran*. İstanbul: Beta.

Wenig, E. (2015, September 6). This is how much cash Iran is spending to keep Asad alive. *The Daily Caller*. Accessed September 30, 2015, from http://dailycaller.com/2015/06/09/this-is-how-much-cash-iran-is-spending-to-keep-Asad-alive/#ixzz3pUtiTVdL

Wilkins, H. (2013). *The making of Labenese foreign policy understanding the 2006 Israeli-Hezbollah war*. New York, NY: Routledge.

Wright, R. (2015, October 26). Iran's generals are dying in Syria. *The New Yorker*. Accessed October 31, 2015, from http://www.newyorker.com/news/news-desk/irans-generals-are-dying-in-syria

Yazd, A. (2014, July 10). 'Iran: From 'axis of evil' to 'last best hope' in the Middle East'. *CNN*. Accessed May 1, 2015, from http://edition.cnn.com/2014/07/09/opinion/iran-u-s-alliance-opinion/

Zarakol, A. (2011a). *After defeat how the east learned to live with the west*. Cambridge: Cambridge University Press.

Zarakol, A. (2011b). What makes terrorism modern? Terrorism, legitimacy, and the international system. *Review of International Studies, 37*(5), 2311–2336.

Zarakol, A. (2014). What made the modern world hang together: Socialisation or stigmatization? *International Theory, 6*(2), 312–313.

The Contagion of the Syrian Civil War into Turkey Under the Impact of ISIS and YPG Cases: Conditioning Factors and Diffusion Mechanisms

Emel Parlar Dal

1 Introduction

This paper is intended to investigate the contagion of the Syrian civil war into Turkey with reference to two VNSAs: ISIS and the YPG. In doing so, the rise and transformation of violent non-state actors (VNSAs) in the realm of the Syrian civil war will not be addressed as a stand-alone trend but will rather analyze their changing role in and impact on the Syrian civil war in light of the conditioning factors and diffusion mechanisms of this conflict. The paper thus draws on the assumption that conflicts easily diffuse to neighboring states and regions under specific conditions and by direct or indirect diffusion mechanisms. The diffusion of civil wars is, therefore, a multifactorial process which must be assessed in terms of its catalyzing conditions and its mechanisms of diffusion. Such a twofold analysis of the diffusion of the Syrian civil war into Turkey provides a robust framework to examine the complete Syrian picture. In the first part of this chapter, the background of the diffusion of the Syrian civil war will be discussed using four mass-level conditioning factors: structural, political, economic-social, and cultural/perceptional. In the second part, the conflict's direct and indirect diffusion mechanisms will be used to investigate their various effects on Turkey via ISIS and YPG.

Given this background, the main research question asks under which conditioning factors and by which diffusion mechanisms have the Syrian civil war has spread to Turkey between 2011 and 2016 via ISIS and the YPG. Additionally, this paper also seeks to examine in which ways and under the influence of which driving conditions and mechanisms did ISIS and the YPG impact the contagiousness of the Syrian conflict in the Turkish case. The diffusion of civil wars or conflicts and

E. Parlar Dal (✉)
Faculty of Political Sciences, International Relations Department, Marmara University, Istanbul, Turkey
e-mail: emelparlar@yahoo.com

Ö.Z. Oktav et al. (eds.), *Violent Non-state Actors and the Syrian Civil War*,
DOI 10.1007/978-3-319-67528-2_11

VNSAs is rarely studied in the IR literature in general and in conflict and security and terrorism studies in particular. A restricted number of studies on ethnic and ethno-sectarian conflicts in Turkey have been published, regardless of the existence of a still unresolved ethnic-originated separatist conflict in the country between the PKK and the Turkish state (Parlar Dal 2017). Nevertheless, a flourishing literature, albeit limited, can be found on the same topic in international conflict and IR studies. On international conflicts, Michael E. Browns' edited book entitled *The International Dimensions of Internal Conflict* offers a comprehensive framework on the conditioning factors and proximate causes of conflicts. The idea of the spread of conflicts from one area to another, or spillover, was first challenged by conflict scholars such as Brown (1996), Cordell and Wolff (2009), and Simowitz (1998). Lake and Rothchild (1998) and Wolff (2006) contributed to the shifting of attention away from internal conflicts to internationalization of conflict. On the spillover of conflict, Danneman and Ritter (2014, p. 7), Murdoch and Sandler (2002, p. 92), Buhaug and Gleditsch (2008), De Maio (2010, pp. 25–27), Gleditsch et al. (2008, p. 3), Saideman (2001, 2012), Salehyan and Gleditsch (2006), and Auton and Slobodien (2016) all contributed extensively to the existing literature on the various aspects of the topic. Given this theoretical background, this study seeks to fill the conceptual and empirical lacunae in the conflict studies literature with its comprehensive framework by linking the driving factors behind civil wars to their diffusion to neighboring regions and states. A second novelty of this paper is its attempt to theoretically and empirically apply the concept of diffusion of conflict/civil war to the topic of "the Syrian civil war and Turkey." A third novelty of this study is its attempt to integrate ISIS and the YPG, as cases of VNSAs, into the comparative study of conflict diffusion.

2 From the Causes to the Diffusion of Regional Civil Conflict: A Theoretical Framework

Diffusion simply refers to the image of the spread of something across space. Similarly, this term is seen by scholars as either an outcome or a process. For others, there exists a duality of diffusion as both cause and effect. In the conflict studies literature, the concept of "diffusion" signifies the spread of instability from one geographic area/region to another. Since a conflict can diffuse internally, or in other words inside the national borders, or externally beyond the boundaries of the conflicted country or region, its effects are generally observed at the multiple levels of national, regional, and international.

The diffusion of regional civil conflicts into the neighboring and other countries in close proximity and its extent and end results or impact may be best grasped by the use of a two-layered framework consisting of the conditioning factors of diffusion and direct and indirect diffusion mechanisms.

2.1 Conditioning Factors of Civil War

According to most scholars of violent conflict claim, conflicts may only diffuse from one geography to another under the existence of a certain number of conditioning factors and thanks to a series of diffusion mechanisms categorized as direct and indirect. Conditioning factors are structural, political, socioeconomic, and cultural. As stated by Michael Brown (1996), these four key categories may lead, either individually or collectively, to the outbreak of a violent conflict which is also prone to diffusion through the functioning of diffusion mechanisms.

Structural Factors The structural framework through which actors engage in different types of sociopolitical relations has proven to be one of the most important factors behind the acceleration of the diffusion process. As Brown has already propounded, regions in which malfunctioning state structures are accompanied by diversified security problems and ethnic diversity are prone to conflict. It is possible to argue that the same factors of weak state structures, security problems, and ethnic sophistication have profound impact on making such regions fertile for the diffusion of the various effects of civil wars. The most common reasoning that appeals to scholars in explaining the accelerating impact of the structural factors on the diffusion of regional civil conflicts is the logic that such conditions restrain the state experiencing the civil war from taking the necessary steps such as the full deployment of military counter programs, in-depth investigation, and cleansing of conflicting groups or deterring actions for preventing the contagion of the conflict. The permissive conditions within each of these "structural" categories of conditioning factors of diffusion can be organized under three subcategories: weak states, intrastate security concerns, and ethnic geography.

Weak States As agreed on by most conflict scholars, the decrease of statehood and the state monopoly of the use of force act as facilitating factors in the spillover of conflict (Elbadawi and Sambanis 2000; Hegre et al. 2001; Salehyan 2007, p. 225). In the conflict literature, the concept of "weak state" refers to the lack of state monopoly against violence and to its inability to protect its territory against rebelling groups located in neighboring states or any military intervention by its neighbors.

Intrastate Security Concerns In the case of weak state structures, individual groups within these states engage in assuring their own defense and take military initiatives of their own, generally leading to the emergence of a security dilemma by threatening the security of other groups within the weak states. The gradual armament and militarization of these individual groups inevitably increase intrastate security concerns (Brown 1996, p. 15).

Ethnic Geography Ethnically heterogeneous societies are generally considered to be more prone to violent conflicts and civil war. As stated by Brown, "countries with intermingled societies are less likely to face secessionist demands because ethnic groups are not distributed in ways that lend themselves for partition"

(Brown 1996, p. 16). States with ethnic groups living in different regions or provinces are more prone to secessionist movements. States formed within the divided territories of the former empires generally possess complex demographics that may lead to serious ethnic problems emanating from the contentious minorities.

Political Factors In addition to the overwhelming tendency in explaining conditioning factors of diffusion with regard to structural factors, the literature has produced compelling arguments about the relevance of political factors in the diffusion process as well. These political factors have been utilized in the literature not only as the source of the conflict itself but also an important component of the diffusion process. Indeed, the political factors behind the origin and the diffusion process of conflicts can reveal important details about the systemic links behind these processes. Brown subsumes such political factors under four categories, each of which contributes to the diffusion process to a certain degree: discriminatory political situations, exclusionary national ideologies, intergroup politics, and elite politics.

Discriminatory Political Situations This first criteria of political factors establishes a connection between the incomprehension of the political institutions and the emergence or diffusion of the conflict with regard to the accumulation of resentment by shunned groups and actors. Excluded from the political participation processes, groups tied by strong ethnic or ideological bonds in particular may try to channel their demands by employing violent tactics and could easily trigger further violent actions.

Exclusionary National Ideologies This second criteria serves as an additional characteristic for the emergence and diffusion of conflicts while boosting the further eradication of the first criteria of discriminatory politics as well. The existence of a strong and predominant ideology, whether national or religious, renders the trajectory of excluded and minority groups in a way that they may result to the means of conflict in overcoming the impacts of strict dominant ideologies that narrows their elbow room.

Intergroup Politics Conflicts in one country may influence groups in another to increase their extreme demands. The likely demands of the groups in one state, for instance, may be emulated by the other groups in the other states, and this may also lead to the mobilization of the latter. This "demonstrative effect" has generally become influential in the diffusion of ethnic conflicts from one country to another.

Elite Politics The politics formulated in the hands of state elites of a country and their relative interests may precipitate similar conflicts in another country. Conflicts may lead elites in one country to revise their beliefs about the costs of protest or violence. On the other hand, elite groups' expansionist or antidemocratic policies may facilitate the spillover of an internal conflict from one country to another. Diffusion may occur as a result of either a mass or elite-led level process (Rodt n.d.). Elites of a country may intentionally seek to cause an internal conflict to spill over into outside regions in order to maximize their political gains from regional instabilities.

Economic-Social Factors First, *economic problems* in a developed or underdeveloped country may increase the risk of both the emergence of an internal conflict and of its contagion into neighboring countries. Inflation, unemployment, law, income-related problems, and resource competitions have potential in increasing tensions, alienations, and frustrations in societies that may also create a convenient ground for the diffusion of conflicts to the outside regions. Second, *the existence of discriminatory economic systems* may end up with the apparition of high levels of frustration in a country and therefore are more prone to the generation and diffusion of violence. Third, aside from economic development, *modernization* may ease the apparition and diffusion of internal conflicts since as a result of industrialization and the use of new technologies, profound social changes like urbanization and migration may damage the existing political institutions and weaken family and social systems, literacy, and education rates. Societies where expectations of people are not met appear to be more prone to the internal crisis and their diffusion to neighboring regions.

Cultural/Perceptional Factors Two cultural and perceptional factors influence the contagion of internal conflicts: patterns of cultural discrimination and problematic group histories. First, the existence of cultural discrimination against minorities in a country reflected on unequitable education opportunities and legal and political limitations on the use of minority languages and on religious freedom may be considered a source of both internal conflict and its diffusion. Second, certain groups' past histories about the perceptions of themselves and other groups in their close proximities may also increase the risk of the contagiousness of internal conflicts since their unchanged beliefs and mutually exclusive perceptions of the "other" may increase the provocation on either side.

2.2 *Diffusion Mechanisms*

2.2.1 Direct Diffusion Mechanisms

The three-layered framework proposed by Buhaug and Gleditsch (2008) provides a comprehensive ground for studying direct diffusion mechanisms with the help of the analytical tools of *bad neighborhood(s)*, *interaction opportunities and ties,* and *conflict characteristics*. In this context, the geographic settings which are prone to conflict due to their ambient conditions are conceptualized as *bad neighborhood(s)*. The logic behind this first layer is that it is highly likely that conflicts in historically unsteady regions easily diffuse across such geographies. By analyzing the cluster of conflicts in relation with impoverishment, Buhaug and Gleditsch argue that one of the underlying characteristics of such geographies is the density of poverty, where conflicts may easily originate and diffuse (Buhaug and Gleditsch 2008, pp. 4–5).

The second layer of direct diffusion mechanisms, *interaction opportunities and ties,* includes seven other factors, each of which contributes to the contagion of civil war: "the distance to the nearest conflict zone, the length of the boundary with the conflict neighbor, the existence of ethnic ties to the neighboring conflict population, refugee population from the conflict neighbor, the severity of the neighboring conflict, the nature of the neighboring conflict and the size of the neighboring country experiencing conflict" (Buhaug and Gleditsch 2008, p. 216). The final layer of *conflict characteristics* looks at the varying characteristics of conflicts and how they relate to the diffusion of conflicts across regions. This factor argues that the conflicts that are separatist in nature are more prone to diffuse into neighboring regions (Buhaug and Gleditsch 2008, p. 223).

2.2.2 Indirect Diffusion Mechanisms

Indirect mechanisms or demonstrative effects of diffusion signify the processes whereby conflicts spread to other groups or regions mostly through the use of specific tools of inspiration such as learning, emulation, mimicry, etc. Whether diffused through learning, emulation, or mimicry, the outcome of these processes results in the emergence of a variety of lessons indirectly triggering the diffusion in neighboring countries. In his study, Saideman (2012) outlines four categories of lessons resulting from such indirect diffusions: *new tactics or strategies, new ideas and delegitimization of previous approaches, revised expectations about the likely behavior of key outside actors, and revised expectations about the chances of success.*

New Tactics or Strategies The learning of new tactics or strategies is one of the most common indirect diffusion mechanisms observed in civil wars and regional conflicts where various actors copy the best ways of conventional and ideological combat from each other through emulation and learning (Börzel and Risse 2012, p. 5). In contemporary conflicts, violent non-state actors proved to be the most prevailing agents of the indirect diffusion of new tactics or strategies whereby they lift the effectiveness of their actions resulting in further violent mobilization across the neighboring regions. This argument is not only valid for the behaviors of the violent non-state actors but also accounts for their organizational transformations in explaining how they restructure their internal dynamics by copying each other's organizational schemes. It is also an acknowledged fact that the validity of direct mechanisms (such as bad neighborhoods or ethnic ties) in a given regional or civil conflict encourages the conflicting parties to learn and carry out each other's tactics and strategies more easily.

New Ideas and Delegitimization of Previous Approaches One common denominator in contemporary diffused conflicts is the belief in certain set of values contaminating a number of mindscapes not only about ideological worldviews but also about certain policy practices of the actors they fight against. As Lake and Rothschild argue, the diffusion of conflicts has a strong relation with the information flows influencing other groups in the neighboring regions (Lake and Rothchild 1998, p. 4). The circulation of ideas across the conflicting regions not only helps the agents of the conflict attract more supporters, fighters, and sympathizers but also triggers the generation of grievances among other groups in different regions by delegitimizing the prevailing beliefs and policies, etc. Delegitimization attracts new supporters through the dissemination of new ideologies and sowing the seeds of further grievances and serves as the most reliable indirect mechanism for violent non-state actors in civil conflicts.

Revised Expectations About the Likely Behavior of Key Outside Actors Under the civil conflicts condition, state or non-state actors, whether violent or not, influence outside actors' actions by changing their expectations of the likelihood of conflict. The civil war may be more contagious when there are transnational ethnic ties among groups located in two or more states. Changing attitudes toward an ethnic group in the conflicted country by key outside actors may raise the expectations of other groups in neighboring countries with ethnic kinship. The outside actors' handling of the civil wars and their support of non-state actors involved in these crises explicitly play an undeniable role in directly and indirectly shaping the strategies of the other state and non-state actors in the country to which conflict diffuses.

Revised Expectations About the Chances of Success The effects of an internal conflict in a state may be highly contagious if a non-state group, violent or not, in the conflicted country achieves relative success in the face of the weakened state apparatus. If the gains of the rebel groups or non-state actors increase in a civil war context, it is highly probable that similar expectations would be increasingly pronounced in the neighboring countries facing similar dissatisfaction from some parts of society or an ethnic group. This certainly affects the way these oppositional or ethnic groups continue their political or military struggle against the central authority. The demonstrative effect of a conflict will certainly be high in terms of emulation when there exists a strategic interaction between two ethnic groups located, respectively, in the conflicted and contaminated countries (Lake and Rothchild 1998, p. 18).

3 Unpacking the Conditioning Factors Catalyzing the Diffusion of Syrian Civil War

3.1 *Structural Factors*

Syria's ongoing civil war steadily undermined its state sovereignty, making the country more vulnerable to growing violence of diverse VNSAs. Syria has gradually become a conflict-torn state unable to protect its territory against rebel groups based in its territory. This preexisting weak state structure also made the country open to foreign interventions by major and regional powers with differing interests. Added to this are the growing intrastate security concerns among various non-state armed groups in the country acting under fragile and volatile coalitions. The struggles between some VNSAs also lead to increasing of intrastate security concerns. It is an acknowledged fact that the Syrian political geography was based on ethnic cleavages, i.e., the Kurds, Turcomans, Druzes, and others. Indeed, the existence of such an ethnic geography laid the groundwork for the spread of violence once intrastate security concerns were stimulated. That is to say that the rather peaceful relations between different ethnic groups in Syria deteriorated with the emergence of threat perceptions among these ethnic groups. In other words, once groups began to take to the streets in an organized manner, others felt the necessity to replicate such an action, leading to a reactionary pattern. For instance, the organizational mobility among the Kurdish groups does indeed trigger the Turcoman groups to do the same in Syria. Therefore, it is possible to argue that the existence of an ethnic geography in Syria paved the way for the operationalization of intrastate security concerns.

3.2 Political Factors

Four political factors impact both the emergence of an internal conflict and its dissemination to other states: discriminatory political situations, exclusionary national ideologies, elite politics, and intergroup politics. The first factor, discriminatory political situations, can be exemplified by the fact that, as a closed and authoritarian system in Syria, the current Syrian regime under the Bashar Al-Assad government generated significant resentment, especially in 2011 when the necessary democratic and political reforms were not been realized and the opposition was restricted. The Syrian Ba'ath party, since taking over of the administration in 1961 after a coup d'état and Hafez al-Assad's arrival to power as president in 1971, has pursued a discriminatory policy favoring Alawite groups rather than the majoritarian Sunni groups. Hafez al-Assad's authoritarian and repressive was also been characterized by its emergency laws, discretionary arrests, and a discriminatory system based on the granting of privileges to certain groups supporting its regime. The policy of ethnic discrimination and national persecution against Sunni, Christian, and Kurdish groups continued under the rule of Bashar al-Assad and helped fuel the uprisings in late 2010. The ascendance of non-Sunni Muslims to positions of power in the Syrian government and bureaucracy also illustrates how the Hafez and Bashar al-Assad governments adopted *exclusionary national ideologies* for more than a half century. Although early on Bashar tried to open up the country in terms of political representation after his father's strict authoritarian and repressive rule, eventually he ended up pursuing the same strict policies. The Assad family's undisputed power in Syria and its family members' privileged positions in the main organs of the state, especially the military, can also be seen as a reflection of Syria's long-lasting *elitist policies*. In the Syrian context, the prospects for violence were great since the multiple ethnic and religious groups in the country have diverging political, ideological, and religious characteristics and confrontational strategies. It can also be claimed that the dynamics of Syrian intergroup politics also made the Syrian conflict more likely given the incompatible objectives of the diverse ethnic and religious groups.

3.3 Economic-Social Factors

The economic-social factors have also set the groundwork for conditioning an adverse social environment driving a wedge not only between the ruling elites and the society but also between various social groups themselves. It seems plausible to argue that although structural and political factors had a more solid impact on the outbreak and the diffusion of the civil war, economic problems sowed seeds of discontent among the society in Syria. With regard to economic problems, first and foremost, it must be noted that since the Syrian economy depended on the agricultural sector to a great extent, the devastating drought and dust storms in Syria between 2006 and 2011 in the absence of advanced irrigation infrastructure not only caused a blow to the economy but also forced the population to leave the countryside in large numbers and move to urban centers (Polk 2013). Such significant internal movement combined with growing numbers of unemployed helped the already existing opposition legitimize their grievances in the eyes of the masses. Such a shock in the agricultural sector also posed significant problems in food security (Gleick 2014, p. 338).[1] Moreover, the termination of state-sponsored food subsidies negatively impacted society and constituted further sources of grievances (Tomass 2016, p. 165). In addition to the disruption of the flow of cheap oil from Iraq after the 2003 invasion, the oil sector in Syria was also in decline with falling numbers of produced barrels, an important part of which were consumed for energy and industry in the country.

Put broadly, the most important established sectors of the Syrian economy, agriculture and oil, no longer provided the people with economic stability. It is possible to argue that Syria also lagged behind in keeping pace with economic development and modernization and thereby failed to diversify the economy in order to integrate the growing numbers of population to the economy. In addition, economic corruption and nepotism were part of the basis of a discriminatory economic system. The concentration of economic power in the hands of the extended families of the ruling elite, most notably the Alawite circles, not only gave them more political power but also spurred other groups to be easily captivated by the opposition movements. In short, economic problems, the failure to

[1]The situation deteriorated so much in Darah that the clergymen even declared eating the meat of cat and dog would be allowed under these circumstances.

modernize the economy and the existence of discriminatory economic systems catalyzed the diffusion of political and civil unrest among the Syrian society.

3.4 Cultural/Perceptional Factors

Cultural/perceptional factors analyzed in conflict studies have come into prominence both before the outbreak and during the diffusion process of the Syrian civil war. It is an indisputable fact that the modern roots of the Syrian sociopolitical complex were constructed on a state-led sectarian ideology limiting the elbow room of other shunned groups. Although Syria was politically portrayed as the most secular country in the Middle East redressing the balance between state and religious institutions (Haran 2016, p. 3), it was a common belief among the Syrian society that the Alawites had easier access to top political positions. This was also valid for the military ranks, so that most of the higher ranks of the Syrian military came from Alawite circles. Whether such an argument represents the truth or not, this perception was strongly embedded in the discourse of the opposition even before the uprisings erupted in Syria. For instance, the head of the Reform Party, Farid Ghadry, pointed out as early as 2011 that the conflict was perceived from a sectarian point of view by the masses: "many Syrians I have spoken with inside the country are seething with anger over the Alawite-led government's butchering of Sunnis" (Pipes 2011).

With regard to the patterns of cultural discrimination, it can be argued that the social aspect of the Syrian puzzle is overwhelmingly shaped around ethnic/tribal cleavages. Many different ethnic groups, most notably the Kurds and Yezidis, have historically been subject to Arabization policies of the Baath party in Syria. As a highly heterogeneous society in terms of ethnic and tribal groups, Kurds, Druzes, Turkomans, and other groups were culturally and politically excluded from fair and effective political representation. However, it is important to note that although such a cultural and perceptual discrimination against different groups was a common practice of the ruling Syrian elites, it did not result in the emergence of separatist ideologies for all of groups concerned.

What is more, even with the existence of such a state-led policy discriminating against various ethnic/cultural groups, it did not cause the formation of severely problematic relations as was the case in Iraq. Despite the state ideology, these groups did not perceive each other as enemies. That is to say that, with regard to the cultural/perceptional factors in Syria, although the patterns of cultural discrimination were evidently led by state policies, it did not evenly lead to the formation of problematic group histories among the Syrian society.

Drawing on this retrospective analysis, it is possible to argue that these conditioning factors of the Syrian civil war also played catalyzing roles to certain extents in the diffusion process of the conflict into Turkey via violent non-state armed actors, most notably ISIS and the YPG. An overall comparative analysis suggests that the diffusion of the impacts of ISIS and the YPG was catalyzed mostly by the *structural* and *political* factors leaving the *economic-social* and *cultural/perspectival* factors less efficient. Given the *structural* factors, it is evident that the existence of *weak states* served the interests of all VNSAs in the country and paved the way for the rapid expansion and territorial control of ISIS and the YPG in Syria. However, what contributed more to the diffusion of the YPG's impact among the structural factors was the existence of a strong *ethnic geography* with various Kurdish groups located in Syria, Iraq, and Turkey. In addition, the political factor of *discriminatory political situations* was an effective factor in the diffusion process of the YPG's impact into Turkey since the Kurds in Syria and Turkey have raised the same rhetoric of political discrimination for many years.

Indeed, it is clear that this rhetorical juncture stemming from *discriminatory political situations* between the Kurds in Syria and Turkey accelerated the diffusion process for the YPG. In the ISIS case, in addition to the existence of *weak states*, the *structural factor* of *intrastate security concerns* played a significant role as with the intensification of the conflict smaller armed groups joined ISIS ranks in order to survive. The existence of such a security dilemma among groups in the country helped the growth of ISIS and diffused its impact across the borders into Turkey. Again, it can be argued that during the origin process of ISIS violence, the *political factor* of *exclusionary national ideologies* played a legitimizing role for the shunned Sunni groups in Iraq and Syria to join the ranks of the network. As noted earlier, both the *economic-social* and *cultural/perceptional* factors laid a general groundwork for the diffusion of the ISIS and the YPG cases. However, what is remarkable was the role of the *cultural/perspectival factor* of *patterns of cultural discrimination* in triggering the diffusion process of the YPG since its ideology is much more grounded on ethnic/nationalist themes than the universal jihadist ideology of ISIS.

4 Impact of Diffusion Mechanisms of the Syrian Civil War into Turkey: ISIS and PYD/YPG Cases

4.1 Assessing Direct Diffusion Mechanisms Within ISIS and PYD/YPG Cases

This section applies the three-layered framework of *bad neighborhoods(s), interaction opportunities and ties,* and *conflict characteristics*, partly borrowed from Buhaug and Gleditsch (2008), to assess the degree of the contagious effects of the Syrian civil war on Turkey.

Bad Neighborhood(s) Geographic distribution is vital in assessing the diffusion of conflicts in the sense that under suitable conditions they can easily trigger conflicts in neighboring countries via cross-border sanctuaries, military infiltration, refugee flows, and political and ideological infection and ethnical ties. In this regard, this neighborhood effect proposes that, albeit stable in political and economic terms, countries in the conflict zones are prone to diffusion effects (Gleditsch et al. 2008; Sambanis 2002). Even the early stages of the Arab Spring, which witnessed the rapid spread of opposition movements from one country to another including Tunisia, Egypt, Libya, and Yemen, partly confirms this argument and proves that the Arab geography contains the elements of these bad neighborhoods. When the Turkish case is taken into consideration, it is possible to argue that the first 2 years of the quagmire in the Arab geography did not pose significant security challenges to the country, but rather Turkey felt challenges more related to economic and foreign policy domains. As seen in Table 2, it could easily be argued that the emergence of ISIS and the YPG as important players in the Syrian scene stimulated the operationalization of this bad neighborhoods mechanism in the Turkish case and made the latter feel security threats spilling over from the Syrian civil war. As will be discussed in detail below, the rise of VNSAs rendered the fate of the contagion process for Turkey in a way that it almost made the effects of the diffusion unmanageable for the latter, especially after 2014. Furthermore, in the subsequent 2 years, the diffusion effects of bad neighborhoods not only remained in the economic and foreign policy domains but also affected Turkey in terms of security with the violence coming from ISIS and the YPG.

4.1.1 Interaction Opportunities and Ties

The direct diffusion of the Syrian civil war into Turkey has also been highly affected by the seven factors outlined under the interaction opportunities and ties: (1) the proximity of nearby conflicts, (2) the existence of a common border and the length of the border with the conflict neighbor, (3) the existence of transnational ethnic ties to the neighboring conflict population, (4) the existence of the influx of refugees from a conflict neighbor, (5) the severity of the neighboring conflict, (6) the nature of the neighboring conflict, and (7) the size of the neighboring country experiencing conflict. The existence and activation of each of these seven factors in the course of the Syrian civil war contributed to making Turkey feel the impact of the diffusion of the conflict into Turkey.

In this regard, it is possible to argue that, as also shown in Table 2, the factors of proximity and the existence of a common border and the length of the border became much more influential in directly triggering the cross-border diffusion. Herein, it must also be reminded that Turkey's "open border policy" allowing the refugees to cross the border freely also played into the hands of ISIS and the YPG for recruiting militia through Turkish territory, also giving the "foreign fighters" phenomena access to the conflict zone. What is important here is to note that the existence of such a long land border with Syria (937 km) made it hard to control the effects of the diffusion mechanisms for Turkey.

The existence of ethnic ties to the neighboring conflict population, the third factor, has been studied in the literature with regard to how the transnational ethnic ties may diffuse the impacts of conflicts from one country to another by increasing ethnic awareness reviving political demands, etc. (Forsberg 2008; Halperin 2008; Kuran 1998; Lake and Rothchild 1998). Drawing on the arguments raised in these studies, it could be argued that the YPG case, as demonstrated in Table 2, seems to be the most relevant case of direct diffusion with regard to the existence of ethnic ties. As the course of the Kobane events already revealed, the existence of strong ethnic ties between the Kurds in Syria and Turkey can easily transfer the unrest from one country to another via these ties. Indeed, the Kobane events, through these transnational ethnic ties, triggered the diffusion of the conflict into Turkey in two ways. First, since Turkey hesitated to support the YPG openly in its fight against ISIS, rapid and firm reactions from the insurgent Kurdish groups in Turkey were witnessed. Second, Kobane events taught the PKK new tactics of insurgency in such a way that they changed their strategies from attacking rural areas to combatting in urban areas in southeastern cities of Turkey, which was inspired by the warfare tactics of the YPG in Syria.

The influx of refugees, the fourth factor of interaction opportunities and ties, also became very influential in directly diffusing the negative impacts of the conflict from Syria to Turkey. In addition to the financial burden of hosting millions of refugees inside the country, Turkey spent almost $11 billion on humanitarian aid for Syrian refugees (Avrupa Komisyonu 2017, p. 2). Turkey deeply felt the difficulties of integrating such a high number of Syrians in Turkish society. Therefore, the influx of refugees, one aspect of the diffusion of the conflict, resulted in financial and social burdens inside the country.

The severity of the neighboring conflict, the nature of the neighboring conflict, and the size of the neighboring country experiencing conflict have become highly operational in the diffusion process of the Syrian civil war into Turkey. When the severity of the conflict is taken into consideration, it could easily be argued that the Syrian civil war is one of the most violent events witnessed in recent years, given the existence of chemical attacks, proliferation of conflicting opposition groups, the rapid rise of VNSAs, most notably ISIS, and the intervention of external countries such as Russia and Iran. The coexistence of these factors intensified the conflict itself and contributed to the contagion process, all of which affected Turkey to various degrees. Indeed, these factors became much more influential in the case of the direct diffusion of the conflict to Turkey than any other immediate neighbors of Syria. Since what is emphasized more in the literature is the parallel relationship between the country size and the risk of diffusion (Buhaug and Gleditsch 2008, p. 221), the Syrian case also proves its validity during the contagion process into Turkey. In terms of a comparative analysis between the role of VNSAs, it seems clear that, as also demonstrated in Table 2, the diffusion through the YPG case seems to be much more affected by the interaction opportunities and ties than the ISIS case.

4.1.2 Conflict Characteristics

As indicated in the theoretical part, the layer of conflict characteristics looks at the connection between the varying types of conflicts and their differing consequences in terms of diffusion. In this regard, the shared argumentation in the literature is that the conflicts that are separatist in nature may easily diffuse to the neighboring countries. Furthermore, Buhaug and Gleditsch argue that conflicts can be further categorized as the conflicts that only involve the aspect of "territory" and the conflicts that are related to "government control" (Buhaug and Gleditsch 2008, p. 222). An empirical analysis of the Syrian conflict suggests that the Syrian scene witnessed almost all different types of conflicts during the course of the civil war: YPG's struggle for exerting autonomy in the northern part of Syria, the ideational strategy of ISIS for territorial expansion based on the understanding of Islamic caliphate, and the fight of various groups for government control. A deeper investigation, also indicated in Table 2, suggests that since the conflict characteristic of the YPG is a separatist one, it became an influential force behind the direct diffusion of the impacts of the Syrian conflict into Turkey.

Drawing on the foresights of the literature focusing on conflict characteristics, it is evident that the Syrian conflict from the very beginning has the possibility of externalities due to the various ethnic and religious groups in neighboring countries subject to the same claims shaping the conflicts in Syria (Oktav et al. 2017). Given the fact that the coexistence of religious and ethnic conflicts is an acknowledged phenomenon in Syria, Turkey appears to have been affected by the impact of the direct diffusion mechanism of conflict characteristics in varying degrees.

4.2 *Indirect Diffusion Mechanisms of Diffusion Within the ISIS and YPG Cases*

4.2.1 New Tactics or Strategies

The ISIS and YPG cases present important examples of how new tactics and strategies emerged as a result of the indirect diffusion of the civil conflict into Turkey in the course of the Syrian civil war. It is possible to argue that Turkey has been affected by the indirect diffusion mechanism of the emergence of new tactics or strategies within the ISIS and YPG cases both on domestic and foreign policy levels.

One of the most important examples with regard to the emergence of new tactics and strategies has been brought with the expansion of ISIS as a solid force on the ground in Syria. Wide international repercussions came after the territorial advancement of ISIS against the Kurdish strongholds, most notably Kobane, and Turkey found itself in the midst of pressures regarding its reluctance to give support to YPG forces in their fight against ISIS. The course of events resulted in a remarkable transformation in the discourse of Kurdish circles in Turkey and expanded their agenda to that of the Kurds in Syria and blamed for the losses in Kobane. These discourses did not remain only at the political level but also found practical correspondence in the streets with wide violent protests in the eastern part of Turkey, which had to be suppressed by Turkish armed forces. For instance, prominent Kurdish leaders in Turkey, Selahattin Demirtas and Pervin Buldan, called for resistance and explicitly stipulated that the fate of the peace process would be connected to the events in Kobane (Gürcan 2014). In this regard, Turkey had to alter its strategy in the Kurdish populated cities of eastern Turkey and undertook tight measures including new urban counter-insurgency tactics. This was important in the sense that the short-lived mutual understanding between Turkey and the PKK came to an end, and government policies began to focus on wiping the PKK presence out of eastern Turkish cities, rather than letting them pass unchallenged from mid-2015 onward (Ünal 2016, p. 93). In this regard, Turkey's Kurdish strategy of a solution process with the participation of the HDP, the political party mainly composed of Kurdish politicians, crumbled. This example well illustrates how ISIS's move affected another VNSA, the YPG, and how the latter altered the fate of domestic politics in a neighboring country through the existence of strong ethnic ties.

The quick expansion and spread of these two VNSAs in the Syrian territories and across the Turkish border have also transformed Turkey's operational strategy and tactics in the Syrian conflict from hesitant support to active involvement. Despite openly calling for international intervention, Turkey has not attempted to undertake a unilateral military action in the Syrian territories. In this sense, Turkey supported the rebels and the anti-Assad coalitions in Syria. However, it was just after ISIS and the YPG spread territorially that Turkey undertook the decision to change its strategy and launch military operations. Accused by the international media of being reluctant to fight against ISIS, Turkey launched its own military operation in August 2016, "Euphrates Shield," in order to support the Free Syrian Army to clear its border from ISIS forces and send back the Kurdish militia to the east of the Euphrates River. Although ending in March 2017, this move was very important in explaining how the presence of the two VNSAs across the Turkish border altered Turkey's reluctant and hesitant strategy and left Turkey no choice but to intervene militarily in the Syrian territories. In this regard, it is possible to argue that the diffused effects of the Syrian civil war via ISIS and the YPG have reflected themselves in Turkey with the emergence of a new strategic perception of labeling/identifying Turkey as an independent security actor in the Middle East.

4.2.2 New Ideas and Delegitimization of Previous Approaches

The Syrian civil war's indirect diffusion to Turkey via ISIS and YPG activities and strategies, especially after 2015, also obliged Turkish authorities to renew the country's border policy and national security strategy. In its changing national security architecture, Turkey seems to have adopted a more comprehensive and responsive approach facing the emerging threats, particularly coming from the two most active VNSAs in the Syrian theatre, ISIS and the YPG. The ethno-religious characters of these two VNSA's fight against the regime forces of Assad also explain the high risk of contagion of the civil war into Turkey since both VNSAs possess a developed network of supporters and sympathizers in Turkey. The existence of a high number of ISIS networks and cells in Turkey and of a significant number of Turkish citizens of Kurdish origin favorably welcoming the PYD-YPG's efforts in reinforcing Rojava status in Syria as an autonomous canton clearly illustrates the necessity for the Turkish authorities to take lessons from their precedent unproductive approaches to ISIS and the YPG. As a response to the rising threat of ISIS networks in the country in 2016, Ankara intensified its efforts to detain ISIS members, which seemed to bring results in the short run in terms of diminishing the number of ISIS's attacks in the country. In addition, Turkey launched strikes against Sinjar and Rojava on 25 April 2017 as the first strike of Turkish air forces against PKK positions in northeastern Syria (Gordon and Kakol 2017). This may also be interpreted as an output of Turkey's new security "idea" against the rising threats of ISIS and the YPG-PKK which is based on a preemptive strategy rather than a defensive one.

Another example with regard to the launch of new ideas as the third dimension of indirect diffusion of the Syrian conflict to Turkey is Ankara's recent efforts in establishing a new trilateral coalition between Russia, Turkey, and Iran, the Astana talks, as a complementary process to the ongoing Geneva peace talks under the surveillance of the UN. This alternative effort may also be seen as a lesson drawing attempt by Turkey aiming to give a breath of fresh air to the existing peace process and save it from the unique monopoly of the UN. This last point also proves Turkey's new approach to crisis management which can also be considered an additional effort of Ankara in diversifying the peace process mechanisms.

4.2.3 Revised Expectations About the Likely Behavior of Key Outside Actors

Another demonstrative effect of the Syrian war on Turkey can be seen in the gradual transformation of its Syrian policy over time as a response to the changing strategies of its allies, particularly the USA at the very beginning of the crisis. The Turkish authorities expected its allies to approve their anti-Assad strategy and support the diverse oppositional groups against Assad. Here it must also be mentioned that Turkey's ISIS strategy has also been criticized by some Western political and media circles, accusing Turkey of not having taken part in the international coalition against ISIS at the initial stage and of not having effectively prevented the flow of foreign fighters to ISIS (Yalcinkaya 2017). The absence of Turkey on the ground in a coalition against ISIS—at the beginning at least—has also disturbed the USA, which was expecting a more active role from Turkey in their fight against ISIS. Despite its initial cooperation with the USA on the "train and equip" program, which ended up not yielding the expected results, Turkey remained isolated among both its Western allies and other regional allies in its anti-Assad and static Syrian strategy. On the other hand, its allies, mainly the USA, preferred to prioritize the neutralization of the ISIS threat rather than the Assad regime. Added to this is the US military and political support to and acknowledgement of the YPG as a reliable local force on the ground in their fight against ISIS. In the face of this attitude of legitimizing the YPG as a regional security partner mostly due to the latter's "secular" posture as opposed to the jihadist ISIS, Turkey, despite their strict opposition, sought to lower its expectations of its main ally, the USA, and revised its expectations on the creation of a no-fly and a safe zone ("Turkey 'ends' Euphrates Shield campaign in Syria" 2017). The announcement on 30 March 2017 by Turkish authorities on the ending of the Euphrates Shield's operation just after it become clear that Turkey would not be allowed to join the possible Raqqa operation by the USA or another key actor of the Syrian crisis is also an important indicator that Turkey's new "autonomous" and "preemptive" Syria strategy will be shaped in accordance with the changing conditions in and role expectations about its security capacity/position in the Syrian context.

As seen in Turkey's recent joint initiative to launch a new peace talk process in the Astana talks with the participation of Russia and Iran, Ankara seems to embrace the idea that cooperating with the USA only in Syria is not be compatible with its interests. Furthermore, Turkey learned through experience that the breakdown in relations with Russia following the downing of the Russian jet pushed Turkey further out of the picture in Syria. As a result, Turkey felt the increasing necessity of redressing the balance between the USA and Russia in the Syrian equation. In this regard, following the rapprochement of Turkey and Russia in the immediate aftermath of the assassination of the Russian ambassador in Ankara, Turkey's position improved by working, albeit to a limited extent, with Russia on the ground.

Ankara also revised its expectations with the EU as a result of the continuing Syrian crisis. In fact, troubled EU-Turkey relations, aggravated by the Syrian refugee crisis, grew even more complex, particularly after 2015. The refugee crisis served as a lesson for Turkey in two ways. First, the EU's strategy based on non-engagement (Ozer and Kacar 2017) prevented it from being largely impacted by all the spillover effects of the conflict, with the exception of those created by the growing refugee flows to Europe and the rising ISIS threat in some European capitals (Kardaş and Özdemir 2014). In the eyes of the Turkish authorities, only the refugee crisis was able to prompt the EU to take an active role in the Syrian crisis and thus believed that a refugee deal with Brussels was necessary. The signing of the refugee deal with the EU Commission in 2016 showcases how Turkey engaged in redefining its relations with the EU on a new ground as a result of its shifting expectations in the context of the evolving Syrian conflict. Second, despite the non-operationalization of the refugee deal due to the existing cleavages between Ankara and Brussels, Turkey still holds the refugee deal card in its hand against the EU, which may certainly be seen as an illustration of Ankara's renewed expectations from the EU regarding the ongoing warfare in Syria.

4.2.4 Revised Expectations About the Chances of Success

The indirect diffusion of the Syrian civil war has indeed led both the VNSAs and the outside actors to revise their calculations and expectations on their chances of success in the face of ISIS and the YPG. The proliferation of VNSAs in the Syrian scene triggered each other's actions and became sources of inspiration for each other. It is possible to argue that this puzzle has become operational partly due to the fact that, one way or another, some VNSAs have managed to spread out in the Syrian territories and were emulated by other groups. Apart from the fact that the two most important VNSAs of the Syrian civil war, ISIS and the YPG, have provoked each other with their territorial advancements across Syria (Lawson 2017), they have also given fillip to mobility inside Turkey as well. With its universal jihadist ideology, ISIS has managed to diffuse and revive such networks in the Turkish countryside and suburbs. Various underground networks and cells have opened in Turkey attempting to spread their ideology and arouse sympathy and financial support. By mobilizing the already existing Salafi networks inside the country, ISIS cells have endeavored to propagate religious indoctrination through their Turkish members and Turkish publications, which was followed by, as noted before, the launch of a series of raids operated by Turkish intelligence circles and police forces (Stein 2016). The same argumentation also applies to the YPG case since an increased sympathy toward the Kurdish movement was generated in Turkey through the heroization of Kurdish militias fighting in Syria against ISIS. It is even possible to argue that the success of the Kurdish dominated HDP in the June 2015 parliamentary elections, surpassing even the Turkish Nationalist Movement Party (MHP), stemmed from the increasing popularity toward the Kurdish movement generated after the Kobane crisis. The more the YPG militias were portrayed as the only remaining defiers against ISIS, the more PKK circles in Turkey increased their expectations of the further legitimization of their case inside the country. Even burial ceremonies of dead bodies of militias who had joined the YPG from Turkey sparked tense debates, stirring up further indignation inside the country (Lawson 2016, p. 489).

On the other side of the coin are the revised expectations about the chances of success of the Turkish state itself. After intense engagements with these two VNSAs, Turkey had to develop a new strategic understanding based on the idea of standing on its own feet. Drawing on the "successful" legacy of the Euphrates Shield operation, Turkish leaders began making statements indicating the future posture of Turkey as an autonomous and reflexive security actor in the region, which would not hesitate to act unilaterally. Most recently, Turkish president Erdogan declared on 29 April 2017 that Turkey "can turn up abruptly one night" ("Erdogan: Turkey and US can wipe out ISIL in Raqqa" 2017) referring to possible further military operations. Indeed, just a few days before this statement, Turkey bombed PKK positions in Iraq and Syria. Together, these events point toward Turkey positioning itself as an active and responsive security actor against the threats posed toward its borders. This is a clear result of the revised expectations of success raised by the Turkish state as the Turkish military operations in Syria have proven to create positive reactions inside the country, even from the opposition ("main opposition CHP welcomes end of Euphrates Shield operation in Syria" 2017). Although such revised expectations have generated the formation of a more reflexive Turkish military policy across its borders, some also portray Turkey's autonomous reactions as a step taken by Turkey to test the reactions of the USA and Russia and their acceptance of further Turkish military presence far beyond its borders (Gürcan 2017). At any rate, the effects of the indirect diffusion of the Syrian civil war into Turkey appear to have brought about a change in Turkey's security role/position in the Middle East by rendering Turkey's approach more preemptive and self-ordained.

5 Conclusion

In a closer investigation of the conditioning factors of civil wars, all four clusters of drivers of *structural, political, economic, and cultural* can be seen in the Syrian civil war context and have made it even more predisposed to violence over time. As seen in Table 1, in the assessment of the reasons behind the Syrian civil war and its diffusion to neighboring states like Turkey, political and structural factors weighed more heavily than the other two clusters of factors, economic-social and cultural/perceptional. Among the four sets of conditioning factors leading to the triggering of the civil conflict, political factors appear as the strongest in catalyzing the Syrian civil war, followed by structural, cultural/perceptional, and economic-social factors, respectively. The surveying of these four sets of factors that make the Syrian civil war more prone to violence is not however sufficient for a clear and nuanced understanding of the contagion of the Syrian conflict into Turkey with reference to its two main spillover cases, ISIS and the YPG. Since civil wars are generally prone to diffusion to neighboring states, a more comprehensive analysis of the Syrian civil war's direct and indirect diffusion mechanisms with reference to their diffusion or contagion effects is likely to offer a proper and complete assessment of the Syrian picture including complexities regarding its non-resolution, key and regional actors, and their diverging responses and strategies over time.

Regarding the direct mechanism of influence, as the Table 2 showcases with reference to the two spillover effects, ISIS and YPG, the first two sets of factors, *bad neighborhood* and *interaction opportunities and ties,* led more to the diffusion

Table 1 Conditioning factors of the diffusion of the Syrian civil war

Structural factors	*Weak states*	Strong
	Intrastate security concerns	Fair
	Ethnic geography	Strong
Political factors	*Discriminatory political situations*	Strong
	Exclusionary national ideologies	Strong
	Intergroup politics	Strong
	Elite politics	Strong
Economic-social factors	*Economic problems*	Fair
	The existence of discriminatory economic systems	Fair
	Modernization	Fair
Cultural/perspectival factors	*Patterns of cultural discrimination*	Strong
	Problematic group histories	Weak

of the conflict into Turkey than the third layer conflict characteristics (Table 2). The bad neighborhood as a systemic effect negatively influenced Turkey's capacity to manage the risk of conflict. Compared to the *bad neighborhood(s)* effect, the second set of direct diffusion mechanisms, *interaction opportunities and ties,* has more potential to increase the contagiousness of the conflict from Syria to Turkey. The diffusion of the Syrian civil war is still an ongoing process which might be countered only by the signature of a long-term cease-fire among the parties. A deeper analysis of factors classified under the cluster carrying the highest risk of contagion, *interaction opportunities and ties*, illustrates that the spillovers of ethnic ties and refugee movement factors appear as the two spillover factors that will be most difficult to tackle in the short term. The two other factors under the same cluster, the distance to the nearest conflict zone and the length of the boundary with the conflict neighbor, remain secondary. The remaining three factors, the severity of the neighboring conflict, the nature of the neighboring conflict, and the size of the neighboring country experiencing conflict spillover, explain the likelihood of contagion in Turkey to a lesser degree than the first four main factors.

The indirect diffusion mechanisms of the Syrian conflict are largely based on Turkey's lesson drawing of its precedent strategies, ideas, expectations, and relations with the other key and regional actors involved in the conflict. All four factors classified under indirect diffusion mechanisms have already led and still contribute to the contagion of the Syrian civil war to varying degrees. In the assessment of the indirect contagion of the Syrian conflict to Turkey among the four factors, the first two factors, new tactics or strategies and new ideas and delegitimization of previous approaches, are likely of greater weight than the other two indirect diffusion factors. Table 3 underlines which landmark events associated with the four indirect diffusion mechanisms contributed to the contagion of the Syrian conflict to Turkey and outlines/summarizes the possible outcomes of the indirect diffusion of the conflict with reference to ISIS and the YPG.

It is possible to conclude that the long-standing Syrian conflict and its most influential non-state actors, ISIS and the YPG, have profoundly affected Turkey's domestic and foreign policy behaviors. Faced with the rising challenge of these

Table 2 Impact of the direct diffusion mechanisms of the Syrian civil war into Turkey

		ISIS	YPG
Bad neighborhoods		Strong	Strong
Interaction opportunities and ties	*Proximity of nearby conflicts*	Weak	Strong
	Common border and the length of the border	Strong	Strong
	Ethnic ties	Weak	Strong
	Influx of refugees	Fair	Weak
	Severity of the conflict	Strong	Strong
	Nature of the conflict	Strong	Strong
	Size of the country	Weak	Weak
Conflict characteristics		Weak	Strong

Table 3 Impact of indirect diffusion mechanisms in the diffusion process of the Syrian war into Turkey through the ISIS and YPG cases (2014–2017)

	Landmark events		Key impacts on Turkey
	ISIS	YPG	
New tactics or strategies	– Kobane assault	– Changing Kurdish discourse	– Stalling of the Kurdish "peace" process
New ideas and delegitimization of previous approaches	– Foreign fighters	– Territorial control in the example of Rojava canton	– Increased border security – Preemptive cross-border strikes
Revised expectations about the likely behavior of key outside actors	– Becoming the main target in the US view	– US train and equip program	– Skepticism about the US role – Rapprochement with Russia – Rocky relations with the EU
Revised expectations about the chances of success	– Jihadist networks	– Heroization of militias	– Increased surveillance and raids in the country – Increased motivation for unilateral operations

armed non-state actors, Turkey was preoccupied with finding ways to solve the complex domestic and foreign policy puzzles triggered by the diffusion of the Syrian conflict. Having outlined the transformations experienced in Turkish domestic and foreign policies, further internal polarization, stalling of the peace process, tighter security measures, rapprochement with Russia, and the construction of an autonomous and preemptive security role, the overall framework of this study argues that a deeper investigation based on the intricate but interconnected bundle of conditioning factors and diffusion mechanisms is needed to properly reveal the wider impacts of civil wars and conflicts on neighboring regions. Lastly, this study further illustrates that such an approach serves not only academic purposes, but it is possible to propose that future policy calculations for countering the contagious effects of civil wars should take these various factors into account for executing reliable and sustained solutions.

References

Auton, G. P., & Slobodien, J. R. (2016). The contagiousness of regional conflict: A Middle East case study. *Journal of International Affairs, 69*(2), 3–12.

Avrupa Komisyonu: İnsani Yardım ve Sivil Koruma. (2017). *Türkiye: Mülteci Krizi*. http://ec.europa.eu/echo/files/aid/countries/factsheets/turkey_syrian_crisis_tr.pdf

Börzel, T. A., & Risse, T. (2012). From Europeanisation to diffusion: Introduction. *West European Politics, 35*(1), 1–19. https://doi.org/10.1080/01402382.2012.631310

Brown, M. E. (1996). *The international dimensions of internal conflict*. Cambridge, MA: MIT Press.

Buhaug, H., & Gleditsch, K. S. (2008). Contagion or confusion? Why conflicts cluster in space. *International Studies Quarterly, 52*(2), 215–233. https://doi.org/10.1111/j.1468-2478.2008.00499.x

Cordell, K., & Wolff, S. (2009). *Ethnic conflict: Causes, consequences and responses*. Malden, MA: Polity.

Danneman, N., & Ritter, E. H. (2014). Contagious rebellion and preemptive repression. *Journal of Conflict Resolution, 58*(2), 254–279. https://doi.org/10.1177/0022002712468720

De Maio, J. (2010). Is war contagious? The transnationalization of conflict in Darfur. *African Studies Quarterly, 11*(4), 25–44.

Elbadawi, I. A., & Sambanis, N. (2000). *External interventions and the duration of Civil Wars* (No. 2433). World Bank.

Erdogan: Turkey and US can wipe out ISIL in Raqqa. (2017, April 29). Aljazeera. Accessed May 21, 2017, from http://www.aljazeera.com/news/2017/04/erdogan-turkey-wipe-isil-raqqa-170429112610087.html

Forsberg, E. (2008). Polarization and ethnic conflict in a widened strategic setting. *Journal of Peace Research, 45*(2), 283–300. https://doi.org/10.1177/0022343307087185

Gleditsch, K. S., Salehyan, I., & Schultz, K. (2008). Fighting at home, fighting abroad: How civil wars lead to international disputes. *Journal of Conflict Resolution, 52*(4), 479–506. https://doi.org/10.1177/0022002707313305

Gleick, P. H. (2014). Water, drought, climate change, and conflict in Syria. *Weather, Climate, and Society, 6*(3), 331–340. https://doi.org/10.1175/WCAS-D-13-00059.1

Gordon, M. R., & Kakol, K. (2017, April 25). Turkish strikes target Kurdish allies of U.S. in Iraq and Syria. *The New York Times*. Accessed May 21, 2017, from https://www.nytimes.com/2017/04/25/world/middleeast/turkey-kurds-airstrikes-iraq-syria.html

Gürcan, M. (2014, October 8). Kurdish activist violence brings Kobani conflict to Turkish streets. *Al Monitor*. http://www.al-monitor.com/pulse/originals/2014/10/turkey-syria-kurds-kobani-pkk-street-violence.html

Gürcan, M. (2017, April 28). Does Turkey plan to continue airstrikes in Iraq, Syria? *Al-Monitor*. Accessed May 21, 2017, from http://www.al-monitor.com/pulse/tr/originals/2017/04/turkey-attacks-on-targets-in-syria-iraq-increase-tension.html

Halperin, E. (2008). Group-based hatred in intractable conflict in Israel. *Journal of Conflict Resolution, 52*(5), 713–736. https://doi.org/10.1177/0022002708314665

Haran, V. (2016). *Roots of the Syrian crisis* (IPCS Special Report No. 181). Institute of Peace and Conflict Studies.

Hegre, H., Ellingsen, T., Gates, S., & Gleditsch, N. P. (2001). Toward a democratic civil peace? Democracy, political change, and civil war, 1816–1992. *The American Political Science Review, 95*(1), 33–48.

Kardaş, T., & Özdemir, Ö. B. (2014). *The making of European foreign fighters* (Analiz No. 11). SETA.

Kuran, T. (1998). Ethnic dissimilation an its international diffusion. In D. A. Lake & D. Rothchild (Eds.), *The international spread of ethnic conflict: Fear, diffusion, and escalation*. Princeton, NJ: Princeton University Press.

Lake, D. A., & Rothchild, D. (Eds.). (1998). *The international spread of ethnic conflict: Fear, diffusion, and escalation*. Princeton, NJ: Princeton University Press.

Lawson, F. H. (2016). Explaining the spread of ethnosectarian conflict: Syria's civil war and the resurgence of Kurdish militancy in Turkey. *Nationalism and Ethnic Politics, 22*(4), 478–496. https://doi.org/10.1080/13537113.2016.1239460

Lawson, F. (2017). The assistance front versus the popular protection units versus the Islamic state: Reciprocal mobilization and the ascendance of violent non-state actors in the Syrian civil war. In O. Z. Oktav, E. Parlar Dal, & A. M. Kursun (Eds.), *Violent non state actors and the Syrian civil war: The ISIS and YPG cases*. Springer.

Main opposition CHP welcomes end of Euphrates Shield operation in Syria. (2017, March 31). *Hürriyet Daily News*. Accessed May 21, 2017, from http://www.hurriyetdailynews.com/main-opposition-chp-welcomes-end-of-euphrates-shield-operation-in-syria.aspx?pageID=238&nID=111455&NewsCatID=338

Murdoch, J. C., & Sandler, T. (2002). Economic growth, civil wars, and spatial spillovers. *Journal of Conflict Resolution, 46*(1), 91–110. https://doi.org/10.1177/0022002702046001006

Oktav, Ö. Z., Parlar Dal, E., & Kursun, A. M. (2017). Reframing and reassessing the VNSAs in Syrian conflict: An introduction. In O. Z. Oktav, E. Parlar Dal, & A. M. Kursun (Eds.), *Violent non state actors and the Syrian civil war: The ISIS and YPG Cases*. Springer.

Ozer, Y., & Kacar, F. (2017). The EU's stance towards VNSAs in dealing with the Syrian crisis and its effects. In O. Z. Oktav, E. Parlar Dal, & A. M. Kursun (Eds.), *Violent non state actors and the Syrian civil war: The ISIS and YPG cases*. Springer.

Parlar Dal, E. (2017). Impact of the transnationalization of the Syrian civil war on Turkey: Conflict spillover cases of ISIS and PYD–YPG/PKK. *Cambridge Review of International Affairs, 29*, 1–25.

Pipes, D. (2011, March 30). "Syria after Assad": Sunnis vs. Alawis. *Daniel Pipes – Middle East Forum*. http://www.danielpipes.org/blog/2011/03/syria-after-asad

Polk, W. R. (2013, December 10). Understanding Syria: From pre-civil war to post-Assad. *The Atlantic*. Accessed May 21, 2017, from https://www.theatlantic.com/international/archive/2013/12/understanding-syria-from-pre-civil-war-to-post-assad/281989/

Rodt, A. P. (n.d.). Diffusion of conflict. *The Princeton Encyclopedia of Self-Determination*. Accessed May 21, 2017, from https://pesd.princeton.edu/?q=node/235

Saideman, S. M. (2001). *The ties that divide: Ethnic politics, foreign policy, and international conflict*. New York, NY: Columbia University Press.

Saideman, S. M. (2012). When conflict spreads: Arab spring and the limits of diffusion. *International Interactions, 38*(5), 713–722. https://doi.org/10.1080/03050629.2012.726186

Salehyan, I. (2007). Transnational rebels: Neighboring states as sanctuary for rebel groups. *World Politics, 59*(2), 217–242. https://doi.org/10.1353/wp.2007.0024

Salehyan, I., & Gleditsch, K. S. (2006). Refugees and the spread of civil war. *International Organization, 60*(2), 335–366. https://doi.org/10.1017/S0020818306060103.

Sambanis, N. (2002). A review of recent advances and future directions in the quantitative literature on civil war. *Defence and Peace Economics, 13*(3), 215–243. https://doi.org/10.1080/10242690210976

Simowitz, R. (1998). Evaluating conflict research on the diffusion of war. *Journal of Peace Research, 35*(2), 211–230. https://doi.org/10.1177/0022343398035002004

Stein, A. (2016, April 6). The Islamic state in Turkey: A deep dive into a dark place. *War on the Rocks*. Accessed May 21, 2017, from https://warontherocks.com/2016/04/the-islamic-state-in-turkey-a-deep-dive-into-a-dark-place/

Tomass, M. (2016). *The religious roots of the Syrian conflict: The remaking of the fertile crescent*. New York, NY: Springer.

Turkey "ends" Euphrates Shield campaign in Syria. (2017, March 30). *BBC News*. Accessed May 21, 2017, from http://www.bbc.com/news/world-middle-east-39439593

Ünal, M. C. (2016). Is it ripe yet? Resolving Turkey's 30 years of conflict with the PKK. *Turkish Studies, 17*(1), 91–125. https://doi.org/10.1080/14683849.2015.1124020

Wolff, S. (2006). *Ethnic conflict: A global perspective*. New York, NY: Oxford University Press.

Yalcinkaya, H. (2017). Foreign fighters of ISIS and their security threat: The experience of Turkey (2014–2016). In O. Z. Oktav, E. Parlar Dal, & A. M. Kursun (Eds.), *Violent non state actors and the Syrian civil war: The ISIS and YPG cases*. Springer.

Kolibri 360 GmbH
Ferdinand-Jühlke-Straße 7
99095 Erfurt, Deutschland
produktsicherheit@kolibri360.de